SALT

SALT The Moscow Agreements and Beyond

Edited by **Mason Willrich**
and
John B. Rhinelander

*Published under the auspices of
the American Society
of International Law*

 THE FREE PRESS
A Division of Macmillan Publishing Co., Inc.
New York

Collier Macmillan Publishers
London

The Free Press
A Division of Macmillan Publishing Co., Inc.
866 Third Avenue, New York, N.Y. 10022

Collier-Macmillan Canada Ltd.

Library of Congress Catalog Card Number: 73–10698

Printed in the United States of America

printing number

1   2   3   4   5   6   7   8   9   10

Library of Congress Cataloging in Publication Data

Willrich, Mason.
    SALT: the Moscow agreements and beyond.

    "Published under the auspices of the American
Society of International Law."
    1.   Atomic weapons and Disarmament. 2.   United
States--Foreign relations--Russia. 3.   Russia--
Foreign relations--United States. I.   Rhinelander,
John B., joint author. II.   American Society of
International Law. III.   Title.
JX1974.7.W56   327.47'073   73-10698
ISBN 0-02-935370-X

Contents

Foreword

Nuclear war would have devastating consequences for all mankind. In 1945 two atomic bombs destroyed two cities and killed tens of thousands of people in Japan, bringing World War II to a rapid end. In the 1970s both the United States and the Soviet Union possess strategic nuclear forces capable of destroying thousands of cities and killing hundreds of millions of people. Each nuclear superpower can devastate the other, but only at the cost of self-destruction. Mutual deterrence between the two superpowers is thus a fact, not just a theory.

Convinced of the necessity of preventing nuclear war, the United States and the Soviet Union have taken the first significant step into what President Nixon has called "a new era of mutually agreed restraint and arms limitation." That step is embodied in the Treaty on the Limitation of Anti-Ballistic Missile Systems (ABM Treaty) and the Interim Agreement on Certain Measures with Respect to the Limitation of Strategic Offensive Arms (Interim Offensive Agreement) which were signed by President Nixon and General Secretary Brezhnev on May 26, 1972 at the Moscow Summit meeting. Thus the first phase of the strategic arms limitation talks—SALT—was concluded successfully after more than four years of intricate preparations and intensive negotiations.

Though the SALT I agreements constitute an important, indeed essential step toward control over the nuclear arms race, they do not close off all avenues of competition in strategic armaments. Even as the second phase of SALT began in November 1972, the United States and the Soviet Union were increasing the quantity and quality of their strategic forces not limited by agreement.

As this is written, no one can say whether or when a SALT II agreement will be reached. It is clear, however, that the issues involved are more difficult and the stakes are even higher than in SALT I.

This book brings together under one cover the views of ten authors who have first-hand knowledge of the subject of strategic armaments and arms control. While many details of the SALT I negotiations and strategic arms are, and will remain, classified, there is a wealth of information in the public domain scattered among a great many sources. Our objective is to increase general knowledge and understanding of issues that affect the security and welfare of everyone. The book is written to be comprehensible to readers who are unacquainted with the jargon and theories of the experts and the implications of nuclear weaponry and missile technology. We are dealing, however, with a complicated area where excessive simplification can be a disservice. Thus, we expect that general readers will find parts of the book difficult going, but we trust they will also find it rewarding.

At the outset, Chalmers M. Roberts provides a broad historical overview of the nuclear age and the negotiations that led up to the SALT I agreements. Jack P. Ruina analyzes the characteristics and effectiveness of the U.S. and Soviet strategic arsenals in relation to the policy objectives these forces are intended to serve. Alton Frye describes the U.S. decision-making process for SALT, including both the executive and the legislative branches of government, and the evolution from the Johnson administration through the first Nixon administration. Marshall D. Shulman examines the role of strategic arms and arms control in the foreign policy of the Soviet Union and the way in which decisions regarding SALT were reached within the Soviet government and Communist Party.

With this essential background in mind, John B. Rhinelander explains the product of SALT I—the ABM Treaty, the Interim Offensive Agreement, the Accident Measures and revised Hot Line Agreements—making clear the meaning and effects of the initial agreements. Herbert Scoville, Jr., traces the growth of national technical capabilities, whereby each party can verify that the other is complying with the limitations which the agreements impose on its strategic nuclear forces, and assesses the future implications of the SALT I verification arrangements.

The SALT I agreements have important implications for the countries of Europe, principally the U.S. allies within NATO, and of Asia, mainly China and Japan. The perspectives of SALT from these two regions differ markedly from both the U.S. and the Soviet viewpoints. Ian Smart analyzes perspectives from Europe, while Morton H. Halperin examines the diverse impacts of SALT on China and Japan.

Turning toward the future and SALT II, George W. Rathjens, Jr., surveys the options available for more comprehensive strategic arms agreements in the years ahead and assesses the likelihood of their success. In conclusion, Mason Willrich appraises the outcome of SALT I, focusing primarily on the underlying political forces that have shaped the process thus far and that will condition the prospects for further agreements. The appendix includes the texts of the SALT I agreements and interpretive matters, the Jackson Amendment, which became a focal point of congressional reactions to the ABM Treaty and Interim Offensive Agreement, and material from the June 1973 Summit.

The general theme of the book supports the results of SALT I and urges the need for more comprehensive strategic arms limitations in the years ahead. As a group, we believe strongly in this theme. However, no group of ten persons should be expected to hold identical views about an issue as value-laden as international security in the nuclear age. Least of all can this be expected from ten individuals who act in different roles and apply different skills in dealing with strategic nuclear problems. In writing the chapters of this book we met frequently as a group and gave each other's work our searching criticism. This has enabled us to lay a common factual foundation for the book and to sharpen our individual thoughts about the range of problems we discuss. We have not, however, attempted to develop a consensus on every major issue or a common position on any important value question. Rather, our goal has been to present our best thinking on SALT.

Research for the book was conducted under the auspices of the American Society of International Law by a working group of the society's Panel on Nuclear Energy and World Order, which is under the chairmanship of Bennett Boskey. The work was funded by a grant from the National Science Foundation. We express our warm appreciation to the society which provided a home for our labors, to Bennett Boskey who ably chaired our meetings, and to the National Science Foundation which supported our project. Of course, the views expressed in this book are those of the authors individually, and they do not necessarily reflect the views of any government agency or institution.

MASON WILLRICH
JOHN B. RHINELANDER
Project Directors and Editors

July 1, 1973

About the Authors

Chalmers M. Roberts is a free-lance writer who retired recently from the staff of the *Washington Post* where he worked as a reporter since 1949, chiefly in the field of diplomacy. Among other assignments, he covered summit meetings, the SALT talks and the national security debate in the U.S. Mr. Roberts is the author of several books, including *The Nuclear Years* (1970) and *First Rough Draft* (1973). He has received the Raymond Clapper Memorial Award, the Sigma Delta Chi Award, and various American Newspaper Guild awards for his reporting. He is a graduate of Amherst College (1933) from which he received an honorary Doctorate of Humane Letters (1963).

Jack P. Ruina is a professor of electrical engineering at Massachusetts Institute of Technology. He is a member of the General Advisory Committee of the U.S. Arms Control and Disarmament Agency and serves as consultant to various government agencies. Dr. Ruina was formerly president of the Institute for Defense Analyses (1963–65). He served in the Department of Defense as director of the Advanced Research Projects Agency (1962–63), and as assistant director of Defense Research and Engineering (1960–61). He was a recipient of the Fleming Award as one of the outstanding young men in government. He is a graduate of CCNY (1944) and received his master's and doctorate from Brooklyn Polytechnic Institute (1949, 1951).

Alton Frye is senior fellow of the Council on Foreign Relations and the Woodrow Wilson International Center for Scholars. He was a member of The RAND Corporation (1962–68) and a research associate of Harvard's Center of International Affairs (1965–66). Dr. Frye is currently national security consultant to Senator Edward W. Brooke, whom he served as Administrative Assistant (1968–71). The author of *Nazi Germany and the American Hemisphere* (1967), he has also contributed to a number of other books and journals, including *The Atlantic, Foreign Policy,* and the *Bulletin of the Atomic Scientists.* He is a graduate of St. Louis University (1958) and received his Ph.D. from Yale University (1961).

Marshall D. Shulman is professor of government and director of the Russian Institute at Columbia University. He was formerly professor of international politics at the Fletcher School of Law and Diplomacy at Tufts University (1961–67), and associate director of the Russian Research Center at Harvard University (1956–60). Dr. Shulman's major publications include *Beyond the Cold War* (1966) and *Stalin's Foreign Policy Reappraised* (1963). He is a graduate of Michigan (1937) and received his master's and doctorate from Columbia (1948, 1959), and, also from Columbia, the Certificate of the Russian Institute (1948).

John B. Rhinelander is now General Counsel of the Department of Health, Education, and Welfare. He served as legal adviser to the U.S. SALT Delegation from April 1971 until the SALT I agreements were concluded, and then entered private law practice in Washington, D.C. He was a law clerk to Justice John M. Harlan (1961–62), practiced law in New York City (1962–66), and served as special civilian assistant to the Secretary of the Navy (1966–68), chief counsel and acting deputy director of a balance of payments regulatory program (1968–69), and deputy legal adviser of the Department of State (1969–71). He is a graduate of Yale (1955) and the University of Virginia Law School (1961), where he was editor-in-chief of the *Virginia Law Review.*

Herbert Scoville, Jr., has been director of the Arms Control Program of the Carnegie Endowment for International Peace. He was assistant director for Science and Technology, U.S. Arms Control and Disarmament Agency (1963–68). Prior to that, Dr. Scoville served with the Central Intelligence Agency as deputy director for research and as assistant director for scientific intelligence. He is the author of *Toward a Strategic Arms Limitation Agreement* (1970) and co-author of *Missile*

Madness (1970) and articles on security policy in *Foreign Affairs, Scientific American,* and other journals. He is a graduate of Yale University (1937) and the University of Rochester (Ph.D. 1942).

Ian Smart is deputy director and director of studies at the Royal Institute of International Affairs (Chatham House) in London. He was formerly a member of the British diplomatic service (1958–69), serving in London, the Middle East, and Washington, and thereafter assistant director of the International Institute for Strategic Studies (1969–73). He is the author of the International Institute for Strategic Studies Adelphi Papers "Future Conditional: The Prospect for Anglo-French Nuclear Cooperation" (1971) and "Advanced Strategic Missiles: A Short Guide" (1969), and of numerous articles on arms control, European security, and East-West strategic relations. He is a graduate of Oxford University (1955).

Morton H. Halperin is senior fellow at the Brookings Institution. He was formerly a member of the staff of the National Security Council in the White House (1969) and served as deputy assistant secretary of defense in the Office of International Security Affairs, Department of Defense (1966–69). He has been assistant professor of government and research associate at the Center of International Affairs, Harvard University (1960–66). He is the editor of *Sino-Soviet Relations and Arms Control* (1967), author of *China and the Bomb* (1965), and co-author of *Communist China and Arms Control* (1965), and *Strategy and Arms Control* (1961). He received a B.A. from Columbia University (1958) and a Ph.D. from Yale (1961).

George W. Rathjens is professor of political science at the Massachusetts Institute of Technology. He was Director of the Systems Evaluation Division of the Institute for Defense Analyses (1965–68). He was formerly special assistant to the director, U.S. Arms Control and Disarmament Agency (1964–65), deputy assistant director, U.S. Arms Control and Disarmament Agency (1962–64), and chief scientist (1960–61) and deputy director (1961–62), Advanced Research Projects Agency, Department of Defense. Dr. Rathjens has been a participant in the

Pugwash Conferences and is the author of *The Future of the Strategic Arms Race: Options for the 1970's* (1969). He is a graduate of Yale (1946) and received a Ph.D. from the University of California at Berkeley (1951).

Mason Willrich is professor of law at the University of Virginia. He was formerly assistant general counsel, U.S. Arms Controls and Disarmament Agency (1962–65), where he participated in arms control policy planning regarding the Nuclear Test Ban and Non-Proliferation Treaties. During that time, he also served on the U.S. delegations to the Conference of the Committee on Disarmament in Geneva and to the Safeguards Committee of the International Atomic Energy Agency in Vienna. He has been a consultant to the Ford Foundation, The RAND Corporation, and the U.S. Arms Control and Disarmament Agency. Mr. Willrich is the author of *Global Politics of Nuclear Energy* (1971), *Non-Proliferation Treaty: Framework for Nuclear Arms Control* (1969), and editor and co-author of *International Safeguards and Nuclear Industry* (1973) and *Civil Nuclear Power and International Security* (1971). Mr. Willrich is a graduate of Yale (1954) and received his J.D. from the University of California at Berkeley (1960).

Glossary

ABM (anti-ballistic missile). Either (1) a missile designed to intercept and destroy or neutralize an incoming warhead/reentry vehicle or (2) a system of launchers, radars, computers, and missiles designed to defend some specified target or geographic area against ballistic-missile attack.

Area defense. A system designed to defend a widespread geographic area, such as several urban complexes, against an attack.

ASM (air-to-surface missile). A missile fired from an aircraft against a target on the ground.

Assured destruction capability. The ability to inflict on an adversary an "unacceptable" level of damage under all foreseeable circumstances, even after absorbing a full-scale first strike.

ASW (antisubmarine warfare). The detection, identification, tracking, attacking, and destruction of hostile submarines.

Backfire. A new Soviet medium-range supersonic bomber having only limited intercontinental capabilities.

B-1. A large U.S. intercontinental supersonic bomber that is currently under development.

B-52. A large U.S. intercontinental subsonic bomber currently deployed.

B-70. A proposed U.S. intercontinental bomber that was never deployed.

Ballistic missile. A missile that, after initial launch, follows a "ballistic" trajectory under the influence of gravity alone.

Bear (Tu-20). A NATO designation for a Soviet four-engine turboprop intercontinental strategic bomber.

Bison (Mya-4). A NATO designation for a Soviet four-engine turbojet intercontinental strategic bomber.

BMEWS (ballistic-missile early warning system). A U.S. electronic defense network, based in Greenland, Scotland, and Alaska, established in the early 1960s to give early warning of incoming transpolar ballistic missiles.

Bus. A missile-launched vehicle with limited propulsion which enables it to maneuver after the initial boost so as to dispense multiple warheads sequentially at different targets.

CEP (circular error probability). A measure of the accuracy of offensive missile attacks on point targets. It is the radius of a circle around the target within which half of the attacking warheads can be expected to fall.

Chaff. Bits of metal or other material dispersed around an incoming warhead in order to confuse radar by reflecting multiple signals.

CSCE (Conference on Security and Cooperation in Europe). A conference on European security involving thirty-five countries. The first phase, held in Helsinki, was concluded on July 7, 1973. The second phase was scheduled to be held in Geneva, beginning in September 1973.

Counterforce capability. The ability to destroy an adversary's strategic offensive forces through attacks on missiles in silos, submarines, or other launchers and bombers at air fields before any of these forces can be launched.

Cruise missile. A missile powered by rocket or jet engines which flies within the atmosphere like an airplane along most of its trajectory.

D-class submarine. A NATO designation for a new Soviet ballistic-missile submarine capable of launching twelve SLBMs with a range of about 4,000 nautical miles. See Y-class submarine.

Damage-limiting capability. A term describing the measures employed to reduce damage to a country from a nuclear attack by an enemy. These measures include counterforce attacks against adversary forces, active defense, and passive defense.

Decoy. A penetration aid designed to complicate the problem presented to a defense system. A decoy (or decoys) simulates the vehicle carrying the warhead and thereby increases the number of targets with which a defender must contend.

Delivery system. The collection of components—aircraft, missiles, or submarines, and their supporting equipment—which gets a weapon to its target.

Depressed-trajectory missile. A ballistic missile fired at a much lower angle than normal. Such a missile rises above the line-of-sight radar horizon at a later stage of flight than a normal parabolic trajectory, making detection and interception more difficult. Its use implies a smaller payload and less accuracy.

Deterrence. The strategy which seeks to persuade an opponent that in his own interest he should avoid certain courses of action, or, in a nuclear sense, that the costs and risks attendant to nuclear aggression clearly outweigh any calculable gains to be drawn from such aggression.

Endoatmospheric defense missile. A defense missile, such as the U.S. Sprint, designed to carry out interception of an offensive vehicle after the latter has reentered the earth's atmosphere. The interception thus is designed to take place in the terminal phase of the offensive missile's flight.

Exoatmospheric defensive missile. A defensive missile, such as the U.S. Spartan and Soviet Galosh, designed to carry out interception of an offensive vehicle while the latter is still outside the earth's atmosphere.

FBS (forward-based system). U.S. aircraft and other capabilities that could deliver nuclear strikes against the Soviet Union from bases outside the United States, although such systems are designed primarily for missions in Western and Central Europe in support of NATO ground forces.

FB-111. A U.S. supersonic bomber. FB-111 squadrons based abroad are generally included in the concept of forward-based systems (FBS).

First strike. The launching of an initial nuclear attack before the adversary attacked has launched any strategic nuclear weapons.

FOBS (fractional orbiting bombardment system). A missile that achieves an orbital velocity but fires a set of retrorockets before the completion of one revolution in order to slow down its reentry system and to drop the warhead that it carries into a normal ballistic trajectory toward a target on the earth's surface. The payload of FOBS delivered by a given propulsion system is generally smaller than with an ICBM, and the accuracy is generally poorer.

G-class submarine. A NATO designation for a Soviet diesel-powered submarine, which can carry two or three ballistic missiles.

Galosh. The NATO designation for the Soviet exoatmospheric ABM which is emplaced around Moscow.

Hardening. The protection of military facilities against damage from nuclear explosions. Land-based missiles are usually hardened by installation in underground silos with protective covers.

Hard-point defense. An ABM system designed to defend a local hardened target, such as an ICBM site, and not a large area, e.g., cities or soft targets.

H-class submarine. A NATO designation for a Soviet nuclear-powered submarine which on the average carries three missiles.

ICBM (intercontinental ballistic missile.). A long-range (4,000 to 8,000 miles) multistage rocket capable of delivering nuclear warheads, defined, for the purposes of SALT, as any missile whose range exceeds the shortest distance between the northeastern extremity of the continental United States and the northwestern extremity of the continental U.S.S.R.

Inertial guidance system. The basic guidance system for ballistic missiles; an integral part of the missile, it is capable of detecting and correcting deviations from planned trajectory and/or velocity.

Interceptor missile. A surface-based missile used as part of either an anti-aircraft or an anti-ballistic missile defense system. ABM interceptor missiles are divided into two classes: those designed for exoatmospheric interception, such as the U.S. Spartan or Soviet Galosh, and those designed for endoatmospheric interception, such as the U.S. Sprint.

Invulnerability. The condition in which a nuclear force is protected from destruction by an enemy counterforce attack. Invulnerability is sought in several ways (1) dispersal, whereby nuclear forces are positioned at multiple staging areas; (2) development of pre-attack warning systems, such as the U.S. BMEWS; (3) development of mobility and concealment capabilities, such as the U.S. Polaris SLBM system; and (4) hardening.

IRBM (intermediate-range ballistic missile). A ballistic missile with a range of roughly 1,500 to 4,000 nautical miles. The U.S. has scrapped its Thor and Jupiter IRBMs, but the Soviets still carry some IRBMs in their operational inventory.

KT (kiloton). A unit of explosive force equivalent to 1,000 tons of TNT. See also Yield.

MFR (mutual force reductions). Arms-control concepts for Europe that would provide for reduction in the military forces of NATO and the Warsaw Pact.

Minuteman. A U.S. solid-fueled ICBM. There are currently 1,000 in the U.S. arsenal. The Minuteman I and II versions have single warheads; Minuteman III is equipped with MIRVs.

MIRV (multiple independently targetable reentry vehicle). A system in which a missile carries several warheads, capable of being directed against the same number of widely separated targets. MIRVs are incorporated in the U.S. Minuteman III and Poseidon missiles. The Soviets have tested MIRVs recently and could place them on the SS-9 and other ICBMs.

MRBM (medium-range ballistic missile). A ballistic missile with a range of from 600 to about 1,500 nautical miles. The United States has never developed MRBMs, but the Soviets have deployed about 300 such missiles.

MRV (multiple reentry vehicle). A system in which a single missile carries multiple warheads that are not independently targeted but are dispersed over a general target area. The U.S. Polaris A-3 carries MRVs and the Soviets have tested them.

MSR (missile site radar). Part of the U.S. Safeguard ABM system. Performs surveillance and detection, target track, missile track, and command functions for the Sprint and Spartan missiles.

MT (megaton). A unit of explosive force equivalent to 1,000,000 tons of TNT. See also Yield.

PAR (perimeter acquisition radar). A long-range radar of the Sentinel and Safeguard ABM systems. Used for initial detection and tracking of incoming warheads.

Penetration aids. Devices to aid the entry of aircraft or missiles through enemy active defenses. Penetration aids for missiles include decoys, chaff, and electronic jammers.

PSI (pounds per square inch) overpressure (i.e., pressure greater than normal atmospheric pressure). The measure commonly used to determine the capability of an object to withstand the pressure exerted by a nuclear blast. Current Minuteman silos in the U.S. are estimated to be hardened to withstand approximately 300 PSI overpressure or more.

Polaris. A U.S. missile of which there have been three versions (A-1, A-2, and A-3). The Polaris system includes a nuclear-powered, missile-launching submarine carrying sixteen missiles (SLBMs).

Poseidon. An advanced U.S. submarine-launched missile being deployed in nuclear-powered submarines. Poseidon missiles have better accuracy, longer range, and higher payload than Polaris missiles and carry MIRVs.

Preemptive attack. First strike against an adversary's offensive forces, population, or industry in anticipation of a possible attack by him.

RV (reentry vehicle). That part of a missile which is designed to reenter the earth's atmosphere and to deliver a functioning warhead to the earth's surface.

SA-5. A NATO designation for a Soviet ground-to-air missile which has been extensively deployed.

Safeguard. The modification of the Sentinel ABM system announced by President Nixon on March 14, 1969. It differs from Sentinel in that it was designed primarily to protect ICBM sites and ultimately to provide only light defense of population centers.

SAM (surface-to-air missile). A missile launched from the earth's surface to intercept a target in the air.

SAM-D. A U.S. ground-to-air missile now under development as a defense against aircraft and potentially against certain low-speed missiles.

Second-strike capability. The capability to carry out a major nuclear attack on an adversary after absorbing a first strike.

Sentinel. An American ABM system approved by President Johnson capable of protecting cities against small-scale attacks and potentially expandable into a "thick" system offering protection against larger attacks. See Safeguard.

SLM (submarine-launched missile). A missile mounted on long-range submarines which can be used to attack either tactical targets such as ships, harbor defenses, etc., or strategic targets such as bomber bases and urban and industrial targets. Divided into: SLBM (submarine-launched ballistic missile), such as the U.S. Polaris and Poseidon missiles, and SLCM (submarine-launched cruise missile).

Soft facilities. Missile sites, command and control centers, and other potential targets that have not been hardened to a degree sufficient to protect against the effects of nearby blasts.

Spartan. A long-range exoatmospheric antimissile missile which is a part of the U.S. ABM system.

Sprint. A short-range endoatmospheric antimissile missile which is a part of the U.S. ABM system.

SRAM (short-range armed missile). An air-to-surface missile first deployed on some U.S. strategic bombers in 1972 by the United States.

Stable strategic deterrence. A situation in which potentially opposing nuclear powers have available weapons systems so numerous and diversified that no single power or combination of powers can hope to upset the balance either through war or through technological innovation.

Strategic nuclear forces. Those forces defined as having the capability of delivering nuclear weapons against targets on the territory of a potential adversary; also defensive forces designed to defend against such attacks. In the superpower context, such forces are commonly thought to include those offensive weapons having intercontinental capabilities, such as long-range bombers, ICBMs, missile-launching submarines, and defenses built to counteract such offensive capabilities. The Russians also include in this category FBS which can attack the U.S.S.R.

SS-9. A large, Soviet liquid-fueled ICBM.

SS-11. The liquid-fueled missile that makes up more than half of the Soviet ICBM force.

SS-13. The first Soviet ICBM to employ solid fuel. In range, payload, and accuracy, it is considered roughly equivalent to the American Minuteman I.

Tallinn. A defensive SAM system deployed by the U.S.S.R.; it takes its name from the fact that some of the facilities were located near Tallinn, Estonia. The prevailing view in the U.S. intelligence community today is that the Tallinn system is an antiaircraft system with no significant capability to intercept ballistic missiles.

Terminal defense. A defense designed to intercept a missile during the final part of its trajectory.

Throw weight. The total payload [reentry vehicle(s), warhead(s), possibly MIRV bus and associated hardware] that the booster stage(s) of a missile places in a ballistic trajectory.

Titan II. A liquid-fueled U.S. ICBM carrying a warhead of several megatons. The U.S. still deploys fifty-four Titan II ICBMs.

Triad. The term used in referring to the basic structure of the U.S. strategic deterrent force. It is composed of land-based ICBMs, the Strategic Air Command (SAC) bomber force, and the Polaris/Poseidon submarine fleet.

Trident (formerly ULMs or underwater long-range missile system). A proposed U.S. nuclear-powered submarine and SLBM system presently in the early stages of development. The submarines would be very large and carry a larger number of missiles than Polaris or Poseidon submarines, and the Trident SLBMs would have a greater range than the Poseidon or Polaris missiles. The first version of the Trident missile, designated C-1, could be retrofitted into existing submarines, but a second version, designated D-1, is designed only for the Trident submarine.

Warhead. That part of a reentry vehicle containing the nuclear explosives, fuses, and other components necessary for a nuclear explosion.

Y-class submarine. A NATO designation for a modern Soviet nuclear-powered submarine which has sixteen SLBM launchers. A newer version, referred to as a stretched Y-class or D-class, has twelve SLBM launchers designed for a new longer-range Soviet missile (SS-N-8).

Yield. The total effective energy produced in a nuclear explosion. Usually expressed as an equivalent tonnage of TNT (kilotons or megatons). Nuclear explosion effects include nuclear radiation, thermal radiation, and blast.

Part 1

CHAPTER ONE
The Road to Moscow
Chalmers M. Roberts

"I sometimes wonder," wrote Senator Arthur H. Vandenberg in his diary on October 26, 1945, "whether the wit of man is competent to deal with this murderous discovery." Now, almost thirty years later, the senator's question about nuclear arms remains open. Yet, although incredibly tumultuous history has passed across the international stage, no nuclear weapon has been fired in anger despite growing arsenals in first one, then two, three, four, and five nations and with several more now able to enter the "nuclear club" if they make the political decision to do so.

Crude but vastly destructive atomic bombs in the sole possession of the United States have evolved into two complex strategic nuclear systems with the lethal power of each increased by quantum jumps. Each superpower now commands hydrogen bomb warheads atop intercontinental ballistic missiles that can span the distance between them in a mere thirty minutes. Added to these weapons, to form a triad of nuclear delivery systems for each superpower, are manned bombers and nuclear-powered submarines capable of firing, from beneath the sea, nuclear-tipped missiles at great distances from potential targets.

Today, although the weapons have not been used since Hiroshima and Nagasaki, the nuclear beast has not been caged. At long last, however, it has been restrained by Soviet-American agreement signed in Moscow on May 26, 1972, by President Richard M. Nixon of the United States and Leonid I. Brezhnev, general secretary of the Central Committee of the Communist Party of the Soviet Union.

A long, tortuous, and often disheartening road led first to a number of peripheral agreements and then, finally, to the first mutual restraint on the nuclear arsenals of the superpowers themselves. In the course of on-and-off and on-again negotiations between five succeeding administrations in Washington and several succeeding leaders and Kremlin majorities in Moscow, certain fundamental facts have become clear.

1. The control of nuclear arms (and conventional weapons and military manpower as well) is possible only if there is a congenial larger framework of international political relationships. This applies in the first instance to the bilateral Soviet-American relationship. Secondly, it applies to what the superpowers perceive to be the military and political interests of their respective allies and other friendly powers.

2. Those political relationships are altered and changed by the perceptions which the United States and the Soviet Union have of each other's motivation and intent at any given moment. They are affected, specifically, by the interaction of Soviet and American perceptions of each other's political moves in various parts of the world and, in general, by the relationship of economic and psychological forces operating between the United States and the Soviet Union and between the two blocs in which each is paramount.

3. There is in the affairs of nations an action-reaction phenomenon akin to the laws of physics. This is as true in nuclear weapons development as it has been in international political relationships. Each superpower views nuclear weaponry as a principle part of its total arsenal designed, at a minimum, to assure national survival by deterrence and, at a maximum, for the enhancement of its stated and unstated global goals. Thus as political move begets political move, so weaponry advance on one side produces counteradvance on the other.

4. Governmental doctrines on how to secure or to enhance national security, on what is necessary in one nation's arsenal to deter the use of another's nuclear arsenal, rest essentially on the available science of weaponry and on the attainable expenditures of national resources to procure such weapons. Ideological and conceptual approaches to the balance of power tend to be fashioned more from the nuclear facts of life than vice versa.

5. Nuclear arms limitation agreements become possible only when the superpowers believe they are at a relative, if rough, state of parity in weaponry. Their political relationship and their respective economic conditions must be such that each is prepared to accept some encumbrance on its freedom to extend and expand

its nuclear arsenal. Peripheral agreements, however, are possible without nuclear parity provided they appear to advance national interests without inhibiting arms development.

6. Nuclear and allied sciences often move faster than diplomacy, creating from time to time (at least thus far) breakthroughs in weapons and their deliverability. Changes in weapons produce alterations, even complete turnabouts, in negotiating postures. Man's capacity to invent and to circumvent, as well as the deeply ingrained differing Soviet-American ideological views of the nature of the governance of the world, serve in combination to make control, rather than abolition, of nuclear arms the most that can be expected.

It is against the backdrop of these half dozen fundamental principles of relationships between national states in the nuclear age, above all between the United States and the Soviet Union, that one must view the history of arms control negotiations from 1945 through 1973. Throughout these years the decision-making process has centered in the White House and the Kremlin. Yet political leaders on both sides have been, and remain, to a considerable degree, prisoners of their advisers, particularly those with technical competence in the complex area of nuclear weaponry and delivery systems. The advisers on the American side include scores of men who move in and out of government to and from academic and other pursuits. Those outside government are often more free to speak out in the United States and at unofficial international scientific gatherings than are those in government who are restrained by the policy of the moment. Many American technicians first thought out among themselves and then argued out with their Soviet opposite numbers (who, of course, lack the disassociation from government that Americans can enjoy) problems that only much later were resolved in Soviet-American negotiations.

Although the nuclear age cannot be neatly compartmentalized, it does fall into four rather distinct periods of intricate efforts, of failure and success, to find negotiated agreements to limit the nuclear arms race.

The American Nuclear Monopoly and the
Baruch Plan for International Control:
1945–1952

On July 24, 1945, during the Potsdam Conference, President Truman told Josef Stalin that the United States had developed a bomb far more destructive than any ever known and that it planned to use the bomb soon unless Japan surrendered. Stalin replied only that "I am glad to hear it and I hope you make good use of it against the Japanese." This was the first formal Soviet-American conversation, however brief, on nuclear weaponry. But behind it lay a story that foreshadowed much of what would occur in subsequent years.

The American Manhattan Project had been initiated by Albert Einstein's famous August 1939 letter to President Roosevelt suggesting the possibility of an atomic bomb, although the decision to launch the project was not made until September 1942. Sometime in June 1942, Soviet scientist Georgi N. Flerov wrote the Soviet State Defense Committee to plead that "it is imperative, without delay, to produce a uranium bomb." The same Russian account published in 1966, which disclosed Flerov's letter, stated that sometime "earlier"—no date was given—"the Soviet government had already learned that in Germany and the United States priority work connected with development of a new, high-powered weapon was being carried out in strictest secrecy." This apparently was an *ex post facto* acknowledgment of Soviet espionage, probably the work of Klaus Fuchs who, when later arrested, confessed that he had begun in 1942 to pass atomic information from Britain and later from the United States.

On December 2, 1942, the first chain reaction was achieved at the University of Chicago. The comparable Soviet achievement came on December 24, 1946. The Soviet Union did not produce sufficient plutonium for a nuclear bomb test until 1949, more than four years after the first American test at Alamagordo, New Mexico, about which Truman had just been informed when he spoke to Stalin at Potsdam.

The United States and the Soviet Union were wartime allies against Hitler's Germany, but they did not share atomic secrets. Instead, hidden from both peoples, the American lead in atomic bomb development produced alarm in the Soviet government. News of the Alamagordo test (at which Fuchs had been present) was received in Moscow, according to a Soviet account of 1963, "with mixed feelings of disappointment, satisfaction and some apprehension." The Americans had been first, hence "disappointment"; a nuclear explosion had been achieved, hence "satisfaction" that it could be done. "Apprehension" probably was a moderate term, however, for the feeling in the Kremlin. The retrospective Soviet view of the years of the American nuclear monopoly (1945–1949) was that "unrestrained nuclear blackmail was initiated, the 'Cold War' of the United States with its ally of yesterday —the Soviet Union—was begun." And: "The U.S.S.R. government called on the scientists and engineers to create an atomic bomb as swiftly as possible" because "it was necessary to defend the homeland against the new disaster hovering over it."

After the atomic bomb had been dropped on Hiroshima, President Truman declared in a report to the nation that "the bomb is too dangerous to be loose in a lawless world." Hence Britain and the United States, which had jointly created it, "do not intend to reveal the secret until means have been found to control the bomb so as to protect ourselves and the rest of the world from the danger of total destruction." Thus, the news of the achievement of nuclear fission burst on most of the world for the first time on August 6, 1945. But by then Stalin had long known what the American and British were doing in secrecy and the Russians were racing to catch up. It was not a congenial framework of Soviet-American and East-West relations in which to seek an arms control agreement.

On June 14, 1946, Bernard Baruch told a meeting of the newly created United Nations Atomic Energy Commission that "we are come to make a choice between the quick and the dead. . . . We must elect World Peace or World Destruction." He presented the plan that was to bear his name, worked out within the American government in the preceding nine months. The Baruch Plan, much of which had come from the Acheson-Lilienthal Report, called for an International Atomic Development Agency that would have exclusive ownership of "all atomic energy activities potentially dangerous to world security." If the Soviet Union would agree to such far-reaching international controls, the United States was prepared to hand over to the new agency both the data on which its own achievements were based and its stockpile of atomic weapons. At the United Nations, with Truman's approval, Baruch added the sanction of "swift and sure punishment" of violators of such an agreement, which would include the great powers relinquishing their veto in the Security Council in such cases. The assumption was that only the Soviet Union was a potential violator.

To many Americans the Baruch Plan was a generous offer, indeed to some it was far too generous. But the offer appeared to the Soviet leaders to be a device to impose on the U.S.S.R. and the rest of the world a *Pax Americana*. In 1962, Nikita Khrushchev retrospectively described the Baruch Plan as having been designed "not to ban nuclear weapons or destroy them," but through an international agency to "interfere in the economic life of nations." The U.S. "wanted to prevent the development of the atomic industry in other countries, leaving the monopoly of nuclear arms to the United States. We, of course, could not agree to this."

The Baruch Plan had such wide appeal in the war-weary world of 1946, however, that Stalin's public response was to play for time with obfuscation and counterproposals. An official Soviet statement in 1963 described what had been the private Soviet view in 1946:

> In the early years after the United States developed nuclear weapons, when the U.S. had a nuclear monopoly and the security of the socialist countries was thus endangered, the Soviet Government proceeded from the consideration that the main thing was to deprive the U.S. of this advantage. That could be achieved either through a complete ban on nuclear weapons which would have been tantamount to taking them away from the only nuclear power of the day, the United States, or through developing nuclear weapons of our own which would serve to protect the security of all the socialist countries.

The Soviet Union, in fact, proceeded on both tracks. A vast propaganda effort, culminating in the 1950 Stockholm Appeal for "the absolute banning of the atom weapon," was mounted while Soviet scientists worked to produce their own bomb. They succeeded with the test explosion of August 23, 1949, three years and two months after the proffer of the Baruch Plan. Aerial sampling by U.S. planes off Japan picked up evidence of the test and Truman announced it one month later.

By then the Cold War was on in earnest. Czechoslovakia had been taken over by the Communists. The plan for four-power rule in Germany had failed and Stalin had tried to drive the Western powers out of West Berlin by a blockade. The Truman Doctrine had been proclaimed. One day after the first Soviet nuclear test, the North Atlantic Treaty came into force. Five months after the test, Fuchs confessed to espionage. Four days after that shocking news reached Washington from London, Truman announced the decision to go ahead with development of the hydrogen bomb, a quantum jump in explosive power. In December 1949, China finally fell to Mao Tse-tung; in June 1950, the Korean War erupted. In the United States, the search was on for both rogues and scapegoats; Alger Hiss was convicted of perjury and Senator Joseph McCarthy was in full cry.

The Baruch Plan was doomed from the outset. Any attempt to negotiate a substitute was hopeless, given the uncongenial character of the Soviet-American political relationship. Though the American nuclear monopoly was broken, Washington was determined to maintain a weapons lead in view of what it saw as the twin threats of a vastly superior Soviet conventional force that could sweep over Western Europe and a possible Soviet nuclear first strike at the continental United States.

As the Cold War rang down the Iron Curtain between East and West, each superpower, its allies huddling close by, sought security through arms. The Warsaw Pact was created to counter NATO, and NATO began to discuss the affiliation of West Germany, which was achieved finally in 1955. Thus action-reaction was in full swing on the political level. In the weapons field, each superpower sought the quantum jump to the H-bomb, achieved experimentally by the U.S. on November 1, 1952, and by the U.S.S.R. the following August 12. These weapons were initially conceived for delivery by bomber aircraft, as were A-bombs, but the vastly greater explosive power of the H-bomb made missile delivery practical despite considerable inaccuracy in guidance systems in early versions of ICBMs. Scientists and war planners in both Moscow and Washington knew the missile age lay ahead, and by the time this initial period in their relationship ended in early 1952, both nations had begun to explore missilry—the Americans leisurely, the Russians intensively.

New Leadership and Reassessment: 1953–1960

General Dwight D. Eisenhower entered the White House on January 20, 1953; Stalin died on March 5. New leadership in both capitals meant major reassessments of foreign and military policies (and of supportive domestic policies as well). It took more than two years for each of the superpowers to clarify its thinking and determine new postures and negotiating proposals. In those two years, both nations achieved deliverable H-bomb capabilities and moved much closer to ICBM capabilities. Science did not wait for politicians.

The transition to new leadership was easier in the United States than in the Soviet Union. General Eisenhower as president inspired confidence in the nation's security. His "new look" at defense policy meant less manpower in the armed forces, once the Korean War was ended six months after he took office, and more emphasis on nuclear weapons. "More bang for the buck" became the slogan of the fiscal conservatives, and Secretary of State John Foster Dulles turned the budget doctrine into a politico-military dogma which became known as "instant massive retaliation." Dulles ringed the Soviet Union and Communist China with a series of defense treaties, adding to NATO in Europe, SEATO in Southeast Asia, the Baghdad Pact in the Middle East (though the United States was not a member), ANZUS in the South Pacific and bilateral ties to Japan, Nationalist China, South Korea, and the Philippines.

Vast nuclear superiority provided the weaponry to enforce containment of communism worldwide. Communism was viewed as an international conspiracy centered in the Kremlin, both immoral and expansionist. If the 1952 Republican campaign rhetoric of a "rollback" of communism was quietly abandoned when uprisings occurred against communist rulers in Eastern Europe, political, economic, and psychological warfare pressures were maintained and often stepped up.

Yet Eisenhower instinctively knew that arms alone, however massive and destructive, were not enough for peace. "Since the advent of nuclear weapons," he said in an off-the-cuff speech in 1954, "it seems clear that there is no longer any alternative to peace, if there is to be a happy and well world." The year before he had rejected a proposal to make public details of what a nuclear war would mean; instead he proposed the use of "atoms for peace" as a positive alternative under international safeguards. In March 1955, Eisenhower named Harold Stassen as his special assistant for disarmament, with cabinet rank, the first such post in American history. By then Senator McCarthy was finished, although the virus he had spread remained for years in the body politic to affect U.S. attitudes toward the Soviet Union and China.

In the Soviet Union, on Stalin's death, there was a massive struggle for power from which Khrushchev finally emerged in 1957 as the undisputed leader. Georgi Malenkov, named premier on Stalin's death, declared in 1954 that "with the existence of the modern means of destruction" a new world war "would mean the destruction of world civilization." This was a deviation from the Leninist doctrine of the inevitability of a "frightful conflict" between capitalism and communism. A doctrinal struggle in the Kremlin, intertwined with personal political maneuvering, ended in Malenkov's ouster. But the breach had been made. Soviet military and political leaders began to face up to the nuclear facts of life and to turn to another of Lenin's principles: peaceful coexistence between states with differing social systems. In practical terms, this meant an effort to control the nuclear arms race lest the weapons destroy communists as well as capitalists.

The first result, the origins of which still remain unclear, was the Soviet proposal of May 10, 1955, presented at a United Nations disarmament session. Here for the first time, the Western powers felt, was a serious Kremlin arms control proposal. It retreated from such hitherto standard fare as banning the bomb and total disarmament to a phased plan, including an end to nuclear tests and the stationing of foreign control personnel at "large ports, at railway junctions, on main motor highways and in aerodromes" of both the superpowers and of their key allies.

Eisenhower wanted a positive response. Stassen and others, including Nelson Rockefeller, then a White House aide, set about drafting various proposals. Dulles, with little faith in arms control and fearful that "euphoria" might loosen the cement of fear that held together the Western alliance, looked on with suspicion, hoping the result would be no more than a propaganda victory. An internal battle began, and continued for years, within the Eisenhower administration. Dulles wanted to deal only "from a position of strength." Stassen sought to reverse the doctrine that the administration would accept no arms control measure that was not to the "net advantage" of the United States. He only partly succeeded because the very idea of strategic parity was an anathema.

The internal Kremlin struggle produced a majority in favor of such new political moves as ending the breach with Yugoslavia's Tito, signing an Austrian State Treaty that included withdrawal of the Red Army from its occupation zone of that country and, most important, opening a dialogue with the United States. The Austrian treaty led to the 1955 Geneva Summit. For that meeting Eisenhower's staff (more

Rockefeller than Stassen) produced the "open skies" proposal which the President sprang on Khrushchev and his nominal superior, Premier Nikolai Bulganin, on July 21. It was a dramatic proposal for a swap of military blueprints and for flights by planes of each superpower across the territory of the other to make sure, in the American phrase of the day, that no "nuclear Pearl Harbor" was in the making. It was still the age of the manned bomber.

But "open skies" was not to be. First of all, there was not yet a sufficiently congenial atmosphere for such a quantum jump politically. Secondly, the strategic disparity was far too great. Rival nuclear weapons stockpiles then were at least, by estimate, 5,000 to 1,000 in the American favor. The United States had just launched the first nuclear-powered submarine and the first of the huge B-52 bombers had just entered combat-ready units. Smaller so-called tactical nuclear weapons were being multiplied and the United States had atomic artillery on station in Western Europe. The American preponderance was massive and Khrushchev's instant reaction to the Eisenhower proposal was that it was an espionage device. To Khrushchev it seemed an obvious attempt to rob the Soviet Union of its greatest strength, the secrecy shrouding its nuclear inferiority and hiding its economic weakness.

At Geneva, in 1955, Secretary Dulles pressed for Soviet acceptance of the reunification of Germany on terms that meant, in Soviet eyes, the forward thrust of Western power into East Germany. The Kremlin leaders rejected that proposal. Later, in what amounted to a counter, they leap-frogged the Dulles containment line in the Middle East by proffering arms to Egypt which had turned to Moscow after an American refusal. The political scene became even less congenial to arms control with the opening of this new Soviet-American area of confrontation which continues to this day.

Stassen, however, kept trying. At the 1957 London disarmament meetings he was able to propose several schemes for aerial surveillance in the Northern Hemisphere in which the Russians indicated interest. But Stassen overstepped himself by disclosing one of the schemes to the Russians before telling the British and West Germans. Dulles used the opportunity to bring Stassen's career to an end as well as to protect his own political aims in Germany. Eisenhower was embarrassed because he then was attempting to repair Anglo-American relations in the wake of the disasterous British-French Suez crisis in which the United States, briefly, was aligned with the Soviet Union against its own long-term allies.

There were other, more ominous developments though only a few people knew about them. When he had come back from Geneva, disappointed by the Soviet rejection of "open skies," Eisenhower had given the go-ahead for the U-2 spy plane and the first flights over Russia began in mid-1956. Action had produced reaction; Soviet secrecy produced a daring scheme to penetrate it. In Moscow the Soviets had taken a gamble to hurdle the bomber age, in which they were hopelessly outclassed by the Americans, with a jump into the missile age. On August 26, 1957, Moscow announced the first test of an ICBM. Six weeks later came Sputnik.

Eisenhower created the Gaither Committee and shortly it reported in secret to the president, so he stated in his memoirs, that by late 1959 the Soviet Union would be capable of launching 100 ICBMs against the United States. Though the "missile gap" was later proved to be a myth, it was accepted as fact in the final period of the Eisenhower administration. The phrase entered the 1960 presidential campaign, employed by Senator John F. Kennedy against Vice President Nixon. The Rockefeller Panel report on defense, largely the work of Henry A. Kissinger, said for the public much of what the Gaither Report said in private. Khrushchev intensified American fears with his "rocket rattling." In reality, however, the Soviets put first priority on intermediate- and medium-range ballistic missiles (IRBMs and MRBMs) to be targeted against Western Europe rather than on ICBMs targeted on the United States. But this was unkown in Washington.

Nonetheless, the search continued for arms control measures. In 1958, following a worldwide outcry against pollution of the atmosphere by nuclear tests, an eight-nation conference of technical experts at Geneva agreed on an East-West scheme for test monitoring posts and onsite inspection in both superpowers. The United States, the Soviet Union, and Britain thereafter tried to reach political agreement on a test ban but could not get over the inspection hurdle. Eisenhower offered a ban on atmospheric tests only, but Khrushchev refused. Finally, after each side had conducted a series of massive tests, both Eisenhower and Khrushchev unilaterally suspended further tests.

Then, on May 1, 1960, Francis Gary Powers' U-2 was shot down over the Soviet Union. The Soviet-American-British-French Summit about to begin in Paris was torpedoed and East-West talks abruptly halted.

Americans feared a missile gap, and the spy flights were intended to produce information that would justify or dispel that fear. However, Khrushchev, as he would say much later, was seriously wounded politically by the U-2 affair. In Peking, Mao Tse-tung, by now, had come to the end of the road with Khrushchev. According to the Russian account, in the wake of Sputnik in 1957, Mao had gone to Moscow where he declared that the "East wind" was "prevailing over the West wind" and argued for Soviet exploitation of its new power by nuclear blackmail of the United States or even by nuclear war. According to the Chinese accounts, Khrushchev had agreed to help China make its own nuclear weapons but two years later "tore up" the agreement. Mao accused Khrushchev of being afraid of the American "paper tiger" but Khrushchev retorted that "the paper tiger had nuclear teeth." The Eisenhower-Khrushchev efforts produced no concrete results other than the creation of the International Atomic Energy Agency in 1957 and the 1959 Antarctic Treaty, but they did begin a thaw in the Cold War. They also helped to widen the chasm between Moscow and Peking to unabridgeable proportions.

In this second period of the nuclear age, 1953–1960, the United States and the Soviet Union, with their allies largely in train, were driven by mutual fears to serious consideration of the meaning and potential use of nuclear weapons and thus they attempted the first serious arms control negotiations. But political problems seemed to grow more than to contract while developments in weaponry raced ahead. The action-reaction phenomenon was at work in both politics and science. The nuclear disparity was too great to produce more than the first peripheral agreements. The United States insisted on retaining nuclear "superiority" and the Soviet Union saw this as nuclear blackmail to force political concessions that it could not, or would not, proffer.

However, at the single Paris summit session at which Eisenhower, Khrushchev, DeGaulle, and Macmillian sat down together, one exchange occurred that would have important subsequent meaning. The president defended the U-2 flights as necessary in view of Soviet secrecy. DeGaulle remarked that in recent days a Soviet satellite had been passing over France and for all that he knew might be taking reconnaissance photographs. At this, as Eisenhower later recounted, "Khrushchev broke in to say he was talking about airplanes, not about satellites. He said any nation in the world who wanted to photograph the Soviet Union by satellite was completely free to do so."

THE CUBAN MISSILE CRISIS AND LIMITED ARMS CONTROL AGREEMENTS: 1961–1968

Immediately following President Kennedy's inauguration, Khrushchev resumed his dialogue with the United States. Kennedy's debacle at the Bay of Pigs in April 1961 early in his administration had an important influence on the Soviet leader. At their Vienna Summit in mid-1961, Khrushchev pushed the new president hard, creating a new Berlin crisis. (Khrushchev's 1958 Berlin ultimatum to Eisenhower had been dissolved, finally, when Eisenhower invited him for his long-sought visit to America.) The new storm that blew up in Soviet-American relations did not end until after the Cuban missle crisis in 1962.

On August 31, 1961, Khrushchev formally announced renewal of nuclear testing in the atmosphere. Four days earlier he had dropped a hint to an American visitor, John J. McCloy, of a fantastic 100-megaton bomb. The largest of the Soviet tests was estimated in the 60-megaton range, from which it would be possible to extrapolate the programmed 100-megaton device. This was larger than any test before or since by either superpower. American officials deprecated the big bomb, but it added to pressure in the United States both to resume testing, which was done in September, and to enlarge American strategic nuclear forces.

Despite the resumption of nuclear testing that same September, Congress approved Kennedy's campaign pledge to create a new agency devoted exclusively to disarmament. But the congressional dichotomy on the subject was evident when the name was compromised as the Arms Control and Disarmament Agency. At Vienna Kennedy and Khrushchev had talked fruitlessly about a test ban. Then arms control was relegated to the sidelines by new crises over Berlin and Laos.

Once in office the new secretary of defense, Robert S. McNamara, determined that it was not the United States but the Soviet Union that was suffering from a missile gap. Nonetheless, the action-reaction phenomenon incited by Soviet ICBMs and Sputnik was at work in Washington, and Kennedy approved massive increases in the American strategic force, though they were less than the military wanted. The Polaris missile-firing submarine had received Eisenhower's approval after the Gaither Report and Kennedy speeded up the program. He also accelerated development of the ICBM force to an eventual 1,054 land-based missiles, 1,000 of them the solid-fueled, quick-firing Minuteman protected in hardened concrete silos. The result was to widen the missile gap in the American favor, which helped to tempt Khrushchev into the Cuban crisis. In 1967, McNamara stated that the 1961 buildup of Polaris and Minuteman "was necessitated by a lack of accurate information" and that "clearly the Soviet buildup" which began after Cuba in 1964 was "in part a reaction to our own buildup since the beginning of this decade."

But none of this was apparent in 1962 when U.S. aerial photography produced clear proof that Soviet medium-range missiles were being secretely emplaced in Cuba. From Cuba, Fidel Castro was calling for Soviet help to prevent another American invasion attempt he feared was coming. Khrushchev, so he said in his memoirs, discussed the Cuban problem with his Kremlin colleagues and concluded that "the logical answer was missiles." There was another, doubtless more compelling, logic to the move: the forty or so MRBMs and IRBMs sent to Cuba would, in one stroke, increase by nearly 50 percent the Soviet Union's first-strike capability against the United States. It is now widely believed, as Kennedy then suspected, that Khrushchev's intention was to confront Kennedy with a vastly altered strategic balance and then to employ it to force American concessions in Berlin and on NATO issues, such as the removal of American missiles then in Italy and Turkey. The secret deployment of missiles in Cuba was a vast gamble, in which the safety of that Latin American Communist regime was incidental, to alter the international political scene in Moscow's favor.

Kennedy's rejoinder was not only a "quarantine" of Cuba but also a direct threat to strike the Soviet Union if any missiles were fired from Cuba. "It shall be the policy of this nation," he said in disclosing the crisis, "to regard any nuclear missile launched from Cuba against any nation in the Western Hemisphere as an attack by the Soviet Union on the United States, requiring a full retaliatory response upon the Soviet Union." Khrushchev, in previous crises, had rattled his rockets and threatened to rain destruction on the West, but never in such chilling words as those Kennedy used. Given the unfavorable logistical and conventional warfare situation in which the Soviet Union found itself, Khrushchev backed down. When it was over he commented that there had been "a smell of burning in the air." Kennedy had said during the confrontation that "we are in as grave a crisis as mankind has been in." Both were correct.

Krushchev's programs had improved the Soviet strategic posture, but his missile developments were not, in fact, as Cuba demonstrated, the equivalent of the image he sought so skillfully to create in the United States and around the world. Of all the many and varied consequences of the Cuban missile crisis, by far the most important was a Kremlin determination to end forever the Soviet missile gap. It is still uncertain whether this determination was formally reached before or shortly after Khrushchev's ouster from power in October 1964. It is beyond dispute, however, that the action-reaction phenomenon was working more forcefully than ever before.

But it would take time for the Soviet strategic forces to approach parity with those of the United States. After Cuba, Khrushchev turned to diplomatic *détente* and in this new atmosphere the two superpowers, with help from Britain but with disdain from France and China, agreed in 1963 on the limited nuclear test ban treaty.

Two important factors on the international scene helped bring it about. One was Kennedy's American University speech of June 10, 1963, in which he disavowed a *Pax Americana* and called on Americans to reexamine their own attitudes toward the Cold War. "We are both caught up in a vicious and dangerous cycle in which suspicion on one side breeds suspicion on the other, and new weapons beget counterweapons," the president said. On July 2, Khrushchev accepted the proposal he had refused when it was offered by Eisenhower: a ban on nuclear tests in the atmosphere, outer space, and underwater, but not on tests conducted underground.

The other factor working toward superpower agreement on a test ban was China, but the extent of its impact on Kremlin decision making is evident only in outline. The Sino-Soviet chasm by then was wide and deep. Three years earlier, Khrushchev had suddenly pulled his technicians out of China and Peking had labeled the move a "gift" to Eisenhower. The Chinese called Khrushchev's effort in Cuba "adventurism" and they termed his failure "capitulationism." Furthermore, almost coincident with the Cuban crisis was the Sino-Indian border war in which Khrushchev, to China's anger, took a neutral stand. Peking called the test ban treaty "a criminal concoction by the two nuclear overlords" designed "to consolidate their nuclear monopoly."

(A month before the limited test ban treaty was agreed upon, Moscow and Washington established a "hot line," a teletype link for communication in time of crisis which proved its worth during the 1967 Arab-Israeli Six-Day War. The system is being upgraded technically, using satellites, under terms of a 1971 Soviet-American agreement.)

Less than two months after Senate approval of the test ban treaty, President Kennedy was assassinated. Kennedy's successor, Lyndon B. Johnson, had little time for arms control in his first months in the presidency. In Moscow, Khrushchev found his power declining. He was weakened politically by the Cuban affair and apparently opposed by a Kremlin faction because he was proposing new overtures to the West on the German issue. While widespread acclaim of the limited test ban showed that most of the world's communist parties sided with him rather than the Chinese, many of his Kremlin colleagues seemed unhappy on how far he had pushed the break with Peking. Khrushchev had stirred opposition among the military by downgrading naval forces and by cuts in Red Army manpower. His emphasis was on ICBMs.

Khrushchev was ousted from power the day before China tested its first nuclear device and became the fifth member of the nuclear club. (The first French test was on February 13, 1959.) Twenty days later Johnson was elected to a full term in the White House.

In dealing with the new Kremlin duumvirate of Premier Alexei Kosygin and the party chief, Leonid Brezhnev, Johnson sought to continue the Kennedy-Khrushchev *détente*. As the Vietnam War escalated, President Johnson was particularly anxious to show that the conflict there did not make impossible agreements with the Soviet Union. He sought a treaty prohibiting the use of outer space for military purposes, including a ban on placing nuclear weapons in orbit, which was signed on January 27, 1967. Here was a conjunction of interests, an agreement to bar what neither superpower seriously considered doing.

Since 1956 there had been intermittent discussions on a treaty to prevent the spread of nuclear weapons to still more nations, and the talks on this subject were renewed under Johnson and Brezhnev and

Kosygin. Here again was a conjunction of interests. The Russians' primary interest was to keep the West German finger from the nuclear trigger. In London in 1967, Kosygin said flatly that "we will not allow" West Germany "to have nuclear weapons and we will take all measures to prevent it getting nuclear weapons. We say it with utter resolution." The Americans did not favor such weapons for the West Germans either, but they also worried about India, Japan, Israel, and other states with the capability to produce them. The Non-Proliferation Treaty (NPT) was stalled for a time by the American scheme for a multilateral nuclear force (MLF) within NATO which, to Moscow, seemed to open the way to a West German finger on the trigger. Lengthy discussion of the proposed NPT at the Disarmament Conference in Geneva (where France continued to refuse to take her seat) produced numerous third-nation efforts to break a Soviet-American deadlock.

At the end of 1966, the MLF was quietly buried by Washington and Moscow softened its demand on the NPT. But then came the Six-Day War in the Middle East. China's first H-Bomb test on June 17, 1967 intensified Indian and Japanese doubts about such a treaty in the absence of American, Soviet, or joint Soviet-American guarantees against China. However, the two superpowers made a number of concessions to the other nations to win their adherence to NPT and it finally was signed in London, Moscow, and Washington on July 1, 1968.

The previous February Kosygin had said that "in light of American aggression" in Vietnam "we cannot have normal relations with the U.S. as long as it continues the war." But the Kremlin imperative of denying nuclear weapons to West Germany, and probably its interest in further isolating China, prevailed. Still, NPT has yet to be signed or, if signed, to be ratified by a number of important potential nuclear powers, as well as by France and China. Whatever its value, NPT was another peripheral agreement in the control of nuclear weapons as far as the two superpowers were concerned. President Johnson hoped for more than that, however. And because the action-reaction phenomenon again was at work, he and the Russians moved toward what later became the strategic arms limitation talks (SALT), the most serious and centrally oriented arms control negotiations since the splitting of the atom.

The Age of Parity and the SALT Talks: 1968–1972

In November 1966, Johnson and his top aides gathered at his Texas ranch. From this meeting came the first overtures for the SALT talks which would begin three years later when President Nixon had succeeded to the presidency. The Texas meeting was sparked in part by intelligence that the Soviet Union had begun to deploy around Moscow an anti-ballistic missile (ABM) system, called Galosh in Western nomenclature, which would provide limited defense against American Minuteman missiles. The Russians had begun an ABM defense around Leningrad in 1962 but, apparently for technical and/or economic reasons, had halted work. The Americans for years also had worked on an ABM system, first the Nike-Zeus and then the more advanced Nike-X, but despite heavy expenditures and considerable pressures from Congress to deploy such a system, both Kennedy and Johnson had taken the position that its potential usefulness was too minimal to justify the cost. News of the Galosh system, however, increased pressures from Congress to build an American ABM and brought Johnson face-to-face with a choice of going ahead with the Nike-X system or trying to negotiate an agreement with the Russians to bar ABMs.

The aborted Leningrad system had been a substantial factor in the U.S. decision to develop a countermeasure: multiple warheads for penetration of such defenses. An initial MRV (multiple warhead reentry vehicle), carrying a cluster of warheads for a buckshot effect, already had been installed on some Polaris submarine missiles (the A-3) and work was accelerating on an independently guided multiple warhead known as a MIRV. The Texas meeting, McNamara announced, had considered "possible production" of Poseidon, a new MIRV missile under development for Polaris submarines, but had concluded it was "much too early" to decide on ABM deployment either against Soviet missiles or against the expected Chinese development of ICBMs.

In December 1966 and January 1967, Johnson began what turned out to be a three-year effort to engage the Russians in a strategic arms control dialogue, a period that overlapped American escalation in Vietnam. It was a period of arguments in the Kremlin, the details of which are only partly known. In February 1967 in London, Kosygin defended the Soviet ABM as simply "defensive." Five days later, Pravda reported that Kosygin had declared (though in fact he had not) that the U.S.S.R. was "ready to discuss the problem of averting a new arms race, both in offensive and defensive weapons." A few days later, the two governments agreed that talks would cover both aspects and thus the general parameters of SALT were established. But still Moscow would not set a date. Johnson again pressed Kosygin without success when they met in June 1967 at Glassboro, New Jersey, in the wake of the Arab-Israeli Six-Day War.

While the news of Galosh was the spark for the eventual SALT talks, it was only part of a larger alarm felt in Washington. As already noted, the Kremlin leaders had decided after the Cuban crisis to build up their own strategic nuclear forces at least in the direction of parity with the United States. But this was not clear to the U.S. until at least 1966 and even by the end of the Johnson administration in January 1969, officials contended that the American overall nuclear "superiority" would continue into the indefinite future.

The Johnson-Kosygin jockeying over beginning SALT came to a climax in mid-1968. There were three related developments. In early 1967 Johnson remarked in an off-the-record talk that soon became public that American "space photography" had shown that "our guesses were way off" on the number of Soviet missiles. "We are harboring fears we didn't need to harbor." By now both Moscow and Washington were regularly flying observation satellites over each other's territory and elsewhere, and other forms of intelligence gathering had also vastly improved and expanded.

In September 1967, McNamara in a San Francisco speech declared a nationwide or "thick" ABM system to be useless because, if emplaced, the Russians "would clearly be strongly motivated to so increase their offensive capability as to cancel our own defense advantage." Nonetheless, he announced a go-ahead on a "thin" ABM system known as Sentinel. His chief justification was that it would protect the United States against Chinese missiles and against accidental Soviet launches. It was in this speech that McNamara said that "what is essential to understand here is that the Soviet Union and the United States mutually influence one another's strategic plans" and that "there is a kind of mad momentum intrinsic to the development of all new nuclear weaponry."

In a June 1968 Moscow speech, Soviet Foreign Minister Andrei

Gromyko alluded to what apparently was the argument going on within the Kremlin over Johnson's call for SALT by assailing "good-for-nothing theoreticians who try to tell us . . . that disarmament is an illusion." Gromyko said Moscow was ready for "an exchange of opinion" on "mutual restrictions and subsequent reduction" of both offensive and defensive strategic weapons "including antimissile." By August 19, Moscow and Washington had agreed in private to a Johnson visit in September to the Soviet Union, at which SALT would be launched.

The next day, the Red Army invaded Czechoslovakia to destroy the regime of liberal communist Alexander Dubcek. The imperatives of arms control were not as important to the Kremlin as the crushing of the Czechoslovak heresy. Thus SALT was shelved until the Nixon administration came to power, although at the very end of his term Johnson tried to revive the talks when the Russians were anxious to take the spotlight off Czechoslovakia.

Czechoslovakia, as part of the Soviet defense-in-depth in Europe, took political and ideological priority in the Kremlin over pursuit of strategic arms limitations. Militarily, Moscow continued to press forward its massive strategic buildup which included not only new ICBMs, especially the massive SS-9s, but numerous nuclear-powered ballistic-missile submarines, referred to as Yankee class (or Y-class) in the West, to match the American Polaris fleet. Moscow was moving toward numerical equality in ICBM launchers, though it had not reached it by the time the SALT talks first were scheduled to begin. In international terms, the Brezhnev-Kosygin leadership was widening its overall role around the world to that of a global power rivaling the United States for the first time in history.

It is, of course, questionable how far the SALT talks might have gone had they begun in September 1968 before the change of administrations in Washington. Open to question is what changes, if any, might have been made in the American development of MIRV, the first test flights of which occurred in August 1968. On the Soviet side there is some evidence, though it is not conclusive, that the SS-9 program was a response to the Johnson administration's Sentinel ABM plan. In any case, the "mad momentum" was at work. The international political climate hampered efforts at negotiation while fostering rival arms developments.

In the United States the idea of "nuclear parity" was hard to swallow, both for the public and for military and political leaders, given the long history of "superiority." McNamara and others at times hinted that enough was enough, that an "assured destruction capability" did not require a vast lead over the Soviet Union. American ICBM and SLBM force levels remained unchanged as the Soviet totals grew, but American MIRVs multiplied while the U.S.S.R. was still working on MRVs.

Nixon came to office a strong backer of "superiority." As a candidate he had charged the Johnson administration with permitting a "security gap" to develop. He had called "parity" a "peculiar, unprecedented doctrine" and he had said that "it appears that the closer we approach strategic parity, the further we move from a stable peace." He hoped, he had said, to be able to negotiate with the Russians "from a superior standpoint."

At his first presidential press conference, however, Nixon accepted "sufficiency" as his verbal doctrine, a term that took the political sting out of the word "parity." The new secretary of defense, Melvin Laird, in time substituted what he called "realistic deterrence" for McNamara's "assured destruction capability." All these verbal gymnastics reflected the new nuclear facts of life.

On the international political scene, Nixon began in 1969 a slow withdrawal of American forces from Vietnam, coupled with intermittent efforts to negotiate an end to the war. He had come to office in the belief that the route to peace with Hanoi was through Moscow, but he found the Soviet leaders for several years to be unwilling and/ or unable to do more than facilitate discussions with North Vietnam. Nixon tried at the beginning of his term to link SALT to political issues, to the Middle East as well as Vietnam, but that, too, had limited results. The Soviet willingness to limit its commitments to Egypt and the other Arab states that are against Israel seemed designed more to protect Moscow's own huge political, military, and economic investment than to produce a permanent peace in the Middle East. Still, the Kremlin did practice restraint to a degree that helped make the world scene more congenial for the SALT talks.

It may be argued that Nixon, with the aid of Henry Kissinger, long a student of nuclear weapons and foreign policy, took much too long to evolve an American negotiating posture and that the U.S. position was too limited. In any event, it was not until October 25, 1969, that Moscow and Washington finally set the opening date for SALT in

Helsinki on November 17, more than a year after the election. By what surely was more than coincidence, October 25 was the very day on which Sino-Soviet talks began on their border dispute that in preceding months had escalated to serious military clashes. The Chinese, in turn, played on Soviet fears by agreeing in December 1969 to resume in Warsaw Sino-American talks that had been broken off two years earlier.

During a stop on Guam on July 25, 1969, the president announced what came to be known as the Nixon Doctrine, a formulation for the gradual scaling down of American commitments around the world. The United States would continue to provide, he later explained, "a shield if a nuclear power threatens the freedom of a nation allied with us, or of a nation whose survival we consider vital to our security and the security of the region as a whole." But other nations, especially Asian nations, would, in the future, have to take primary responsibility for their own military defense. As for Europe and NATO, this meant the allies should pay a larger share of the cost and provide a greater proportion of the manpower for defense. This doctrine and the winding down of the Vietnam War, together with Nixon's overall declared purpose to move from "an era of confrontation" to one of "negotiation," it is safe to assume, all played a part in the Kremlin decision to enter the SALT talks, as in Peking's later invitation to Nixon to visit China.

There was another reason, hinted at by Gromyko in a July 1969 speech. Discussing the control of strategic arms, Gromyko alluded to the spiraling costs without producing greater security for either side. Then he spoke of the "increasingly autonomous" nature of nuclear delivery systems, noting that "the human brain is no longer capable of assessing at sufficient speed the results of the multitude of instruments." The decisions adopted by man depend in the last analysis upon the conclusions provided by computers, he noted and, hence, the governments "must do everything possible to be able to determine the development of events and not to find themselves in the role of captives of the events." American MIRV development was then racing ahead with the first deployments only nine months away. The Soviet arms "momentum," Laird had hinted before Gromyko's speech, was by now so great that the SS-9 could be taken to indicate a Kremlin intention to achieve a first-strike capability.

Much of the public talk on both sides was psychological warfare, but behind it each government realized the strategic nuclear arms race was moving to a new plateau at multibillion dollar costs to each nation unless the "mad momentum" was halted by a SALT agreement. Nixon had scaled down Johnson's Sentinel ABM program and converted it to his own Safeguard system, setting off a major debate that culminated in Senate approval by a single vote in August 1969. The congressional, especially the Senate's, desire for arms control was evident. In the fall of 1969, the NPT won Senate approval. A multilateral treaty banning nuclear weapons from the world's seabeds was also reached. It was another of the peripheral arms control agreements.

SALT opened ceremoniously in Helsinki on November 17, 1969, but it would take two and a half years and hundreds of meetings, formal and informal, plus direct intervention at key points by Washington and Moscow, to produce the Moscow agreements of May 26, 1972. During the course of the talks, action-reaction continued unabated, both at the negotiating table and outside, as the Soviet and American delegates sat in seven sessions, four in Helsinki and three in Vienna. The sessions were in Helsinki in November–December 1969, Vienna in April–August 1970, Helsinki in November–December 1970, Vienna in March–May 1971, Helsinki in July–September 1971, Vienna in November 1971–February 1972 and Helsinki in March–May 1972. The formal sessions took place alternately in the American and Soviet embassies, generally twice a week. At these sessions, a prepared statement was read by one side and interpreted; the other side then did the same, and informal discussion followed. As the talks progressed, less formal discussions occurred, both at the embassies and elsewhere, and toward the end of the last session, informal meetings were held daily. Some major breakthroughs occurred during the weekend trips arranged once in each session by the host government, Finland or Austria. At the end of the seven negotiating sessions, however, nothing was officially made public beyond a bland communique devoid of substance.

The U.S. delegation, appointed by the president, was headed by Gerard C. Smith, director of the Arms Control and Disarmament Agency (ACDA). The other delegates were Ambassador Llewellyn E. Thompson (succeeded by Ambassador J. Graham Parsons) from the State Department; Paul H. Nitze for the Defense Department; Lt. Gen. Royal B. Allison, USAF, representing the chairman of the Joint Chiefs of Staff; and Dr. Harold Brown, president of the California Institute of Technology and former Pentagon official. In addition, there were about twenty governmental experts and advisers; Raymond L. Garthoff was the delegation's executive secretary. The U.S.S.R. delegation similarly represented the various major power centers in the Soviet government. The delegation head was Vladimir S. Semenov, a deputy foreign minister. The other delegates at the first session were Col. Gen. Nikolai V. Ogarkov, first deputy chief of the General Staff; Pyotr S. Pleshakov, first deputy minister of the Radio Ministry; Dr. A. N. Schukin, an academician; Col. Gen. N. N. Alekseev, Ministry of Defense; and Georgy Kornienko of the Foreign Office. Ogarkov and Alekseev were later succeeded by Lt. Gen. Trusov. Kornienko was succeeded by Oleg Grinevsky, deputy chief of the Ministry of Foreign Affairs, and Roland Timerbaev, also a deputy chief of that department, who attended one session. The Soviet delegation also had its complement of experts and advisers. The executive secretary of the delegation was Nikolai S. Kishilov.

Of the non-SALT issues forming the backdrop to the negotiations the most important were the Sino-American-Soviet triangle of relationships, the continuing Vietnam War culminating, just before the Moscow summit conference, in Nixon's stepped-up bombing of North Vietnam and the mining of Haiphong Harbor, the West German Ostpolitik (the West German policy toward East Europe that created a new East-West relationship of *détente* in Europe), and the continuing Arab-Israeli conflict in the Middle East. Through the course of SALT, these political currents exerted both positive and negative influences in Moscow and Washington, though each superpower denied during this period any "linkage" between arms control and political issues.

Peking, in part apparently fearful of a Soviet preemptive strike against its developing nuclear establishment, opened the way for the Nixon visit and thus to a continuing dialogue with the United States. Moscow, more and more bitter about China's apostasy, as Moscow saw it, increased its conventional and probably its nuclear military strength on the Chinese border while moving to secure its western flank by new agreements with West Germany and with the three Western allies on Berlin. Washington and Moscow worried that their Middle East clients might suck them into a direct conflict and both worked to dampen that prospect, although there were anxious days after Soviet surface-to-air (SAM) missiles were moved forward in the Suez Canal zone at the time of the August 1970 cease-fire.

Perhaps most critical of all, and most revealing of the Kremlin's attitude toward SALT, was the Soviet reaction to Nixon's blocade of North Vietnam together with massive new air assaults on Moscow's socialist ally announced on May 8, 1972. If these moves had come early or in the middle of the SALT talks, Moscow probably would have shelved the discussions at least for a time. When the moves did come, however, SALT was close to agreement obviously to the satisfaction of the Kremlin majority. Moreover, Nixon already had been to Peking, and the Moscow summit was only two weeks away. In the larger interest, the Soviet leaders overlooked the smaller interest. Thus the political atmosphere remained congenial.

The SALT talks themselves related to political issues as well as to continuing weapons development. The talks fell essentially into three parts: defining the parameters of possible agreements, hammering out many of the noncentral details and, finally, arriving at compromises on the key issues in the two eventual pacts. The asymmetry between the two superpowers—in political outlook, in each nation's knowledge of the other's basic military doctrine, in the nature of and felt need for particular arms for differing needs, and in the relationship of arms control to the respective allies and their interests—made bargaining especially difficult. There were, too, differing perceptions within the two rival governmental establishments in Moscow and Washington as well as between them, making necessary constant referrals from the conference table and numerous recesses in order to work out agreed national positions on a host of issues. Nonetheless, once having embarked on SALT, both sides were driven forward not only by the prospects of success, but also by the potential consequences of failure.

A basic argument took place over what constituted the strategic nuclear weapons, offensive and defensive, they had agreed to try to curb. The Russians argued that any weapons that could fall on Soviet soil and their delivery systems should be included, as well as ABM systems designed to prevent missile attacks. To Moscow, this meant inclusion not only of ICBMs, ABMs, and American long-range bombers, but also tactical bombers and other nuclear-armed aircraft based in Western Europe and on carriers plying the waters of the Mediterranean, the North Atlantic, and the Northwestern Pacific. The Americans contended that these latter categories, known as forward-based systems (FBS), were not basically strategic weapons aimed at Soviet soil but rather a counter to Soviet IRBMs and MRBMs, estimated at

630 in number, based in the western regions of the U.S.S.R. and targeted on the European NATO allies. In the end, the FBS weaponry was left out of the agreements, subject to later consideration along with American long-range bombers and comparable Soviet aircraft.

The negotiating process was long and complex. At the beginning of the lengthy second session in Vienna (April–August 1970), the U.S. tabled two "approaches" covering both offensive and defensive systems. Toward the end of the session, the U.S. put forward a comprehensive proposal, with various options, covering both offensive and defensive strategic systems. It called for either "zero ABM" or a single ABM site in each country to protect each national capital. At this point in the talks, both sides made MIRV proposals but each was apparently couched in terms so clearly unacceptable to the other that the subject was basically dropped for the remainder of SALT I.

It soon became apparent that the Soviets were predominantly interested in halting the American ABM system. During the November–December 1970 session in Helsinki, the Soviets proposed an ABM-only agreement, with limitation of offensive systems left for SALT II. Early at the March–May 1971 session in Vienna, the Soviets tabled a complete ABM draft treaty which proposed a single ABM site for each nation to protect its capital. The Americans continued to insist on the interrelationship of offensive and defensive strategic systems and the necessity of limiting both. But the U.S. still did not table a draft agreement and its thinking on ABM limits was changing. By this time, the Nixon administration had widely publicized what it called the Soviet "momentum" in offensive arms, especially the SS-9 development, and it became more and more firmly committed to the position that there must be both offensive and defensive agreements.

As this impasse over the offensive-defensive relationship began to develop, President Nixon initiated an exchange of correspondence with Kosygin in early 1971. The outcome breaking the deadlock was a Washington-Moscow agreement announced on May 20, 1971. In it the two governments declared that they had "agreed to concentrate this year on working out an agreement for the limitation of the deployment" of ABM systems and they "also agreed that, together with concluding an agreement to limit ABMs, they will agree on certain measures with respect to the limitation of offensive strategic weapons."

In the light of the May 20 announcement, the United States opted for a new ABM position. It proposed, in drafts tabled at Helsinki in

July 1971, a choice for each superpower between four ABM sites for defense of respective ICBM silos and one ABM site each for national capital defense. It seemed evident that if there were to be such a choice, the U.S. would elect the former and the U.S.S.R. the latter. At the same time, the United States proposed that submarine-launched ballistic missiles (SLBMs) and ballistic-missile submarines be included in its proposal for a freeze on offensive weapons, a position which over the next year hardened from a proposal to an insistence.

Toward the end of the July–September 1971 session in Helsinki, a U.S.-U.S.S.R. working group began preparing joint draft texts of the ABM document in English and Russian with disagreed provisions in brackets, a normal negotiating technique. There was significant progress on noncentral issues as well as agreement in principle that some matters could be handled outside the texts of the agreements, as eventually was done in the form of "agreed interpretations" and "unilateral statements."

The May 20, 1971 announcement prompted the Soviets to proffer a plan to cover offensive systems. They did this in December when they tabled a draft interim agreement to freeze, as of July 1972, the levels of rival ICBMs, their own total already having surpassed that of the United States. While significant progress was made on the language of both the offensive and defensive agreements, two central issues remained unresolved: (1) the U.S. ABM proposal, by now calling for either one site for capital defense or two sites for ICBM defense for each nation, and (2) the Soviet position that SLBMs, in which the U.S. still had the numerical lead, should not be included in the initial agreement on strategic offensive systems.

As SALT moved into the seventh and last session in the spring of 1972, a session that did not end until after the Nixon-Brezhnev Moscow Summit conference had begun, the U.S. position on inclusion of SLBMs hardened to an absolute precondition. This position also was made known publicly. The Pentagon leadership, both civilians and the Joint Chiefs of Staff, was insistent on SLBM inclusion.

By late April, after further high level Moscow-Washington exchanges by use of highly secret "back channel" communications known only to a few people and including Henry Kissinger's Moscow visit that month, a number of issues approached resolution. In addition, exchanges in Helsinki indicated what might be feasable compromises on the remaining issues. The Pentagon had decided that if there were to be only two ABM sites, it wanted one for ICBM defense and the other to protect Washington. Therefore, when the May Summit began, all key issues in the ABM Treaty had been basically agreed upon between SALT delegations in Helsinki, and the remaining problems were in the Interim Offensive Agreement. While the delegations in Helsinki had worked out a variety of possible approaches to the outstanding issues, the political deadlock was resolved by Nixon and Brezhnev, with a few aides, who worked out the final arrangements involving ICBMs, SLBMs, and permissible substitutions if Soviet submarine construction continues. The ABM Treaty is of unlimited duration, whereas the offensive arms pact is an interim agreement of up to five years' duration, subject to later negotiation of a permanent treaty.

During the course of the SALT talks, two subsidiary arrangements were made: the previously mentioned technical upgrading of the U.S.-U.S.S.R. "hot line" and an agreement to take certain measures designed to "reduce the risk of outbreak of nuclear war between them," especially as the result of accidental or unauthorized use of nuclear weapons. Both agreements were worked out by special negotiating teams within the two SALT delegations and signed on September 30, 1971. For the accident measures talks, the special group was headed by Ambassador Parsons for the U.S. and Minister Timerbaev, followed by Minister Grinevsky, for the U.S.S.R. For the "hot line" talks, communications experts Clifford May and Vladimir Minashin came from Washington and Moscow to work out technical recommendations and eventual agreement. It was agreed to add, in addition to the existing "hot line" cable and communications, two satellite circuits, the U.S. choosing the Intelsat system and the U.S.S.R. the Molniya II system, with multiple terminals in both nations. The net gain will be increased invulnerability and flexibility of communications when the systems are operational, which is estimated to be 1974.

The Accident Measures Agreement, in essence, codified common sense provisions which the two governments would normally consider adopting in anticipation of and during any such emergency. Quite likely such a codification impels each government to review and revamp its own internal procedures to prevent accidental or unauthorized launches and to prepare procedures in advance—including use of the "hot line"—in case any such grave incident occurred.

Also during the course of the SALT negotiations, but in the forum of the multilateral Conference of the Committee on Disarmament meeting in Geneva, the two nations and other powers agreed in 1972 to ban biological warfare weapons, although they could not agree to a similar ban on chemical warfare weapons.

The two SALT agreements, signed in Moscow, were accompanied by moves forward in other Soviet-American relationships. The totality of these agreements and contacts was enveloped in a unique statement, signed by Brezhnev and Nixon, of "basic principles of relations" between the U.S. and U.S.S.R. The first substantive paragraph of this declaration sums up the principles on which the two nations had reached the SALT accords and on which they were proceeding in other fields:

> They will proceed from the common determination that in the nuclear age there is no alternative to conducting their mutual relations on the basis of peaceful coexistence. Differences in ideology and in the social systems of the U.S.A. and U.S.S.R. are not obstacles to the bilateral development of normal relations based on the principles of sovereignty, equality, non-interference in internal affairs and mutual advantage.

Here, in this document of mid–1972, were incorporated both essential views and fragments of language distilled from Eisenhower, Kennedy, Johnson, and Nixon on the American side and Malenkov, Khrushchev, Kosygin, and Brezhnev on the Soviet side. The reality of the newly proclaimed Soviet-American relationship, however, was more frankly put by Kissinger the next month when he spoke to members of Congress:

> We are ideological adversaries and we will in all likelihood remain so for the foreseeable future. We are political and military competitors and neither can be indifferent to advances by the other in either of these fields. . . . Although we compete, the conflict will not admit of resolution by victory in the classical sense. We are compelled to coexist. . . . In recent months, major progress was achieved in moving toward a broadly-based accommodation of interests with the U.S.S.R., in which an arms limitation agreement could be a central element. . . . The SALT agreement does not stand alone, isolated and incongruous in the relationship of hostility, vulnerable at any moment to the shock of some sudden crisis. It stands, rather, linked organically, to a chain of agreements and to a broad understanding about international conduct appropriate to the dangers of the nuclear age. The agreements on the limitation of strategic arms is thus, not merely a technical accomplishment, although it is that in part, but it must be seen as a political event of some magnitude.

The Aftermath of SALT I

At the same congressional briefing at which Kissinger spoke those words, President Nixon indicated what he considered to be the limitation of the SALT accords. He said that "Mr. Brezhnev and his colleagues made it absolutely clear that they are going forward with the defense programs in the offensive area which are not limited by these agreements." This became the rationale for the subsequent congressional-approved acceleration of the long-range missile-firing Trident submarine program and of the increased development work on the new B-1 long-range bomber. Just as the ABM had been pictured by the Nixon administration and its congressional proponents as a useful "bargaining chip" at SALT I, so the "modernization" of offensive weapons systems in the form of Trident and B-1 became the potential "chip" for SALT II. In his report to Congress on his return from Moscow, Nixon declared that "no power on earth is stronger than the United States. of America today. And none will be stronger than the United States of America in the future."

The action-reaction phenonemon had begun anew. Neither superpower, it appeared, was prepared to go very far in restraining those of its own nuclear weapons programs not covered by limitation agreements. The ABM Treaty was endorsed by the Senate (by an 88 to 2 vote); but before the Senate gave its approval to the Interim Offensive Agreement (also by an 88 to 2 vote), it added (by a 56 to 35 vote) to the joint resolution of approval an amendment sponsored by Senator Henry M. Jackson. The amendment, which the House later accepted, urged and requested the president to seek a treaty replacing the Interim Offensive Agreement that "would not limit the United States to levels of inter-continental strategic forces inferior to the limits provided for the Soviet Union. . . ." Jackson stated this meant that the U.S. should insist on "equality" in numbers of ICBMs, SLBMs, and long-range bombers, but omitted MIRV'd warheads where the U.S. had a significant lead and was adding an average of three warheads a day. To some within the administration, as well as in Congress, the Jackson Amendment was yet another bargaining chip for SALT II.

The SALT I agreements rested on two pillars: a general parity in rival strategic nuclear forces and a political environment congenial to such accords. In Peking, however, Premier Chou En-lai saw the agreements as the beginning of a new stage of the arms race between the two superpowers.

It has now been almost thirty years since Senator Vandenberg wondered "whether the wit of man is competent to deal with this murderous discovery." By official American calculation, the total gross national product in the United States in that period had been approximately $15 trillion, of which approximately $1.3 trillion had been spent on defense. Out of the Soviet Union's more than $4 trillion in GNP, an estimated $1 trillion had gone for defense. There are few signs that such expenditures will do other than continue apace. Yet, over more than a quarter century, no nuclear weapons had been fired in anger. The decision makers in Washington, Moscow, and elsewhere continue today to apply their "wit" to keep it so.

CHAPTER TWO
U.S. and Soviet Strategic Arsenals

J. P. Ruina

INTRODUCTION

The world has become accustomed to seeing a steady flow of new strategic weapon systems introduced into the arsenals of both the United States and the Soviet Union. Such systems cost more than $200 billion dollars over the decade preceding the opening of SALT negotiations in 1969.

Many of the strategic systems developed and deployed in this period seemed appropriate in the political and military environment of that time. But all too often there was intense pressure to acquire strategic systems using justifications that were custom-tailored rather than based on reasoned objective analysis. Looking back, it appears that neither political leadership, nor stated policy goals, nor the programs and activities of the opposite side can account for the full range and large quantity of strategic armaments that came into being. The nuclear arms race developed a "mad momentum" of its own which seemed disconnected from external factors. This phenomenon cannot be explained adequately by an action-reaction process whereby each side was overreacting to the actual or perceived military and technical developments of the other.

Careful observation and reflection regarding the genesis of weapons systems suggest that self-restraint on one side is generally not reciprocated by the other. The reduction or elimination by side A of a weapons system which had been the justification for a particular weapons development on the part of side B did not necessarily alter

34

B's ongoing program. Prime examples are the continued development and deployment by the U.S. of multiple warheads ostensibly to penetrate Soviet anti-ballistic missiles (ABMs), even after it became clear that a large-scale Soviet ABM was not about to materialize, and the continued full-scale development by the Soviet Union of the modern Tallinn air defense system even after the U.S. B-70 had been cancelled and it was clear that there would not be a new high performance U.S. bomber for at least a decade.

It appeared that the momentum of the arms race could only be tempered by formal agreement—presumably to moderate the action-reaction cycle for both parties—but, in fact, to give each side the courage of its own convictions about exercising self-restraint and the means to do so.

Viewed from a broad perspective, the U.S. and Soviet strategic arsenals were quite similar when SALT began in 1969. Both had large intercontinental ballistic missile (ICBM) forces that constituted the prime elements; both had substantial, submarine-launched ballistic-missile (SLBM) forces; both had effective, but aged, long-range bombers; both countries were proceeding with ambivalence on relatively ineffective ABM systems. In addition, each side also had large numbers of nuclear delivery systems not specifically included in the strategic category such as carrier-based nuclear-armed aircraft and tactical nuclear weapons in Europe in the case of the United States; and medium-range ballistic missiles, nuclear-armed tactical aircraft, and submarine-launched cruise missiles in the case of the Soviet Union. Though often ignored in comparisons of nuclear strength, these non-strategic systems were nevertheless capable of inflicting horrendous destruction on the Soviet Union and the Warsaw Pact countries or conversely on the United States and its NATO allies.

When examined closely, however, the technical characteristics of the strategic systems of each country appeared quite different. Also, the demographic and geographic factors which were included in detailed analyses of force effectiveness differed for each country. Great stress was placed on these differences, but they paled by comparison with the overriding reality that, throughout the decade prior to SALT, each side was capable of inflicting overwhelming destruction on the opponent's major urban and industrial centers, even after an all-out preemptive first strike.

Strategic Policy Considerations

The primary policy justifications for the acquisition of strategic nuclear weapons systems in the United States have been (1) to maintain an adequate nuclear deterrent; (2) to maintain an appropriate nuclear image; (3) to develop flexible response possibilities; (4) to limit damage if deterrence fails; and (5) to acquire bargaining chips in arms control negotiations.

Varying combinations of these purposes have been used at different times by U.S. political leaders to provide a policy framework for strategic weapons programs. We can infer that the Soviets employed a similar set of goals in justifying strategic programs to their own bureaucracy, but with somewhat different timing and emphasis and perhaps without the elaboration necessary in the U.S. where so much more information is available.

Nuclear Deterrence

The first and foremost U.S. policy objective has been to maintain an adequate deterrent force. This is to be achieved by the development of an *assured destruction* capability, defined as the ability to inflict *unacceptable* retaliatory damage on the Soviet Union, even after a Soviet preemptive first strike. This meant possession of a strategic nuclear force that would survive any possible Soviet preemptive strike in sufficient numbers to penetrate existing Soviet defensive systems and destroy much of Soviet society. We assume that no Soviet leader, knowing that we had such a capability, would conceivably order a nuclear attack on the United States; and likewise, that if the Soviet Union had such a deterrent force, the United States would not initiate a nuclear attack.

In order to translate this policy objective into specific requirements for the quantity, quality, and variety of weapons systems, it is necessary to make assumptions about factors that are not readily quantified. How *assured* must the destruction be that we can inflict? How much damage is *unacceptable* to the Soviet leaders? What kind of strategic capability will the Soviet Union have in five or ten years when weapons they now have in the planning stage might be fully deployed? Needless to say, estimates for each of these factors vary widely. Some analysts believe that a small, carefully selected strategic force less than one-tenth the current size of the U.S. force would suffice. Others are concerned that the existing U.S. force is hardly sufficient and that our deterrent will soon be in jeopardy unless we urgently proceed with major new strategic programs.

From what we know about present Soviet strategic capabilities, we have essentially 100 percent assurance that we can devastate the Soviet Union in a retaliatory strike. In fact, only a small fraction of the U.S. strategic force could readily destroy about 30 percent of the Soviet Union's urban/industrial resources. (This is equally true for the Soviet capability against the U.S.) The pressure for more and different weapons stems from an interest in maintaining the same degree of assurance no matter what changes might conceivably occur in the quality and quantity of Soviet weaponry. Although some of the postulated Soviet developments that are feared are technically feasible and politically credible, others strain credulity on either or both counts. In any event, a first-strike capability requires assurance of being able to destroy essentially all retaliatory weapons, whereas deterrence requires assurance that sufficient weapons would survive a first strike to cause an adversary to doubt the success of a first strike.

A consequence of the U.S. interest in maintaining a high degree of assurance for its deterrent in the years ahead has been the maintenance of three central elements in the strategic offensive force, each having somewhat different potential vulnerabilities: (1) long-range bombers, (2) ICBMs, and (3) sub-launched ballistic missiles. The original concept was that this triad of forces, in combination, would provide us with an assured destruction capability. For some, the triad concept has come to mean that *each* element of the force should be independently capable of assured destruction of the Soviet Union. Compounding assurances in this way leads to great pressure for constant modernization of each of these elements of the strategic force.

Regarding drawing the line between what a country might or might not consider "unacceptable" damage, McGeorge Bundy wrote in *Foreign Affairs* in 1969:

> In the real world of real political leaders—whether here or in the Soviet Union—a decision that would bring even one hydrogen bomb on one city of one's own country would be recognized in advance as a catastrophic blunder; ten bombs on ten cities would be a disaster beyond history; and a hundred bombs on a hundred cities are unthinkable.

On the other hand, some gloomy analysts feel that tension between the U.S. and the Soviet Union could conceivably reach the point where, in order to settle differences with the United States in their favor once and for all, Soviet leaders might accept destruction in their country several times more severe than they received during World War II.

In the mid-1960s when the U.S. Department of Defense was intent on quantifying strategic analyses as much as possible, unacceptable damage came to be defined as the equivalent of 400 one-megaton nuclear bombs exploded on Soviet urban/industrial centers. This definition has more or less persisted as a measure of assured destruction within the U.S. defense community. We must note in passing that one megaton is about 50 times the power of the Hiroshima bomb and can cause indescribable havoc in any city no matter how large. It would be more than enough to obliterate cities of the size of San Francisco or Boston with an area of about 50 square miles and a population of about 750,000. The 400 largest cities in the U.S. contain 60 percent of its total population and over 80 percent of its industrial capacity while the 400 largest cities in the Soviet Union have 40 percent of the Soviet population and over 70 percent of its industrial capacity.

Discussions of deterrence often assume an oversimplified, first-strike scenario. Because some retaliatory devastation can never be avoided, it does not seem credible that either superpower would deliberately develop a military capability for a premeditated, all-out nuclear surprise attack. But the concept of unacceptable damage must also persist and guide decisions on both sides at a time of extreme crisis, such as might have been the case if the Cuban missile crisis or an earlier Berlin crisis had escalated further than they did. In such situations, national leaders might fear that war was inevitable and if they perceived a military advantage in initiating a nuclear strike, the pressure to do so would be great. Non-nuclear preemptive first strikes have occurred frequently in history. (A notable example is the Israeli initiative in the 1967 Arab-Israeli Six-Day War.) Of course, the very existence of nuclear weapons on both sides would change such scenarios drastically. Nevertheless, the only conceivably realistic scenario for preemptive nuclear strikes relates to such extremely critical periods when military pressure on political leadership to initiate a nuclear exchange might prove to be irresistible.

Maintenance of an Appropriate Image

After some fears prior to 1961 of a missile gap, which was later determined to be illusory, U.S. nuclear superiority was universally accepted up to the time SALT began. The United States had larger numbers of nuclear weapons that could be delivered against targets in the Soviet Union and its delivery systems were technologically superior to those of the Soviet Union. The political significance of such a superior nuclear posture, although unclear, cannot be dismissed even if its military significance, given the tremendous destructive capability possessed by each side, may have been meaningless.

Robert McNamara, as secretary of defense, simultaneously proclaimed U.S. strategic superiority and denigrated the military significance of an excess of nuclear weaponry. For the public, nuclear superiority represented security, in the form of insurance that the Soviets would not dare escalate a crisis to the brink of a nuclear exchange. Besides, McNamara had to contend with U.S. military leaders who argued that a deterrent capability was not all that was required. The military were concerned about the outcome of a nuclear exchange if deterrence failed and they believed that the nation which had military superiority would suffer less and be better able to recover.

The effect on other nations' political behavior based on their perceptions of the comparative nuclear posture of the U.S. vis-à-vis the Soviet Union has always been of great concern. For example, the ready departure of the Soviet missiles from Cuba in 1962 has been attributed to the combination of U.S. strategic nuclear superiority and local conventional military superiority. If that were the case, then the crisis probably was a powerful stimulus for the massive buildup of the Soviet missile force that began about that time. Now that the superpowers have become nuclear peers, U.S. leaders are beginning to express deep-rooted fears about the possibility of a Soviet appearance of superiority and its consequence for U.S. foreign relations.

What contributes to the perception of military strength in the eyes of political beholders does not necessarily coincide with the significant military characteristics of a strategic force. Since there is no accepted international accounting system for nuclear prowess, it is simple and natural to use only the grossest parameters for its measurement. Perhaps as a consequence of concerns expressed by U.S. leaders about

Soviet ballistic-missile strength, the international focus now seems to be on ballistic missiles. Nuclear-armed long-range bombers and most of the qualitative parameters related to strategic systems, although mentioned, are strongly discounted on the political front. What the world views as the key measures of strength can change with time and most certainly will change if the SALT negotiations between the U.S. and the Soviet Union result in their using other measures themselves to compare their nuclear arsenals. But the important considerations to bear in mind are that, as far as deterrent capability is concerned, the U.S. and the Soviet Union have been nuclear peers for many years, and that fine measures are not appropriate for making comparisons of nuclear capability.

Flexibility

President Nixon has repeatedly stated that the United States strategic force should not be limited to providing only assured destruction. For example, in the 1972 Foreign Policy Report to the Congress, he said:

> Our forces must be maintained at a level sufficient to make it clear that even an all-out surprise attack on the United States by the U.S.S.R. would not cripple our capability to retaliate. Our forces must also be capable of flexible application. A simple "assured destruction" doctrine does not meet our present requirements for a flexible range of strategic options. No President should be left with only one strategic course of action, particularly that of ordering the mass destruction of enemy civilians and facilities.

It is hard to imagine that the leaders of any country would order the destruction of an adversary, and consequent assured destruction of their own country, for any level of provocation whatsoever. However, the president's expressed concern is that if nuclear forces on both sides were structured to be capable only of mutual annihilation, these forces would be useless in deterring provocations less than all-out nuclear strikes. In order to extend the utility of the nuclear force to deter lesser aggressions, the force should be capable of small, as well as large, amounts of destruction; it should be capable of precise control by the political leaders; it should be capable of destroying single targets, such as special industrial or military facilities, with minimal damage to nearby population centers; and it should be capable of being used in a deliberate, planned, and limited manner even during extreme crisis.

It is relatively easy to structure both U.S. and Soviet strategic forces to include a great deal of flexibility. It is not necessary that they be designed only for all-out retaliation. Weapons can be designed for use one at a time, and they can be equipped to be targeted and retargeted on very short notice. With little or no ABM capability on the opponent's side, a missile-launched nuclear weapon will almost certainly destroy its target. While the desire for some flexibility seems reasonable and justifiable and can be easily satisfied, demands for extreme flexibility provide a rationale for unlimited weapons systems development and could be interpreted by an adversary as demands for a first-strike potential. There is clearly a point of diminishing political returns for the expenditures required in pursuit of flexibility.

Damage Limitation

Until very recently, Soviet political leaders and writers about strategic matters stressed the need for defensive systems. They indicated that ABM systems were not aggressive and were needed to limit the damage that might be inflicted by a potential nuclear aggressor. In the mid-1960s, U.S. strategic policy extended this argument to the more general concept of damage limitation. Damage-limiting systems obviously include defensive systems, but also include offensive weapons that would be capable of destroying some of the opponent's nuclear forces before they could be used.

Stated U.S. defense objectives were to provide a force both to deter nuclear aggression and also to minimize damage to our population and industrial capacity if deterrence failed. This goal sounded simple and attractive in principle, but the technical difficulty and costs of developing the hardware that would have a substantial, damage-limiting effect were high compared with the difficulties and costs to the opponent of compensating measures in his own offensive forces. Also, the quality of the military hardware required for damage limitation was almost identical to that required for developing a first-strike capability. After all, pursuit of a damage-limiting capability, if carried to its extreme, is identical with development of a first-strike capability, and it should be expected to create deep concern on the other side. By the time SALT began, the political leadership of both sides recognized the hazards in pursuing a policy of damage limitation in their strategic weapons acquisition and both de-emphasized the need for such forces in their publicly stated strategic goals.

Bargaining Chips

With the prospect of SALT negotiations in the offing, a new strategic force objective came into being, namely that U.S. forces include systems which could be used as bargaining chips. The argument was made that limits on strategic arms must have some inherent symmetry in order to be negotiable. If one side was interested in stopping a particular program of the other, it must have something to offer in exchange.

To be a good bargaining chip, a strategic system would have to be particularly irritating or threatening to the other side and yet not be so attractive to one's own constituency that it could not be curtailed or cancelled. ABM systems seemed to meet these requirements precisely. The Soviets had probably not developed their ABM system around Moscow originally as a bargaining chip, but the U.S. ABM program was, in good part, justified on this ground. Emphasizing strategic bargaining chips can result in expensive and unnecessary arms procurement and can even be dangerous since some chips may prove to be nonnegotiable.

STRATEGIC WEAPONS

Having considered various strategic policy objectives, we turn now to examine the salient technical characteristics of U.S. and Soviet strategic forces and their effectiveness in meeting those policy objectives. Information about U.S. systems, those that are under development as well as those already deployed, is generally known to the public from official government releases and from statements of political and military leaders, particularly from their testimony before various committees of the Congress. Information about Soviet systems also comes from Western sources and therefore is not nearly as complete as that available about U.S. forces. Nevertheless, the broad outlines and the gross technical characteristics of deployed Soviet systems are known. However, when a Soviet system is observed in development, it is not known whether it will actually be deployed, and even if we know a new Soviet system is in production and being deployed, we still do not generally know the numbers planned for the force. Although there is considerable guesswork in ascertaining the details of Soviet systems during the early days of testing and development, the critical parameters of any particular system are usually known by the time there is any significant deployment.

Nuclear Weapon Technology

The first U.S. nuclear weapons developed and tested were fission bombs in the 15- to 20-kiloton range which weighed about 10,000 pounds each. Within the following two decades, fusion bombs were developed up to a yield of about 20 megatons (one thousand times the yield of the first bombs) and still weighing about 10,000 pounds. At the other end of the spectrum, small bombs weighing about one hundred pounds were developed giving yields of a fraction of a kiloton. Most of the larger yield bombs were developed for strategic purposes and the smaller yield bombs for tactical use. At a larger yield, it is possible to get more efficient weapons (more yield per pound) than at smaller yields since larger weapons permit more efficient nuclear fuel utilization and the weight associated with the auxiliary devices (i.e., detonating mechanisms, etc.) is not strongly dependent on the yield of the weapon.

Nuclear weapons technology progressed at least as rapidly in the Soviet Union as it did in the United States, particularly in the case of larger yield weapons. Although the first Soviet nuclear explosion occurred in 1949 (five years after the first U.S. explosion), by 1961 they had developed and tested a 60-megaton prototype of a 100-megaton weapon.

The technology of large yield weapons has now reached a point of diminishing returns in terms of what is obtainable for a given set of weight, size, and shape constraints. Both the U.S. and the Soviet Union are able to develop large weapons with yields sufficiently close to the theoretical limit so that much higher efficiencies will be hard to come by. However, new nuclear weapons are still being developed for strategic systems either to improve efficiency at lower yields, or to meet weight, shape, and other specifications required to optimize the performance of new delivery systems.

Large yield weapons are less effective per unit of yield than small yield weapons. Only four or five one-megaton explosions would destroy as much area as one ten-megaton explosion. Also, large weapons may have excessive yields for some purposes (i.e., the destruction of an airbase or a small city). If a target can be totally destroyed by 50 kilotons, then one megaton is clearly unnecessary.

It should be noted that U.S. assessments of Soviet strategic weapons systems generally infer bomb yields from what U.S. technology can produce, rather than from direct observation of tests of bombs known to be installed in a particular Soviet system.

In the early stages of the nuclear competition between the U.S. and the Soviet Union, emphasis was on the number and size of nuclear weapons in the stockpile of each country rather than on delivery vehicles. After ballistic missiles were developed and it became clear that the nuclear weapons technology of both countries was reaching the point where additional advances were losing significance, the emphasis shifted to delivery vehicles. Although the Soviet 60-megaton explosion in 1961 came as a surprise and received worldwide attention, its major effect was political because it increased concern about Soviet intentions. Its military significance was soon recognized as minimal. In a way, this broad recognition that even such a spectacular weapon was of little strategic consequence marked the beginning of public doubt about the continued importance of further development of nuclear weapons technology for national security.

Ballistic Missiles

The current U.S. and Soviet ballistic-missile forces consist of land-based ICBMs located at fixed sites and SLBMs which are released while the submarine is submerged. Some consideration has been given to basing long-range strategic ballistic missiles on surface ships and on aircraft, but neither side has fully developed such systems. Assuming that operational missiles work reliably, the technical characteristics of a missile force which are most significant in determining its effectiveness are pre-launch survivability, missile throw weight, and accuracy.

Pre-launch Survivability

Can the force survive and remain operational after an all-out nuclear attack? To increase the survivability of ICBMs, their launchers are emplaced in "hardened" underground silos carefully designed to withstand great blasts with over pressures of hundreds of pounds per square inch (psi). The blast from a one-megaton surface explosion, which could destroy a frame house at a distance of 15,000 feet, would have to be closer than 2,100 feet to a 300-psi hardened silo to destroy it, and closer than 1,300 feet to a 1,000-psi hardened silo. At the present time, neither the U.S. nor the Soviet Union has an ICBM force with a sufficient combination of numbers of warheads, yield, and accuracy to destroy the bulk of the ICBM force of the other side in the ground.

Another method of achieving a high level of ICBM survivability is by placing individual missiles on mobile launchers designed to move on rails or on roads. Survivability is achieved by virtue of the fact that an attacker would not know at any time precisely where all of the targets were. Neither the U.S. nor the Soviet Union has land-mobile ICBMs in operation although the Soviets do have operational mobile medium-range ballistic missiles and have expressed interest in mobile ICBMs.

There are serious operational problems both in achieving high mobility over vast land areas and quick response capability and also in maintaining good communications and control. Mobile ICBMs also present special difficulty for arms control since once a mobile force is in being, it is difficult for the other side to ascertain with high confidence the number of missiles so deployed. However, as accuracy of warhead delivery improves, thereby jeopardizing the survivability of fixed land-based missiles, interest in land-mobile ICBMs will certainly increase.

To maintain survivability, SLBMs depend on submarines hiding in vast oceans. With long-range missiles, submarines can operate in isolation in remote areas of the oceans. The longer the missile range, the more the ocean area that is available for operation. At the present time, both the U.S. and the Soviet Union can be certain that their SLBM forces are not vulnerable to an all-out surprise attack.

Fears have been expressed that a technological breakthrough might alter this situation but no known, definable technology has the potential of seriously endangering a deployed submarine fleet with total simultaneous destruction. There are difficult technical problems involved in detecting and locating a single submarine in a specified area with any reliability. Designing a system that within a short period of time can detect, locate, and destroy a whole fleet of submarines deployed on a worldwide basis is inconceivable with current technology.

Moreover, steps can be taken to improve the technical characteristics and operational procedures for submarines to minimize any potential vulnerabilities. Therefore, we can state very conservatively that, for the next decade at least, the U.S. and Soviet SLBM forces can remain secure from destruction by a surprise attack. There is little indication that even after a decade SLBM forces would be vulnerable to a first strike.

Missile Throw Weights: Single and Multiple Warheads

The deliverable payload, or throw weight, of a missile depends on many design parameters and launching techniques, but it is limited primarily by the total size or volume of the overall missile. Large payloads require physically large missiles. However, a substantial increase in throw weight for a given missile can be obtained by using an added "zero stage" to propel the missile out of its silo with some reasonable velocity. This permits larger missiles to be installed in a given silo and allows the main booster to use its full energy more effectively. The net result is that by using a pop-up technique it is possible to increase throw weight by a factor of two or more. Both the U.S. and the U.S.S.R. have investigated the use of a zero stage for ICBMs, and the Soviets have actually begun field tests of this method of land-based missile launch.

All of the early U.S. and Soviet missiles were equipped with single warheads. However, in the early 1960s, U.S. studies regarding the effectiveness of ballistic-missile defense concluded that a simple tactic to saturate and overwhelm an ABM system is to use a cluster of nuclear-armed multiple reentry vehicles (MRV) in the payloads of each missile. Although the total yield that can be packaged in the payload of a missile is decreased when mutliple warheads are used, the overall destructive capability may not change appreciably since, as previously mentioned, the effectiveness in destroying targets is greater per unit yield for low yield weapons than for high yield weapons. To destroy large targets such as cities, multiple warheads could be designed so that they scattered over a large area.

More sophisticated still are multiple independently targetable re-entry vehicles—MIRVs. Here each missile payload can include several reentry vehicles (i.e., warheads), each capable of being accurately guided to a designated target. With MIRVs, each reentry vehicle from a single launcher can be specifically aimed to provide maximum destruction of a complex of targets or they all can be accurately directed to a single hard target in order to increase the probability of its destruction. A MIRV system can also be used to get large separation of the reentry vehicles from a single launcher to avoid their simultaneous destruction by a single large ABM interceptor. But most important, MIRVs can provide one ballistic missile with the capability of destroying many separate targets if each target could be destroyed by only a fraction of the yield of a single bomb that the same missile could carry.

Examples of missile payload options are given below to provide a general idea of some of the trade-offs that may be involved. The numbers used are only approximate and depend on many design details.

Example 1

Throw weight = 2,000 pounds

For a single RV	Yield = 3 megatons
3 MIRVs	Yield of each RV = 200 kilotons
	Total yield = 600 kilotons
5 MIRVs	Yield of each RV = 80 kilotons
	Total yield = 400 kilotons

Example 2

Throw weight = 5,000 pounds

For a single RV	Yield = 10 megatons
3 MIRVs	Yield of each RV = 1 megaton
	Total yield = 3 megatons
5 MIRVs	Yield of each RV = 400 kilotons
	Total yield = 2 megatons
10 MIRVs	Yield of each RV = 100 kilotons
	Total yield = 1 megaton

Example 3

Throw weight = 10,000 pounds

For a single RV	Yield = 25 megatons
3 MIRVs	Yield of each RV = 4 megatons
	Total yield = 12 megatons
5 MIRVs	Yield of each RV = 1.4 megatons
	Total yield = 7 megatons
10 MIRVs	Yield of each RV = 500 kilotons
	Total yield = 5 megatons
25 MIRVs	Yield of each RV = 50 kilotons
	Total yield = 1.3 megatons

The throw weights of current operational strategic missiles vary from about 1,000 to 15,000 pounds. Small missiles are less expensive, easier to handle, and, in the case of ICBMs, have launch facilities that are easier to harden. In the case of SLBMs, the missile size is also limited by the very high cost of large submarines.

There is clearly a point of diminishing returns in producing missiles with larger throw weights if they are to deliver only single large yield weapons. On the other hand, if MIRVs are deployed, the number of usable warheads of any given yield is almost directly proportional to the throw weight of each missile, making throw weight capability a meaningful measure of potential effectiveness. As of September 1973, the United States had two MIRV designs in production and being deployed, one for ICBMs (Minuteman III) and one for SLBMs (Poseidon). The Soviets have also tested a MIRV system but were clearly behind the U.S. in this technology.

Missile Accuracy

Probably the most important performance factor determining the strategic significance of MIRVs is the accuracy with which they can be delivered on target. Accuracy of reentry vehicle delivery, combined with nuclear explosion yield, determines the degree of vulnerability of different categories of targets to a missile attack. Generally, large urban and industrial complexes do not require high accuracy warhead delivery, but small hardened military targets do. A missile system capable of no better accuracy of delivery than several miles can still cause great damage to a city, but it may require ten or more times greater accuracy to give high assurance of destroying a hardened silo.

Obtaining sufficient missile accuracy even for urban targets was considered a major technical milestone in the early days of ICBM development. In the 15 years since ICBMs became operational, miss distances have been reduced by a factor of 8 approximately. Now, rather naively, some analysts assume that the same rate of improvement in accuracy (i.e., a factor of 2 every 5 years) will continue for the next decade or longer.

The usual measure of missile accuracy is the Circular Error Probability (CEP) defined as the radius of the circle centered on the target within which the reentry vehicle is expected to land with a 50 percent probability. In the early missile systems, when CEPs were greater than one mile, accuracy was limited by guidance system errors in sensing position and velocity of the missile (during powered flight). Because of impressive improvements in inertial guidance systems, other sources of error have become relatively more significant.

First, there are geodetic errors stemming from uncertainty in the precise location of the target and the launch site. Launch site location errors can be made very small for fixed land-based missiles but may be important for moving launchers such as submarines. Second, there are errors derived from the interaction of a reentry vehicle with the atmosphere during reentry. This category includes imprecise prediction of drag and lift forces on the reentry vehicle, displacement of the reentry vehicle by unpredictable winds in the target area, and deviation from the predicted trajectory during reentry caused by local variations in atmospheric density. Third, errors occur because of insufficient knowledge of certain geophysical data (particularly anomalies in the earth's gravitational field) to predict with precision the free-flight trajectories of reentry vehicles. Fourth, errors arise from imprecise control of the rocket thrust and steering and of the release of reentry vehicles. By careful design (and with perhaps some added complexity) this error source can be virtually eliminated and should not limit overall missile accuracy.

Substantial improvement in missile accuracy over what is currently attainable will require:

1. Highly innovative design and fabrication of inertial sensors (gyroscopes and accelerometers) for extremely accurate, reliable,

and stable performance. Techniques have already been suggested which would provide major improvements over what we now have.

2. Accurate target location determination. Large, soft targets such as cities do not require precise targeting. Small, hard military targets can probably be located on the ground to several hundred feet if necessary.

3. Survey of the earth's gravitation field in the region of expected reentry vehicle trajectories to measure significant anomalies, which then must be included in the guidance computation. Other geophysical error sources are probably too small to require special corrections.

4. Substantial reduction in reentry errors. This can be done in two ways. First, reentry vehicles can be designed so that the drag is as low as possible. The closer the reentry vehicle trajectory (on reentry) is to a ballistic trajectory, the better. With a truly streamlined design and short transit through the atmosphere, reentry errors can be reduced to about 300 feet. Second, reentry errors can be reduced by some means of terminal guidance. This can be achieved by including in each reentry vehicle a precision inertial guidance package to sense deviations from the predicted trajectory and a control mechanism (aerodynamic or rocket-powered) to make the small corrections in flight for accurate targeting. Another method of terminal guidance is to substitute for the inertial system an optical or radar system to observe the terrain in the reentry area and guide the reentry vehicle to target.

There are no fundamental technical reasons why missile accuracy cannot be made as precise as desired and some guidance experts have suggested CEPs of 100 feet as realistic goals. However, further improvements in accuracy at the same rate we have had may be much more difficult. Extrapolations from past improvements are not necessarily valid. Improved accuracy is no longer achieved only by improved guidance systems—many limiting factors enter the picture as CEPs get lower. It may be that they will all be amenable to technical circumvention, but as the number of factors gets larger, the probability that they all give way gets smaller.

It is important to note here that 2,000 feet CEPs are clearly achieveable with existing technology and that the ability of a single reentry vehicle to destroy a hard target with a reasonable probability depends on weapon yield and target hardness, but is in the region of 500 feet to 1,500 feet. How soon operational (not research and development) missiles can achieve such high accuracies remains uncertain, but money, time, and determination would surely make it come to pass.

A Comparison of Strategic Offensive Systems

ICBM Forces

ICBMs have been the prime element in the strategic force of both the U.S. and U.S.S.R. Of the three central strategic forces, they are the least expensive and the most amenable to tight command and control. For the present, we can retain confidence in their survivability. However, unless some means are found to limit improvements in accuracy, confidence in the survivability of a fixed land-based ICBM force will certainly diminish.

In July 1972 the U.S. ICBM force consisted of 1,000 relatively small, solid-fueled Minuteman missiles and 54 old, large, liquid-fueled Titans. The Minuteman force level was planned in the early 1960s and achieved by 1967. Since 1967, the major emphasis in the U.S. ICBM program has been upon upgrading the force for improved accuracy, greater payload, longer range, better command and control, and greater versatility.

The Soviet ICBM force grew very slowly at first, substantially lagging behind U.S. levels until the late 1960s. In the early and mid-1960s, it was generally assumed that U.S. missile superiority would remain unchallenged and that the Soviets would not commit the resources necessary to build their ICBM forces to U.S. levels. However, a massive Soviet ICBM buildup was observed starting in 1967 and was viewed in the U.S. first with perplexity, and then with deep apprehension. By 1969, U.S. superiority in ICBM numbers vanished, but the Soviet buildup did not slacken until 1971. In July 1972, the Soviet force consisted of over 1,500 operational ICBMs with approximately 90 additional ICBM launchers under construction.

The table below shows the buildup of U.S. and Soviet operational ICBMs:

	1960	1961	1962	1963	1964	1965	1966	1967	1968	1969	1970	1971	1972
U.S. ICBMs	18	63	294	424	834	854	904	1054	1054	1054	1054	1054	1054
Soviet ICBMs	35	50	75	100	200	270	300	460	800	1050	1300	1510	1528

In July 1972 the U.S. ICBM force consisted of:

1. 54 Titan 2s: These are the last and only survivors of a series of large, liquid-fueled U.S. missiles. They were deployed in 1962–1963 in hardened silos and carry a single warhead. They have been kept in the force because of their long reach (over 7,000-mile range) and large warhead (approximately five megatons). Newer U.S. ICBMs and SLBMs also have adequate range to be directed at targets in the deep interior of the Soviet Union; they also have greater accuracy and are far less expensive to maintain so that interest in maintaining Titans in the force has waned.

2. 1,000 Minutemen: These are small, solid-fueled missiles with hardened launchers. They come in three types: Minuteman I, first deployed in 1962 and being phased out; Minuteman II, first deployed in 1966, carrying a single warhead of 1- to 2-megaton yield; and Minuteman III which has been replacing Minuteman I since 1970. Minuteman III contains a MIRV'd payload of three warheads, presumably of 200-kiloton yield each. Minuteman III deployment in 550 of the 1,000 Minuteman silos is scheduled for completion in 1975. Full deployment of Minuteman III in all silos has not yet been authorized.

In July 1972 the Soviet ICBM force consisted of:

1. 210 SS-7s and SS-8s: These are old, large, liquid-fueled missiles, first deployed in 1961—mostly in soft (i.e., above ground) configurations. The payload consists of a single 5-megaton warhead. These missiles are not likely to remain in the Soviet force much longer.

2. 288 SS-9s (plus 25 additional launchers under construction): These are very large, liquid-fueled missiles, first deployed in 1965 in hardened silos with a throw weight capacity over 10,000 pounds. An SS-9 can carry a single warhead estimated to be about 25 megatons, or a cluster of three warheads of five megatons each that are not independently guided. The SS-9 has also been observed testing a fractional orbiting bombing system (FOBS). FOBS utilize a low altitude satellite which reenters the atmosphere after less than one full orbit. They can bypass certain existing U.S. early warning radars and de-

stroy targets in the U.S. The military utility of FOBS is marginal at best, since their payloads are necessarily smaller and less accurate than what can be delivered with conventional ballistic trajectories, and other radars can be built to provide early warning. It is not known whether, or to what extent, FOBS and triplet warheads are deployed on operational SS-9s.

3. 970 SS-11s (plus about 65 additional launchers under construction): These are also liquid-fueled and launched from hardened silos and have been deployed since 1966. Although physically larger than the U.S. Minuteman II, the payload is about the same, i.e., a single 1- to 2-megaton warhead. SS-11s have been observed in test with multiple (but not independently guided) warheads.

4. 60 SS-13s: The SS-13 is the newest and only solid-fueled Soviet ICBM and has a small payload, i.e., a single one-megaton warhead. Deployment is limited and has probably stopped.

For some time, the U.S. has been concerned about the potential threat to its own ICBM force of the large throw weight capability of the Soviet ICBMs. If the Soviets were to develop MIRVs successfully and to improve their accuracy to about 1,000 feet CEP or less, then simple calculations demonstrate that they could destroy all but a small fraction of the U.S. ICBMs with 300 missiles, each having the estimated throw weight of the SS-9.

While the focus has been on Soviet SS-9s with their gigantic throw weights, very high accuracy payloads mounted on missiles no larger than the SS-11 or Minuteman could also be effective in destroying the opponent's ICBMs, particularly if a zero stage were added for launch. The capability to destroy hard military targets is much more dependent on accuracy than it is on yield (an increase by a factor of 8 in yield is equivalent to an increase in accuracy by a factor of 2). It is hard to judge whether the U.S. with its higher accuracy ICBMs (estimated to be a factor of 2 better than Soviet missile accuracy) and developed MIRV technology is closer to developing a truly threatening counterforce capability than are the Soviets with their enormous total ICBM throw weight (estimated to be a factor of 3 to 4 greater than that of the U.S.). But, lest we forget what has already been stated, neither side had such capability in 1972 when SALT I was concluded, nor is either side likely to have such capability before the 1980s.

SLBM Forces

The first U.S. Polaris submarine carrying nuclear-armed ballistic missiles was deployed in 1960 and by 1967, forty-one boats were in operation—each boat carrying sixteen missiles. The design of the first ten boats was based on a modification of the nuclear-powered attack submarines that were already in the U.S. fleet, while the next thirty-one boats were specifically designed for delivery of SLBMs.

Currently, the U.S. SLBM force operates from overseas bases in Scotland, Spain, and Guam, thereby decreasing substantially the fraction of time each submarine requires to transit from port to station.

Several generations of U.S. missiles have been built for submarine launching. The first of the series, the A-1, had a range of about 1,200 miles. The succeeding A-2 and A-3 each had a longer range and a heavier payload capacity than its predecessor in the series. In 1972, the U.S. was in the midst of a retrofit program, installing the next in its series of operational SLBMs, the C-3 (also known as the Poseidon) in all but the 10 oldest Polaris submarines. The C-3 has a range of about 2,500 miles and carries 10 or more MIRVs, each of approximately 50-kiloton yield. As of July 1972, 10 boats were equipped with C-3s and 10 were undergoing conversion so they could be equipped with C-3s. When the full retrofit program is completed in 1976, the number of independently targetable warheads in the Polaris/Poseidon fleet will have increased from 656 to over 5,000.

The C-3 could have been designed to carry a single warhead of approximately 10-megaton yield instead of 10 warheads totalling a half megaton that it now carries. The primary motivation for installing multiple warheads on each SLBM was to saturate any conceivable ABM that the Soviets deployed and to extend the U.S. missile force destructive capability to a very large number of smaller soft targets.

During SALT I negotiations, the U.S. was designing still another missile, this one to be operational by 1977, for the Polaris boats. The new SLBM, the C-4, has a design range of approximately 4,000 miles, thereby vastly increasing the area of the ocean (particularly to include the Indian Ocean) from which submarines can fire and reach most of the important targets in the Soviet Union.

In 1972, the U.S. was also starting to develop the Trident submarine for production. This new, large, and costly boat would begin operation in 1978 and carry 24 SLBMs of the C-4 class, or of yet a newer type SLBM, the D-5. The D-5 is expected to have a range of approximately 6,000 miles—the distance between Los Angeles and Moscow. Equipped with C-4 or D-5 missiles, U.S. strategic submarines would essentially be on station while still in U.S. home ports. Full-scale Trident development provides the United States with the option of enlarging its SLBM force in the late 1970s or, at the very least, of replacing the 10 older Polaris boats which cannot carry Poseidon missiles. By being quieter and by having substantially larger ocean operating areas than existing submarines, Trident would also provide a hedge against some conceivable technical breakthroughs in antisubmarine warfare.

Critics of the Trident submarine program argue that there is no military need for an increased SLBM force; that most of the benefits of a longer range SLBM can also be obtained by the far less costly option of retrofitting the C-4 missile on existing Polaris submarines; and that the useful life of a submarine is at least 25 years, so no submarine replacements will be needed until the mid-1980s. Further, they claim that the Trident submarine will be much too costly and may well have the wrong characteristics to cope with whatever new antisubmarine technology might develop in the next decade.

The first Soviet Y-class submarine carrying SLBMs of the Polaris type was deployed in the mid-1960s. At the time the SALT negotiations were completed in 1972, the Soviets had approximately 29 boats of this class in operation and were building them at the very high rate of about eight a year. At that rate of production, the Soviets might have as many as 70 modern ballistic missile submarines by 1977. In addition, the Soviets retain in their SLBM force ten older H-class nuclear-powered submarines, each carrying three ballistic missiles with about a 700-mile range, and some G-class diesel-powered submarines. In 1972, the Soviets also started testing a longer range SLBM (i.e., 3,000–4,000 miles) intended for a new larger version of the Soviet Y-class submarines which has only 12 launch tubes per boat. The first of these submarines, referred to by the U.S. as Delta class, was launched in early 1972.

The technical quality of the Soviet SLBM force lags behind that of the U.S. The payload and range of the Soviet SLBMs deployed in 1972 were comparable to those of the early U.S. A-1 missiles; and the Y-class boats are not as quiet as the Polaris submarines. In addition, the Soviets have fewer ports from which to operate their submarines and no overseas bases. Even if U.S. submarines operated out of U.S. ports, geography would favor the U.S. It takes U.S. submarines less time to arrive on station from the U.S. east coast than it takes Soviet boats to reach mid-Atlantic stations, since they have to travel across the Norwegian Sea down past the narrow Greenland-Iceland or Iceland-United Kingdom gaps. These geographic and basing considerations could tend to make the Soviets put a high premium on increasing the range of their SLBMs in order to have more time on station and also to avoid having their boats navigate in the potentially unsafe region on either side of Iceland.

Strategic Bombers

Comparing bomber forces is difficult. The payload of any given bomber depends heavily on the mission range, the speed and altitude chosen for each leg of its flight, the number of in-flight refuelings, and whether the aircraft is intended to return to home base, to land at a post-strike base in a foreign country, or simply to engage in a one-way flight. Also, U.S. and Soviet strategic bombers will encounter very different air defense systems—since the Soviet air defenses are much more substantial than those of the U.S. Even simple numerical counts of aircraft can be ambiguous, since it is not always clear whether or not a medium-range bomber, no matter how it is categorized, may also be usable (with refueling) for strategic missions. The categorization used in this chapter is consistent with that used by the International Institute for Strategic Studies in their annual *Military Balance* and by U.S. Defense Department officials in their congressional testimony.

Neither the United States nor the Soviet Union has built heavy, intercontinental strategic bombers in more than a decade. By continually upgrading their older type bombers, both countries have managed to retain the military utility of their strategic bombers for a much longer period than had been expected.

The U.S. strategic bomber force consists of about 400 long-range subsonic B-52s and about 65 shorter range, supersonic FB-111s. Several models of the B-52 have been produced; the most recent (the B-52G and the B-52H) were first deployed in 1959. The life of the aircraft has been extended substantially by reinforcing some of the basic structural elements and by redesigning the aircraft control system to minimize the in-flight mechanical stress on the wing and tail sections. The FB-111 was first deployed in 1969 after encountering both a political controversy and serious technical problems during development. The FB-111 is a much smaller aircraft than the B-52.

In addition to "gravity" bombs, a part of the U.S. strategic bomber force is being equipped with new Short-Range Armed Missiles (SRAMs), each of which carries a nuclear warhead probably very roughly comparable in yield to that of each of the three RVs in Minuteman III. Equipped with such standoff missiles, each separately targetable, a bomber with SRAMs is comparable to the first stage of a missile system with a MIRV payload. Based on SRAMs alone, the FB-111 is perhaps the equivalent of one or two Minuteman III missiles and the B-52 is equivalent to five or six such missiles. Therefore, if all B-52s and F-111s were equipped with SRAMs, the destructive potential carried by the U.S. bomber force would be approximately twice that of the full U.S. ICBM force, or approximately equal to the sum of the U.S. ICBM plus SLBM forces.

To survive a surprise attack, bombers must be capable of getting off the ground on short notice. Early warning radars can give ten to fifteen minutes' warning of a massive ICBM attack, giving enough time for most bombers on ground alert status to get out of danger. The potential threat of Soviet submarines, stationed off the U.S. coast and capable of launching missiles on very low, short flight time trajectories, has forced the United States to disperse strategic bombers to many inland bases to assure survivability. If bomber survivability is threatened even more seriously, the U.S. has the option, albeit a very expensive one, of keeping a sizable fraction of its bomber and tanker force in the air at all times or at least during times of crisis.

In non-nuclear encounters during and since World War II, a few percent of the bombers penetrating heavily defended regions were destroyed on each raid. An attrition rate of 10 percent destroyed was considered very high indeed and for most missions has been considered unacceptable. On the other hand, in an all-out nuclear exchange where the destructive capability of each bomber is enormous, almost perfect defense is required to avoid massive destruction in a raid. It is almost certain that U.S. bombers can readily cope with Soviet air defenses. The bombers are equipped with a variety of sophisticated electronic countermeasures to jam or deceive air defense radars; they can fly very low to avoid long-range detection and tracking; and they can use stand-off missiles to avoid the need to penetrate defense systems around the target area. The existence of heavy Soviet defenses certainly limits the flexibility of the U.S. bomber force and would exact a toll of U.S. aircraft. But considering that even one tenth of the U.S. bomber force can, in principle, inflict damage equivalent to perhaps a thousand Hiroshima bombs, it is hard to see how Soviet air defenses can jeopardize the deterrent capability of this force.

The Soviet strategic bomber force consists of about 100 TU-95s (Bears), a long-range turboprop bomber first introduced into operation in 1956. The force also includes about 40 shorter range, jet-powered Bisons introduced into service about the same time.

Although the Soviet strategic bomber force is older, less capable, and much smaller than the U.S. bomber force, it still represents a substantial deterrent. The U.S. is not nearly as heavily defended as the Soviet Union and a fleet of bombers could readily penetrate U.S. air space, and simple calculations demonstrate the tremendous damage even a small, penetrating force could inflict.

In July 1972, the U.S. was in the early phases of developing and producing a new, long-range heavy bomber, the B-1, for initial deployment in the late 1970s. The B-1 is designed to fly supersonically at high altitudes and at about the speed of sound at low altitudes. It is designed to be based at a large variety of airfields. The requirement that it be capable of supersonic operation makes it expensive to produce and technically risky. The argument that the B-52 will soon have to be replaced if the U.S. is to maintain a bomber component in our central strategic forces is compelling. However, the U.S. Air Force has been less convincing in its arguments that the replacement aircraft must be supersonic and that a modern version of a B-52 type aircraft would not suffice. It may well be that the B-1 will not encounter serious difficulties and be a technical tour-de-force. Even so, it may not be cost-effective since it probably will be too expensive to buy in any reasonable quantities.

In 1972, the Soviets were in the early stages of flight testing a new supersonic bomber, the Backfire, which is larger than the U.S. FB-111 but smaller than the B-1. The detailed characteristics of the Backfire are still uncertain, but the best estimates indicate that it is a medium-range bomber intended for the European theater rather than for intercontinental use. This is not to say that the Backfire might not also be intended to reach U.S. targets with in-flight refueling, but only that its primary mission is not directed against targets in the U.S.

Both the U.S. and Soviet strategic bombers have relatively little utility for counterforce or surprise attack since they give warning signals long before they can release their nuclear weapons. Bomber activity, observable on early warning systems, can thus provide a useful means of deliberate communication with an opponent, although there are also circumstances when the observation of an adversary's air alert status or other activity with his bomber force might cause an unintended intensification of a crisis. This type of signalling has no counterpart for a missile force since the alert status of the force is not observable.

Anti-ballistic Missile (ABM) Systems

Although systems to defend against a ballistic-missile attack have been under development in both the U.S. and the Soviet Union since the mid-1950s when long-range offensive ballistic missiles first seemed feasible, there is little promise that an effective defensive system can ever be developed and, as a consequence, neither country has deployed any meaningful level of ABM.

The U.S. has spent over four billion dollars in various ABM programs. First, we had a program of full-scale development of the Nike-Zeus. This was followed by full-scale development of the more advanced Nike X. Although the hardware (i.e., radars, computers, interceptors, etc.) performed well in both systems, neither was able to cope adequately with the extremely difficult problems presented by the ballistic-missile threat that was envisaged—that is, an attack by a large number of missiles, each with multiple warheads and each containing effective penetration aids (i.e., decoys, jammers, chaff, etc.).

In addition to the Nike-Zeus and Nike X developments, both of which employ nuclear weapons on the defensive missiles, the U.S. ABM programs included research and exploratory development of exotic types of ABM, including attempts to use various kinds of electromagnetic or particle radiation to destroy reentry vehicles. These were pursued as last ditch efforts to be sure that no technical approaches that might possibly lead to an effective solution of the ABM problem were left unexplored.

Because the operational effectiveness of ABM is marginal and the cost of deployment so high (some estimates were up to 50 billion dollars), the U.S. decision, after anguished appraisals each year from the late 1950s until 1967, had been to continue development but not to initiate deployment. Finally, in 1967, presumably due to perceived pressures from Congress and also to frustration about Soviet responsiveness to his approach to arms control, President Johnson authorized the deployment of a truncated version of Nike X to provide defense of the whole country against a very light attack. The system, called Sentinel, was justified as a means of defense of the entire U.S. population and territory against a potential Chinese ICBM force or an accidental or unauthorized launch from the Soviet Union.

To the surprise of many observers, the decision to deploy Sentinel aroused great objection from a growing segment of the U.S. Senate, which was disillusioned with continued heavy expenditures, and from the public, which had previously been rather apathetic about the ABM issue. Opposition to Sentinel centered about several aspects of the system: its high cost and limited effectiveness against even a light attack; the placement of nuclear-armed interceptors close to populated areas, particularly Boston, Chicago, and Seattle; and probably most significant, that Sentinel deployment opened the door to a whole new dimension in the arms race which would probably escalate both U.S. and Soviet nuclear arms activity to new high levels without any increase in the security of either side.

The essence of the argument that ABM for the protection of population would be escalatory, and perhaps even dangerous, ran something like this: ABM was technically very difficult and prohibitively expensive, while offensive missiles to destroy cities were relatively cheap. Any efforts at defense would be countered at a fraction of the cost by increasing the size and sophistication of the opponent's offensive force. In fact, to compensate for any uncertainties in its assessment of the defensive system's capabilities, a nation facing an ABM would enlarge the size of its offensive force more than necessary. The net result would be that even modest ABM efforts on both sides would result in much larger offensive arsenals for both, and perhaps an unending offensive/defensive systems race for both. An inference from this argument is that if ABM were kept from being deployed, there would be hope for levelling off offensive systems and, perhaps some day, major reductions.

Interesting to note is the fact that, in principle, these arguments against ABM defense of cities do not apply to ABM systems deployed to defend strategic bases. Defense of strategic offensive systems is a way of strengthening one's own deterrent force and discounting an opponent's preemptive strike, while defense of cities has the effect of reducing an opponent's deterrent capability. The paradox that ABM to defend cities and people may escalate the arms race, while ABM to defend missile forces may not, is a consequence of the high cost and low effectiveness of ABM. If a truly effective ABM were possible, the argument would no longer be valid.

In 1969, the Nixon administration reviewed and subsequently modified the Sentinel program into the Safeguard ABM system, emphasizing protection of Minuteman sites against a possible Soviet preemptive strike rather than nationwide defense against China. The full Safeguard system, as proposed, had 12 sites and would have provided a thin defense of all of the U.S., as well as defense of Minuteman silos. Each ABM site included one large, phased-array radar referred to as a Missile Site Radar (MSR) and about 100 Spartan and Sprint interceptors. The Spartan, with a range of hundreds of miles, provided a first tier defense while the very agile Sprint, with a range of only 25 miles, provided a second tier defense. In addition, some sites included a very large Perimeter Acquisition Radar (PAR) to provide radar surveillance for large sections of the country.

Only Phase I of the program, which included four ABM sites located to protect Minuteman silos in Missouri, Wyoming, North Dakota, and Montana, was authorized, and Congress later limited appropriations to allow the completion of only two sites: those at Malmstrom in Montana and Grand Forks in North Dakota. Congress never viewed favorably an ABM defense of the National Command Authority, which meant a site near Washington, D.C.

Safeguard, which incorporated components originally intended for an urban defense system, has been shown to be far less cost-effective than it might otherwise be. Specifically, the MSR was much too vulnerable and too expensive to have more than one or two at each site, the Spartan was ineffective against the kinds of penetration aids the Soviets could use, and the reach of the Sprint was not long enough to protect the MSR and many Minutemen silos. Consequently, in 1972, the U.S. started development of a new ABM system specifically designed to protect Minuteman silos. It had smaller and cheaper radars than the MSR so that many (i.e., 10–20) can be deployed at each site and was designed to operate compatibly with deployed Safeguard batteries.

The Soviet Union deployed its first ABM defense around Leningrad in the early 1960s. The system was soon dismantled, probably because of technical difficulties. In the mid-1960s a more substantial ABM was built around Moscow, but the system was not deployed with any great speed and it never reached the size that both U.S. observers anticipated and the Soviet military must have planned. At the time of SALT I, the Moscow system (also referred to as Galosh) consisted of two large, phased-array radars (referred to as Dog House Radars by the U.S.), several sets of smaller mechanical-scan radars (called Try Adds in U.S. nomenclature), and a total of 64 interceptor missiles at four operational complexes. Even if the system worked perfectly, it would be of only minor consequence to the strategic balance, since it was only capable of destroying 64 of the thousands of warheads the U.S. has mounted on its strategic ballistic missiles. Moreover, the technical performance of each of the key components of the system (i.e., radars, interceptors, and data processing equipment) is considered by U.S. observers to be substantially lower than that of the U.S. Safeguard system.

There were no indications that Soviets planned to deploy the Galosh ABM at any other localities. In spite of avowed Soviet interest and commitment to defensive systems, fundamental technical inadequacies may have kept them from deploying ABM in meaningful quantities.

Before leaving the subject of ABM, it is important to note that designing a system which can play a militarily useful role in defending hardened silos is much simpler than designing a system to protect cities and people. To be effective in protecting population, an ABM defense can allow few, if any, reentry vehicles to penetrate. To be effective in protecting missile silos, a defense need only reduce significantly the likelihood that a preemptive strike would succeed in destroying essentially all the silos. Also, missiles in silos are hard targets —and can only be destroyed by explosions that are very close—while people and houses are not. People are also very vulnerable to radioactive fallout, while missile silos are not.

These significant differences between the defense of missile silos and urban areas suggest that perhaps a small, non-nuclear, and inexpensive system might be designed to handle what is referred to in

U.S. terminology as hard site defense. Indeed, several attempts have been made at designing simple ABM systems, but the painful conclusion from these efforts is that, with current technology, even hard site defense requires relatively large radars, big computers, and nuclear-armed interceptors. These components would, of course, be smaller and less expensive than those required for an urban area defense, but there is not a vary large difference between the two types of ABM systems in cost and size.

AIR DEFENSES

For the past decade, the U.S. has been steadily reducing its continental defenses against aircraft attacks. Older components are not being replaced as they become obsolescent. The air defense system that remains is a skeletal version of what was planned in the early 1950s in the pre-missile era. Although the current system provides early warning, it provides little defense against a determined, massive bomber attack which the Soviets can mount, particularly if such an air attack were preceded by a missile attack devised to destroy U.S. defenses. For some years, feeble attempts were made by the U.S. Department of Defense to modernize the U.S. air defense system. These could not arouse much enthusiasm or support since the costs were too high for the slight improvement in capability they provided. Besides, capability in air defense seemed futile since the U.S. was completely vulnerable to destruction by the existing Soviet missile force.

The Soviet Union has maintained interest in air defense and vigor in its air defense programs. The backbone of the Soviet air defense system, which is the most extensive in the world, is made up of the SA-2 and newer SA-5 long-range systems and the SA-3 short-range-low-altitude system. These and some older surface-to-air missile systems (SAMs) are deployed throughout the Soviet Union with a total of 10,000 interceptor missiles (compared to fewer than 800 for the U.S.). In addition, the Soviets retain more than 3,000 interceptor aircraft, about six times the number in the U.S. air defense system. Detailed analyses of the effectiveness of Soviet air defenses against a large-scale strategic bomber attack and the vulnerability of the system itself to a missile attack (against which it cannot protect itself) indicate that the system would have little military utility in an all-out nuclear exchange.

Continued Soviet investment in air defense systems is indeed puzzling to Western analysts. It seems too simple and unconvincing to see Soviet activity as only a consequence of their traditional interest in defensive systems. It is conceivable that by modifying their SA-2 and SA-5 air defense systems and moving them to new locations, the Soviets could develop some limited effectiveness against a ballistic missile attack, a possibility which caused uneasiness within the U.S. defense community. Some feared that the existence of large numbers of Soviet air defense systems might tempt the Soviets to a "cheap and dirty" ABM development. Other U.S. analysts regard the possibility of upgrading *existing* air defense systems to provide a meaningful ABM capability as fanciful speculation, too remote to be taken seriously. On the other hand, there is general agreement that any *new* air defense systems designed to handle small, bomber launched air-to-surface missiles, would require a technical approach not much different from the design of a system to handle ballistic missiles. Consequently, an effective future air defense system would have to be designed to have some dual capability.

Forward-Based Systems and Other Nuclear Forces

In addition to the strategic forces discussed above, both the United States and Soviet Union have other nuclear forces which play, or at least have the potential of playing, a strategic role.

The U.S. has hundreds of modern aircraft based in Europe and on aircraft carriers. These aircraft are capable of delivering nuclear warheads on Soviet territory. Paticularly relevant are the roughly 70 F-111s stationed in England and the A-6 and A-7 aircraft on carriers in the Mediterranean and Western Pacific. The U.S. F-4 aircraft stationed in Europe may be capable of reaching the periphery of Soviet territory, but are certainly not capable of deep penetration. These forward-based systems (FBS) have been a special matter of contention. The Soviets claim that they are clearly strategic since they can deliver nuclear weapons on Soviet territory, while the U.S. claims that they are not strategic but part of our general purpose forces. Particularly, since they are themselves vulnerable to an all-out nuclear attack, they cannot play a major role as a deterrent force and therefore cannot be equated with the central strategic forces.

The Soviet nuclear forces include about 600 intermediate- and medium-range missiles in soft emplacements and about 20 older G-class diesel submarines carrying three missiles each—about half carry short-range ballistic missiles and half carry short-range cruise missiles. The Soviets also have about 700 medium-range bombers that can carry nuclear weapons. All of these are probably directed at European and Asian targets. However, the submarines can be moved to operate off the U.S. coast and the bombers can be made to reach the U.S. with refueling. The Soviet G-class submarine force is old and is expected to be retired in the near future.

CHAPTER THREE
U.S. Decision Making for SALT

ALTON FRYE

To appraise the SALT I agreements of 1972 requires an analysis of the way in which the United States government shaped its decisions on the myriad details of these complex understandings. Let it be said at the outset that the story is not one of good men versus bad men, of reason versus passion, or of liberals versus conservatives. Rather it is a tale of contending rationalities, as strong-minded and dedicated men brought differing perspectives to bear on the task of framing a policy regarding strategic arms which would serve their individual visions of American security and international peace.

THE INTELLECTUAL AND POLITICAL CONTEXT

U.S. policy concerning strategic arms limitation evolved in the changing context of the 1960s and early 1970s. Perhaps the most fundamental international change was the achievement by the Soviet Union of rough strategic parity with the United States. However, that change was itself a function of U.S. behavior which was determined primarily by a number of domestic factors.

In particular, the strategic parity which was a prerequisite for strategic arms limitation could not have come about except for conscious restraint on the part of the U.S. government. That restraint owes much to the remarkable change of perspective which occurred in the Department of Defense (DOD) during the incumbency of Robert McNamara as secretary. Had McNamara and his colleagues persisted in

the policies of strategic superiority followed by their predecessors—
and indeed by themselves during the early 1960s—the extraordinary
growth of Soviet armament during recent years would have spurrred
an even greater extension of the American strategic inventory.

After the rapid buildup of American strategic forces in the Kennedy administration, provoked by what proved to be a false alarm regarding the rate of Soviet strategic expansion, the principal defense
officials in the United States grew more sensitive to the hazards of
a seemingly endless, evidently expensive competition in strategic
arms between the United States and the Soviet Union. Though still
wary of Soviet intentions, U.S. decision makers acquired confidence
that the margin of U.S. military capabilities afforded an ample guarantee of deterrence through the threat of retaliation. They saw that
massive additions to American force levels would pose new threats to
strategic stability without enhancing deterrence in any measurable
way. Furthermore, after the early theoretical exercises regarding counterforce and damage-limiting operations against the emerging Soviet
strategic forces, the perception spread within the U.S. government that
both great powers possessed such lethal weapons that even modest
forces surviving on either side would be able to inflict unacceptable
damage on the other. The quest for counterforce and damage-limiting
weapons would continue to be pressed by a few, but the realization
gradually became more widely accepted that such weapons could not
protect the American people; they could only provoke the Soviets.

The consequences of these altered attitudes were profound. Under
pressure from the military services to maintain the vast quantitative
advantage which the United States had enjoyed throughout the postwar era, Defense Secretary McNamara persuaded President Johnson
not to race ahead with additional deployments beyond those achieved
by the mid-1960s. The focus instead would shift to maintaining a
qualitative lead over Soviet technology. Thus, initial Air Force proposals to deploy well over 2,000 Minuteman missiles were trimmed to
about 1,700 and eventually the United States held the Minuteman
force to a level of only 1,000. Similarly, developmental difficulties and
strategic considerations led the McNamara Pentagon to resist pressures
for early deployment of a new, manned strategic bomber. In this
manner, the United States reached and maintained a kind of plateau
in its strategic posture, albeit with continuing and substantial technological innovation in the force structure.

Official U.S. acceptance of Moscow's capacity to inflict lethal damage on the American people was the result not of a linear and automatic process but of a calculus in which various factors inclined in different directions. Attempting to cope with a rapidly changing strategic environment, U.S. national security policy was itself in a state of high flux produced by intellectual, political, and operational forces.

On the intellectual plane, the 1960s saw the growth of a highly sophisticated and fully informed literature demonstrating not only the compatibility of certain kinds of arms limitation with national security planning, but the need for appropriate forms of arms control as a complement to the force deployments on which governments were accustomed to rely. A large body of analyses and arguments in the 1950s had emphasized the novelty of the nuclear balance and the necessity for a kind of collaboration between adversaries to manage the perils of the modern strategic equation. It is noteworthy that the bulk of these studies came not from career military officers but from the sizeable number of civilian analysts who turned their attention to the dilemmas of nuclear strategy. The most important work of the strategic analysts concerned the intricate psychological and military facets of nuclear deterrence.

Perceiving the intolerable costs of a thermonuclear Pearl Harbor and gradually accepting the improbability of an ironclad defense against either bombers or intercontinental missiles, defense experts concentrated increasingly on the requirements of a reliable system of deterrence. They discerned what many consider to be the key to stable deterrence: the possession of a sufficient number of invulnerable strategic weapons that could survive a nuclear attack and be used to retaliate on a scale which promised to destroy the aggressor as a functioning society. From the adoption of a survivable second-strike force as a primary planning factor, there ensued a chain reaction of adjustments in American strategic doctrine.

U.S. preoccupation with maintaining an invulnerable second-strike force (or an assured destruction capability, as it would be known in the McNamara years) led inexorably to the knowledge that deterrence could not be unilateral if it were to be stable. Stable deterrence is necessary to ward off the holocaust. But deterrence between great powers armed with nuclear weapons can be stable only to the extent that both parties are confident neither could successfully launch a nuclear strike without inviting certain devastation in response. Therefore, deterrence must be mutual.

Elaborated through years of study and experience, the syllogism grew in power and persuasiveness. Yet even for analysts, not to mention responsible decision makers, it was excruciating to accept the corollary principle that the Soviet Union, as well as the United States, must possess a secure second-strike force. To grant any nation the right to hold millions of Americans hostage was an agonizing prospect. Yet, mutual deterrence required mutual vulnerability. To protect the American people from nuclear attack, they must be left naked to precisely that contingency. To deter the dreaded strike, the invulnerability of U.S. weapons must be assured at precisely the time when the utter vulnerability of U.S. citizens must be acknowledged. The paradox prompted deep skepticism in some circles, while it provoked caricature in others.

Had there been an apparent technological solution to these dilemmas, it is doubtful that the basic concept of mutual deterrence and its implications for strategic arms control could have gained sway in any government. In some respects, it was the failure no less than the success of modern technology which impressed analysts with the inevitability of a condition of mutual deterrence. As the decade wore on, it became more and more clear that nothing either side could do would enable it to deny to the other a residual capacity to deliver a devastating strike. The doctrine of mutual deterrence did not so much state a strategic objective as describe a technological fact. It was just this fact which loomed larger and larger in the succession of strategic posture statements which Robert McNamara presented to the Congress.

Though intellectual acceptance of mutual deterrence was increasing, the political context of U.S. decision making, informed by quite different considerations and articulated by spokesmen of divergent views, was by no means uniform. Leading members of Congress, especially the ranking membership of the House and Senate Armed Services and Appropriations Committees, were allied with certain elements of the national security bureaucracy in a deep-seated and chronic mistrust of the Soviet Union. On numerous occasions since 1945, senators like Richard Russell and congressmen like Mendel Rivers had seen Moscow reject what they considered exceedingly generous proposals to limit arms. Their Cold War experience with a deceptive and dangerous adversary made them doubt whether any dependable arrangements could be reached with the Soviet Union. These men were skeptics, not simpletons. Few members of Congress were strong advocates of the strategic logic which argued that a situation of mutual deterrence was probably the best the United States could achieve. By no means oblivious to this line of reasoning, their perception of the Soviet Union inclined them to support the most vigorous efforts to escape from the condition of mutual deterrence. In practical terms, this meant substantial support from a number of senior members of the Congress for energetic development of ABM systems and for a broad variety of measures to enhance America's offensive capabilities, including counterforce technologies.

Surely, there were countervailing influences at work in the Congress. From the 1950s onward, Senator Hubert Humphrey and other members of the Foreign Relations Subcommittee on Disarmament formed a growing chorus of legislators who stressed the overriding hazards of the arms race. These figures achieved a signal success in the creation in 1961 of the Arms Control and Disarmament Agency (ACDA) as an executive agency responsible for explicit emphasis on these aspects of national security planning. The work of this subcommittee proved seminal in several respects, providing a fertile seedbed for a broad range of arms control ideas and helping to recruit such tough-minded and respected security experts as Senator Stuart Symington to the cause of restraining superfluous weapons. Nevertheless, just as ACDA remained an agency of limited potency in executive planning, the arms control bloc in Congress held limited influence until a broader coalition emerged at the time of the debates over ABM deployment in 1968–70.

The inherent tension between the intellectual and political context of American strategic planning might never have been resolved except for basic changes in the operational context in which these several factors mingled. Soviet opposition to dependable verification measures became a symbol of putative bad faith on their part, suggesting a Russian intention to enter only those agreements which they might subvert to their advantage. But in the course of the 1960s the progressive development and installation of a number of intelligence technologies gave American authorities greater confidence that, for a number of possible arms limitations, an adversary would not be able to cheat, at least on a scale sufficient to alter the basic stability of the strategic equation. As useful and welcome as these systems proved to be, their introduction faced formidable political and operational obstacles.

Despite Nikita Khrushchev's oblique endorsement of space-based surveillance, Soviet military and legal literature of the early 1960s persistently damned intelligence collection via satellite as an intolerable intrusion and a violation of national sovereignty. Russian commentators occasionally coupled their critique of observation satellites with their claims to a right to employ antisatellite weapons against them. Given the Soviet Union's previous repudiation of the Eisenhower proposal for an "open skies" system of mutual inspection, American officials took most seriously the possibility that Moscow might actually begin to destroy U.S. satellites. These fears and the desire to avoid the political controversy, which might well flow from any suggestion that Washington had managed unilaterally to impose the equivalent of the open skies procedures denounced by Moscow, help explain the obsessive secrecy surrounding U.S. observation satellite programs.

It took time and familiarity with the results for those at the pinnacle of the U.S. political system to learn to trust the output of the novel technologies which were placed at their disposal during the early 1960s. Thus, the propensity remained high for the American government to hedge against the danger that Moscow might steal a march on Washington with grave consequences internationally and calamitous results domestically for the officials responsible. Eventually, however, satellites and other modern observation technologies paved the way to reconciling the intellectual and political contexts we have described.

One glimpses irony here. For years, ranking American politicians concerned with national security had hoped for a technological fix to the mortal jeopardy in which expanding Soviet nuclear capabilities placed the United States. The politicians' hopes were fueled by the claims of eager weaponeers who, mistrusting political approaches to national security problems, held to the idea that only more and better technologies could provide safety for the country. Only slowly did it become clear that technologists could not solve the problem they had created by fashioning weapons of mass destruction. However, the fabrication of observation satellites and other surveillance instruments constituted a technological contribution of a wholly different character. It meant that weapons which could not be defeated technologically might at least be managed politically, to the mutual benefit of the adversaries. In short, the rapid progress of observation technology moved the broad objectives of arms control theory closer to the realm of political feasibility.

Planning for SALT: The Johnson Administration

On January 21, 1964, in a message to the Conference of the Eighteen-Nation Disarmament Committee presented at the first session following achievement of the limited nuclear test ban, President Johnson proposed that Moscow and Washington explore a "verified freeze of the number and characteristics of strategic nuclear offensive and defensive vehicles." The truth is, however, that the United States was woefully unprepared to pursue negotiations at that time.

The president's reference to a possible freeze triggered a broad range of study activity in and out of the U.S. government. It provided decisive impetus to moving the U.S. arms control effort beyond the sterile exercise of drafting plans for general and complete disarmament—a proclivity sparked by propaganda battles with the Soviets at previous disarmament conferences.

Early in 1965, a special studies group of the Joint Chiefs of Staff began to evaluate various freeze proposals in some depth, as did the Arms Control and Disarmament Agency. These studies, plus a number performed at private research centers, helped to clarify the complex relationships between various types of offensive and defensive systems. Then and later, expert opinion was not unanimous. Some observers saw a golden opportunity for effective reduction of the lethal potential of the two arsenals, if offensive weapons were tightly constrained while defensive systems were permitted to grow to reasonably high levels. To the extent that ABM systems proved effective, the levels of damage which an attacking nation might inflict would decline.

Other analysts, however, and in time the preponderance of them, concluded that deployment of large-scale defensive networks by either country would only spur the other to augment its offensive forces in the same or greater proportion. Each side would be determined to maintain an unquestioned capacity to retaliate and would increase or improve its strategic forces in any way necessary to guarantee penetration of an ABM system. Though contested by advocates of ballistic-missile defense on the Joint Chiefs of Staff, the view that large ABM systems would threaten strategic stability began to permeate the defense community.

Meanwhile the Soviet Union, historically and bureaucratically attracted to major investment in defense systems, began to deploy an ABM system. In the military establishment and in Congress, pressure for the United States to reciprocate began to mount. In the advisory channels of the executive branch, a number of prominent technologists, including former director of Defense Research, Herbert York, and others affiliated with the president's science advisory committee, argued the futility and danger of a matching ABM deployment. The burden of technical advice reaching President Johnson was opposed to fielding an ABM system, but countering that advice was the insistence of the Joint Chiefs of Staff and influential legislators that the United States must begin a defensive network of its own.

The result was a kind of long stall, in which the president sought to assuage the anxieties of his former colleagues on Capitol Hill, while making repeated overtures to the Soviets to join in serious negotiations to limit both offensive and defensive weapons. But so long as Moscow proved unresponsive, Johnson could not hope to fend off Congress indefinitely. In 1966, the legislators approved, against the administration's wishes, more than $160 million for advance preparation to deploy an ABM system. Early the next year, still lacking Soviet agreement to begin strategic arms limitation talks, Johnson felt obliged to ask authorization of $350 million to begin an ABM deployment. He assured the Congress that unless the Soviet Union demonstrated real determination to support mutual arms limitations, he would begin to use the contingent authorization before the year was out. At the Glassboro Summit Conference of July 1967, Johnson and McNamara tried in vain to enlist Soviet interest in avoiding an ABM race. Premier Alexei Kosygin seemed insensitive or indifferent to the consequences of an interacting competition in offensive and defensive weapons.

A few weeks later in San Francisco, Secretary McNamara announced that the United States would soon begin to install a thin ABM system designed to cope with the type of relatively light attack of which China might be capable in coming years. The so-called Sentinel system would also be capable of meeting inadvertent launches and of providing some protection for strategic bombers and ICBMs against moderately heavy counterforce attacks from the Soviet Union. But the secretary's extensive discussion in that speech left no doubt of his conviction that it would be folly to build a thick defense in an attempt to ward off the burgeoning nuclear weaponry of the Soviet Union.

The impact of the U.S. decision to deploy Sentinel will long be debated. Did it speed diplomacy on its way to strategic arms limitation? Or did it impede negotiations by adding another complication to the balance of forces between Moscow and Washington? Lacking access to the inner councils of the Soviet government, no one can say with confidence. What one can assert is that many influential congressmen and senior defense officials of the Johnson administration and subsequently the Nixon administration became convinced that only an active U.S. ABM program would induce the Soviet Union to bargain in good faith. In consultations with the Senate Armed Services Committee, Clark Clifford, McNamara's successor as secretary of defense, emphasized his support for the planned Sentinel deployment and stressed the program's value in persuading Moscow of the desirability of mutual arms limitations.

The notion of ABM as a useful bargaining chip gained credence during the 1968 congressional debate on the Sentinel system, when a favorable Senate vote was followed by Moscow's belated public expression of interest in strategic arms talks. Actually, quiet communication between the two capitals had already begun to reveal a 180 degree turn in Moscow's previous insistence that ABM systems were nonprovocative; but to Senator Henry Jackson, Congressman Melvin Laird, and other key legislators, it was more than coincidence that the Kremlin published its willingness to talk at the very moment the United States was launching an ABM program of its own. The so-called bargaining chip rationale for an American defense network had won a place in the national security debate.

During the first half of 1968, a series of probes between the governments of the two superpowers tested the water and explored whether, in fact, concrete negotiations on strategic arms would take place. Somewhat surprisingly, considering the fact that the United States had for years sought Soviet agreement to enter into serious discussion of strategic arms limitation, the summer of 1968 still found the American government without an agreed position for such negotiations. Only when the talks appeared imminent did President Johnson direct intensive preparation for the undertaking. A committee of principals, including Secretaries McNamara and Rusk and other senior national security officials, was ordered to coordinate the U.S. effort. The deputy director of the Arms Control and Disarmament Agency, Adrian Fisher, headed an interagency working group to perform the detailed analyses.

The guidelines, modus operandi, and sheer velocity of the Johnson administration's planning for SALT contrast sharply with the later preparations of the Nixon administration. Mr. Johnson made clear that he wanted the national security bureaucracy to devise an intelligent and workable proposal which both American and Soviet observers would recognize as a genuine basis for serious bargaining. With customary concern for his domestic flank, Johnson also demanded that the proposal represent a consensus of views, especially between the military and civilian participants in the process. He was anxious to head off the possibility of discontented elements engaging in sniping or recrimination at a later stage. These presidential impulses registered effectively throughout the government. The Joint Chiefs of Staff, no less than civilian planners, recognized that they were obliged to produce a substantive and affirmative set of proposals rather than a mere negotiating posture. One measure of JCS sensitivity to the White House's determination to move forward promptly with the negotiations was the assignment of Air Force General Royal Allison to serve as the Chiefs' principal agent in the enterprise. With past service in the JCS Special Studies Group, Allison was an experienced senior officer who brought both competence and stature to a field which had previously been something of a stepchild to the military.

The Fisher working group, with participants from the Departments of State and Defense as well as the intelligence agencies, bore formal responsibility for presentations to the committee of principals. The crucial bureaucratic bargaining, however, took place within the Department of Defense, where leadership of the SALT exercise was vested in the Office of International Security Affairs (ISA) under Paul Warnke. A strong supporting contribution came from the potent Office of Systems Analysis which, with the Joint Chiefs of Staff, completed the major triangle of the intra-DOD planning group. The Office of the Director of Defense Research and Engineering (DDR&E) under Dr. John Foster, an effective skeptic of the SALT venture, was only peripherally involved in the planning process, although DDR&E frequently made known its views to the secretary of defense; informally, Dr. Foster and his staff served as a kind of intellectual backstop for the work of the JCS.

Virtually all of the major questions which later occupied planners in the Nixon administration surfaced during this first round of planning for SALT in the summer of 1968. Should ABM systems be banned entirely? If not, what level should be prescribed? Should the incipient MIRV technology be prohibited, and if so how? Should the agreement call for a literal freeze on offensive deployments or should systems then under construction be allowed to proceed to operational status? Should the agreement cover bombers or not? And should the signatories have freedom to substitute systems between categories of weapons, e.g., phase out land-based ICBMs in favor of additional missile-launching submarines? Permeating the discussion of these and other issues was the chronic problem of verification. Should the U.S. package include only those items which could be verified absolutely or should it contain an interlocking set of provisions with somewhat less stringent verification requirements?

Under ISA leadership, General Allison and his colleagues engaged in a more flexible and intimate collaboration than the formalistic exchanges of letters often employed in communications between the civilian leadership of the department and the Joint Chiefs. Pressed to implement the president's directive for a consensus position, the Defense participants joined in a fruitful prenegotiation of disputed points. Questions were not presented formally to the JCS until they could be framed in a manner calculated to elicit concurrence. For example, despite the simplifying advantages of a zero-level ABM proposal, the predictable JCS insistence on some latitude for defensive deployments persuaded other DOD officials not to advance such a proposal. Other disputes were similarly muted or finessed, including the complex problem of controlling multiple independently targetable reentry vehicles (MIRV).

In the Defense Department and the Arms Control and Disarmament Agency, there were many who were concerned about the destabilizing counterforce potential of MIRV systems. Nevertheless, the Air Force and Navy were so committed to MIRV deployment that neither within the Defense Department nor at the committee of principals was there a concerted campaign to include a MIRV ban in the SALT package. The issue was considered too contentious to resolve in advance of talks with the Soviets. Once the U.S. was directly engaged in negotiations with the Soviet Union, some officials hoped that Moscow's own concern about MIRV deployment would justify the bureaucratic friction of thrashing out an agreed American position on the matter.

The outcome of these several levels of SALT preparation was a position which called for a limitation of ABM systems together with a freeze on ICBM and SLBM deployments and no freedom to mix between those latter categories of weapons. Although the broad elements of this proposal mark the direction which the United States would pursue for several years, as then formulated they undoubtedly concealed a number of bureaucratic squabbles which were bound to emerge in the event of actual negotiations. Nevertheless, this planning phase recorded a number of singular achievements, several of which were summarized in a letter from Secretary Clifford to the president, conveying the Defense Department's endorsement of the SALT recommendations. In this endorsement, the Joint Chiefs of Staff for the first time concurred in an arms control package constructed primarily around national means of verification rather than onsite inspection. The corollary of this approach was recognition by the U.S. government that the goal should be to control activities for which unilateral verification was probable rather than certain, a less absolutistic and more prudent standard than previous requirements posed by the JCS. Moreover, of the greatest significance, the military and civilian leadership of the Defense establishment joined in the opinion that the nation's security could better be served by cooperative diplomacy than by competitive deployments.

As it happened this tentative consensus would not be tested in hard bargaining with the Soviet Union that year. Scarcely had the United States prepared a position for strategic arms limitation talks when the Soviet invasion of Czechoslovakia in August 1968 cast a fatal chill in the atmosphere. Neither President Johnson's hopes for prompt SALT negotiations nor his desire for a Moscow Summit conference would be fulfilled.

The diplomatic delays arising out of the Czech crisis proved extremely costly. In no respect was this so true as in the effect of these delays on the evolution of MIRV technology. With a two-year program of MIRV testing in prospect prior to deployment, and with an early beginning of arms limitation talks expected, Defense Secretary Clifford saw no reason to slow down the U.S. MIRV effort. Although he would later change his mind, Mr. Clifford seems to have been comfortable with the "we arm to parley" axiom. An ongoing U.S. campaign to perfect MIRV technology was calculated to heighten Russian interest in prompt and productive negotiations. Unfortunately, by the end of August 1968, the talks were off and the tests were on. In coming years, this drastic transformation of American missile systems would invite a matching Soviet effort and would pose a grave challenge to a stable arms control arrangement.

Thus, the first hectic effort to design an American position for strategic arms limitation came to naught. Yet by forcing the bureaucracy to think through the relevant issues, the initial attempt laid the groundwork for the definitive planning and negotiations which were to come.

PLANNING FOR SALT: THE NIXON PHASE

A man well-versed and keenly interested in foreign policy, Richard Nixon came to the presidency still new to questions of nuclear strategy. He had campaigned for the office in 1968 with outworn shibboleths alleging the value and feasibility of American strategic superiority. He seemed to favor a sizable ABM deployment, downplaying the probability of successful negotiations with an adversary which he continued to view as ruthless and untrustworthy. Yet the new president moved swiftly to adapt his views to the demands and opportunities of the modern strategic condition. Early in his term, Nixon dropped the ritual invocation of strategic "superiority" in favor of acceptance of strategic "sufficiency." This was a welcome and serviceable euphemism for the unavoidable nuclear parity which was then impending. Its corollary was a presidential commitment to seek negotiated limits on strategic arms rather than to risk heating up the arms race in a vain attempt to recapture superiority.

Unlike his predecessor, Nixon was not prepared to accept the bureaucracy's definition of the strategic problems facing the nation or its prescription of a single negotiating option. During the transitional period between the two administrations, the president-elect conferred extensively with his national security adviser, Dr. Henry Kissinger, and laid out a sequence of planning and decision making on strategic matters. It was clear from the outset that Mr. Nixon would not be rushed into premature talks with the Soviet Union. An examination of the U.S. strategic posture would precede the elaboration of an American diplomatic position regarding arms limitation.

At the risk of conveying to Moscow a declining U.S. interest in strategic arms limitation talks, the president did not immediately seize upon the Soviet Union's reiteration of interest in early negotiations. On January 21, 1969, a National Security Study Memorandum (NSSM 3) launched a general review of American military posture. This was but one of a barrage of NSSMs which flooded the bureaucracy during the early months of the Nixon administration. Its importance as a prelude to SALT planning was widely perceived and, at the suggestion of the National Security Council staff, Deputy Secretary of Defense David Packard agreed to facilitate SALT preparations by expediting the strategic force evaluation. The studies harvested by NSSM 3 eventually led to a National Security Decision Memorandum (NSDM) setting forth several criteria for strategic sufficiency. The sufficiency concept would perform valuable service in molding the Nixon administration's SALT position. That position began to take shape on March 13, 1969 when NSSM 28 called for the several interested agencies to identify and analyze the principal issues and options for SALT.

The emphasis was on options. President Nixon and Dr. Kissinger made very clear that they did not want an agreed bureaucratic recommendation. According to NSSM 28, an interagency committee chaired by Gerard Smith, director of the Arms Control and Disarmament Agency, was to canvass a broad variety of approaches to strategic arms control. A number of the people who provided supporting data and analyses for the Smith Committee, including members of the National Security Council (NSC) staff, the DOD office of Systems Analysis, and Central Intelligence Agency, had participated in the Johnson planning process. Apprehensive regarding the hazards of reopening bureaucratic maneuvering on the SALT agenda, several of the holdovers hoped the president would pick up the Johnson plan and move forward swiftly with the negotiations.

This was not to be. While adoption of the previously prepared SALT position was not precluded in advance by the president, his demand for options created a wholly different setting from that which prevailed the previous year. For those opposed to one or more facets of the earlier plan, it was now open season on the old proposal. Furthermore, the early results of the Smith Committee's work did not impress Kissinger favorably. The NSC chief and the president seemed to grow even more wary of the prepared positions flowing from the bureaucracy.

One reason for this heightened suspicion at the presidential level was the fact that the papers responding to NSSM 28 highlighted a number of issues which had been relatively invisible in the final documentation of the Johnson administration's SALT position. Many additional arguments now surfaced regarding the difficulties of verification. Allegations regarding possible improvements in Soviet air defenses to make them effective against ballistic missiles—the "SAM upgrade" hypothesis—were now treated with a seriousness they had not received in the Johnson years. A cardinal explanation for the injection of these issues lies in the altered complexion of the groups which NSSM 28 brought into the planning process. Where a vigorous staff in the Office of International Security Affairs had led Defense Department planning in 1968, the action office in DOD was now the Office of Defense Research and Engineering, still directed by Dr. Foster. Less committed to arms control objectives and more inclined to depend on technological solutions to security problems, DDR&E would prove to be a major source of new complexities in SALT planning.

During this period, as the executive branch began to address the questions posed by NSSM 28, two other significant events occurred. The president reoriented the ABM program from defense of cities to a primary mission of defending the American deterrent, and he sought to moderate possible Soviet fears that the thin anti-Chinese defense planned by the United States might become the base for a thick defense against the Soviet Union. Nixon candidly stated his reluctant conclusion that there could be no effective defense against the level of offensive forces possessed by the Soviet Union. He also sought to persuade the Soviet Union of the vital importance of avoiding provocative weapons innovations, repeatedly indicating his intention not to engage in programs which appeared to threaten the Soviet deterrent. Though employing the basic components of the earlier Sentinel technology, the Nixon Safeguard deployment program represented a constructive attempt to meet some of the criticism of the U.S. ABM program.

For criticism was mounting steadily. To the dismay of ABM advocates, the country's reaction to the Sentinel proposal had been very mixed. In 1968 army planners had feared serious public outcry from those regions not covered by the thin ABM deployment being proposed. Unexpectedly, the complaints came from citizens and congressmen in areas where ABM facilities were to be installed—Boston,

Chicago, Seattle. By the end of 1968, more than 40 senators had cast one or another vote against ABM deployment and in favor of limiting the system to developmental activities. The leaders of this incipient coalition were two widely respected senators, John Sherman Cooper of Kentucky and Philip Hart of Michigan. Thus the Nixon administration was on notice that it would face substantial political opposition in attempting to build the Sentinel system. While strategic calculations undoubtedly account for the president's shift to the Safeguard plan, these political considerations also argued for the more palatable scheme of concentrating initial deployment in the relatively isolated areas surrounding U.S. ICBM fields.

Political sources outside the executive branch impressed upon the president another strategic controversy. In April, a few weeks after the Safeguard announcement, Senator Edward W. Brooke met privately with the president to urge him to seek an immediate joint moratorium with the Soviet Union on MIRV testing and deployment. For some months, Senator Brooke had pressed behind the scenes to concentrate Senate energies on the imminent hazards of MIRV technology rather than exclusively on the problems of ABM. Orally and in writing, he now sought to convince the president to give priority to the MIRV problem.

It was clear that President Nixon had not faced the destabilizing implications of a potential MIRV deployment, and he received the Brooke overture with an open mind. He promised a thorough executive branch study of the possibility of a test moratorium. Coincidental with the senator's approach to the president, the MIRV question was arising in the proceedings of the Smith Committee, in which the Arms Control and Disarmament Agency spokesmen were advocating an immediate standstill in the strategic competition under a formula known as SWWA—Stop Where We Are. With considerable reinforcement from the State Department and other agencies outside DOD, ACDA now began to press the case for a MIRV ban.

The questions of whether one could monitor a test moratorium and whether such a moratorium would provide sufficient guarantees against MIRV deployment dominated the attention of all parties. With mounting concern that the large Soviet missiles known as the SS-9 might eventually become a threatening MIRV system with counterforce capabilities, the National Security Council took an intense interest in the possibilities of a MIRV limitation. General Earl Wheeler, chairman of the Joint Chiefs of Staff, questioned whether the verification procedures suggested by ACDA would suffice and made his doubts known in quite sharp language at an early NSC meeting to consider the SALT planning process. Responding to Wheeler's pointed criticism, Gerard Smith proposed a special study of the MIRV ban verification problem. Smith's memorandum to the president on this point marked the start of a drastic shift in the locus of SALT planning. An ad hoc committee chaired by Henry Kissinger examined the MIRV verification issues in great detail during the early summer of 1969. From this experience, there emerged a standing Verification Panel, appointed on July 21, through which Dr. Kissinger and the NSC Staff assumed and retained the principal role in planning for SALT.

The Verification Panel functioned through working groups led by senior Kissinger aides and drew on the technical resources of the entire government. Although its title was a misnomer, suggesting a more confined role than it actually performed, the panel seems to have been well-designed to meet the president's preference for active White House control of the planning and review process which attended the negotiations. At the same time, the relative frequency of panel initiatives and meetings (as compared with the NSC itself) energized the work of the bureaucracy by providing constant reminders of the president's interest in the arms limitation effort. On balance, though encumbered by some familiar habits of intragovernmental bargaining, the panel became an effective instrument for forging U.S. positions in advance of and during exchanges with the Soviets. It certainly added to Mr. Nixon's confidence that the government had "done its homework" and that he could make his decisions on a sound analytical basis.

As the Nixon administration undertook these preparations, several convictions formed and gained force at the top levels of the government. In Dr. Kissinger's opinion it was important for the United States not to present the Soviet Union with a single comprehensive position. To do so, in his judgment, would guarantee that the United States thereafter would be negotiating with itself, as the Soviet Union made counterproposals requiring the United States to modify its initial plan. Until more was known of Soviet intentions, it seemed wiser to set forth an array of possibilities to which Moscow might respond, rather than a single preferred design to which the United States was already deeply committed.

The "options approach" served other functions as well. Mr. Nixon's procedures permitted him to delay the hardest decisions until he discovered the degree of Soviet interest in a particular option. Thus the president did not have to face prematurely the static which would predictably occur when he elected the preference of one element of the bureaucracy over that of another.

There was much to be said in favor of sketching the broadest possible framework in which to explore common concerns and potential accommodations with the Soviet Union. Yet implicit in this procedure were real difficulties, which would grow more apparent in the many months of negotiation following the opening of the SALT talks at Helsinki in November 1969. The very multiplicity of options adduced by the American negotiators may actually have added a measure of confusion to the talks. It is possible that the Soviet Union had a simpler notion of the type of strategic freeze which it expected to consider. In particular, weighing the kind of messages conveyed by the United States at Glassboro and through other channels, the Kremlin probably planned and certainly preferred to concentrate on limiting ABM systems. Moscow may well have perceived the elaborate, multifaceted presentation of the U.S. delegation as a delaying device, permitting the United States to go forward during the talks with ABM and MIRV deployment. A parallel suspicion of delay soon emerged in the United States, as many Americans came to perceive Soviet procrastination in SALT as a cover for quantum increases in the Soviet ICBM and SLBM forces. Many participants in the SALT process are convinced that extensive discussions with the Soviets of a broad variety of offensive and defensive limitations were necessary to educate both delegations and to lay the foundations of mutual confidence necessary for agreement. They may be correct. Yet it is not carping to note the similarity between the SALT agreements of 1972 and the U.S. plan of 1968 for a low level limitation on ABM and a freeze on additional offensive deployments.

Another serious problem lurked in the options approach. By laying out possible limitations ranging on the defensive side from a zero level ABM—inserted by presidential direction after the bureaucracy had not recommended such a proposal—to a moderately high level deployment, and on the offensive side from a limit on the numbers of ICBMs and SLBMs to a ban on MIRV testing and deployment as well as controls over strategic bombers, the United States was providing a sort of menu from which the Soviet Union might choose. This mode of diplomacy left the United States literally in the position of waiting upon the

Soviet Union, guiding its concrete proposals in light of the specific topics in which Moscow displayed serious interest. Again the argument in behalf of this approach is obvious and strong; focusing upon identified areas of mutual concern would seem to maximize the probability of agreement. Unfortunately, this procedure tended to produce agreement on the lowest common denominator, without encouraging the wider area of understandings which might have emerged from more energetic efforts by one or the other side to persuade its diplomatic partner of the importance of some issues on which there was not evident agreement. This was notably true with regard to MIRV. Reluctant to forgo a technological asset and preoccupied with the verification problem, the U.S. discussion of MIRV at SALT envisaged a ban on testing and deployment accompanied by onsite inspection. The Soviets, still hostile to onsite inspection and unwilling to grant the United States a technological lead in the MIRV field, responded by proposing an unverifiable ban on production but not a limitation on testing.

These exchanges prompted the negotiators not to entertain hard bargaining to bridge the gap on this crucial problem, but to drop the MIRV issue as an unpromising candidate for negotiation. Foolish though it may seem, the Soviets were unwilling to take the lead in efforts to curb MIRV deployment, lest they acknowledge inferiority in such technology. They may also have looked toward a future advantage if they could couple a workable MIRV device to their gigantic missiles, a possibility widely advertised in the U.S. strategic debates. One Russian diplomat remarked that MIRV was a U.S. problem and the United States should advance proposals for dealing with it. From the United States' standpoint, the failure of the Soviets to evince serious interest in a MIRV ban meant that President Nixon never found it necessary during SALT I to make the hard, refined judgment necessary to resolve the continuing bureaucratic conflict over the desirability and feasibility of a MIRV moratorium. In this respect, an option which should have been high on the agenda generated only tepid conversation and moved too quickly out of the realm of serious discourse.

Negotiating at SALT I

The formal SALT I negotiations took place in seven sessions, alternating between Helsinki and Vienna. Although SALT I consumed thirty months of elapsed time, about half of the time being in actual negotiations, one may summarize the basic movements and key decisions rather briefly. In the opening session in Helsinki in November–December 1969, the United States took the initiative to talk through with the Soviet delegation the option of a moderately high ABM deployment along the lines of the proposed twelve-site Safeguard system, together with a freeze on further ICBM installations. During the following session in Vienna from April through August 1970, the U.S. delegation outlined more extensive prospects, including submarine limitations as well as the possibility of a MIRV ban and a zero ABM level.

Among the specific ABM limitations described by the U.S. delegation was an arrangement for each country to build a single ABM site to protect its national capital or national command authority (NCA), as it came to be known. Alone among the possibilities outlined in the long, drawn-out negotiations of SALT I, the single-site NCA defense option elicited immediate Soviet interest. Little more than a week after the United States proposed the NCA defense scheme on April 20, 1970, Moscow responded affirmatively. The rapidly shifting strategic balance, however, had altered U.S. interest significantly in the months since Secretary McNamara had pressed the urgency of an ABM ban as the priority objective. The Nixon administration was already deeply committed to curtailing expansion of Soviet ICBMs; it would not consider a separate deal on ABM.

Soviet preference for an ABM treaty only, and the NCA option in particular, whetted suspicions that American officials had gained during 1969, when, after Secretary of State Rogers announced U.S. willingness to enter talks, Moscow appeared to delay the start of negotiations in hopes that Congress would defeat the president's ABM proposal. On August 6, the Senate came within a hair of doing so, dividing 50–50 on one variation of the Cooper-Hart Amendment which would have precluded Safeguard deployment and diverted development funds to more advanced ABM technology. Although new evidence discounted the likelihood that multiple warhead tests of the SS-9 in fact constituted an emerging MIRV capability, the dark surmise persisted that the Soviets were seeking a substantial capacity to demolish the Minuteman ICBM force. In this context, Moscow's interest in the NCA option only, without an indication of a willingness to curb supersized offensive missiles, could be read as malevolent. And the very nature of the ABM debate in Congress, with its repeated invocations of the emerging Soviet counterforce threat, now made it imperative for the United States government to obtain matching restraint in Soviet ICBM deployment for any American defensive limitation. Whatever one may say of the objective strategic circumstances, these were the political perceptions in the White House.

Thus the United States did not promptly pick up the Soviet interest in an NCA defense, nor did it care for Moscow's reiteration later in 1970 of a preference for a separate ABM agreement only. That the United States backed away from an option it had itself developed in the early rounds of SALT may well have raised doubts in the Kremlin about American intentions, though one should note that the option had been presented in the context of a comprehensive agreement. There was already a basis for some confusion in Moscow in the fact that, while proposing a single-site defense of national capitals as one option, the United States was, in fact, starting to build its ABM network far from Washington in the heartland of the country. Observing this kind of dynamic in the sluggish discussions, one sees how mutual suspicion continued to compete with efforts to build mutual trust.

By the time the delegations convened for the relatively fruitless third session in Helsinki during November and December 1970, the possibility of diplomatic paralysis was very real. The Soviet Union's ICBM deployments were approaching 1,500 launchers, half again as many as the United States', while Russian submarine production was now running at seven to eight Y-class ballistic-missile submarines a year. On the U.S. side, another hard-fought legislative battle had produced a narrow victory for President Nixon's proposal of a third site for the Safeguard system, but Congress had begun to signal more clearly its doubts whether the initial four-site, defense-of-the-deterrent program should eventually grow into a twelve-site defense against China, an objective still being entertained by the administration.

Disturbed that the United States was proceeding to install its first generation MIRV systems before exhausting the possibilities of a mutual ban on such weaponry, a large number of senators had joined together in May 1970 to pass a resolution proposed by Senator Brooke and modified in committee by Senator Cooper. Senate Resolution 211 highlighted the instabilities that could flow from MIRV deployment and urged a prompt standstill freeze on further deployments of offensive and defensive weapons by the two superpowers. Nonetheless, in June 1970, the United States had begun to deploy the Minuteman III with MIRV warheads, and, shortly thereafter, the Poseidon MIRV systems also began to enter service on Polaris submarines which were converted to carry the larger missiles. On both sides, partially as a perverse result of the quest for diplomatic leverage, the arms race was spurting ahead of diplomacy.

To resolve the incipient stalemate, President Nixon wrote secretly to Soviet Premier Alexei Kosygin in January 1971, calling for the most serious efforts to move the negotiations forward and to find a basis for accommodation regarding the problem of Berlin as well. Nixon did not offer a detailed set of prescriptions, but the letter to Kosygin engaged the energies of the highest levels of both governments. More importantly, it inaugurated a series of so-called back channel communications which were to prove crucial to the two sides' later efforts.

In a pattern which repeated itself periodically during the first Nixon administration, there now occurred a series of wide-ranging consultations between Henry Kissinger, the president, and Soviet Ambassador Dobrynin in Washington. There was no involvement of the American embassy in Moscow and the American SALT team was reportedly uninformed. Working directly with Dobrynin, the White House prepared the way for a joint statement of May 20, 1971, which broke through several obstacles to further SALT negotiations. The announcement pledged both governments to concentrate in 1971 on an ABM agreement, a draft of which the Soviets had recently tabled in Vienna, but it also established a definitive link between a proposed limitation of defensive weapons and the offensive constraints which the United States considered essential. The talks surrounding the joint announcement also succeeded in severing the so-called forword-based systems (FBS) problem from the initial offensive agreement toward which the parties were working; at this point, the Soviet Union relaxed its previous insistence that the definition of strategic weapons include U.S. tactical nuclear systems deployed on carriers and at forward bases on the European continent. The SALT negotiations would continue to seesaw back and forth on many controversial points, but the May 20th statement constituted a crucial intervention by the political leadership of the two countries.

The hyper-cautious groping toward a balanced agreement exacted a heavy price in options foreclosed. In the course of selling his Safeguard ABM program to the Congress, the president had enlisted the assistance of leading legislators, some of whom had become totally convinced of the need to deploy at least the four-site defense of the Minuteman force. The chairman of the SALT Subcommittee of the Senate Armed Services Committee, Henry Jackson, concluded from the Soviet SS-9 deployment that the United States must retain the option for active defense of its ICBMs. During 1970 and 1971, Jackson argued with Dr. Kissinger and his associates for a shift in the U.S. bargaining stance on ABM. Instead of the zero level ABM or an NCA option, Jackson strongly contended that the United States should insist upon the right to a four-site defense of the Minuteman fields, taking care to distinguish it from the population defense begun by the Soviet Union around Moscow. Jackson developed these views most extensively in a letter to the president in October 1970 and restated them frequently in the months to follow. As the man who had borne the brunt of carrying the administration's Safeguard program through the Congress, Senator Jackson had a large claim to be heard in administration councils. These and other legislative pressures combined with intra-executive argumentation to produce a change in the U.S. bargaining position.

Toward the end of the fourth session in Vienna, the U.S. SALT delegation began to prepare the first unofficial draft of an ABM Treaty. It was designed to expedite the presentation of an American text and to flush out issues that appear only when a detailed document is prepared. Some key details, such as the proposed ABM level, were left blank. This draft was hand-carried back to Washington and revised between the fourth and fifth sessions. The drafting process brought to the surface for the first time the "future systems" question—that is, whether the ABM agreement should just limit ABM launchers, missiles, and radars, or whether it should prohibit all ABM systems except those ABM components specifically permitted, thereby foreclosing future systems such as land-based lasers. (The latter position was eventually adopted as the U.S. position in August while the fifth session was underway, and the Soviets accepted it at the end of the sixth session.)

Between the fourth and fifth sessions, there was general agreement that the preparation of two draft agreements in Washington would lead to endless haggling and that the best procedure would be for the delegation to prepare the drafts while abroad and cable the texts to Washington. In this way, bureaucratic comments would be controllable since the senior members of the delegation would have reached a consensus on many issues and each senior member could help dampen criticism in his own bailiwick at home. Accordingly, when the U.S. delegation returned to Helsinki in early July 1971 for the fifth session, it carried drafts of both an ABM agreement and an Interim Agreement which had already been reviewed by its senior members in Washington. While the U.S. delegation described some aspects of the substance of its position to the Soviets in the first three weeks of the fifth session, the session was off to a slow start and the two draft agreements prepared by the U.S. were not tabled until late July. Even then, the draft ABM agreement tabled by the U.S. included one blank article since the U.S. position on future systems was not resolved in Washington for another month.

The instructions with which the delegation had returned to Helsinki are generally acknowledged to have been one of the poorer NSC products, being both incomplete and internally inconsistent. These hastily concocted directives, transmitted as National Security Decision Memorandum (NSDM) 117, were the product of many convergent pressures which hyperactivity in the NSC system had been unable to resolve. Kissinger and Nixon were under great stress as their several diplomatic initiatives began to peak that summer, and a serious bureaucratic snarl was developing on SALT. The delegation successfully appealed a number of points in the instructions and new guidelines were forwarded before the month was out. Nevertheless, a good many wires were crossed, including those communicating the American ABM position.

On orders from Washington, the SALT delegation advanced a four-site to one-site package, the U.S. defense-of-the-deterrent program in exchange for the Soviet defense of Moscow. The program would have allowed the Soviets to deploy up to 100 interceptors while the United States would have been able to install 400 interceptors to defend the

Minuteman fields. This significant U.S. change of position, though not unreasonable, seems to have shaken the negotiations noticeably. Moreover, it was hardly credible since the president and Henry Kissinger had already offered a three-to-one package via the back channel, although the front-channel negotiators, at least in the U.S. delegation, may not have known this. The Soviets quickly objected to any such unequal arrangement and, despite vigorous U.S. presentations, seemed unwilling to accept the different functions proposed for the two deployments. Moscow insisted on an equal number both of sites and of ABM interceptors. Gradually, the U.S. delegation's position shifted to a three-for-one arrangement, and eventually to a two-for-one scheme.

Soviet nervousness was also enhanced at this time by Henry Kissinger's trip to Peking. Possibly interpreting the shifting ABM proposals as merely a bagaining tactic, the Kremlin responded with some posturing of its own. Ambassador Semenov, chairman of the SALT delegation, intimated that any of a variety of other ABM limitations would be acceptable. The Russians offered three options: NCA defense only, two sites around administrative centers, or two city defense sites in the Soviet Union in exchange for the first of the U.S. Safeguard sites being installed at Grand Forks. The only plausible rationale for the latter seemed to be a tacit acknowledgement of the superiority of U.S. ABM technology, particularly the possibility that long-range interceptors like the Spartan ABM missile would have significant area defense potential, even when deployed in the interior of the United States.

This flurry of unpromising give-and-take seems to have disabused the United States of the hope that it could obtain the full-fledged defense of the deterrent in exchange for limited area defense in the Soviet Union. Much to the distress of Senator Jackson and his associates, the United States did not stand firm with the four-for-one proposal, and in early 1972, the negotiations gravitated toward a two-site arrangement for both countries, seeking to define where those sites could be and whether they could mix the function of defense of the deterrent with that of defending the population centers. In the internal U.S. deliberations, faced with a choice of insisting on two sites to defend Minuteman fields or one Minuteman installation plus defense of the national capital, the JCS ultimately chose the latter. The Chiefs calculated, against the apparent odds, that Congress would actually fund an NCA defense, if the agreement finally provided for it. While a symmetrical two-site ABM limit seemed in the offing, the

U.S. refused to pin it down until limits on offensive forces were further delineated in the seventh and last session in Helsinki (March–May 1972).

In the winter of 1971–1972, Secretary of Defense Melvin Laird recommended that the United States proceed with an advanced ballistic-missile submarine system to be known as the Trident. Recognizing that the system could not enter service until late in the 1970s and increasingly wary of the rapid rate of Soviet SLBM production, Laird prevailed upon the president to demand that submarine-based ballistic missiles (SLBM), as well as land-based ICBMs, be covered by the prospective offensive agreement.

With private exchanges continuing between the White House and the Soviet Embassy in Washington, as well as between the SALT delegations at Vienna (sixth session) and later at the concluding session in Helsinki, many issues remained difficult to settle. A glimpse of the possible compromises surfaced during Henry Kissinger's pre-Summit visit to Moscow in April 1972 when the Soviet leadership came down hard in favor of a matching two-site ABM limit, including defense of the NCAs, offering in return an interim offensive agreement covering launchers for ICBMs and SLBMs, but permitting Moscow to expand its ballistic-missile submarine fleet if it phased out older land-based ICBM missiles. This persistent Soviet effort to maintain its considerable momentum in force modernization sustained the mistrust of U.S. Defense Department officials and led them to redouble their efforts to launch major modernization programs for U.S. strategic forces, despite congressional misgivings about premature commitment to the Trident SLBM system and the B-1 bomber program. Even as agreement seemed near, the seeds were being sown for intensified competition in strategic technology.

Kissinger's April visit to Moscow was crucial to forging an agreement, since the Soviets had previously been adamant against curtailing submarine-launched ballistic missiles in the Interim Offensive Agreement. Nevertheless, some participants in the SALT delegation believe that a more stringent submarine limitation could have been achieved. In particular, some Americans associated with SALT feel that the suggested high ceiling on the Russian submarine fleet could have been diluted by inclusion of all the older diesel-powered (G-class) and nuclear-powered (H-class) Soviet submarines in the overall limit. Some American officials, as well as some of the congressmen monitoring the negotiations, are also convinced that a stronger effort during Kissinger's visit or the subsequent Summit conference could have attained a two-for-one ABM arrangement, in view of the Soviet gains under the Interim Offensive Agreement. These possibilities remain imponderables in assessing the final outcome.

By the time President Nixon arrived in Moscow on May 22, 1972, the SALT delegations, still laboring in Helsinki, had explored in great detail the contentious issues. Yet they still awaited political decisions on numerous specific points: What would be the exact number of ballistic-missile submarines permitted under the offensive agreement? Where would the second Soviet ABM site be located? At what stage in their construction should SLBMs be counted as operational systems? Would there be agreed definitions tied in with the prohibition on converting launchers for light missiles to heavier launchers? The president and his advisors in Moscow expected and preferred that the Summit would resolve the lingering issues in broad political terms, leaving it to the technical competence of their respective SALT delegations to put the argrements into operational terms. To their surprise, Secretary Brezhnev, who had superseded Kosygin as the Soviet principal in SALT, and his colleagues proved extremely eager to resolve even technical details directly at the Summit itself.

This precipitated considerable confusion since the SALT delegations in Helsinki were still pursuing the final resolution of key issues. Once the Summit meetings were underway, however, the Soviet delegation almost stopped talking at Helsinki. One infers that the Soviet delegates were not being currently informed of the deliberations underway in Moscow and, lacking fresh instructions, were unable to carry matters further. Despite concerted efforts to maintain communications between the U.S. delegation in Moscow and the SALT team in Helsinki, events moved too rapidly to keep the regular American SALT negotiators fully abreast of the movement toward agreement.

Brezhnev's inclination to deal at the top might be construed as an attempt to maximize the diplomatic advantage he enjoyed by working at close proximity to the technical resources of his government while President Nixon was relatively isolated from his. The Americans who participated in the Summit question this speculation. Though Brezhnev was indeed moving back and forth between sessions with the president and consultations with senior associates in the Soviet hierarchy, the U.S. participants at Moscow are satisfied that the Soviet leader

was seeking to expedite reasonable agreement, not to extract some un-
due advantage through last minute, high-pressure tactics on the visiting
American president. Those with an intimate glimpse of the proceedings
tend to concur in this opinion, being uniformly impressed at the
businesslike nature of the Summit working sessions.

The escalation of extraordinarily complex technical issues on which
the U.S. SALT delegation was better informed than the American
negotiators in Moscow posed an inordinate burden for the president's
staff. Indeed the Summit became a physical ordeal for Dr. Kissinger
and others called upon to conduct the substantive negotiations. These
arrangements also engendered much bad feeling on the part of the
U.S. SALT team, which considered Dr. Kissinger and his staff less well
prepared to cope with a number of questions than those working in
Helsinki. The talks in the two cities occasionally got out of phase, for
example, regarding the treatment to be accorded the differing classes
of Soviet ballistic-missile submarines.

The result was some unavoidable ambiguity in the agreements
finally concluded and possibly less satisfactory arrangements than
might have been made on a few specific points. The process was undoubtedly cumbersome but, in this writer's judgment, nothing of substance was sacrificed in the hectic proceedings at Moscow. Moreover,
the staff supporting the president's work at the Summit and the chief
executive himself were sufficiently well-prepared and alert to the
major nuances of the impending agreement to avoid the pitfalls that
could have befallen less skillful negotiators. One instance of a potential pitfall concerned the Soviet indication that mobile land-based
ICBMs would not be foreclosed by the Interim Offensive Agreement.
The president and Dr. Kissinger made clear the United States reservations on this point, leaving no doubt that the United States would
have to reconsider its position if mobile long-range missiles complicated the U.S. capacity to verify the size and deployment of the Soviet
strategic missile force.

The unexpectedly hectic Summit discussions also confirmed the
longstanding American inference that the Russian foreign ministry
officials most visible in the SALT negotiations held limited influence
in the inner circles of the Kremlin. Until the Moscow meeting, the
United States had been dealing with a remote and relatively impotent
extension of the Soviet government. Now the opportunity presented
itself to deal forcefully and effectively with men who had both the

power and the competence to bargain for conclusive understandings. That opportunity was too vital to be missed.

The Domestic Politics of SALT Ratification

To political intimates, President Nixon confided his anxieties that the historic SALT understandings might create domestic political difficulties. On the plane returning from Moscow, he speculated that the conservative Republican candidacy of John Ashbrook, an Ohio congressman challenging Mr. Nixon in a number of primaries, might benefit from reaction in some quarters against the SALT I agreements. The California primary was just weeks ahead and the president, recalling the lethal disaffection of conservative Republicans in his race for governor of that state in 1962, thought the Ashbrook vote might be inflated by ten percentage points or more. This did not occur but other storm warnings had already begun to gather. Even before the president had returned from Moscow, Senator Henry Jackson had begun to criticize both the procedure and the product of the strategic arms negotiations conducted at the Summit. Along with Senator Cooper, who had worked strenuously to speed the negotiations to a conclusion, Jackson had been one of a small number of legislators following the work of the SALT delegation and the Verification Panel in close detail. To lend maximum impetus to the ratification efforts, the president returned directly to the Capitol to discuss the results of the historic meeting.

Mr. Nixon respected Senator Jackson both for his judgment and his political savvy, qualities which had prompted the chief executive to offer the Washington Democrat the post of Secretary of Defense in 1968. Nixon was also a close student of Woodrow Wilson's career and was doubly cautious of the danger that a debacle reminiscent of Versailles might occur. Both the instincts and the political calculations of those in the White House argued for tactical reassurance of Senator Jackson and other critics who felt the Moscow arrangements had been a bad trade for the United States. Nixon had also been deeply impressed by the fact, as he reported, "that Mr. Brezhnev and his colleagues made it absolutely clear that they are going forward with defense programs in the offensive area which are not limited by these agreements." Rejecting the counsel of congressmen and commentators who saw the Moscow pacts as an invitation to slow a number of proposed projects not prohibited by the language of the agreements themselves, the administration adopted the stance of strong support for further work on such ventures as the Trident submarine and the B-1 bomber. Many questioned the wisdom of the administration's posture on these matters, but the president judged them essential to obtain prompt congressional approval of the Moscow accords and to facilitate follow-on negotiations to achieve a permanent treaty controlling offensive forces.

It was clear that the overwhelming majority of Congress wanted to see a lid placed on the strategic arms race, but the extended strategic debates over ABM and other weapons systems from 1969 to 1971 had generated a number of crosscurrents which affected the process of ratification. The argument over ABM in 1969 had focused upon complex technical issues and had revolved around the basic question of whether the Safeguard system would in fact work. By 1970, the technological arguments had shifted significantly against the Safeguard deployment, with a number of advocates admitting that the system, employing Sentinel technology, might be overwhelmed by modest increments in the Soviet SS-9 force. Trying to cope with this contingency, the Department of Defense was beginning to look seriously at more advanced technology for hardsite defense of the U.S. deterrent.

In 1970 and the following year, the balance of congressional votes was tipped in favor of Safeguard less by persuasive arguments that the system would function as intended than by the president's claim that he required an ongoing ABM program as a bargaining chip in the SALT negotiations. Earlier, the administration had quietly signaled that it was willing to negotiate away the anti-China element of the Safeguard system if that were necessary to achieve a Soviet-American limitation. Taking its cue, the Senate Armed Services Committee had explicitly indicated in 1970 and again in 1971 that it did not believe the anti-China defense was warranted, though it continued to endorse progress on the defense of the Minuteman fields against the Soviet counterforce threat. One upshot of these years of debate in the Capitol was the conclusion that, despite Defense Department confidence that the legislators would go along, Congress was most unlikely to authorize the ABM defense of Washington, the so-called NCA site, which the ABM Treaty would permit. To Senator Jackson and others who had fought hard to move the Safeguard ICBM defense along its perilous legislative course, the ABM options agreed upon at Moscow were essentially worthless. Jackson, in particular, was left with little regard for the administration's diplomatic prowess.

From another perspective, the relatively modest limitations contained in the Interim Offensive Agreement left many U.S. analysts and officials gravely disturbed. They foresaw an intensification of a qualitative arms race in which the Soviet advantage in numbers of delivery vehicles and payload would shortly be transformed into a significant Soviet lead in numbers of deliverable warheads. Not all of them were satisfied with the reassurance that the low limits on ABM virtually guaranteed that even qualitative improvement in the Soviet offensive forces could not be meaningful in terms of jeopardizing the U.S. capacity to retaliate after any Russian attack.

The possibility of a qualitative arms race was already a concern among high officials of the administration. Ambassador Smith had conveyed to the Soviet negotiators the American view that Russian installation of a counterforce MIRV capability might force Washington to reconsider the ABM Treaty. In the few weeks following SALT I, Dr. Kissinger, Secretary Rogers, and others alluded to the problem of technological change as the principal agenda item in SALT II. The theme won its greatest endorsement some months later, when Secretary Brezhnev paid a reciprocal visit to the United States. Focusing once more on ways to spur the continuing SALT negotiations, the two leaders issued a set of basic principles which set the goal of signing another agreement in 1974 and specifically anticipated that limitations would govern both qualitative and quantitative aspects of strategic weapons. The Washington Summit of June 1973 also revealed considerable interest in expediting supplementary agreements on what Dr. Kissinger described as "some issues that are time-urgent," by which he was understood to mean certain MIRV programs. The problems had grown more acute as the Soviet Union belatedly began to test a MIRV device of its own.

There was a substantial prehistory on this subject, and some of the administration's actions seemed to belie its newfound concern for restricting qualitative arms changes. Foremost was the administration's uneven performance regarding the possible development of a MIRV system for the U.S. Minuteman III that would be capable of destroying hard targets such as ICBMs in silos. In exchanges with Senator Brooke and testimony before the responsible committees, Nixon administration spokesmen had gradually formulated a declaratory policy which would limit the United States to a strictly retaliatory MIRV capability, refraining from more advanced technology capable of attacking hardened missile silos. In late 1969, the administration had declined to recommend an Air Force program to develop a larger warhead and more accurate reentry vehicle for the Minuteman III system. The first generation MIRV payloads were performing better than expected, but their small size precluded their effective use as counterforce weapons. From time to time, however, the government appeared quite erratic, with the Air Force chief of staff, General John Ryan, and others referring to the counterforce potential of an improved MIRV system.

In the aftermath of the Moscow Summit, while top administration figures were focusing publicly for the first time on the challenge of qualitative arms control, the Defense Department resurrected plans for a hard target MIRV system. With a general but vague mandate from the president for some additional research and development activity deemed appropriate in light of the SALT I agreements, the DOD sought funds in June 1972 to begin development of a higher yield and more accurate reentry vehicle for MIRV application. Defense officials seemed oblivious to the inherent contradiction between such a scheme and the goal of forestalling an escalation in destabilizing technologies. However, determined efforts, centered in the Senate Armed Services Subcommittee on Research and Development, chaired by Senator Thomas McIntyre, succeeded in deleting authority and funds for the hard target MIRV reentry vehicle. But the incident did not speak well for the administration's capacity to orchestrate its diplomacy and its defense planning.

By the late summer of 1972, the House and Senate were moving toward ratification of the ABM Treaty and approval of the Interim Offensive Agreement. With the House Foreign Affairs and Senate Foreign Relations Committees favorably disposed, overwhelming ratification seemed assured. But the administration was extremely interested in assuaging Senator Jackson's concerns, both to win his personal endorsement of SALT I and to maintain a constructive working relationship with him for the future. An immediate problem had arisen in connection with the fiscal 1973 defense authorization; a sharp division in the Senate Armed Services Committee heralded real trouble for the Trident submarine program and for other presumed bargaining chips for the next round of SALT. Partially to enlist Senator Jackson's support for the Trident program and partially for the broader purpose of healing the breach that was beginning to open between the administration and the shrewd Washingtonian, Dr. Kissinger agreed to support an amendment Jackson was preparing to offer to the joint resolution of approval of the Interim Offensive Agreement. The senator's proposal led to many days of fierce debate during August and September and the administration's on-again-off-again support for the Jackson Amendment—but not for the senator's interpretation of it—marked a low point in its uniformly poor record of congressional relations.

Seemingly innocuous on its face, the Jackson Amendment was a sophisticated maneuver to enhance the leverage which he and the Armed Services Subcommittee on SALT would have on future strategic arms negotiations. Displaying his customary parliamentary skills, Jackson enlisted well over one-third of the Senate as cosponsors even before serious debate on his amendment began. The proposal filled an evident political need for many legislators; almost any member who entertained subliminal doubts about the understandings reached at Moscow could hedge his approval by endorsing Jackson's formulation of principles for the next round of negotiations. Though Senators Fulbright, Cooper, and others who were prominent supporters of the SALT accords felt the Jackson Amendment would call into question American good faith in the bargain just struck, a modified version of Jackson's language won handily when put to a vote on September 14, 1972.

As enacted, the Jackson Amendment stressed that the "supreme national interests" of the United States demanded a more complete strategic offensive arms agreement to insure the survivability of American deterrent forces. The provision further urged that the principle of "equality" reflected in the ABM Treaty be adopted as the standard for SALT II negotiations on offensive arms, insisting that the United States should not be limited to levels of intercontinental strategic forces inferior to those authorized for the Soviet Union. And the amended resolution also expressed congressional approval for a vigorous research and development and modernization program for U.S. strategic forces. These broad themes were obviously susceptible of varying interpretations. Nevertheless, Jackson's success in enacting them promised to enhance his influence over the coming SALT II negotiation.

To dilute the unique impact of the Jackson proposal, Senator Mansfield and others succeeded in adding other language to the resolution of approval, endorsing relevant portions of the Declaration of Basic Principles of Mutual Relations Between the U.S.A. and U.S.S.R. which President Nixon and Secretary Brezhnev had promulgated in Moscow. Other amendments commended the president's success in concluding the agreements and urged him to seek actual arms reductions at the earliest practicable date. The Congress also adopted a proposal by Senator Brooke urging "the preservation of longstanding United States policy that neither the Soviet Union nor the United States should seek unilateral advantage by developing a first strike potential." This was the latest attempt to build a legislative barricade against the recurrent threat of counterforce technology.

Thus, at the end as at the beginning of SALT I, the Congress signaled to the president and to the Soviet Union a diverse set of impulses. In varying degrees, congressmen and senators wished to voice their relief and gratitude that something constructive had been achieved; to signal their demand that something better would be required for the future; and to endorse a sufficient program of continued defense expenditures while restraining zealous military professionals from undermining the possibility of stable arms limitation by superfluous technological innovation.

Conclusion

The influences which impinged on U.S. decision making for SALT include many factors not addressed here. Yet the most striking feature of recent national security decision making in the American government is that there was adequate political support in both the executive branch and the Congress for a patient and prudent search for stable arms arrangements. It seems clear that, in contrast with many previous occasions, Congress was a helpful force for strategic restraint. Those legislators who fought to slow the movement toward ABM deployment made a signal contribution. Had the Sentinel and Safeguard proposals proceeded as originally intended, while diplomacy followed its snaillike course, it would have been far more difficult to attain a low-level limitation on ABM systems. And without such a low limit on defenses the complexities of bargaining for an offensive accord, even on an interim basis, might well have proved insurmountable. Similarly, it was Congress, rather than the expert community associated with the executive branch, which publicly explicated the hazards of MIRV technology and other aspects of qualitative change —the central challenge to subsequent strategic arms negotiations.

Though one may fault the executive branch on a number of points, the Nixon administration's initial success in curbing strategic armaments could prove decisive for long term stability. Measured against this unprecedented achievement, the U.S. governent's diplomatic and analytic shortcomings pale into insignificance. An imperative task has at last begun.

CHAPTER FOUR
SALT and the Soviet Union*

Marshall D. Shulman

Among the many questions that come to mind in any consideration of the Soviet approach to strategic arms limitations, the following three are of most immediate interest:

1. Does the Soviet participation in SALT represent a continuation or a departure in Soviet foreign policy objectives?
2. How much is the Soviet behavior in SALT influenced by the interplay of domestic politics?
3. Do the Soviet leaders think about SALT and the strategic balance in the same way that we do, and if not, how much does this matter?

These are matters on which systematic scholarly investigation is difficult, obviously. There is a fair-sized volume of commentary, both Soviet and Western, but there is not much that can be called hard evidence. Thus, the answers to the questions posed are necessarily impressionist and tentative.

SALT AND SOVIET FOREIGN POLICY

It seems a fair guess that, in the perspective of decades, SALT and the other Summit agreements of 1972 are likely to be regarded as a major turning point in Soviet policy, less for the specific details of what was agreed upon than for the implied acceptance of a changed

* Research for the material in this chapter was supported in part by grants from the American Council of Learned Societies, the International Research and Exchanges Board, the American Academy of Arts and Sciences, and the Russian Institute of Columbia University.

definition of the terms of competition with its main adversary. From the Soviet point of view, one of the most important aspects of the Summit encounter—an aspect which received relatively little attention in the United States—was the acceptance by the United States in the Statement of Basic Principles of Relations of the formula of "peaceful coexistence" as the basis for relations between the superpowers. What appeared to the West as a penchant for rhetorical declarations was hailed in the Soviet post-Summit commentary as a major achievement, for it signified to the Soviet leadership a codification of the ground rules for a competition for political influence around the globe in which the role of strategic weapons would be subordinated. The commitment of the Soviet leadership to this mixture of competition, constraint, and cooperation as a long-term mode of advancing its interests represented a qualitative advance over previous Soviet tactical forays in this direction.

Five elements combined to make a move in this direction possible at this moment: (1) a decade of strenuous effort through which the Soviet Union had overcome the inferiority in nuclear weapons under which it had lived since World War II, as a result of which the principle of "equal security" could now be invoked; (2) a growing realization by the Soviet political leadership of the limited political utility of strategic weapons and of the futility and high cost of an unregulated strategic competition; (3) a crystallization of the preference of the Party leadership for obtaining long-term increases in the flow of grain, technology, management, and goods from abroad as a way of dealing with economic shortcomings in the Communist system, rather than the alternative of institutional modifications; (4) a tentative acceptance of the possibility that the political leadership of the United States was prepared to move in the same direction ("the era of negotiation"); (5) a mounting concern by the Soviet leadership with the rise of China in international diplomacy, and the desire to offset developing relations between China and the United States.

The principle of "equal security" not only means that the Soviet Union feels that a SALT agreement would not now have the effect of freezing it into a position of permanent inferiority; it implies to the Soviet leadership an acceptance of the status of the Soviet Union as a coequal great power, not subject to threat or intimidation. It also carries the implication for the Soviet Union that the United States would no longer be able to follow a policy of "positions of strength" as a basis for negotiations on strategic military matters.

Still, there is a paradox in the present Soviet situation, a consciousness of both strength and weakness, a need for consolidation, and an expectation of continuing political gains. In historical perspective, the Soviet Union has entered upon a phase of national growth like that which many other great nations experienced in the nineteenth and early twentieth centuries. It has become a global maritime power, self-conscious and proud of its status. In the present ambiguous flux of international politics, the Soviet Union anticipates that it will play a role of increasing political influence, responding to opportunities arising from the decline in the influence of its chief rival. In the Soviet perspective, the United States has passed its zenith as the leading world power. At the same time, however—this is the other side of the paradox—the Soviet leadership is constrained by some serious limitations: a lag in productivity and industrial technology, a continuing conflict with China, and some possible political vulnerabilities at home and in Eastern Europe.

The logic of this paradox of strength and weakness, of the need for consolidation, and the hope of political advances leads the Soviet Union to a futher evolution of the line of policy known as "peaceful coexistence." In the early days of the Soviet Union, this term had the connotation of a temporary breathing spell, when circumstances required an easement from the effects of a more militant policy, and war with the West was regarded as a less than remote possibility. During the last two decades, events have moved the political leadership of the Soviet Union toward a more explicit recognition that peaceful coexistence is the only prudent path toward the validation of the Communist view of history. The term now is associated with a long-term political strategy, carrying the implication of a restrained mixture of political competition and limited cooperation with an adversary who is characterized in much more differentiated terms than was the unmitigated imperialist enemy of the past.

SALT brought the matter to a head when it was proposed in 1967. For sixteen months there was no reply. The alternatives were debated, and meanwhile the strategic gap was being narrowed. By the spring of 1968, the first tentative acceptance of the SALT overture was exploratory, with the essential issues still unresolved in the internal debates. First Czechoslovakia and then the election of a new American president held the matter in abeyance for another year. By that time, the critical factors had fallen into place in the internal Soviet debates. Parity ("the favorable relations of forces") was within sight. The economic consequences of a continuing strategic competition as against the opportunity for a repair of the technological lag at home were more starkly evident. Not least in importance was the growing acceptance of the possibility that SALT represented a real option rather than a trap, based upon the conviction that the offer of an "era of negotiation" by a conservative American president rested upon genuine necessities in the situation in which the United States then found itself.

The importance of China as a factor in Soviet motivation is difficult to measure, but at this point and subsequently, China clearly played a significant role in Soviet calculations. In the spring of 1969 came the outbreak of fighting on the Sino-Soviet border, which gave added reason to the regulation of Soviet relations with the West. In October 1969, the opening of Sino-Soviet negotiations on border questions coincided, to the day, with the announcement that SALT would begin the following month. In July 1970, the Soviet representative unsuccessfully proposed joint action with the United States against provocative steps by third nuclear powers. Later, the development of the United States' relations with China and the emergence of China from its diplomatic isolation appeared to stimulate Soviet interest in more rapid progress in SALT and in its Western policies generally, to forestall a Sino-American alliance, and to assure at least a quiescent Western front in the event of further difficulties along the Chinese border.

The step to enlarge the context of SALT, to codify the political rationale for a decisive commitment to a broad policy of peaceful coexistence, came at the XXIV Congress of the Communist Party of the Soviet Union in the spring of 1971, and during the months leading up to the congress and to the drafting of the Ninth Five-Year Plan for the Soviet economy. A clear primacy was given to the need for upgrading science and technology in the Soviet Union as the key requirement for a strong economic base in the future. It followed that a foreign policy of low tension was required to facilitate trade and technology transfer and to encourage trends toward neutralism in Western Europe and Japan. The logic of these requirements led not only to an affirmation of support for the treaty with West Germany and for the prospect of a Conference on Security and Cooperation in Europe, but to a signal of interest in the "normalization" of relations with the United States, which had previously been relegated to a lower rung on the *détente* ladder. What "normalization" meant was made explicit by General Secretary Brezhnev, who committed his personal prestige to this course of action: not only a stabilization of the strategic competition in SALT, but a broad context of interdependency—an expansion of trade, a range of measures of cooperation in science and technology, health, space, and environment—with the reservation, however, that peaceful coexistence in these matters should not be understood as marking any diminution of zeal for unflagging opposition to American imperialism or for the ideological commitment to Marxism-Leninism. Operationally, this multilevel differentiation of relations with the United States has its difficulties for the Soviet leadership. To contend with the Chinese for leadership of the anti-imperialist movement in the world while consorting with the leading imperialist power; to maintain a mobilized ideological élan at home while exchanging visits and toasts with the ideological arch-adversary; to prevent the penetration of foreign influences at home and in Eastern Europe while multiplying the number of cultural, political, and economic contacts —all this takes careful management. The famous question in Soviet politics—"Who-Whom?" (or, more exactly, "Who does what to whom?")—under conditions of a *détente* policy presents itself in the form of a historic gamble: which side can most advantageously balance the gains and risks of political competition in a situation of diminished polarity?

It seems at least possible that the transformations taking place in international politics will work to the advantage of both sides, while they produce evolutionary changes not presently foreseen or intended. In responding to immediate felt needs, actors in history may be part of a pattern which they do not intend and of which they may be unaware. Or, to put the matter in Soviet terms: the objective consequences may turn out to be different from the subjective intent. The residual long-term effects of an expansion of trade and technology transfer will make it difficult for the Soviet Union to resume its fundamental commitment to economic autarchy. In time, the web of multiple interdependencies projected at the Summit in 1972 is likely to begin to modify, in a substantial degree, the historical commitment to an adversary outlook, if the process is not seriously interrupted by episodes of high tension.

One of the most interesting questions involved in this evolving situation is: will SALT turn out to be central or peripheral to the whole web of relationships? Or, to put the question in another way: to what extent can the plane of strategic competition be insulated from the vicissitudes of the political competition? In logic, the self-interest of the two countries in damping down their competition in strategic weapons is not dependent upon the level of tension in other aspects of their relationship—but how far can this logical separability be made politically viable? Vietnam and Czechoslovakia were temporary impediments to SALT, but the mining of Haiphong harbor was not. One can only guess whether this marked a learning trend, or whether it reflected special factors in this instance, such as the prospect of increased trade with the United States, the need to offset the developing Chinese-American relationship, and the momentum of prior decisions.

The way in which the Soviet Union has approached the SALT negotiations is an indication of some degree of separability of strategic and political questions. All participants have testified to the businesslike deportment of the Soviet negotiators. Their observance of the secrecy of the proceedings may be taken as a mark of seriousness. There has not been any systematic Soviet effort to exploit the negotiations for propaganda purposes which has sometimes characterized other diplomatic engagements.

The Soviet Union has not sought a "linkage" between SALT and political objectives, and it has strenuously objected to reported American efforts to do so at an early stage in the negotiations. During the early months of 1969, when the Soviet government was pressing the new Nixon administration to speed up its restudy of the American positions, it unwittingly created the impression that the Soviet Union was more eagerly interested in SALT than was the United States. As a consequence, there began to be heard in Washington suggestions that the Soviets could be made to pay a price for a SALT agreement, in the form of cooperation in the settlement of the Vietnam conflict, restraint in the Middle East, or progress on the Berlin issue. The Soviet Union learned its lesson, and its representatives were instructed to "play it cool." In the following months, Soviet diplomats were elaborately casual in letting it be known, with a shrug, that it was all the same to them whether SALT went forward or not.

No one would argue that there can be a total compartmentalization of negotiations on strategic arms limitations, but there is at least a clear separation in the Soviet mind between SALT agreements and a political rapprochement. It may be that experience will teach both sides to insulate the SALT negotiations from the inevitable episodes of tension in other aspects of their relationship, within reasonable limits.

There are, however, other uncertainties to reckon with. If the effort at strategic stabilization proves successful, will the effect be to loosen inhibitions on the margins of risk the Soviet Union is willing to accept in conventional military confrontations? So far the answer would appear to be negative; in the Middle East, for example, the Soviet Union has continued cautiously to avoid any risk of direct and uncontrollable involvement in a great power confrontation.

There is a question in the other direction which may be more relevant: if, despite the formal agreements, the strategic competition continues unabated or is further stimulated in weapons systems and qualitative characteristics not covered by the agreements, will the effect be to undermine the rationale for entering into arms limitation negotiations? We have learned how much the acceptance by President Eisenhower of personal responsibility for the U-2 overflights undermined Khrushchev's political position and weakened his argument that one could do business with the American leadership. One can only guess at what point Brezhnev would become vulnerable to the charge that the United States had used SALT as a justification for increasing its qualitative superiority, and whether, as a consequence, the entire movement of Soviet policy in the direction of a more differentiated relationship with the United States would be discredited. The possibilities for such a political change and policy reversal, which are ever-present although the threshold is uncertain, might increase if the prospects for trade also prove disappointing. This question involves some judgments about the internal tugs and hauls around SALT issues and brings us to a consideration of the domestic political aspects of SALT in the Soviet Union.

SALT AND SOVIET POLITICS

The politics of arms limitations appear to be about as complex in the Soviet Union as in the United States. However, the political alignments, interplay of interests, and the process of decision making are different, reflecting the differences in the political structures and social systems of the two countries.

In the eight years since Khrushchev, the leadership of the Soviet Union has been characterized by a relatively stable and conservative balance based on consensus. Its main preoccupation has been the state of the Soviet economy. While the growth rate of the economy as a whole was respectable by international standards until 1973, what has caused concern to the Soviet leaders are shortcomings in significant aspects, notably in productivity, agriculture, the consumer sector and, above all, the advanced technological sector. Since these problems involve institutional rigidities in the system, a central issue in Soviet politics has developed between pressures for modernizing reforms and resistance to changes which might have unforeseeable consequences for the Party system of centralized political control.

The decision of the Party leadership at the XXIV Congress to move toward an increase in trade and technology transfer and an easement in the strategic competition has the effect of softening or postponing the debate over institutional reforms, in the expectation that the infusion of advanced technology and modern management from abroad will help to overcome the laggard sectors with the least immediate risk to the integrity of the internal system. To move in this direction, however, implied a willingness on the part of the Soviet leadership to accept a long-term economic interdependency with the capitalist world, in place of the economic autarchy that had become a central principle of Soviet ideology.

That this course was subject to vigorous debate within the Party was evident in the oblique references which appeared in the press and the specialized military and economic journals. Specifically, the decision to move forward to strategic arms limitations in SALT I, within a broad framework of "normalized" relations with the United States and a *détente* with other industrial nations of the West, and such parallel actions as the treaty with the Federal Republic of Germany were subject to challenge from several quarters. Any identification of individual spokesmen for various "hard-line" opposition positions is speculative, but the terms of the debate suggest that orthodox ideologues and some elements of the professional military services combined to articulate the traditional dire forecasts of the consequences of trafficking with the imperialist enemy. The counterargument, bolstered by a new level of sophistication in Soviet studies of the United States, defended the chosen course as the most effective and prudent way to advance

Soviet interests in the light of the vulnerabilities of Western societies, as against the risks and costs of a more militant policy.

Although the debate stopped shortly before the Party Congress, as General Secretary Brezhnev identified himself firmly with the *détente* policy, the constraints imposed by the political reawakening of criticism from the "hard-liners" have been evident in the negotiations. The Soviet General Staff has been prominently represented in the Soviet negotiating team at SALT. Although the Party insists that it is preeminent over all subordinate interests in Soviet politics, including the military, and that there cannot be an autonomous "military-industrial complex" in the Soviet system, it is clear that the military services are a formidable element in Soviet politics and that their interests have to be accommodated in the process of compromise by which the consensus leadership is maintained.

While it would be misleading to speak of "interest groups" in Soviet politics in the sense in which this term is used in Western politics, it is not far-fetched to identify functional interests in Soviet politics as an inevitable outgrowth of advancing industrialization. To the extent that the Party can absorb these functional interests within its ranks, it may keep the interplay of interests indoors beneath the Party roof, at least in part. The technocrat and the marshal may both be members of the Central Committee of the Party, but each continues to have his constituent bureaucracy, his professional preoccupation, his parochial perspective of the national interest.

Although the inaccessibility of the Soviet political processes makes it difficult to go much beyond this impressionistic sketch of the distinctive mechanism by which the Soviet system compromises conflicting interests, it suggests three points to keep in mind. First, SALT is not an encounter between two entities, but an interaction between two constellations of interests. Second, the issues raised by SALT in Soviet politics tend to pit the relative moderation of the technological modernizers against the intransigence of the ideologues and the narrow professionalism of certain of the military services. And third, the balance between these contending interests is, in some measure, affected by the resultant of diverse forces in American politics. If SALT succeeds not only in producing agreements but in restraining the military competition, and if productive trading relations develop, those whose interests are identified with the normalization of relations between the two countries will thereby be strengthened, and this pattern of relationships will be more securely established. Conversely, if the substance of SALT is undermined by a narrow military perspective in the United States, it would be reasonable to expect that analogous pressures on the Soviet side will increase.

Of course, the interacting process works in both directions. Therefore, it is also necessary for the Soviet political leadership to bear in mind the effect of its actions upon the interplay of bureaucratic interests in the United States, if the process of mutual stimulation between the military interests of the two sides is to be brought under control.

Soviet Decision-making Process

The process by which positions on SALT are prepared and decisions made is quite different in the Soviet Union from what it is in the United States. There is no Soviet analogue to the U.S. Arms Control and Disarmament Agency and no precise analogue to the National Security Council and its staff, nor to a presidential advisor with his sweeping responsibilities for coordination of policy and negotiations. Nor is there in the Soviet Union a circulation of defense scientists in and out of government, as in the United States, to provide an independent lobby of knowledgeable experts to form public opinion on arms limitation issues. The Supreme Soviet, the legislative arm of government, does have standing commissions on foreign policy, which approved the SALT ABM Treaty, but there is no equivalent to be found in the Soviet system of the congressional committee hearings, independent of and often critical of the administration position during the period when decisions are being made. Some articles on military strategy relevant to arms limitation matters do appear in the professional journals, and occasionally articles may be found in the general press on U.S. positions which convey a substantial amount of information on arms limitation issues, but public debates of the kind that the U.S. experienced during the ABM controversy are absent in the Soviet Union.

The main locus of work on the preparation of positions for SALT is to be found in the Soviet Ministry of Defense, which has a section charged with this responsibility. It reports to the General Staff, which reconciles the competing views of the various services and represents the military position in the higher councils of the government and the Party. Two high officials of the General Staff have been senior members of the SALT delegation, and half a dozen other Ministry of Defense officials have been attached to the SALT delegation staff.

The Ministry of Foreign Affairs has a section under the International Organization Division on preparations for SALT and other disarmament activities. The Policy Planning Division and the American desk have also been occupied with preparations for SALT I. It appears, however, that the input of the Ministry of Foreign Affairs is largely limited to the diplomatic and political aspects of the negotiations, including the drafting of treaty language, but is quite separate from the technical hardware details of arms limitation problems. Although Vladimir S. Semenov, the chief of the Soviet SALT delegation, is a deputy foreign minister, his role appears to be similarly defined.

The Foreign Ministry has also provided an important supplementary channel of communication and negotiation with the U.S. administration through the Soviet ambassador in Washington, Anatoly F. Dobrynin, by drawing on his experience in interpreting American developments and his relations of confidence with the White House. The Dobrynin-Kissinger channel provided confidential and informal communication between the heads of State, through which an impasse between the SALT delegations was broken by the May 20, 1971 understanding. In the preparations for the Summit and during the Summit, Dobrynin served as explicator and, on occasion, as interpreter when difficulties arose.

The Soviet Academy of Sciences is involved in arms limitation matters in a number of ways. Scientists in the defense sector, a large and influential element in the Academy, are, of course, consulted on the technical aspects of SALT problems affecting weapons systems on which they have worked. But in addition, the scientific community—a prestigious sector in Soviet society—also plays a broader advisory role whose influence, however, is difficult to assess. In the period before the opening of SALT negotiations, a study group was formed in the Academy to prepare recommendations on possible arms limitation positions. Although these do not appear to have won acceptance at the time, it may be that their influence was felt at a later stage in the negotiations, and the director of the study group, Academician Aleksandr N. Shchukhin, has served as a leading member of the Soviet

SALT delegation from the beginning. The Academy has also maintained a Commission on Disarmament, which has served to coordinate the research of subordinate bodies on the subject. Through its contact with foreign scientists, the Academy has been a channel through which information from abroad has flowed into the Soviet system, performing useful exploratory and preparatory functions. It seems probable that these nonofficial contacts between Soviet scientists and independent but responsible scholars on the American side over a period of more than a decade may have been an essential forerunner to SALT, as, for example, in bringing together the Soviet and American positions on anti-ballistic missile (ABM) systems.

Under the Soviet Academy of Sciences, a number of research institutes play important roles in the preparation of SALT positions. Two of them—the Institute of World Economy and International Relations and the newer Institute on the U.S.A.—feed into the system information on relevant political and economic developments in the United States. In addition, each institute has recently established a section on disarmament, staffed in part by retired military officers, which issues increasingly sophisticated reports and articles on strategic and arms control thought in the United States. It is interesting to observe that Soviet studies of the United States in recent years have been increasing dramatically in numbers and in level of competence, while American studies of the Soviet Union in this period have been contracting.

It became apparent during the Summit meetings that between the Ministry of Defense and the Party leadership are a number of important mechanisms for coordinating military policy with political and economic considerations. The Supreme Military Council, with Brezhnev as chairman, proved to be a significant instrument through which the political authorities are involved in the policy-making process on military matters, including SALT. In addition, a previously unknown working level channel between the General Staff and the Party-government authorities involved in the supervision of defense production exists. This channel proved during the Summit negotiations to be a significant link in the decision-making process on SALT affairs, and apparently it has had representation on the SALT delegation. The principal figures involved in the channel are Dmitry F. Ustinov, a candidate member of the Politburo and also a member of the Party Secretariat, and Leonid V. Smirnov, a deputy prime minister in charge

of the Military-Industrial Commission, which oversees the Soviet armament industry. During a critical stage in the Summit negotiations on
SALT, Smirnov was assigned to work with Henry Kissinger in resolv-
ing a number of remaining difficulties, which he did with a considerable measure of authority, despite initial language difficulties. (This
was one instance of the effect of the Summit in bringing American
negotiators into more direct contact with the Soviet decision-making
process on SALT issues.) It is reasonable to assume that this Party-
government channel is a crucial nexus in the consideration of the
resource claims of weapons systems, together with GOSPLAN, the
State Planning Committee, and also in making available to the Party
leadership informed civilian judgments on military technology questions. It has been suggested by some writers, however, that the defense
industry sector, comprising eight ministries, and the large military
research and development institutions under these ministries may so
closely identify their interests with those of the professional military
establishment that they are scarcely likely to function as a source of
critical and independent judgment on military budgetary demands.

Within the Communist Party itself, the Central Committee has
general responsibility for overseeing defense industry, science and technology, and military affairs, which are presumably involved in SALT
questions. Perhaps more actively involved is the staff of the Central
Committee, a group of Party functionaries who are divided into task
forces to coordinate information for the Committee's Politburo on
every aspect of government activity. In the eight years under the
present Party leadership, the Central Committee staff has functioned
with clearer lines of responsibility than heretofore, and it has contributed to the general regularization of the decision-making process
which has developed since the Khrushchev period. It is not clear to
what extent the Central Committee staff occupied with SALT affairs
is involved and competent in the hardware technicalities of weapons
systems, or whether it mainly performs secretariat functions in coordinating information for Politburo decisions, but one has the impression that the latter more limited role seems to be the more probable. To the extent that this is true, its functions differ from those of
the National Security Council in the United States, although it does
seem to be moving in an emulative direction.

Another question of interest in this connection is the degree to which
the Central Committee staff personnel tend to be pragmatic or nar-

rowly ideological in their outlook and the extent of their experience outside the Soviet Union. These qualities in the Party staff could be decisive factors in the shaping of Soviet policy. On this point, it is possible to hazard the impression that the knowledge of the staff regarding other countries may be considerable, for under the *nomenklatura* system, which earmarks positions of high responsibility at home and abroad for members of a select upper Party career service, many of the Central Committee staff have had extensive experience in foreign posts. Although Party regularity is an important requisite for Central Committee staff members, it no longer appears to be regarded as a substitute for competence, and advanced degrees are not now uncommon among staff members. Like the upper level of bureaucracies in other countries, the staff has some of the characteristics of an "old boy" network, in which mutually protective relations based on old associations count for a good deal, but the level of general competence and of pragmatic problem-solving zeal would appear to compare favorably with upper level government bureaucracies in other countries, despite bureaucratic and ideological encumbrances elsewhere in the system.

Finally, the apex of the decision-making structure is, of course, the Politburo of the Party. While the sixteen full and seven candidate members of this group have specialized responsibilities, and although Brezhnev as General Secretary took the lead in the Summit negotiations on SALT and signed the SALT agreements on behalf of the Soviet Union, there does appear to be a process of consultation and a sharing of responsibility within the Politburo as a whole for arms limitation decisions, a mark of collective leadership and perhaps also of elementary precaution. The addition to the Politburo, in April 1973, of the minister of defense, Marshal Andrei A. Grechko, and the foreign minister, Andrei A. Gromyko, regularized the participation of these two government officials in the Party's ultimate decision-making body.

Although primary responsibility for SALT matters appears to have rested with Premier Alexei N. Kosygin during the early phases of negotiations, from early 1971 and particularly after the XXIV Party Congress, the main responsibility for SALT and for overall relations with the United States and for the treaty with the Federal Republic of Germany shifted to General Secretary Leonid I. Brezhnev. Following the Plenum of the Central Committee in April 1973, Brezhnev's hand was perceptibly strengthened, and he showed considerably greater self-confidence and authority in the course of his visits to Bonn and Washington after that meeting. The private communications of President Nixon to the Soviet leadership reflected this shift of responsibility: Kosygin was the recipient of the president's confidential communications prior to 1971; after that time, the addressee was Brezhnev. Although his authority is derived from his position as General Secretary of the Party, Brezhnev was authorized by special action of the Supreme Soviet to sign the SALT documents of May 1972, and the Washington agreements of June 1973, in behalf of the Soviet government.

Between the various bureaucratic channels occupied with specialized aspects of SALT problems, there appears to have been little lateral transfer of information, except at the upper level within the Party. The high degree of compartmentalization within military channels of all details concerning Soviet weapons, including their deployment, their performance, etc., is characteristic of the extreme secrecy of the Soviet system toward all military information. As it affected SALT I, this compartmentalization meant that bureaucracies other than a limited sector within the military were not in a position to consider the technical aspect of arms limitations, lacking data on Soviet weapons systems. Soviet researchers and even Soviet diplomatic representatives were thus in the position of having to use published Western estimates of numbers and performance characteristics of Soviet weapons systems as a basis for calculations regarding possible arms limitation agreements. Moreover, in the SALT discussions, Western nomenclature was used by both sides to refer to Soviet weapons systems, and Soviet military representatives showed uneasiness at the discussion of technical details of weapons systems in the presence of Soviet civilian representatives. As a consequence of the compartmentalization of technical information, the interplay between the military and other bureaucratic elements in the decision-making process has been highly constricted. In any case, the prestige of the military in the Soviet social order is so elevated that it would be difficult to conceive of a public debate on positions advocated by the military services even if the information were available. The memorandum circulated by Academician Sakharov advocating the limitation of armaments, including anti-ballistic missile systems, was an isolated exception.

However, things may never be quite the same after the climactic decision making at the Summit sessions on SALT I. For those few hectic days, Brezhnev, the other top Party leaders, and the principal civilian technical authorities were directly engaged in the negotiating process, learning the problems at first hand, trading directly with the American principals. Only in this way, perhaps, could political concepts of security be brought fully to bear upon technical issues whose resolution ultimately required political judgments. The case for Summit-level contacts as a way of breaking through layers of military and other bureaucratic insulation, of directly informing and engaging the central authorities, was dramatically made during those few days when the action shifted from Helsinki to Moscow, despite the cost and the disorder of not having at hand the experienced SALT negotiating team. As a consequence of SALT I and the Summit stage in the negotiations, the circle of officials informed and involved in arms limitation matters is undoubtedly wider than it was, and the participation of nonmilitary elements in the bureaucratic interplay surrounding SALT II may be substantially greater than it has been in the past.

The Soviet Conceptual Approach to SALT

It has been assumed by many in the West that Soviet thinking about strategic doctrine and arms limitation has been moving along essentially the same track as in the United States, although lagging by a few years. Partly as a result of the negotiating experience connected with SALT, however, we have become aware that this is not altogether correct, and that in some important respects, the Soviet conceptual base is quite different from that which lies behind Western thinking about arms control.

There can be no doubt that the Soviet leadership and people share with the United States the conviction that general nuclear war must be avoided, and that the Soviet approach to these matters is characterized by a considerable degree of sobriety. Nor is there any doubt that Soviet thinking from the time of Khrushchev proceeded from the assumption that the main purpose of strategic forces is to deter the outbreak of general war. While the Soviet Union still remains formally committed to the proposal for General and Complete Disarmament, it has, for all practical purposes, accepted some elements of the more limited but more realistic "arms control" approach as a basis for negotiation, in the name of "partial measures" toward the first stage of general disarmament. This has involved Soviet acceptance of a number of Western arms control concepts, as for example the Gromyko acceptance in 1963 of the nuclear "umbrella" notion, according to which each side would retain a limited number of strategic weapons under a first-stage disarmament agreement, in contrast to the previous Soviet insistence upon a total ban on nuclear weapons at the outset. In the course of the discussion of ABM systems, the Soviet Union moved from the first folk-wisdom position in the mid-1960s that, since ABM was defensive, it must be good, to an acceptance by the end of the decade of the Western arms control argument that ABM could be destabilizing and a stimulus to the further buildup of offensive weapons. Another important idea that travelled from the United States to the Soviet Union was the desirability of increasing the relative invulnerability of strategic forces through hardening, dispersal, or mobility in order to protect a retaliatory second-strike capability from surprise attack, thereby giving some measure of stability to the strategic balance.

However, the general sense in which the concept of deterrence is applied in the Soviet Union contains some major differences from the much more differentiated meanings it has come to contain in Western usage. One reason for these differences may be that the major contributions to strategic theory in the United States since World War II have come from civilians, whereas the Soviet writings on the subject are preponderantly by men with professional military backgrounds.

The nature of the differences can be best illustrated by a reference to the language used. In Russian, the word generally used to express "deterrence" is the same word that was brought into general use after World War II to mean "containment" (*sderzhivaniye*). Occasionally a phrase is added: "by means of intimidation" (*putyom ustrasheniye*). Sometimes "intimidation" is used by itself as a shorthand expression. (The word also conveys the sense of "terror," "threat," or "frightfulness.") One Russian writer has defined deterrence as: "to guarantee a destructive retaliatory blow to any aggressor." To the extent that the Soviet concept of deterrence is explicated, it generally takes the form of a short paragraph which suggests that the imperialists do not commit aggression against the Soviet Union because they know that they would receive in return such a crushing blow against their entire country, including military and industrial targets, that imperialism would never rise again.

What is notably absent in this approach are the distinctions made in American strategic theory between "deterrence" and "defense" or "war-fighting" capabilities; between "counter-value" and "counter-force" targeting; between "minimum," "limited," "finite," "graduated," or other variants of the definition of deterrent functions and capabilities. Generally absent in Soviet strategic theory are the contributions that have entered the American literature on the subject from operations research, game theory, bargaining theory, and such refinements as the efforts to quantify "assured destruction," and "damage limitation;" or to explicate such notions as "nuclear pause," "escalatory levels," or "city-sparing" exchanges.

Some of the ideas involved in these terms do make their appearance in simpler form in the Soviet military and other journals, often through surrogate issues. For example, the arguments over whether there can be such a thing as "winning" a general nuclear war imply a debate between what we would call "deterrent" versus "war-fighting" postures. Similarly, the discussions over whether a nuclear war might be long or short, or whether it is conceivable that a limited nuclear war could remain limited, reflect budgetary competition between the rocket forces and the more traditional services, as well as the kinds of issues raised in the United States by the president's request for the capabilities to exercise "options" short of an all-out response.

From the Soviet point of view, the problem is simpler than is represented in the Western arms control literature, which it tends to regard as intellectual calisthenics, abstract from life, intended to evade real issues if not to deceive. In negotiations, the Soviet representatives are markedly uninterested in concepts, beyond the elementary principle of "equal security." Soviet representatives profess to be puzzled by the attribution to the Soviet Union of elaborate first-strike strategies as an explanation for their deployment of the large SS-9 missile, since we can fit it into no other place in our catalogue of strategies. A deterrent, they say, is meant to frighten, and a big one frightens more, and isn't that what deterrence is all about? We can only guess whether this is a disingenuous argument from civilian officials who might not, in fact, be in a position to know whether their military officials do or do not have a particular strategic doctrine for the SS-9; or whether the weapon grew historically from the earlier preference for large launchers and came to have a demonstrative bargaining utility. However, it seems probable that the Soviet military procurement is determined by less elaborate doctrinal justifications than are set forth in the posture statements of the Secretary of Defense of the United States.

Still, the question is: How much does it matter if there is a substantial asymmetry between the Soviet and American conceptual approaches to strategic doctrine and arms limitation? Is it necessary to close the conceptual gap in order to make substantial progress in arms control?

Without doubt, there is some merit in the Soviet argument that Western arms control theory is sometimes overly abstracted from real life situations. One could go further and acknowledge that strategic doctrine sometimes appears as an after-the-fact rationalization for weapons programs which owe their existence to political or economic pressures that are far from theoretical. Granted all this, it still remains true that the extraordinary development of arms control theory in the United States during the 1950s and early 1960s represented a major step toward an understanding of the complex implications of the revolution that had taken place in military technology. To attain even the minimum intermediate goal of a stable deterrent balance at moderate levels requires that the political leaders of the nations involved proceed from some common understanding of the implications of each of the three words: "stable," "deterrent," and "balance." It cannot be said that this conception is clearly understood and accepted in either the Soviet Union or the United States. The residual effect of pre-nuclear age thought about the putative benefits of a "superior war-fighting capability" for either military or political advantages is still to be seen in both countries.

This means that the difference in conceptual approaches does matter and does need to be worked at, not as abstract theory, but in the political context of the pressures and interests, the perceptions, the uncertainties, the interactions of the two systems and of others as they are involved. Underpinning the negotiating process, there needs to be a continuing effort to enlarge the understanding by the political leaders on both sides of their own real security interests in an age of nuclear weapons, and the extent of their involvement in the internal political processes of the other side.

It is still unclear, for example, whether the Soviet acceptance of the ABM Treaty in SALT I signified an understanding and acceptance of the principle that the deterrent balance rests upon the survivability of the retaliatory forces on both sides, or whether it simply indicated a judgment on the Soviet side that in the absence of such a treaty, the United States might proceed to deploy a superior area defense. If the former, there may be grounds for hope that the logical concomitant in SALT II would be to seek a resting place for the arms competition at the point at which the curve of megatons to destruction begins to flatten out—in other words, at the level of finite deterrence. If the latter, and if the Soviet Union continues to seek technological advantages, for example, in accuracy of warhead delivery, on top of an advantage in numbers and throw weight of missiles, the instability of the present deterrent balance will be increased, and SALT II discussions will retrogress to first principles.

A clear issue thus emerges between the natural reluctance of the Soviet military to accept limitations on further qualitative improvements, and the real interests of the Soviet Union, as of the United States, in stabilizing the strategic competition at the modest level of a deterrent balance.

It should be added, however, that the encouragement of Soviet conceptual understanding in this direction is impeded by the misapplied reliance on the bargaining chip tactic on the American side. When the bargaining chip argument is used to gain support for weapons systems which would not be supported on their merits, the net effect is to stimulate the arms competition rather than negotiations and to obscure our real interests in a stable deterrent balance. It is sometimes argued that the bargaining chip argument in behalf of ABM and MIRV in the United States helped to produce agreement in SALT I. In retrospect, however, it is clear that on balance the bargaining chip tactic as it has been used has raised the military competition to levels more difficult to bring under control. If there is a justification for the use of the bargaining chip tactic, it would apply only where options are held out to the adversary which would clearly be justifiable and necessary in the absence of an agreement and where the programs involved would not be funded if negotiations were successful.

A related argument has centered on the question whether the military preparations of the two countries have developed in response to an action-reaction cycle. Some writers have tended to deny this phenomenon on the grounds that each country has responded to military pressures from within and to the tug of new technology. But the history of the military competition since World War II amply demonstrates that the real, or anticipated, or wrongly perceived military preparations, or even utterances, of each side have often been used to gain support in the interplay of pressures and interest on the other for weapons programs which would not otherwise have been funded.

SALT I opened the door for the leaders of the Soviet Union and the United States to the possibility that they can achieve greater security for their countries and the rest of the world at a reduced level of competition in strategic weapons. When this has been realized, it will become possible to look beyond deterrence to some less dangerous form of security. The process begins, however, with a common understanding of our common predicament. Here perhaps is the real significance of SALT I, for its most important accomplishment is to be found less in the substantive agreements reached than in the educational effect of the negotiating process itself.

Part 2

CHAPTER FIVE
The SALT I Agreements

John B. Rhinelander

INTRODUCTION

SALT I produced four agreements, but only two of them—the ABM Treaty and the Interim Offensive Agreement—deal with arms control as such. Final agreement on some issues relating to these was reached only in Moscow during the 1972 Summit. Although the texts set forth the basic agreement that was reached at the SALT sessions and in Moscow, many subsidiary matters are also recorded in what can best be described as a three-layer approach on agreed matters. First, there are the texts of the two agreements themselves, signed by President Nixon and General Secretary Brezhnev, including the signed Protocol attached to the Interim Offensive Agreement which provides details on the ballistic-missile submarine and SLBM limitations. Second, there are a series of "agreed interpretations" in the form of statements initialed by Ambassador Smith for the U.S. and Deputy Minister Semenov for the Soviet Union on an airplane from Helsinki to Moscow prior to the signing of the texts of the agreements. Third, there are a number of agreed interpretations in the form of "common understandings" that were mutually agreed upon, but not recorded in a document initialed by both sides; some are in the form of statements by one side indicating where agreement is understood to have been reached. In almost all cases, the initialed statements and common understandings were initially proposed for inclusion in the texts of the agreements by one side or the other (more frequently by the U.S.), but for a variety of reasons were relegated to less formal documentation. The "initialed statements" and "common understandings" are as binding on the U.S. and U.S.S.R. as the texts of the agreements. In addition, several note-worthy unilateral statements were made by the U.S. and U.S.S.R. which

125

are important even though they do not necessarily represent agreement.

The presidential papers transmitting the ABM Treaty, the Interim Offensive Agreement, and the various initialed statements, common understandings, and unilateral statements to the Congress also included a detailed analysis of the agreements submitted by the Secretary of State. During the course of the congressional hearings and debate, a legislative record was made which, in certain cases, expressed the U.S. position on provisions that appear ambiguous from the texts of the negotiated documents.

The other two agreements reached at SALT I, the Accident Measures Agreement and revised Hot Line Agreement, are executive agreements which entered into force on September 30, 1971, without congressional debate or approval.

THE ABM TREATY

The ABM Treaty is clearly the most important and most detailed agreement reached at SALT I. By severely limiting ABM systems by various quantitative, qualitative, and geographic constraints, the treaty effectively removes the threat to the penetration capability of U.S. strategic retaliatory forces that survived a first strike. In the view of most observers, the ABM Treaty should eliminate fears on either side of a first strike as a rational policy option. The ABM Treaty contains some highly significant qualitative constraints which should preserve its impact over time, and it provides for a Standing Consultative Commission to promote its objectives and facilitate its implementation. Verification by national technical means, a euphemism for various techniques including orbiting satellites, and provisions against interference with or concealment from national technical means are expressly recognized. The duration of the treaty is unlimited, but it contains various provisions relating to periodic review, amendment, and withdrawal. By its terms the treaty commits the U.S. and U.S.S.R. to continue negotiations for limitations on strategic offensive arms in order to replace the Interim Offensive Agreement with a comprehensive agreement.

ABM Limitations

The Basic Principles: Mutual Vulnerability

Paragraph 2 of Article I of the ABM Treaty sets forth in general terms the fundamental premise agreed at SALT—the U.S. and the U.S.S.R. each agree not to deploy ABM systems which would provide a defense covering substantially the whole of its territory and not to provide a base upon which such an ABM system might be built in the future.

This embodies a political decision of the first magnitude. For the Soviet Union, it represents a significant shift in strategic doctrine by accepting, in a formal international agreement, that Soviet territory is and will remain defenseless against U.S. land-based and sea-based nuclear missiles. While the U.S. had recognized the fact of mutual vulnerability in the event of a heavy nuclear attack and had discounted the feasibility of a "thick" nationwide ABM defense, proposals had persisted for a "thin" nationwide defense as well as for a hard site defense of ICBM launchers with thousands of short-range interceptors around hardened ICBM silos. Both of these possibilities were rejected as policy options by agreement on Articles I and III of the ABM Treaty.

The prohibition on a "base" for a nationwide defensive system precludes, in general terms, the construction of ABM or ABM-capable radars outside one ICBM missile field and the national capital area, as described in Article III, and would appear to limit the capability of ABM missiles deployed inside Article III areas to those that could not provide a thin defense covering substantially the whole of the territory of the U.S. or U.S.S.R. Thus, a "thin" nationwide defense is prohibited, even in the unlikely event that technological advances made feasible thin coverage from the two ABM areas which each side is permitted under Article III. Paragraph 2 of Article I also prohibits the deployment of a regional ABM system, except to the extent permitted under Article III. Reading the ABM Treaty as a whole, the more specific Articles III, IV, V, and VI, and related agreed interpretations, serve to reinforce the basic principles in paragraph 2 of Article I.

ABM Systems and ABM Components

Article II defines ABM systems and the three principal ABM components which are limited by the treaty—ABM launchers, ABM interceptor missiles, and ABM radars. Computer and communications systems, while vital parts of an operational ABM system, are not considered "ABM components" for purposes of the treaty.

An ABM system is defined as "a system to counter strategic ballistic missiles or their elements in flight trajectory." The term "elements" would include separate warheads or reentry vehicles. This definition would preclude an assertion that an ICBM on one side that was targetable at ICBM silos on the other was an ABM system, since such an ICBM and launcher would not be designed to counter an ICBM "in flight trajectory."

Article II defines an ABM system as "currently consisting of ABM launchers, interceptor missiles and radars." The prohibitions of the ABM Treaty are not limited to ABMs with nuclear warheads, although current ABM interceptor missiles are nuclear-equipped. Articles II and III provide the treaty framework for the ban on "future ABM systems," which is spelled out further in an agreed interpretation.*

The future systems ban applies to devices which would be capable of substituting for one or more of the three basic ABM components, such as a "killer" laser or a particle accelerator. Article III of the treaty does not preclude either development or testing of fixed land-based devices which could substitute for ABM components, but does prohibit their deployment. Article V, on the other hand, prohibits development and testing, as well as deployment, of air-based, sea-based, space-based, or mobile land-based ABM systems or components, which includes "future systems" for those kinds of environments. The overall effect of the treaty, therefore, is to prohibit any deployment of future systems and to limit their development and testing to those in a fixed land-based mode. Certain devices, such as telescopes, which are simply adjuncts to, not substitutes for, present ABM components are not covered.

These constraints on future ABM systems, which the U.S. proposed, are an attempt to ensure a long-term, effective limitation on strategic defensive systems in an age of changing technology. Neither laser technology nor any other kind of device now appears to have a signi-

---

* ABM Treaty, Initialed Statement D.

ficant ABM potential; for instance, a land-based laser would not be effective in the event of cloud cover, and the platform for an air-based laser would itself be a vulnerable target. However, the failure to include a broad proscription against future devices might have led to a significant effort by either or both the U.S. and U.S.S.R. to develop esoteric ABM systems. The prohibition in the treaty thus serves the same preventive purpose as the prohibition on placing weapons of mass destruction in orbit which is contained in the Outer Space Treaty of 1967.

Article II defines ABM interceptor missiles and ABM radars in terms of components "constructed and deployed" for an ABM role, or of a type "tested in an ABM mode" subsequent to the date of signature. In earlier years, both sides had unsuccessfully tested air defense systems (SAMs) for possible ABM roles, and the prohibition is understood to apply to tests subsequent to the date of signature of the ABM Treaty.* The definitions are reinforced by the corollary undertaking in Article VI not to give an ABM capability to non-ABM missiles, launchers, and radars and not to test them in the future "in an ABM mode." The latter concept is discussed below in the context of Article VI.

An ABM launcher is defined in Article II in terms of a launcher constructed or deployed for launching ABM missiles. This would include any launcher associated with a missile tested in an ABM mode subsequent to date of signature, even though the launcher was primarily identified with a non-ABM system.

The term ABM radar means radars with target tracking or missile control capabilities essential to command and control of current ABM systems and does not include early warning radars. There is obviously a gray area between early warning radars, which have acquisition and some tracking capability, and an ABM radar, but various criteria, such as location, can be used to determine whether a particular radar should be considered an ABM radar or an early warning radar.

The second paragraph of Article II lists various conditions of ABM components—operational, under construction, undergoing overhaul, etc. These provisions emphasize that the deployment, numerical, and geographic constraints in other articles apply from the moment an ABM launcher or ABM radar is under construction until it is destroyed or dismantled.

---

* ABM Treaty, Unilateral Statement B, by U.S.

Authorized ABM Deployments

Article III authorizes, but does not require, the U.S. and U.S.S.R. to deploy ABM systems in two widely separated areas under various geographic, quantitative, and qualitative constraints. The U.S. and U.S.S.R. are each limited to one ABM deployment area centered on its national capital and one ABM deployment area containing ICBM silos. An agreed interpretation* provides that the location of the two ABM deployment areas must be 1,300 kilometers apart, which precludes an effective area defense. Since the location of present U.S. and Soviet ICBM silos is known and new construction of additional ICBM silos is prohibited by the Interim Offensive Agreement, the treaty effectively limits the Soviets to an ABM system in defense of ICBM silos to a location east of the Ural Mountains and the U.S. to an ABM system located west of the Mississippi River.

Article III prohibits the U.S. and U.S.S.R. from deploying an ABM system elsewhere than on their territories, an obligation also stated in Article IX which prohibits transfers of ABM systems or ABM components to other states. During the negotiations, the U.S. delegation stated its ABM deployment area in defense of ICBM silos would be located at Grand Forks, North Dakota;* the Soviets did not indicate whether they would construct such an ABM system.

At the time the negotiations were completed, the U.S. ABM site at Grand Forks was nearing completion and the Soviet Galosh system around Moscow was already operational although incomplete. In addition, the U.S. had not started construction of an ABM system around Washington (and the Congress refused to authorize the appropriation of funds for that purpose in the summer of 1972 after the treaty was signed), and the Soviets had not started construction of an ABM system located in ICBM fields. While consideration was given at SALT to deferring, by a provision in the text of the treaty itself, the second deployment area for each side, this was not ultimately agreed upon. Thus, while each side has the same ABM deployment options under the treaty, actual deployments are asymmetrical. Upon signing the treaty on May 26, 1972, the U.S. stopped construction of the second Safeguard ABM site in defense of ICBM silos at Malmstrom Air Force

* ABM Treaty, Common Understanding A.

Base in Montana and, under Article VIII, had an affirmative duty to begin to dismantle or destroy this site within the shortest possible agreed periods of time subsequent to the date of entry into force (October 3, 1972).

The two widely separated deployment areas for ABM systems authorized by Article III are limited to circular areas with a radius of 150 kilometers each. Within each circular area, there can be no more than 100 ABM launchers and 100 ABM interceptor missiles "at launch sites." The prohibition relating to "at launch sites" does not preclude a limited number of additional missiles in maintenance sheds within the circular area. The present Soviet Galosh system around Moscow has sixty-four ABM launchers, plus one used for test purposes; the U.S. plans to deploy ninety-seven ABM launchers at the Grand Forks ICBM field. The treaty does not prohibit construction and deployment of ABM launchers and interceptor missiles for test and training purposes in the Article III areas, but if, for instance, the launcher were capable of launching a missile, it would be included in the numerical limitation of one hundred.

The ABM radar constraints are different for the two deployment areas. In the national capital area, ABM radars must be located within six small circles with diameters of only three kilometers; there are no quantitative or qualitative limits on ABM radars in those small areas. The small circular areas are intended to constrain deployment by the Soviets of modern phased-array ABM radars around Moscow that were not operational during SALT I; specific quantitative and qualitative constraints proved nonnegotiable. The limitation of modern phased-array radars to the small circular areas ensures that the ABM system, as a whole, and the national capital area will be vulnerable. An agreed interpretation* provides that the six circle limitations do not apply to the Soviet mechanical scan, dish-type radars (TRY ADDs) which were operational when the treaty was signed. As Article III stands, a defense of either Washington or Moscow limited to one hundred ABM interceptors and ABM launchers, with modern phased-array ABM radars confined to the six small circular areas, cannot be effective against a determined ICBM attack by the U.S. or U.S.S.R. Such a national command authority defense might have some limited utility against an accidental or unauthorized launch directed against the

---

* ABM Treaty, Initialed Statement A.

capital area, but would have no utility beyond the effective range of the ABM radars or ABM interceptor missiles.

For the defense of the ICBM deployment area, each side is permitted two large ABM radars and eighteen smaller ABM radars. The limitations are stated in terms of the "potential" of the radars. (An agreed interpretation defined "potential" of ABM radars as the product of the mean emitted power in watts and the antenna area in square meters, and set the missile site radar [MSR] potential as three million for this purpose.* A further understanding was reached on how to measure potential if a radar has separate antennae for receiving and transmitting.) In effect, these provisions permit the U.S. and U.S.S.R. each to deploy one large ABM radar with a "potential" of the U.S. perimeter acquisition radar (PAR) and a second ABM radar with a "potential" of the U.S. missile site radar (MSR) being deployed at Grand Forks, and eighteen ABM radars, each with a "potential" less than the MSR. Present plans for Grand Forks call for construction of only two ABM radars—a PAR and an MSR. The treaty would permit deployment of additional ABM radars by the U.S., but a hard site defense using twenty ABM radars would not be feasible in light of the limitation of one hundred ABM launchers.

While an ABM defense of 100 or 150 ICBM silos by 100 interceptor missiles could complicate an attack because of the possibility of preferential defenses of certain silos, it could be overwhelmed. The fixed ABM radars are, of course, themselves vulnerable to being knocked out of action in a nuclear exchange. The deployment of a limited ABM defense of ICBM silos by the U.S. does, however, provide some experience with an operational ABM system.

Article III was the most difficult of the articles in the ABM Treaty to agree upon, for a variety of reasons. Its eventual form and content reflect compromises made in Washington and Moscow at different stages to meet various concerns and needs. In the perspective of having reached a treaty that prohibits the deployment of an effective ABM system by either side, and in the event agreement is reached at SALT II on a long-term limitation on strategic offensive systems, Article III could be amended to limit ABM deployments to only one area for each side, or even provide for a total ABM deployment ban.

* ABM Treaty, Initialed Statement B.

ABM Test Ranges

Article IV of the treaty provides that the deployment limitations of Article III do not apply to ABM systems or ABM components used for development or testing and located within current or additionally agreed test ranges. The current Soviet test range for ABM systems is located near Sary Shagan, Kazakhastan S.S.R., and the U.S. test ranges are located at White Sands, New Mexico, and Kwajalein Atoll in the Trust Territories of the Pacific. Because the Soviets refused to discuss the location of present test ranges, and in order to make the negotiating record explicit, the U.S. formally identified at SALT the current ABM test ranges of both countries.*

The effect of Article IV is to prohibit either side from constructing ABM components, for instance, around Leningrad or New York, under the label of a "test range." It should be noted that Article IV refers to "development and testing," not to research. While the delineation between "advanced research" and "development" is not precise, "development" is understood in this article to mean the developmental stage approaching flight testing of missiles. Neither research nor production facilities are affected by the treaty.

An ABM test range might be considered to include the whole corridor from where ICBMs are test-fired to the area where ABM components are located. For the U.S., this would include Vandenberg Air Force Base, California, where ICBMs are launched, to an impact area at Kwajalein Atoll in the South Pacific, where the ABM components are located. To deal with this problem, it was agreed that ABM test ranges encompass the area within which ABM components are located for test purposes.* It was further understood that non-phased-array radars of types used for range safety or instrumentation purposes may be located outside the ABM test ranges. The U.S., for instance, has such radars in Hawaii and deploys Navy picket ships in the Pacific in connection with ABM tests at Kwajalein.

Article IV further provides that the U.S. and U.S.S.R. may have no more than a total of fifteen ABM launchers at test ranges. Because of

* ABM Treaty, Common Understanding B.

Article V, such launchers cannot be mobile, but must be fixed land-based. The number of ABM radars at test ranges is not limited.

Prohibited Environments for ABM Components and Additional Constraints on ABM Launchers and ABM Interceptor Missiles

Article V prohibits the development and testing, as well as deployment, of certain types of ABM systems and ABM components. As used in Article V, "development" has a broad meaning. The word in the Russian text, which means "create," makes this broad sense clearer.

The effect of paragraph 1 of Article V is to limit ABM systems or ABM components which may be developed, tested, or deployed under Articles III and IV to those which are fixed land-based. While paragraph 1 of Article V expressly refers to sea-based, air-based, space-based, or mobile land-based ABMs, the intention was to foreclose ABM components except fixed land-based; therefore ABM components are prohibited not only from the bottom of the sea but also on or in lakes or rivers. The prohibitions in Article V apply to each of the three basic ABM components, as well as the system as a whole, and would therefore prohibit a sea-based ABM radar linked with land-based ABM launchers and interceptor missiles. It would also prohibit future ABM systems, such as an airborne killer laser, as a substitute for a fixed land-based ABM interceptor missile, or a space-based sensor that, coupled with land-based components, was capable of substituting for one or more current ABM components. There are, however, gray areas since the treaty does not limit deployment of sensors or satellites which provide early warning of missile launches.

Agreement on the basic prohibitions in paragraph 1 of Article V was reached relatively early at SALT. Neither side had pushed ABM programs which would be affected by this paragraph, although each possessed various surface-to-air (SAM) or air-to-air missile systems to defend against aircraft, including mobile or transportable SAM systems. The prohibition on mobile land-based ABM components will enhance confidence that each side is complying with the numerical limits on ABM launchers in Article III. To clarify the scope of this provision, an agreed interpretation was reached that the prohibitions on mobile ABM components apply to those which are not of a permanent, fixed type,* thus covering both mobile and transportable systems.

Paragraph 2 of Article V contains further provisions which ensure that the basic Article III numerical limitations on ABM launchers and ABM interceptor missiles are meaningful. This paragraph prohibits the development, testing, or deployment of:

—ABM launchers for launching more than one ABM interceptor missile at a time from each launcher, or the modification of deployed launchers to provide such a capability; and

—automatic, semiautomatic, or other similar systems for the rapid reload of ABM launchers.

A deployment limitation of one hundred ABM launchers would quite obviously be weaker if rapid reload capabilities permitted firing a second ABM missile shortly after the first. While the treaty does not prohibit dual or multiple ABM launchers, each launcher in such a system would count against the numerical limits in Articles III and IV.

In addition to the limitations set forth in the text of Article V, an agreed interpretation† provides an obligation not to develop, test, or deploy ABM interceptor missiles with more than one independently guided warhead. While limitations on MIRV'd ICBMs were not seriously pursued at SALT I, the U.S. and U.S.S.R. did agree to prohibit "MIRV'd" ABM interceptor missiles. Neither side had developed or tested MIRV'd ABMs and such a system could be circumvented by staggering the arrival time of incoming warheads. These factors made a prohibition on MIRV'd ABM systems feasible at this stage.

Constraints on Non-ABM and ABM-Capable Systems

Article VI and related understandings contain limitations on non-ABM systems, such as surface-to-air missile (SAM) systems, which, while not designed for ABM purposes, could be given some ABM capabilities through upgrading. This article also contains geographic and qualitative limitations on early warning and other non-ABM radars. These provisions are particularly important to the U.S. The

---

* ABM Treaty, Common Understanding C.

† ABM Treaty, Initialed Statement E.

U.S.S.R. has deployed approximately 10,000 SAM sites in the Soviet Union. Soviet tests of both ABM and non-ABM systems are conducted at the Sary Shagan test range. Moreover, the Soviets have deployed in various locations a number of large phased-array radars (referred to in the West as "Hen House" radars) for early warning, space track, test range, and other purposes.

Paragraph (a) of Article VI prohibits giving missiles, launchers, or radars (other than ABM interceptor missiles, ABM launchers, or ABM radars) the capabilities to counter strategic ballistic missiles or their elements in flight trajectory. Every SAM system, of course, has some theoretical, even if minimal, ABM capability. There are SAM systems which are clearly not ABM-capable in the practical world, but new SAM systems could possibly be developed to have dual capabilities.

The first paragraph of Article VI also contains a prohibition on testing non-ABM systems "in an ABM mode." (The concept "tested in an ABM mode" is also used in the definitions of ABM interceptor missiles and ABM radars in Article II.) Despite the importance of this term in separating the prohibited from the permitted, there was no agreed interpretation. The U.S. delegation did, however, make a statement* which makes clear the prohibition is on testing non-ABM components for ABM purposes, and not on the testing of either ABM components for ABM purposes or non-ABM components for non-ABM purposes. In addition, the U.S. delegation made clear that the U.S. statement was not intended to imply that ABMs and SAMs could not be tested at the same test range, as at Sary Shagan, but only that they could not be tested at the same time. The U.S.S.R. delegation did not formally respond to the U.S. statement on "testing in an ABM mode" at SALT.

Testing, of course, is a critical step prior to full-scale production or field deployment. It also is subject to monitoring by national technical means of verification. The U.S. statement makes use of illustrative examples rather than quantitative criteria; while examples have the disadvantage of being nonexclusive, criteria would be difficult to negotiate since they would require agreed thresholds and would create the risk that any quantitative thresholds might become a design objective for non-ABM components.

The first example of testing in an ABM mode in the U.S. statement

---

* ABM Treaty, Unilateral Statement B, by U.S.

applies to launchers and is quite simple. If a launcher were used to launch an ABM interceptor missile and were later deployed, it would be considered an ABM launcher and therefore subject to the limitations of Articles III and IV.

The second example in the U.S. statement applies to interceptor missiles. It is more complex and is really three instances of prohibited flight testing of interceptor missiles. One is the flight testing of an interceptor missile against a "target" vehicle which has a flight trajectory with the characteristics of a strategic ballistic missile; the target vehicle need not be an ICBM, MR/IRBM, or SLBM, but could be a much shorter-range missile. The second is an interceptor missile that is flight tested in conjunction with the test of an ABM interceptor missile or an ABM radar at the same test range. Finally, there is the flight testing of an interceptor missile at a higher altitude than that of aircraft flight. Each of these is an example of what the U.S. considers would be testing the interceptor missile "in an ABM mode."

The third example in the U.S. statement applies to radars and raises two separate matters. One is a radar making measurements against a "cooperative" target vehicle with flight trajectory characteristics of a strategic ballistic missile during reentry. The word "cooperative" is used to make clear that the tracking of an orbiting satellite (manned or unmanned) by a radar, for instance, does not mean the radar should be considered an ABM radar. The second is radar measurements in conjunction with the test of an ABM interceptor missile or an ABM radar at the same test range. Because ABM radars are the long lead-time item and a critical component in an effective ABM system and because radars for air defense with a "potential" of less than three million watt-square meters are not constrained by the treaty, the prohibition on testing a radar—except, of course, an ABM radar—"in an ABM mode" has basic importance. The U.S. delegation made clear that radars which are used for purposes of range safety or instrumentation (which do not, under Article IV, have to be located at the test ranges themselves) are not intended to be covered by the U.S. statement.

Paragraph (b) of Article VI limits the future deployment of "radars for early warning of strategic ballistic missiles" to locations on the periphery of the country and oriented outward. Although the number of any such additional radars is not limited, this geographical and directional constraint minimizes the possibility that any additionally deployed early warning radars could contribute to an effective ABM defense in the interior. For instance, the paragraph would prohibit construction of early warning radars on the periphery of either the U.S or U.S.S.R. if they had inland, or "over-the-shoulder," tracking capability. The paragraph does not apply to radars for early warning of tactical missiles, such as might be deployed by U.S. or U.S.S.R. forces in central Europe or on a naval vessel. The paragraph would, however, prohibit deployment in the future of radars for early warning of strategic missiles in third countries, such as the ballistic-missile early warning radars (BMEWs) the U.S. operates in Greenland, but it does not apply to existing systems. It was understood that Article VI was not intended to prohibt the use of phased-array technology for early warning radars.

Finally, an agreed interpretation* provides that phased-array radars having a potential exceeding three million watt-square meters will not be deployed, except as provided in Article III (ABM radars in circular areas), Article IV (ABM test ranges), and Article VI (future early warning radars), and except for the purpose of tracking objects in outer space or for use as national technical means of verification. This prohibits deployment of a SAM system, for instance, with a phased-array radar with such a potential.

Article VI and the related interpretations and statements are one of the most technical parts of the ABM Treaty. It is notable in that the Soviets accepted both explicit corollary constraints on non-ABM systems and qualitative limitations which included specific numbers.

Modernization and Dismantling

Article VII permits modernization and replacement of ABM systems. This is obviously necessary for any weapons system. However, the right is explicitly qualified as being subject to the provisions of the treaty, meaning the various limitations and prohibitions in Articles I, III, IV, V, and VI and in the agreed interpretations. For instance, the Soviet mechanical scan, dish-type radars, now part of the Moscow ABM system, need not be located in the small circles within the Article III areas;† however, they could not be "replaced" by phased-array radars

---

* ABM Treaty, Initialed Statement F.
† ABM Treaty, Initialed Statement A.

unless the latter type of radar were located in one of the six small circles. ABM launchers presently deployed could be replaced, but only within the Article III circular areas.

Article VIII provides for the destruction or dismantling of ABM systems or ABM components which are in excess of the numbers or outside of the areas specified by Articles III or IV (ABM test ranges) or which are prohibited by Article V. Dismantling or destruction shall take place in accordance with agreed procedures, within the shortest possible agreed period of time.

Verification

Article XII on verification, which covers "national technical means of verification" and is identical to Article V of the Interim Offensive Agreement, is a landmark in arms control agreements. Specific "national technical means of verification" are not defined, but they are understood to mean information-collection systems operated outside the territory of the other side. National technical means could include, for instance, satellites carrying photographic or other equipment, radars in third countries, or radars on ships or aircraft operating outside territorial waters or national airspace. The treaty does not require changes from current operating practices and procedures with respect to national technical means of verification.

Paragraph 1 of Article XII provides that the U.S. and U.S.S.R. will use national technical means of verification at their disposal in a manner consistent with generally recognized principles of international law for the purpose of providing assurance of compliance with the provisions of the treaty. This paragraph does not limit verification to national technical means. For instance, embassy officers or attachés are not a national technical means of verification, but information they gather can be used. However, this first paragraph recognizes national technical means and establishes the basis for provisions against interference with these means in the second and third paragraphs.

The relevant general principles of international law are not precise. Although a State has sovereign power over its air space and territorial waters (and the ABM Treaty does not limit these rights of the U.S. or U.S.S.R.), there is no agreed delineation between air space and outer space in international law. States have acquiesced in the operation of satellites which orbit over their territory for peaceful purposes. These and other imprecisions in international law should not have an impact on the SALT agreements, particularly in light of the fact that the U.S. and U.S.S.R. are each aware of what the other has been and is doing, and neither has protested over the past ten years.

The second paragraph of Article XII prohibits interference with national technical means of verifiaction operating in accordance with generally recognized principles of international law. This provision would not prohibit actions against an unauthorized aircraft entering air space of one side, but would prevent interference with an orbiting satellite. Nothing in the treaty prohibits the development or testing of satellites capable of destroying other satellites. Any use of such an anti-satellite, however, to interfere with verification measures of the other side would violate the treaty and would provide a basis for withdrawal from the treaty.

The third paragraph prohibits deliberate concealment methods which impede verification by national technical means, but it explicitly permits continuation of current construction, assembly, conversion, and overhaul practices. The meaning of the word "deliberate" is ambiguous, since it could mean either measures intended to impede verification or measures which had that result although intended for other purposes, such as a cover over a missile launcher to protect it from the weather. Since national technical means cannot discern intentions, this paragraph cannot be limited to the first interpretation. Covered assembly or maintenance facilities as currently used are specifically exempted. The effect of such facilities on verification is not significant in terms of the treaty obligations.

Miscellaneous Provisions

International Transfers

Article IX provides that in order to assure the viability and effectiveness of the treaty, the U.S. and U.S.S.R. will not transfer to other States, and will not deploy outside their national territories, ABM systems or ABM components limited by the treaty. The non-transfer obligation reinforces the constraints contained in Article III which implicitly limit ABM deployment to two areas in the territory of the U.S. and U.S.S.R. The deployment provision in this article does not apply to the current U.S. ABM test range at Kwajalein Atoll. While this article does not apply to radars for early warning of strategic ballistic missiles because they are not considered "ABM radars," Article VI limits future construction of such radars to the territory of the U.S. and U.S.S.R.

The non-transfer provisions in Article IX are supplemented by an agreed interpretation* not to provide to other States technical descriptions or blueprints specially worked out for the construction of ABM systems and ABM components limited by the treaty. This obligation was important to the Soviets who, undoubtedly, were concerned that the U.S. might provide ABM systems to its allies.

The U.S. delegation at SALT made clear in a unilateral statement† that the non-transfer provisions of Article IX did not set a precedent for a treaty limiting strategic offensive arms. The statement reflects the fact, for example, that the U.S. has a special agreement with the United Kingdom relating to the U.K. Polaris submarines.

Amendment and Withdrawal

Article XIV covers amendments to the treaty and periodic formal reviews. The first paragraph of Article XIV, which provides that the U.S. and U.S.S.R. can propose amendments, is not necessary since parties to an international agreement can always do this. However the explicit statement on amendments indicates that the ABM Treaty should not be considered a static document since it deals with changing technology and strategic relationships.

The second paragraph of Article XIV provides for formal review of the ABM Treaty five years after the date of entry into force (which would be October 3, 1977), and at five-year intervals thereafter. This does not preclude amendment prior to that date. While not required by the treaty, the formal review by the U.S. and U.S.S.R. would probably be conducted through the Standing Consultative Commission. The first review date is particularly significant since the Interim Offensive Agreement will terminate then unless extended or previously superseded by a long-term treaty on limitations of strategic offensive arms.

The ABM Treaty is explicitly stated to be of unlimited duration in paragraph 1 of Article XV. This, however, should be read in conjunction with the second paragraph of that article which is a withdrawal

---

* ABM Treaty, Initialed Statement G.

† ABM Treaty, Unilateral Statement C, by U.S.

clause similar to those in the Limited Nuclear Test Ban, Non-Proliferation, Seabed, and other recent multilateral arms control treaties. The withdrawal clause can be invoked at any time and requires six months' notice to the other party prior to withdrawal and a statement of the extraordinary events related to the subject matter of the ABM Treaty which the notifying party regards as having jeopardized its "supreme interests." The determinations made under this kind of clause are unilateral, but the consequences of even giving notice of withdrawal would, of course, be immense.

Nothing in the treaty limits the general right of the U.S. or U.S.S.R. under international law to suspend or terminate performance under the treaty in the event of a material breach by the other. In addition, the treaty is silent on the effect that war, either general or limited, between the U.S. and U.S.S.R. would have on their obligations. Presumably, the effects of such circumstances on their obligations under the treaty would be determined by general principles of international law looking to the purposes of the treaty as a whole.

The U.S. delegation made a significant unilateral statement* on withdrawal which links the ABM Treaty to the achievement of agreement on more complete limitations on strategic offensive arms. The U.S. delegation made the statement after the Soviet delegation had repeatedly stressed that it would be inappropriate to include such language in the text of the treaty itself, which is intended to be long-term. The U.S. statement stresses the objective of constraining and reducing on a long-term basis the threats to the survivability of strategic retaliatory forces and notes that if an agreement limiting strategic offensive systems is not achieved within five years, U.S. supreme interests could be jeopardized and this could constitute a basis for withdrawal. The finely tuned language of the U.S. statement does not mean that failure to achieve agreement at SALT II would lead the U.S. to withdraw from the ABM Treaty.

The Interim Offensive Agreement

The Interim Offensive Agreement is intended to be exactly what the title implies—a temporary agreement constraining certain strategic offensive systems, while a comprehensive treaty is negotiated at SALT II. Although its coverage is limited and the text itself is quite

* ABM Treaty, Unilateral Statement A, by U.S.

short, there are several agreed interpretations and understandings relating to its provisions in addition to a signed Protocol. In general, the Interim Offensive Agreement combines a "freeze" on new construction of ICBM launchers with numerical limits on ballistic-missile submarines and SLBMs.

The Interim Offensive Agreement does not cover the principal ongoing U.S. strategic program—the MIRVing of ICBMs and SLBMs, which is now progressing at the rate of about three additional warheads per day. It does not cover forward-basing of U.S. systems in Europe and at sea. It does not limit strategic bombers, where the U.S. has a significant qualitative and quantitative advantage, or the deployment of SRAMs presently being added to some B-52 squadrons. The accuracy and range of missiles, the throw weight and yield, and number of warheads on each missile are not affected. There are no qualitative constraints, with the exception of limits on ICBM silo dimensions. The Interim Offensive Agreement permits the Soviet Union to continue its active ballistic-missile submarine construction program and would not restrict a Soviet MIRV program. It sets some limits on, but does not prohibit, the retrofit of new ICBMs into present ICBM silos.

The ICBM Launcher Freeze

Fixed Land-Based ICBMs

The freeze concept in Article I bans the construction of additional fixed land-based ICBM launchers except launchers for operational uses. The prohibition applies to both silo and soft-pad, or aboveground, launchers; the latter are relics of earlier days of the missile age and they are highly vulnerable. An agreed interpretation,* which reflects the Soviets' view that "strategic" includes any weapon capable of striking the U.S.S.R., defines an ICBM launcher as a launcher for a missile capable of ranges in excess of the shortest distance between the northeastern border of the continental U.S. and the northwestern border of the continental U.S.S.R. This comes to approximately 5,500 kilometers. This agreed interpretation also makes clear that Article I applies to ICBM launchers whether or not they may be targeted at

* Interim Offensive Agreement, Initialed Statement A.

lesser distances, or are deployed in fields with intermediate- or medium-range ballistic missiles (IRBMs or MRBMs). ICBM launchers are understood to include launchers for fractional orbiting bombardment systems (FOBS). Another agreed interpretation* emphasizes that the prohibition on "additional" launchers in Article I does not include the ninety-one ICBM launchers that were under active construction in the U.S.S.R. at date of signature, but that it does include those launchers in the U.S.S.R. on which active construction had ceased several years ago.

Article I leaves the Soviets with a maximum of 1,618 ICBM launchers and missiles with larger throw weights than the U.S. The U.S., according to present plans, will deploy MIRVs on 550 of its Minuteman missiles, for a total of 2,100 independently targetable warheads on its 1,000 Minuteman missiles.

Although the text of Article I refers to the "freeze" date as July 1, 1972, that date is meaningless as a benchmark. The Soviets had stopped construction of additional ICBM launchers in the summer of 1971 and the U.S. knew it. As a formal matter, the U.S. and U.S.S.R. reached a "standstill arrangement,"† the effect of which applied the freeze from the date of signature (May 26, 1972) until the date the agreement actually entered into force, which occurred on October 3, 1972.

The Soviets would not agree to apply the "freeze" to land-mobile ICBM launchers, perhaps to keep open the option of permitting land-mobiles under a SALT II agreement. The U.S. made a unilateral statement‡ agreeing to defer the issue to SALT II, but stating unequivocally that, in its view, the deployment of operational land-mobile ICBM launchers would be inconsistent with the objectives of the Interim Offensive Agreement. Neither side has deployed such land-mobile ICBM launchers, and the question of a complete ban will undoubtedly be raised at SALT II.

---

* Interim Offensive Agreement, Initialed Statement B.
† Interim Offensive Agreement, Common Understanding C.
‡ Interim Offensive Agreement, Unilateral Statement B, by U.S.

Modern Heavy ICBMs

A principal concern of the U.S. at SALT I was to ensure that a freeze on construction of new ICBM launchers would not be circumvented by the Soviets by allowing them to retrofit very large ICBMs into launchers constructed for smaller ICBMs. The most direct way to handle this would have been with an agreement that *any* missile over a stated size (measured by the volume of the entire missile) would be considered a large missile, and a further agreement not to enlarge silo launchers for "smaller" ICBMs into launchers for "large" ICBMs. This direct approach was not negotiable and Article II uses a less direct and less precise approach. The article classifies ICBMs as "light" or "heavy," and heavy ICBMs are further classified by whether they are "modern" or "older" types deployed prior to 1964. It then prohibits conversion of launchers for light or older types of ICBMs into modern heavy ICBM launchers.

The effect of Article II is to limit the U.S.S.R. to 313 launchers for "modern heavy" missiles. The conversion of ICBM launchers for older heavy ICBMs (the U.S. Titan, the Soviet SS-7 and SS-8) or smaller ICBM launchers (the U.S. Minuteman, the Soviet SS-11 and SS-13) to launchers for "modern heavy" ICBMs (such as the Soviet SS-9) is explicitly prohibited. The 313 Soviet launchers for "modern heavy" ICBMs are viewed by the U.S. as the main destabilizing element in the Soviet strategic force because of the possibility that, with highly improved accuracy and MIRV warheads, the SS-9s could threaten the survivability of the U.S. Minuteman force.

One agreed interpretation* provides that, in the process of modernization or replacement, the dimensions of land-based ICBM silos will not be significantly increased, and a second† provides that "significantly increased" means an increase not greater than 10 to 15 percent of the present dimensions of ICBM silos. These agreed matters supplement the prohibitions against conversion in Article II by limiting "modernization" to small increases in the size of launchers for "light" ICBMs. As drafted, however, the supplemental understandings do not make clear whether agreement was reached that the 10 to 15 percent restriction applies to the cubic volume of the silo, to a 10 to 15

---

* Interim Offensive Agreement, Initialed Statement C.
† Interim Offensive Agreement, Common Understanding A.

percent increase in both depth and internal diameter—which would amount to a fifty percent increase by volume—or to a 10 to 15 percent increase in either depth or interior diameter. In the course of congressional hearings, the administration stated its view that the last construction was the correct one.

Because the U.S.S.R. was unwilling to agree on the need for a definition of a "modern heavy" missile, the U.S. made a unilateral statement* that it would consider an ICBM having a volume "significantly greater" than that of the largest light ICBM then operational to be a "heavy" ICBM. While agreement was not reached on the volume of the largest "light" ICBM, which is the Soviet SS-11, this formulation effectively means a volume significantly greater than approximately seventy cubic meters. Assuming "significantly greater" missiles is used in the same context as "significantly increased" silo launchers, this amounts to a volume increase of between 10 and 15 percent. If the Soviets accept this U.S. unilateral statement, Article II, with its various glosses, limits the size of "light" ICBMs to approximately eighty-five cubic meters, which amounts to less than half the size of the Soviet's SS-9 missile. In any event, the Interim Agreement does not prohibit enlargement for the purpose of hardening silos and does not prohibit a modest increase in the size of "light" ICBMs as part of a modernization program.

Submarines and SLBMs

Article III, the attached Protocol, and an agreed interpretation† on dismantling schedules, all of which deal with ballistic-missile submarines and SLBMs, are the most difficult provisions of the Interim Offensive Agreement to understand. The difficulty is partly derived from imprecise language which reflects the pressure of time and the failure to coordinate negotiations in Moscow and Helsinki. It also reflects the fact that the Soviets have three different classes of ballistic-missile submarines equipped with missile systems of significantly different capabilities, and that this article provides for substitution of certain kinds of ICBMs by certain kinds of SLBMs. The "plain meaning of the words" (a phrase frequently used by lawyers arguing that the

---

* Interim Offensive Agreement, Unilateral Statement D, by U.S.
† Interim Offensive Agreement, Initialed Statement E.

text and not the legislative history should be controlling) is non-existent. Therefore, it is necessary to describe the intended scope.

Article III and the Protocol are based on intermediate limits on SLBM launchers that require dismantling or destruction of other launchers in order to reach the overall SLBM limit. The effect of these provisions can be summarized as follows:

1. The U.S. may not have more than 656 and the Soviets more than 740 "modern SLBM launchers" on "modern" ballistic-missile submarines unless other ICBM or SLBM launchers are dismantled or destroyed.

2. After exercising full rights of substitution, the U.S. cannot have more than 710 and the Soviets more than 950 "modern SLBM launchers" on "nuclear-powered" submarines.

3. The U.S. cannot have more than 44 and the Soviets more than 62 "modern" ballistic-missile submarines after exercising full rights of substitution.

4. SLBM launchers on additional "modern" ballistic submarines may be substituted for "older heavy" ICBM launchers or for launchers for "modern" SLBM missiles on nuclear-powered submarines.

5. The launchers being replaced must be dismantled or destroyed, under agreed procedures, when the replacement submarine begins sea trials.

These principles are straightforward when applied to the U.S. since the U.S. has 41 ballistic-missile submarines of the same basic type; the U.S. did not have any ballistic-missile submarines under construction; both Polaris and Poseidon missiles are considered "modern" SLBMs; and the U.S. has only 54 "older heavy" missiles. The net effect is that the U.S. Trident development program can go forward and, under the terms of the Interim Agreement, the U.S. could replace the 54 Titan missiles with no more than 54 SLBM launchers on 3 Trident submarines without dismantling any of the present Polaris/Poseidon boats. The Trident will not, however, be ready for deployment by 1977 when the Interim Offensive Agreement is scheduled to lapse, and each Trident is apparently designed with 24 launchers.

The situation for the Soviets is more complex for a variety of reasons. There was no agreement as to the exact number of Y-class or stretched Y-class (now referred to as D-class) Soviet submarines which were operational or under construction. There was no agreement whether "under construction" as used in the text of Article III included only those submarines being assembled, as the U.S. proposed, or also included those further back in the production cycle (for instance, beginning with the prefabrication of hull sections). There was also no agreement on the number of SLBM launchers on Soviet submarines under construction, the U.S. uncertainty being complicated because D-class boats have twelve launchers while Y-class boats have sixteen. The substitution provisions are complicated when applied to the Soviets since the U.S.S.R. still has some earlier nuclear-powered ballistic-missile submarines (H-class), and some diesel-powered submarines (G-class) that have older short-range ballistic missiles.

When the basic principles of Article III and the Protocol are applied to the Soviets, the following points are clear:

1. When the Soviet modern ballistic-missile submarine (Y-class and D-class) with the 741st launcher begins sea trials, the Soviets must begin to dismantle a number of launchers equivalent to the number of SLBM launchers on that new submarine.

2. The launchers which can be replaced are 210 SS-7s and SS-8s, which are "older heavy" ICBMs, or the 30 SLBM launchers on the nuclear-powered H-class submarines.

3. The launchers on the nuclear-powered H-class do not count in the 740 threshold number, but are included in the overall 950 limitation; the H-class submarines, however, do not count against the "modern" submarine limit of 62.

4. Launchers on the diesel-powered G-class are not included in either the 740 threshold or the 950 limitation; the G-class boats do not count in the "modern" submarine limit of 62.

5. The Soviets would have to dismantle approximately 180 SS-7s and SS-8s and the 30 SLBM launchers on the H-class submarines, or the 210 SS-7s and SS-8s, if they exercise their full right of substitution.

The agreed interpretation does not require dismantling or destruction of the replaced launchers—whether SLBMs or older heavy ICBMs —until the replacement submarine begins sea trials. This would theoretically permit aggregates of SLBM launchers "operational and under construction" to exceed the numerical ceilings of 710 for the U.S. and 950 for the U.S.S.R. from the period beginning with construction of the replaced submarine through its outfitting. However, this is of little strategic importance, given the aggregate numbers of ICBMs and SLBMs available to both sides. In any event, the replaced launchers are required to be inoperable prior to the completion of sea trials of the replacement boat, which generally takes about six months. The agreed interpretation provides that dismantling will be completed in the shortest possible agreed period of time.

Article III and the Protocol embody a limited application of the principle of "one-way freedom to mix" from land to sea, which the U.S. proposed in August 1970 for inclusion in a comprehensive strategic offensive treaty. The principle is derived from the concept that submarine-based missiles are deterrent, not first-strike, systems and that they are less destabilizing than land-based ICBMs which may threaten the survivability of the ICBMs on the other side. A broad, one-way freedom to mix, including all land-based ICBMs and heavy bombers and without upper limits on SLBMs or ballistic-missile submarines, might be included in a reduction formula in a SALT II treaty. This would leave the U.S. and U.S.S.R. free to choose their own mix of the three basic strategic offensive systems while providing upper limits only on the current inventory of ICBMs and bombers, and overall aggregates for ICBMs, SLBMs, and bombers.

There was no agreed rationale for the higher Soviet numerical limits on SLBM launchers or ballistic-missile submarines. The U.S.S.R. twice made a unilateral statement* toward the conclusion of SALT I which proposed an overall limit for U.S., U.K., and French submarine forces of 50 ballistic-missile submarines and 800 SLBM launchers. The U.S.S.R. statement added that if the Allied forces exceeded these numbers, the U.S.S.R. could increase its numerical limits accordingly. The Soviet statement also asserted that the agreed limits of 62 Soviet and 44 U.S. submarines only partially compensated for the deployment imbalance which results from the forward basing of U.S. ballistic missile submarines. The U.S. twice rejected the appropriateness of including third-country submarines in SALT calculations and the forward base issue.

The Soviet statement on SLBMs makes clear that the "on-station" advantage the U.S. enjoys as a result of its bases in Holy Loch, Scotland, and Rota, Spain, for its submarines in the Atlantic and Mediterranean, and the base on Guam for its submarines in the Pacific; the U.K. and French ballistic-missile submarines; and the FBS issue (fighter-bombers in Europe and on carriers capable of reaching the

* Interim Offensive Agreement, Unilateral Statement by U.S.S.R., and U.S. reply.

Soviet Union) will all be raised by the Soviets in the negotiations at SALT II.

ICBM Launchers for Test and Training Purposes

The texts of Articles I, II, and III of the Interim Offensive Agreement would imply that the construction "freeze" on new ICBM launchers and the submarine and SLBM launcher limits apply to all fixed land-based ICBM launchers and SLBM launchers, whatever their purpose. This is not the case. An agreed interpretation* provides that there shall be no "significant increase" in the number of ICBM and SLBM test and training launchers or in the number of such launchers for modern land-based heavy ICBMs, and further prohibits the construction or conversion of ICBM launchers at test ranges except for test and training purposes. The interpretation, in effect, prohibits construction of "operational" launchers at test ranges, but permits construction of test and training launchers at operational sites.

The U.S. practice has been to construct ICBM launchers for test and training purposes at test ranges only. The U.S. uses special test platforms for tests of SLBMs as well as test firings from the submarines themselves. Soviet practice is more complicated since their operational ICBM fields include launchers constructed for test and training purposes, and some older submarines are used for test and training purposes only. In addition, the U.S.S.R. has more launchers for test and training than the U.S.

Modernization and Replacement

As discussed previously, the ABM Treaty includes qualitative constraints which severely limit the scope of the provisions of the treaty that permit modernization and replacement of ABM systems. This is not the case with the Interim Offensive Agreement, since the only qualitative constraint is the prohibition of conversions to additional "modern heavy" ICBM launchers. Under these circumstances, a provision permitting modernization and replacement might not be viewed as necessary, particularly since the overall context is that anything not

---

* Interim Offensive Agreement, Initialed Statement D.

prohibited is permitted. Nevertheless, such a provision is included in Article IV of the Interim Offensive Agreement. This emphasizes that, among other things, the U.S. MIRV programs for Minuteman III and Poseidon are not constrained, nor is any Soviet MIRV program.

Verification

The text of Article V on national technical means of verification is identical to the text of Article XII in the ABM Treaty. Two more comments are appropriate in connection with the Interim Offensive Agreement. First, although neither the Interim Offensive Agreement nor the agreed interpretations refer to the number of ICBM launchers the U.S.S.R. is permitted under the freeze, national technical means are fully adequate to determine the number of launchers the Soviets had which were operational or under construction and to identify those which are for test and training purposes. National technical means are also adequate to determine the number of SLBM launchers on ballistic-missile submarines in operational status, on sea trials, and being outfitted after launch, even though the exact number of SLBM launchers and submarines under construction in covered facilities can only be estimated. Second, the U.S. made a unilateral statement* on covered facilities which emphasized that a change from the current practice of fitting out or berthing submarines in the open to the use of covered facilities could constitute concealment of this process from national technical means.

Miscellaneous Provisions

Duration and Withdrawal

Paragraph 2 of Article VIII provides that the Interim Offensive Agreement will remain in effect for five years, unless earlier replaced by agreement on more complete measures limiting strategic offensive arms. Accordingly, the agreement should not be viewed necessarily as a five-year agreement, remaining in force until October 3, 1977, particularly since both the U.S. and U.S.S.R. expressed the expectation it would be superseded before then. The text itself provides that the

---

* Interim Offensive Agreement, Unilateral Statement C, by U.S.

objective of the U.S. and U.S.S.R. is to "conduct follow-on negotiations with the aim of concluding such an agreement as soon as possible." On the other hand, the agreement could be extended, by mutual agreement, beyond its five-year term.

Paragraph 3 of Article VIII contains a "supreme interest" withdrawal clause, substantively identical to paragraph 2 of Article XV of the ABM Treaty.

Entry into Force

Paragraph 1 of Article VIII, which covers entry into force, does not refer to any legislative approval. It simply provides that the agreement shall enter into force upon the exchange of written notices of acceptance simultaneously with the exchange of instruments of ratification of the ABM Treaty. This formula served two purposes. First, it made explicit that the Interim Offensive Agreement would not enter into force before the ABM Treaty, meeting a Soviet concern, and also that the ABM Treaty would not come into effect first, which was a U.S. concern. Second, the formulation permitted, but did not require, the U.S. and U.S.S.R. to seek legislative authorization or approval of the Interim Offensive Agreement.

Section 33 of the Arms Control and Disarmament Act of 1961 prohibits the executive branch of the government from taking action under law to "obligate the United States to disarm or to reduce or to limit the . . . armaments of the United States, except pursuant to the treaty making power of the President under the Constitution or unless authorized by further affirmative legislation by the Congress of the United States." The administration could have sent the Interim Offensive Agreement to the Senate, for its advice and consent to ratification by a two-thirds vote pursuant to the Senate's treaty powers, as it did with the ABM Treaty, but it chose not to do so. Instead, the president transmitted the Interim Offensive Agreement, with attached Protocol, to both the Senate and the House of Representatives for approval by Joint Resolution adopted by a simple majority of both houses of Congress. While an unusual procedure to adopt for an arms control agreement, it clearly satisified Section 33 and tended to emphasize that, unlike the ABM Treaty, the Interim Offensive Agreement was a temporary arrangement, pending negotiation of a treaty at SALT II which would require Senate approval.

The president's Letter of Transmittal did not, however, request "approval" by the Congress, but only an "expression of support," and draft resolutions introduced on behalf of the administration in both Houses used similar language. Senator Fulbright immediately introduced an alternative Joint Resolution explicitly providing for congressional approval and ratification of the Interim Offensive Agreement. The administration did not pursue this potential confrontation, but the Joint Resolution nevertheless became the major focus of congressional attention when Senator Jackson introduced his amendment in which he sought "equality" in a SALT II treaty.

THE STANDING CONSULTATIVE COMMISSION

The Standing Consultative Commission established in accordance with Article XIII of the ABM Treaty could be one of the significant results of SALT I. The Commission will have two primary functions—the first relating to the implementation of the treaty and the Interim Offensive Agreement, and the second relating to further negotiations after the conclusion of SALT II.

At SALT I, the U.S. and U.S.S.R. did not agree on matters such as the charter and regulations of the commission, its site, the make-up of the commission, and its relation to SALT II. This was, however, one of the first matters handled at SALT II. The charter of the commission was signed and made public at the end of the first session of SALT II on December 21, 1972. This announcement did not indicate whether the members of the present SALT delegations would also serve on the commission as necessary or whether it would be separately staffed. Ambassador U. Alexis Johnson, who replaced Gerard Smith as the head of the U.S. SALT delegation in early 1973, and Major-General Georgi I. Ustinov were named the first commissioners. In June 1973, when the regulations of the commission were signed and made public and the commission held its first formal meetings, Sidney N. Graybeal became the U.S. Commissioner. Apparently, the commission will meet in Geneva at least while SALT II continues, and the details of discussions will not be made public.

A principal function of the commission will be to consider questions of compliance with the obligations assumed under the ABM Treaty and the Interim Offensive Agreement and related situations which may be considered ambiguous. The treaty does not require any exchange of information, but makes clear that each side may voluntarily provide information which it considers necessary to assure confidence in compliance. One side can raise a question of compliance based on information gathered by national technical means of verification or other national means, and the other can provide information to clarify the matter. While the treaty does not prohibit the offering of onsite inspection, the Soviets made very clear at SALT I their opposition to any requests of this nature.

The commission has the responsibility to consider any questions of interference with national technical means of verification and may also consider questions of deliberate concealment. The commission may consider changes in the general strategic situation having a bearing on the agreements. This is not limited to developments in the U.S. and U.S.S.R., but includes developments in third countries which might affect the SALT agreements. An important and related function is to consider proposals to increase the viability of the treaty, including proposals for amendments; this might include agreement on additional interpretations or understandings. This function could become increasingly important as, inevitably, interpretative issues arise out of ambiguities in the present texts. Amendments to the treaty would have to be submitted to the Senate for its advice and consent pursuant to Articles XIV and XVI.

The commission may also handle other appropriate measures, not specifically enumerated in Article XIII, aimed at further limiting strategic arms. This is broad enough to include further matters relating to the Accident Measures or revised Hot Line Agreements and amendments to these two agreements.

Finally, and most importantly over the near term, the commission will be the vehicle for agreeing on dates and procedures relating to the destruction or dismantling of ABM systems or ABM components pursuant to the mandate of Article VIII of the ABM Treaty and on dates and procedures relating to the SLBM substitution provisions in Article III of the Interim Offensive Agreement and the SLBM Protocol. Early agreement on these matters during SALT II would seem to be the priority matter for the Commission.

REVISED HOT LINE AND ACCIDENT MEASURES AGREEMENTS

The Accident Measures and revised Hot Line Agreements entered into force when they were signed on September 30, 1971. At the signing ceremony, both Secretary Rogers and Foreign Minister Gromyko stressed the resolve of the U.S. and U.S.S.R. that an accident or misunderstanding not lead to a nuclear catastrophe.

The derivation of these agreements goes back to studies conducted in the late 1950s and early 1960s and proposals made by the U.S. in 1962 at the Eighteen-Nation Committee on Disarmament in Geneva (now known as the Conference of the Committee on Disarmament, or the CCD) on measures to reduce the risk of nuclear war through "accident, miscalculation or failure of communication." The Direct Communications Link or Hot Line Agreement was signed on June 20, 1963. It provides for a direct link by teleprinter terminals, with no voice capability, in Washington and Moscow, connected by a wire-telegraph circuit routed Washington-London-Copenhagen-Stockholm-Helsinki-Moscow, and a back-up radio-telegraph circuit routed Washington-Tangier-Moscow.

Revised Hot Line Agreement

The revised Hot Line Agreement, which sets forth measures to improve the present direct communications link, is very short. It modifies, but does not repeal, the 1963 agreement. The details on implementing the arrangements are contained in an Annex negotiated at the same time, which is a basic part of the revised agreement.

The preamble notes that the "hot line" was established for use in time of emergency. The revised agreement is similarly limited, and it would require agreement of the U.S. and U.S.S.R. to use the facilities for other purposes. One purpose which might be considered in the future would be the establishment of direct communication between the U.S. government and the U.S. embassy in Moscow and between the U.S.S.R. government and the Soviet embassy in Washington.

For the purpose of increasing the reliability of the direct communications link, the agreement provides for the establishment of two additional circuits, using a satellite communications system chosen by each party and multiple terminals located in the U.S. and U.S.S.R. The Annex makes clear that the original circuits will be maintained and operated until it is agreed that they are no longer necessary. It is estimated that the two satellite communications systems will not be operational before 1974.

The Annex specifies that the U.S. will provide one circuit via the Intelsat System and the U.S.S.R. shall provide one circuit via the Molniya II system. Intelsat—the International Telecommunications Satellite Consortium—was established by Interim Arrangements in 1963, and eighty nations with more than 95 percent of the world's international telecommunications traffic hammered out the Definitive Arrangements between 1969 and 1971. While the U.S., through COMSAT—the federally-chartered corporation created by Congress—has the strongest voice in Intelsat policies, no country may cast more than 40 percent of the vote, and a two-thirds vote on most issues is required. The U.S.S.R. fully controls the Molniya II system, which is not yet operational.

Article III of the agreement notes that the U.S. and U.S.S.R. agree to take all possible measures to assure continuous and reliable operation of the circuits and systems of governments for which each is responsible. This is not an absolute assurance since the U.S. does not control Intelsat and because technical problems could interfere with service. The U.S and U.S.S.R. each agree as well to communicate to the head of its government any messages received over the hot line from the head of the government of the other.

The frequency and context of the use of the hot line in years past remain classified. Coded messages are sent from the U.S. in English and from the U.S.S.R. in Russian. It would be possible to provide voice channels rather than encoded teleprinter messages. However, it is felt that the accuracy of a written message, which must be translated on the receiving end, is preferable to the necessary simultaneous translation which would be required for voice channels. The twenty-four-hour availability of skilled translators at the various terminals is, of course, an absolute requirement.

Accident Measures

The preamble to the Accident Measures Agreement describes the underlying premise—that nuclear war would be disastrous for all—

and includes the statement that the agreement is in no way contrary to the interests of any other country. Although consideration was given to an accession clause permitting other nuclear powers to become parties, it was decided to keep the agreement bilateral, leaving to both the U.S. and U.S.S.R. the decision whether to enter into similar agreements with other nuclear powers.

Article 1 deals with the physical security and nuclear arrangements of the U.S. and U.S.S.R. The U.S. and U.S.S.R. agree, as each deems it necessary, to maintain and improve their existing organizational and technical arrangements to guard against the accidental or unauthorized use of nuclear weapons under their control. The article does not require either party to divulge its arrangements and does not create an international obligation to take any specific action. However, it declares the intention of each party to take necessary steps and might provide the basis for agreement on further measures at a later stage.

Under Article 2, the U.S. and U.S.S.R. agree to notify each other immediately in the event of an accidental, unauthorized, or other unexplained incident involving the possible detonation of a nuclear weapon if such an incident could create a risk of an outbreak of nuclear war. There has not been any such incident since the end of World War II which, if the agreement had been in effect, would have required notification under this article. In the event of any incident, the U.S. and U.S.S.R. must determine whether a risk of war might occur and, in that event, give immediate notice. Because of the short time involved between the release of any missile and impact, each side, for the agreement to be effective, would have to adopt in advance emergency procedures and messages for use upon proper authorization.

Article 2 also provides that in the event of any such nuclear incident, the party whose nuclear weapon is involved will immediately make every effort to take those measures it considers necessary to render the weapon harmless or to destroy it without its causing damage. There is no assurance, of course, that the side whose weapon is involved has fail-safe procedures or other measures which would be effective once a strategic missile were launched. The agreement does not require the adoption of any such procedures.

Article 3 provides that the U.S. and U.S.S.R. will notify each other immediately in the event of detection by their missile warning systems of objects they are unable to identify or in the event of signs of interference with such missile warning systems or related communications facilities. The article is directed at occurrences that could create the risk of nuclear war between the U.S. and U.S.S.R. and does not contemplate continuous exchange of information. Since it takes about thirty minutes for an ICBM to travel between the U.S. and U.S.S.R., the time period envisaged by Article 3, as well as Article 2, is very short. By the same token, the importance of an immediate exchange of messages and information is clear. The reference to interference with missile warning systems and related communications facilities is broad enough to encompass space-based, air-based, sea-based, or land-based systems and includes interference from any source.

Article 4, which is taken from one of the 1962 U.S. proposals, provides that the U.S. and U.S.S.R. will notify each other in advance of any planned missile test launches, if they are in the direction of the territory of the other and the missile flight will extend beyond the national boundary of the launching state. This article is not confined to tests of missiles for military uses. While the U.S. and U.S.S.R. presently launch test missiles which impact in the Pacific Ocean, the flight paths are not in the direction of the other's territory.

Article 5 is a catchall provision in which the U.S. and U.S.S.R. agree that in other situations related to unexplained incidents involving a risk of nuclear war, each will act in such a manner as to reduce the possibility of its actions being misinterpreted by the other; and that each may inform the other, or request information, when, in its view, this is warranted in order to avoid a risk of nuclear war. The remaining articles provide that the U.S. and U.S.S.R. shall make primary use of the hot line for transmissions in situations requiring prompt clarification; provide for consultations regarding implementation of the agreement, as well as possible amendments; and provide that it shall be of unlimited duration.

While the substance is modest, the agreement serves various purposes. First, it served to build confidence at SALT I while the U.S. and U.S.S.R. were still far apart on the two basic initial agreements, the ABM Treaty and Interim Offensive Agreement. Second, it touches a subject of enormous importance in the age of nuclear missiles, namely the danger to mankind in the event of the accidental, unauthorized, or other unintended release of a nuclear weapon. The Accident Measures Agreement provides a basis for continuing internal review in the U.S. and U.S.S.R. of their procedures and techniques to guard against the release of weapons. Third, it emphasizes that the U.S. and U.S.S.R. should each prepare in advance draft messages and adopt authorization procedures for use of the hot line in one very critical kind of situation. Finally, the Accident Measures Agreement and the revised Hot Line Agreement could serve as models for initial arms control agreements between the U.S. and China at some future date.

Toward a SALT II Treaty

Two agreements relating to SALT were made public during the Nixon-Brezhnev Summit meetings in the United States in June 1973. The first is on the prevention of nuclear war. In several respects it is comparable to the Accident Measures Agreement. It does not limit arms, but instead calls for consultation between the U.S. and U.S.S.R. under specified circumstances, and entered into force without congressional approval. The second agreement deals with the essence of SALT II. It sets forth basic principles for further negotiations on the limitation of strategic offensive arms. Although it is more formal in appearance, this document resembles the May 20, 1971, understanding, which recorded some intermediate understandings on basic issues and set forth the agreed goals for SALT I. The new agreement on basic principles on further negotiations is similarly very general in terms and does not, by its terms, indicate whether agreement on approaches or details was reached. The drawn-out negotiations of the ABM Treaty and Interim Offensive Agreement should be a reminder that agreement in general principle may mask disagreement on fundamental approaches and important details as the SALT II negotiations proceed.

CHAPTER SIX
A Leap Forward in Verification

Herbert Scoville, Jr.

GROWTH OF VERIFICATION CAPABILITIES

Over the past twenty years, verification has probably been the greatest single roadblock to the successful negotiation of arms control agreements. The difficulties in developing arrangements which could provide assurance against possible violations seriously affecting the security of the parties proved insurmountable. During the 1950s, proposed agreements on the reduction of forces all foundered in a large part because of fears that the Soviet Union would clandestinely deploy military forces above those levels that would have been allowed. The secrecy behind the Iron Curtain was so great that U.S. security planners could have no confidence that an agreement would not place our ability to support our critical national interests in jeopardy.

In an attempt to overcome this difficulty, President Eisenhower put forth on July 21, 1955 his celebrated "open skies" proposal, and the U.S. submitted a plan for its implementation to the United Nations Disarmament Commission in August of that year. The inspection phase of the "open skies" plan called for unrestricted, but monitored, overflight of national territories to determine that secret military buildups for a surprise attack were not occurring. This proposal was disparaged by Soviet leaders as legalized espionage, and no headway was made in overcoming the verification problem. Failing to achieve its objective by internationally recognized means, the U.S. proceeded with the secret development of the U-2 photographic reconnaissance aircraft which could fly sufficiently high to be out of reach of Soviet air defenses. The U-2s operated with considerable success during the late 1950s but, because of their secret nature, the number of flights was restricted and the land area that could be surveyed was very limited. Even with many overflights, the area which can be observed by a single aircraft is small. Furthermore, this type of activity, which was not internationally sanctioned, would have been very unsatisfactory for verifying an arms control agreement since the evidence provided might be very difficult to use in denouncing any observed violation. Success in achieving arms control agreements was never realized.

October 4, 1957, however, marked the beginning of a new era which culminated in a radical change in capabilities to verify arms control agreements. On that day, the Soviets orbited their first satellite. It traversed the U.S. and set a precedent for making legitimate the space transit of national territories without permission of the States involved. No request was ever made for permission to carry out this operation, and no complaint was ever voiced by the Soviet Union when the United States followed suit the next year. No other country raised the question of legality, and thus the first steps were taken toward the establishment in customary international law of the freedom of access to outer space for peaceful and scientific purposes.

Of course, these early satellites did not contain any instruments capable of making observations of the territory over which they passed, but the precedent had been set, and it was not long before at least crude reconnaissance capabilities became available. In 1960, without secrecy, the U.S. orbited weather satellites capable of making low resolution photographs of the earth, i.e., photographs which could define large geographical features, such as lakes, but not smaller man-made objects, such as buildings or vehicles. In April 1961, the Soviets placed Astronaut Gagarin in orbit around the earth so that at least limited visual observation would have been possible. Still no complaints were voiced by any nation. Admittedly, these early space flights were of no practical value in monitoring arms control agreements, but they did help to set the stage for international approval of satellite observation.

Meantime, in May 1960, the U.S. U-2 aircraft was shot down over the Soviet Union, and this ended, at least vis-à-vis the U.S.S.R., even this limited source of information for verifying arms control agreements. Fortunately, the U.S. had foreseen the eventual demise of aircraft reconnaissance over foreign countries and had proceeded with a program for developing methods of obtaining similar information from satellites. In 1960, this new technique was still not fully operational. Fears of widespread Soviet ICBM deployment that could then not be verified resulted in the creation of the so-called missile gap, an important campaign issue in the presidential election of that year. There was no disagreement even within the Eisenhower administration that the Soviets had more ballistic missiles than the U.S., only on the size of the gap and its military significance. The Air Force saw the gap as very large and the significance as horrendous, while the president was less concerned since he felt the U.S. bomber deterrent was more than enough to compensate for the reasonably estimated disparity in missile force levels until the U.S. missile programs could catch up. During early 1961, the missile gap began to shrink and by the end of 1961, U.S. authorities confidently discounted the existence of any gap. Apparently the Russians had deployed at the most a handful of their cumbersome first-generation SS-6 missiles. The ability to carry out satellite observation of large areas of the Soviet Union with sufficient photographic resolution to spot missile silos was available to prove that the launchers were not hidden even in remote parts of the U.S.S.R.

The Soviet Union proceeded with a parallel development of observation satellites, and both nations improved the capabilities of their systems throughout the 1960s. By 1964, Secretary MacNamara was regularly reporting publicly on Soviet strategic deployments and in 1967, President Johnson extolled the virtues of the U.S. space program for protecting our security. In recent years, Secretary Laird described the Soviet strategic posture in detail, frequently announcing new construction very shortly after it began. Neither country, however, publicly admitted the method by which this information was obtained in order to avoid a political confrontation and a possible international uproar which might have raised questions of the legality of such operations. Instead, there was a tacit recognition of observation satellite capabilities by both sides and perhaps an increasing realization that the availability of the information to the other nation provided a stabilizing influence.

In addition to its invulnerability and international acceptance, satellite reconnaissance has a number of major advantages over that carried out by aircraft. A satellite in an orbit of 100–300 miles altitude can survey very large areas in a very short time period. If a satellite were launched in a north–south polar trajectory, then the entire earth could be covered, once in daylight and once at night, every twenty-four hours. Thus, a satellite camera platform is ideally suited for searching large areas to determine the presence of military equipment and installations.

A satellite at these altitudes would normally have an orbit period of approximately one and one-half hours, thus permitting sixteen orbits of the earth each day. For complete daily coverage of the earth's surface at 45° latitude, the camera would have to observe a swath 1,100 miles wide. Since most of the U.S.S.R. lies north of the 45° latitude, a camera that could observe 600 miles on each side could photograph the entire U.S.S.R. in successive passes. Since this wide a swath might unduly degrade the quality of the picture, it may be more practical to use a satellite observing a narrower strip of the earth, leaving gaps in the coverage which can then be filled on subsequent days. This gap-filling can be accomplished by selecting an orbital period which is not an even fraction of twenty-four hours so that the identical path over the earth will not be covered on successive days. The satellite programming must, of course, take into account the hours of sunlight, but a complete survey should be obtainable in three to four days. Some areas will inevitably be screened by clouds, so observation of the entire country cannot be counted on in any given flight. Certain parts of the world are often covered by clouds, but they are never covered 100 percent of the time, and thus any area is always potentially exposed to satellite observation.

Since the wider the swath, the poorer will be the photographic resolution, a narrower band would have to be photographed in a single pass for detailed examination of an object. This can be accomplished by longer focal length cameras which can be programmed to look at small areas. Thus, a survey type system might locate a missile silo while a high-resolution system could measure its dimensions and determine its characteristics. Apparently, at the present time, both the U.S. and U.S.S.R. have both kinds of systems, i.e., those that can rapidly photograph large areas with relatively low resolution, and other systems which can focus on specific locations deemed of interest as a result of the large area surveys. Judging by the details reported on Soviet weapons systems, the U.S., and probably also the U.S.S.R., have a capability to resolve objects with a dimension of a few feet or even less. This would permit the observation of most items of military equipment exposed in the open, but the presence and characteristics of those under cover can only be inferred from the nature of the surroundings. The information obtained can be relayed back to earth by TV transmission, in which case the quality and resolution might be degraded, or by returning the photographic film to earth in a recoverable capsule. In the case of TV transmission, the time lag between observation and the availability of the information at a command center can be very short—hours or less—but if the film must be returned to earth, the delay can be days or even a week or more.

For specialized types of information, sensors which record in other regions of the electromagnetic spectrum than visible light can be used. Thus, infrared sensors would be useful for observing missile launchings and other phenomena where large temperature discontinuities exist. Such observations could, of course, be carried out at night as well as in daytime. It is conceivable that certain kinds of radars might also be used for space observation, and passive sensors in space vehicles could be useful for listening to radio waves such as those emitted by large radars. Satellites do not, however, offer any prospect for observation of submerged submarines, regardless of the sensors that are carried.

Of course, satellites are not the only means of verifying arms control agreements. From 1958 to 1963, the primary arms control measure under negotiation was a ban on nuclear weapons testing, and the principal problem in these negotiations was the lack of ability to verify that clandestine testing was not occurring. The chief argument revolved around whether onsite inspections were needed to verify a ban on underground tests, and if so, the number that would be required each year to provide confidence against significant violations. The U.S. believed that seismic means were not adequate and insisted on onsite inspections. With the exception of a short period at the end of 1962, when Khrushchev agreed to accept three onsite inspections per year while the U.S. demanded seven, the Russian position has been consistently against this type of verification. The problem was skirted in 1963 by postponing a ban on underground tests and relying on national technical means to verify the ban in the Limited Nuclear Test Ban Treaty on tests in the atmosphere, underwater, and in outer space.

For nuclear tests in the atmosphere and underwater, acoustic, electromagnetic, and radioactive debris sampling techniques, all of which could be employed outside the boundaries of the Soviet Union, were considered quite adequate to detect any significant forbidden tests. For tests in outer space, these methods could be supplemented by satellites with sensors for measuring neutron, gamma, x-ray, and ultraviolet radiations. Thus, the principle that national technical means including satellites could be used to monitor arms control agreements was clearly established, but no reference to these means is specifically included in the Limited Test Ban Treaty of 1963. At no point during the negotiations was any reference made in the public record to observation of the earth by satellites, although at least crude capabilities for doing so were then available to both sides.

In the early 1960s, while reconnaissance satellites were being gradually improved, debate was simultaneously proceeding on the international legality of such operations. Although the principle of free access to space for peaceful purposes was universally recognized from the outset, considerable debate ensued concerning the definition of the term "peaceful." In 1962, in the Legal Subcommittee of the United Nations Committee on the Peaceful Uses of Outer Space, the Soviet Union proposed that the "use of artificial satellites for collection of intelligence information in the territory of foreign states is incompatible with the peaceful objective of mankind in its conquest of outer space." The U.S., while not accepting that reconnaissance satellites were "incompatible" with the peaceful uses of space, was, nevertheless, a strong advocate of restricting the use of outer space to nonmilitary purposes. This apparent inconsistency in position was clarified by a later U.S. statement that reconnaissance was nonaggressive and, therefore, should be considered peaceful and essentially a nonmiltary use. The U.S. argued that observation from space is consistent with international law just as is observation from the high seas.

The difference in point of view between the U.S. and the Soviet Union was finally resolved in the fall of 1963 when the Soviet Union suddenly dropped its insistence on including a ban on space reconnaissance and negotiated with the U.S. representatives a United Nations resolution* dealing with outer space which called upon all States to refrain from placing nuclear weapons or other weapons of mass destruction in orbit. The U.S. and U.S.S.R. had just previously stated their intentions not to do so without including any reference to the issue of reconnaissance satellites. This public change in Russian atti-

---

* General Assembly Resolution 1884, XVIII, October 17, 1963.

tude may have resulted from their acquisition of a satellite reconnaissance capability of their own, although Khrushchev is reported to have stated earlier that satellite photography was permissible. The 1963 U.N. resolution was broadened in 1967 into a Treaty on Outer Space* which carefully omitted reconnaissance from the banned activities. However, no document during this period ever specifically endorsed the use of space for reconnaissance purposes.

Following the successful negotiation of the Limited Test Ban Treaty and the Treaty on Outer Space, attention in arms control negotiations shifted first to the multilateral Treaty on the Non-Proliferation of Nuclear Weapons and, secondly, to bilateral negotiations between the U.S. and U.S.S.R. to limit strategic delivery systems. In the case of the Non-Proliferation Treaty, the verification problem was directed toward the detection of the diversion of fissionable materials from peaceful to weapons programs. It was foreseen that peaceful nuclear power programs would, in the coming decades, involve the use, production, and processing of large amounts of fissionable materials which could easily be turned into weapons. Thus, inspection and materials accountability of the operating plants were essential, but it was always understood, although never stated, that the construction of a secret or undeclared plant for producing fissionable material for weapons would be susceptible to detection by national means. The negotiation of the agreed safeguarding procedures to detect diversion from declared peaceful plants proved to be extremely difficult and delayed the successful negotiation of the Non-Proliferation Treaty for an appreciable time. Fortunately, it was not also necessary to reach a formal agreement on procedures for detecting clandestine fissionable material production facilities for, if so, we would probably not have a Non-Proliferation Treaty today. Onsite inspections to look for such plants would have been unacceptable to many countries, and the world was probably not yet ready to give a specific endorsement to space observations. Thus, again, national means of verification were implicit, but unstated, in the Non-Proliferation Treaty.

In the area of verification of limits on strategic delivery vehicles, the capabilities of national technical means were clearly recognized from the early 1960s, although until 1968 U.S. positions generally stipulated

---

* Treaty on the Principles Governing the Activities of States in the Exploration and Use of Outer Space, Including the Moon and Other Celestial Bodies.

that these be supplemented by onsite inspections. However, in general, attempts were always made to increase negotiability by designing measures in such a way as to maximize the reliance on national technical means and minimize the need for onsite inspections. Restrictions on deployment, rather than on production, were generally sought since the former was more subject to aerial observation and more difficult to conceal. The success of these attempts was finally demonstrated by the conclusion of the ABM Treaty and the Interim Offensive Agreement.

VERIFICATION OF THE SALT I AGREEMENTS

ABM Treaty

The provisions of both the ABM Treaty and the Interim Offensive Agreement mark a critical milestone along the road toward the solution of the problems of verifying arms control agreements. As discussed in Chapter 5, the identical language used in Article XII of the ABM Treaty and Article V of the Interim Offensive Agreement explicitly recognizes that national technical means of verification shall be used. Perhaps even more significantly, both countries also undertake neither to interfere with such means nor to use deliberate concealment measures to impede them. Thus, not only are these means sanctioned by international treaty, but it now becomes a violation of the treaty to attempt to degrade their effectiveness. While these provisions are not binding on nations other than the U.S. and U.S.S.R., no others have the potential for interfering with satellite observations. Although neither the treaty nor the published interpretations refer specifically to reconnaissance satellites, Secretary Rogers, in forwarding the treaty to the president for transmittal to the Senate, referred to the fact that paragraph 2 of Article XII prohibits intereference with an orbiting satellite being used for verification of the treaty.

The new verification articles are a far cry from May 1960 when the U-2 was shot down; they even go further than the Eisenhower "open skies" proposal. Both countries are now recognizing the right of each side to obtain information about the other nation's military capabilities that is pertinent to the subject of the SALT I agreements. Finally, Article XIII of the treaty established a Standing Consultative Commission to provide, among other things, a means of exchanging information which may well facilitate the verification of both the ABM Treaty and the Interim Offensive Agreement. These specific articles, supplemented by many detailed arrangements negotiated between the two parties, are not only extraordinarily valuable for verifying the SALT I agreements, but they also provide extremely useful precedents for future arms control agreements. However, the prime objective of these verification procedures is to provide assurance to both sides that violations which could significantly affect the strategic balance are not occurring. If they do not work satisfactorily in the case of the SALT I agreements, they might be virtually useless as precedents for the future.

In the case of the ABM Treaty, the basic obligation is to limit each country to two ABM sites, one centered on the national capital and one protecting an ICBM silo complex. Restrictions are placed on the numbers and types of interceptor missiles and of ABM radars at each site. Past history clearly shows that any significant violations of these restrictions can be detected. The deployment of ABM interceptors has been satisfactorily monitored by national means for many years. In 1969, President Nixon had no hesitation in reporting that the Soviets were deploying 64 ABM interceptors in defense of Moscow, and Secretary Laird even amplified on this by stating that construction had been stopped on some additions to these deployments. Even the small U.S. SPRINT interceptor, which is $4\frac{1}{2}$ feet in diameter and 27 feet long, and the associated launcher construction would be easily visible with relatively low-resolution satellite photography. Similarly, ABM radars are extremely large [our smaller missile site radar (MSR) has four faces each with an antenna diameter of $13\frac{1}{2}$ feet, all housed in a building more than 100 feet square. In addition, when they become operational, they continuously emit tremendous quantities of radio wave energy. An agreed treaty interpretation refers to a power-antenna area product of three million for the MSR, the smaller of the two U.S. phased-array radars. This radiation can be picked up by receiving antennas outside the borders of the country or in satellites.

Thus, the potential problem in verifying the ABM Treaty is not the observability of an ABM, but rather the ability to distinguish between a missile defense system and one designed ostensibly for anti-aircraft purposes which could be used as a disguise for an ABM. The fear that aircraft defense missile systems (SAMs) might be upgraded to give them

ABM capabilities has long been the worry of some U.S. ABM scientists. Thus, in order to enhance the assurance of the effectiveness of limitations on ABM systems, Article VI of the treaty provides that not only shall air defense missile launchers and radars not be given the capabilities to counter strategic ballistic missiles, but that they shall also not be tested in an ABM mode. It is this prohibition on testing which provides added confidence that the treaty is not being violated by deploying ABMs disguised as antiaircraft systems. Any defense system that would have a significant capability to destroy ballistic missiles would have to be extensively tested under conditions closely simulating an attempt to intercept a strategic offensive missile. Such tests, particularly when they approached operational conditions, would be subject to observation by national technical means. The U.S. reported as long ago as 1961 on experiments at the Soviet anti-ballistic missile test range near Sary Shagan in which the Soviet ABM systems simulated the interception of incoming ICBM warheads. Undoubtedly, our capabilities for observing ABM testing have improved since that time, and we should be able to detect any Soviet attempt to carry out similar tests using aircraft defense missiles or radars. In this connection, Article IV of the ABM Treaty and its associated interpretations limit ABM testing to "current or additional agreed test ranges" so that any ABM testing at a new, undeclared range would by itself be a violation—a violation which would have a high probability of being detected. This is just one example of where the SALT I agreements contain supplementary detailed provisions which greatly facilitate its verification.

In addition to the basic limitations which the treaty places on ABM deployment, both countries also undertake not to develop, test, or deploy: sea-based, air-based, space-based, or mobile land-based ABM systems; ABM launchers for launching more than one interceptor missile at a time; ABM interceptors with multiple warheads; or systems for their rapid reload (Article V). Although national technical means of verification cannot guarantee that such actions will never occur, the risk that clandestine operations of such a nature would be detected is still appreciable and the potential gains therefrom marginal in view of the limitation on the total number of ABM launchers allowed to each side. The testing of such different types of ABM systems would be particularly susceptible to detection by national technical means. The Sary Shagan ABM test range in southern Russia is subject to observation from outside the U.S.S.R. Many tests under closely simulated operational conditions would be required before a truly effective system could be deployed. The verification capabilities are thus more than adequate in light of the small security risks in the event of a violation of these provisions. In fact, the inclusion of these supplementary prohibitions tends to enhance the overall effectiveness of the verification of the treaty since, were the development and testing of these different types of ABMs allowed, their subsequent deployment might be more difficult to monitor. The ABM Treaty establishes a useful precedent for including in an agreement a number of supplementary arms limitations, any one of which may have a relatively low probability of detection, but which in totality can be adequately verified because of the additive opportunities to monitor at least one of the separate restrictions.

Interim Offensive Agreement

It is considerably simpler to verify the Interim Offensive Agreement than to verify the ABM Treaty since the agreement is restricted to numerical limitations—a freeze on the construction of additional ICBM launchers and a ceiling on the numbers of submarines and their ballistic-missile launchers. Ever since 1961, when extensive satellite coverage first became available and the missile gap fears were laid to rest, the U.S. has been able to observe the deployment of fixed ICBM launchers. ICBM launchers are, by their very nature, large, have extensive support facilities, and many clearly identifiable features. Moreover, hardened underground silos take eighteen months to two years to build so that sufficient time is available to detect construction far in advance of their becoming operational. Although a single, or even a few ICBM silos might be excavated beneath the roof of other buildings or under the guise of some other type of construction, such a clandestine program would have no security consequences in view of the large numbers of missile launchers already available to both sides. There would be no incentive for a small violation of this sort. Furthermore, by paragraph 3 of Article V of the Interim Offensive Agreement, each party involved undertakes not to use deliberate concealment measures, so the very attempt to use different construction procedures for ICBM silos or to camouflage them as oil tank farms would in itself be a violation.

If some unusual activity were observed, one nation could seek an explanation within the Standing Consultative Commission. In fact, it is likely that from time to time perfectly legitimate operations could be confused with missile launcher construction and require clarification in this forum. The Consultative Commission is an excellent mechanism for reassuring both sides about normal activities. We could have profited if such a commission were in existence at the time of the moratorium on nuclear weapons tests from 1958 to 1961 when the alarm bells were continually ringing as a result of unsubstantiated items of intelligence which indicated the possibility of a secret nuclear test. The commission might also have been a useful forum for urging against resumption of tests when preparations were detected.

The numerical limitations on submarines and their missile launchers in the Interim Offensive Agreement can also be monitored easily enough by national technical means. Missile submarines are about 400 feet in length and, in the later stages, construction is normally carried out in open pens so that observation from above is quite easy. Although there was some confusion as to the precise number of Soviet submarines operational or under construction at the time the SALT agreements were signed, the U.S. claiming forty-two and the Soviets forty-eight, this did not result from an inability of intelligence to observe such construction. Rather, it came from a difference in the definition of when construction on a submarine was started. The U.S. figures were based on the time assembly work began on the submarine as a whole, while the Russians included those additional submarines for which the design and fabrication of some parts were already in progress. In addition to the submarines themselves, the number of missile launchers in each ship can be observed. This is substantiated by official reports that some Soviet submarines have three launchers, others sixteen, and now some have twelve. Any change in the present production practices would be a violation of the "concealment" provisions of Article V, and the U.S. delegation even made specific reference to the application of this to the *fitting out or berthing of submarines* in an unilateral statement on May 20, 1972.*

In addition to establishing numerical limits, the Interim Offensive Agreement also places certain restrictions on the conversion of land-based launchers for light ICBMs into launchers for heavy ICBMs, and the negotiators also reached an understanding that the dimensions

* Unilateral Statement C, Covered Facilities.

of silos will not be increased significantly (10 to 15 percent of the present dimensions). The diameters of the U.S. Titans and Minuteman ICBMs are 10 feet and 6 feet respectively, and the interior diameters of their silos about 16 feet and 12 feet. The new, large Soviet missile has been reported as having a diameter of 12 feet, about one third larger than the SS-9. Presumably, the new, large Soviet missile silos are about 16 to 20 feet in diameter. Thus, if the 10 to 15 percent limitation is to be monitored, photographic resolution of 1 to 3 feet would be required. No public statement has been made on whether such resolution is achievable, but based on stated ability to discriminate between these types of missiles and silos, the 1 to 3 feet resolution is probably feasible. Thus, it would appear that the U.S. could adequately verify the 10 to 15 percent criterion of the Interim Agreement.

The Interim Agreement does not include any specific provisions on mobile ICBM launchers, although the U.S. sought to have a complete ban on the deployment of such types of systems included and did make a statement to the effect that it would consider such deployment as inconsistent with the objective of the agreement. Mobile systems do, of course, provide additional complications for verification since, unless near-simultaneous coverage of the entire nation is available (and this is virtually impossible because of cloud cover), it is not easy to obtain an exact count of the numbers of deployed mobile missile launchers. A complete ban, therefore, greatly facilitates such verification since the detection of even one mobile ICBM missile launcher would be evidence of a violation; presumably it is such a ban that the U.S. was proposing. On the other hand, while an exact count of mobile missile launchers is difficult, it is unlikely that the uncertainty in the number of such weapons deployed would ever be so large as to have security significance in view of the fact that both nations have more than 1,000 fixed land-based missiles already deployed.

In sum, the limitations agreed to at Moscow on both ABMs and offensive missile launchers can be satisfactorily verified by national technical means. While detection of every violation cannot be guaranteed, none that might escape could have any significant effect on the security of either nation; there would be no incentive for such violations.

Although the verification issue has been the key problem in most earlier agreements and was frequently raised by opponents of arms control during the course of the SALT negotiations, virtually no objections were raised to the SALT I agreements on this score during the congressional ratification hearings. Evaluation of the verification capabilities was made entirely in closed sessions, primarily in testimony by Richard Helms, director of the CIA, so that the administration never made any detailed public defense of its adequacy. The only nongovernmental witness who even raised the question was Edward Teller, and he only touched on it in passing as he expressed alarm over the disastrous state of our national security. Senator James Buckley also referred to the risks from Russian violations, but apparently the remainder of Congress was satisfied that our security would not be endangered.

The public, without any access to secret information, expressed no concern, perhaps an indication that fears of Russian cheating are now a less critical factor in developing our national security policies. The fact that the U.S. has such large nuclear arsenals that significant cheating has become virtually impossible may at last be understood. Congress and the press have been useful in educating the public regarding our satellite capabilities even though the details are still classified. Thus, the unique verification arrangements negotiated for the SALT I agreements appear to provide satisfactory assurance that undetected violations will not jeopardize U.S. security.

IMPLICATIONS FOR FUTURE ARMS LIMITATIONS

General Implications

The precedents established verifying the SALT I agreements can be extraordinarily useful in easing the way toward the negotiation of future arms limitations. Once certain procedures have become internationally recognized, there is rarely a turning back unless dramatic events occur which prove them to be unworkable. The same phraseology negotiated in one arms control agreement often shows up over and over again in future ones. For example, withdrawal clauses in the Limited Test Ban Treaty, the Non-Proliferation Treaty, the Seabed Treaty, and the SALT I agreements have substantially identical wording. It is quite likely that subsequent agreements related to SALT and even other arms limitations could contain verification clauses similar to those in Article XII of the ABM Treaty.

Although provisions may be added for other means of verification, the right to use national technical means of verification, now established, will almost certainly apply to future arms control agreements. Furthermore, the undertaking not to interfere with such means will have to be extended to future understandings as well. It is hard to imagine that a nation could destroy a satellite that was making observations in support of a comprehensive nuclear test ban treaty while it allowed another, or even the same, satellite to search for forbidden ABM deployment. Moreover, these national technical means are not limited to satellites, but include ships in international waters or instrumentation, such as radars or radio receivers, outside the boundaries of the other State; the only restriction is that they must be used "in a manner consistent with generally recognized principles of international law." It is unfortunate for future applications that the public record does not mention any other technical means than satellites or elaborate on the generally recognized principles of international law, although, presumably, the unpublished records of SALT must have included these subjects.

The provisions of Article XII could perhaps also be made to apply to some agreements which were negotiated before SALT I, even though national technical means were not mentioned specifically in these cases. For example, acoustic or other types of instruments installed in various countries around the world for the purpose of verifying the Limited Test Ban Treaty would now appear to have an even greater legitimacy. Although their existence has never in the past been the subject of any protest, the U.S. and certain other countries have handled their deployment circumspectly in order to avoid raising any issue as to their legality. No one wished to provoke an unnecessary international incident. In the future, fears on this score should be reduced.

The adoption of the undertaking not to use deliberate concealment measures to impede verification can be particularly important in future arms control situations. In many cases, the fear that camouflage or radical changes in operational procedures might diminish the ability to verify an arms control agreement has been a major factor in preventing successful negotiations. This could be especially true in situations where one suspected a violation, but because of the concealment techniques used, evidence for international action could not be obtained. Evidence that a concealment technique was being used would be in itself a sufficient basis for action. In doubtful cases, the Consultative Commission would provide a mechanism for seeking explanations for suspicious activities. In fact, the establishment in the ABM Treaty of the Consultative Commission is in itself a major step forward since the existence of a forum for obtaining information on anomalous observations could be a major factor in providing assurance that violations are not occurring. The Consultative Commission should be evaluated carefully in order to determine how to optimize its operations in support of future agreements as well as SALT I.

In addition to the specific verification articles, the SALT I agreements establish a number of other precedents which can be beneficial for the future. For example, Article IV of the ABM Treaty, supplemented by a common understanding, establishes the location of allowed ABM test ranges and implies that if these are to be expanded, the other side must be notified and concur. Limitations are even put on the number of ABM launchers that are allowed at these ranges. Similar provisions relative to other types of test ranges could be extremely useful in reaching agreement on restricting tests of missiles or other military equipment, a key element if the qualitative arms race is to be brought under control.

Possible Salt II Limitations

The application of the precedents of SALT I to specific arms limitation areas of the future must now be examined in detail. The major loophole in the Interim Offensive Agreement is its failure to place any restrictions whatever on the substituting of more advanced missiles for existing ones, particularly ones with MIRVs, and because of this failure, the arms race is turned from quantitative into qualitative directions. A key goal in SALT II, confirmed by the Nixon-Brezhnev agreement in June 1973, will, therefore, be to place restraints on the replacement of old weapons by new models, to restrict the development of new missile technology and, particularly, to place some controls on MIRVs. Limitations on missile testing seem the most likely approach to halting missile improvements.

In preparing the U.S. positions for SALT I, considerable debate ensued over suitable verification for controls on MIRVs. At one point, the U.S. proposed a ban on the testing and deployment of MIRVs, but coupled this with a requirement for onsite inspections to determine whether deployed missiles had more than a single warhead, although the prestigious Presidential Arms Control General Advisory Committee recommended against the need for such inspections. This proposal for onsite inspection was patently unacceptable to the Soviets and in any case would not have adequately verified a MIRV deployment ban. The onsite inspections could have been easily evaded by replacing a multiple warhead final missile stage with one containing only one warhead before the inspection team arrived. The only practical method of verifying limitations on MIRVs in the Soviet Union would be in the testing phase, and this can be accomplished without onsite inspections.

During the period from 1969 to 1972, there was considerable bebate as to whether the Soviets had actually tested a MIRV system for its large SS-9 missile. There was no difference of opinion on the fact that the Soviets had tested multiple warheads, but only on whether these warheads had the ability to be independently guided to different targets. In 1969, the administration prematurely jumped to the conclusion that the Soviet testing did indicate such an ability, but as more and more data were accumulated, it became apparent that the Russians did not test a true MIRV at all until mid-1973. Since there might always be some confusion on this score, it may be necessary to ban all multiple reentry vehicle testing, not just MIRVs.

The verification precedents established in the SALT I agreements should make it easier to verify limitations on MIRVs and other missile testing in future negotiations. The trajectory of a long-range ballistic missile rises several hundred miles above the earth's surface and the limited land mass of even the Soviet Union necessitates launch or reentry near or beyond its boundaries. Ever since the first Russian ICBM test in August 1957, the U.S. has been making observations on Soviet ICBM test firings from outside the borders of the Soviet Union. National technical means should, therefore, be quite satisfactory for verifying any quota on numbers of missile tests or controls on testing MIRVs or new reentry vehicles. Following the precedent of SALT I, agreement might be reached to restrict long-range missile testing to existing test ranges and, particularly, to those in which the reentry occurred near or beyond the borders of the Soviet Union and the U.S. Such a restriction, although not essential, would be particularly helpful if controls were placed on MIRV testing since it would assure observation of the reentry and thus determination of the number and characteristics of the reentry vehicles. In the past, the U.S. has been able to observe the Russian ICBM tests from ships since their reentry has occurred over the Kamchatka peninsula or over the Pacific. The U.S., in turn, has fired its long-range missiles from Vandenberg Air Force Base in California, over the Pacific toward Kwajalein, or from Cape Kennedy out over the Atlantic. SLBM firings are not necessarily restricted to specific test ranges, so it would be even more useful to reach an understanding on where and when these would occur to facilitate the procurement of desired data.

Interference with the ships making observations in support of an agreement would, in accordance with paragraph 2 of the verification article, be forbidden. Similarly, attempts to jam the radars tracking the missiles in flight would be considered a violation. Disguising the purpose of the tests by using only a single reentry vehicle in a MIRV experiment or by conducting MIRV development in the guise of a space program could be considered attempts at concealment. Although it might not be possible to relate unequivocally such testing to MIRV development, suspicion would almost certainly be raised, and clarification could then be sought through the Consultative Commission. False or misleading explanations would run a high risk of being caught, particularly in view of the fact that the other side would never know the total amount of information available from all sources. For example, if a MIRV system were to be tested in a manner that only one reentry vehicle entered the impact area, the mass characteristics of the reentry component and of the residual vehicle would be inconsistent with those expected in any normal firing (the weight of the expended missile stage would be very much larger than normal). A request for an explanation of such a peculiar test would certainly be in order, and a satisfactory answer might be hard to provide.

Although there is no near-term threat to the Polaris-Poseidon submarine deterrent, attempts should be made after SALT I to place limitations on antisubmarine warfare (ASW) in order to increase confidence that the submarine missile force, the primary element in the deterrent, does not in the distant future become vulnerable to some new unforeseen technology. One suggestion has been to freeze the number of attack antisubmarine warfare submarines in much the same way that a ceiling was placed on the number of missile submarines in

SALT I. The present number of attack submarines is probably not large enough to threaten either the U.S. Polaris-Poseidon or the Soviet Y-class and new D-class fleets. The methods of verifying missile submarines under SALT I are directly applicable to a future freeze on attack submarines. The shipyards at which attack submarines are built could be specified, and changes in construction procedures, which might conceal their production, could be proscribed as has been done in SALT I. The invulnerability of ballistic-missile submarines might also be guaranteed by the agreed establishment of separate ocean areas as sanctuaries for each country's submarines (i.e., an area in which U.S. ballistic-missile submarines could operate freely and Soviet ASW would be banned). The absence of ASW in such areas could be verified by national technical means such as acoustic sensors, an interference with these means either by jamming or other destructive action could be forbidden.

Comprehensive Nuclear Weapon Test Ban

Inability to achieve U.S.-U.S.S.R. agreement on verification procedures has been the public explanation for the past failures in the negotiation of a comprehensive nuclear test ban. Such a ban is again a likely candidate for serious negotiations now that some strategic delivery systems have been frozen. Seismic discrimination between earthquakes and explosions has improved markedly since the Limited Test Ban Treaty of 1963, but there will always be some detected seismic events which cannot positively be identified as either earthquakes or explosions. Although most of these unknowns will be small and therefore it is debatable whether they present significant security risks, such a treaty might, nevertheless, be more stable and assurance against violations might be greater if additional information on their nature were available. If a comprehensive test ban treaty contained an article similar to Article XII of the ABM Treaty, and if arrangements were spelled out for a multilateral international consultative commission to provide a forum for obtaining additional clarification, then the fears from possible violations should be greatly reduced and perhaps even eliminated.

Although a few unidentified seismic events with energies equivalent to or greater than that of a low kiloton explosion are detected each year in the U.S.S.R., most of these originate in the remote wilds of Kamchatka or the Pamir Mountains. Satellite photography of the location of such an unidentified event would, in almost all cases, give satisfactory evidence that human activity of the type required to conduct a deep underground explosion had not occurred at the site. In the rare case where the unidentified seismic event was located near the scene of some drilling or mining operation, then further reassurance could be sought in the consultative commission.

Another verification concern relative to an underground test ban has been that the seismic signals from somewhat larger nuclear explosions could be concealed by conducting the test either in a large cavity deep underground or immediately after a large earthquake. Theoretical studies have shown that a 300 foot diameter hole several thousand feet underground would be required to muffle the seismic signal of a five to ten kiloton explosion sufficiently to make it undetectable. However, the construction of such a cavity with a volume of more than ten million cubic feet at the required depth would be a mammoth engineering operation estimated to take more than four years. It would almost certainly be observable by satellite. Thus, even if the concealment technique were successful in preventing seismic detection, its employment would, by itself provide evidence of a violation. At the very least, an explanation of the suspicious activity could be sought through the consultative commission, and it would probably be extraordinarily difficult to provide a satisfactory rationale for such a construction project. Concealment of a nuclear explosion by the conduct of the test in the immediate aftermath of a large earthquake would also be considered a violation of such an agreement. While the evidence of such an attempt might be more difficult to obtain, it is likely that preparations for such a test would give rise to suspicions. In several ways, therefore, an article similar to that which appears in the ABM Treaty would be a useful contribution toward reassurance that a violation of a comprehensive test ban treaty could not become a security risk.

Limitations on Production of Chemical Warfare Agents

Another arms control area currently under negotiation where verification has been the primary reason for failure to reach any agreement has been limitations on the production of chemical warfare (CW) agents. Verification was ignored in the parallel biological warfare (BW) area, not because it was satisfactory, but primarily because biological warfare, by its very nature, was considered to have very dubious military value and because the U.S. had already decided unilaterally to forgo any offensive BW program and to destroy its existing stockpiles. The incentives, and therefore the risks, for a clandestine biological warfare program in violation of the Biological Weapons Convention did not appear to be sufficiently great to override the benefits from a worldwide ban on this potentially dangerous type of weapon. With chemical warfare (CW), however, the situation is somewhat different. CW can be more carefully controlled and can have some potential military advantages if used for tactical purposes when only one side is equipped with these weapons. Therefore, some assurance against the clandestine production of chemical warfare agents appears desirable.

CW agent production is relatively easy to conceal and can, in many cases, be carried out under the guise of a civil requirement for the chemicals. Thus, a satisfactory solution to the verification problem has so far not been found. The new procedures agreed to for SALT I could perhaps be at least a partial step toward the solution of the problem and might reduce the requirement for extensive inspections. For example, organophosphorus compounds are the most critical types of CW agents. Although the production of organophosphorus insecticides is somewhat similar to that of organophosphorous CW agents, the procedures used to produce these chemicals normally have significant differences. Economically sound chemical processes for insecticides are different from those used to produce CW agents and the safety measures required for CW agents are greater than for insecticides. Agreement might be reached that the unusual procedures for chemical agent production would not be undertaken for the insecticide industry without explaining such actions to the other parties and, perhaps, allowing observation of the specific plant to provide assurance that a chemical agent was not being manufactured. Such an agreement would be similar to the understanding at SALT I that submarine construction procedures would not be changed without consultation with the other side. Similarly, nations might declare the extent of their industrial toxic chemical production and account for its use in order to provide assurance that significant diversion to military purposes was not taking place. Since, at least in the larger nations, very substantial quantities of these materials would be required in order to have any military significance and in small, less developed nations even a small production would be easier to account for, such verification procedures might provide satisfactory assurance that security was not being jeopardized by the agreement.

Mutual Balanced Force Reductions in Europe

During 1973, detailed negotiations are commencing on Mutual Balanced Force Reductions (MBFR) between some of the NATO and Warsaw Pact countries with troops in Central Europe. These discussions will include reductions not only in manpower, but also in a wide variety of weapons systems with very significant asymmetries between the two sides. Furthermore, the geographical proximity of the U.S.S.R. to the potential conflict area, as compared with the U.S., which is an ocean away, makes the problem of resupply a very critical one in attempting to establish a balance. If the U.S.S.R. were able to reintroduce troops and arms clandestinely into the Warsaw Pact area in violation of an MBFR agreement, the NATO countries might be placed at a very significant military disadvantage. Therefore, verification procedures which could prevent such action, or at least detect it in its early stages, become critically important.

Provisions similar to those for verification under the SALT I agreements offer some real promise of solving this problem. The four-power occupation of Germany has used ground observers to keep track of troop movements in both the East and West, but this may no longer be necessary with the legalization of space observation. Certainly the number of inspectors can be reduced. Satellite observation by visible light photography would have a good capability of detecting the movement of troops and weapons during the daylight. Individual infiltration would, of course, be impossible to observe, but extensive troop redeployments in the European theater would provide many potential opportunities for detection. Military equipment would be easier to detect even if attempts were made to camouflage it. An anticoncealment clause in the agreement would be an added deterrent since the evidence of camouflage would be evidence of violation. Such a clause could include an understanding that troops and military equipment would only cross the border at specific points, and then only during the daytime. In such a situation, even a single observation of a forbidden movement would constitute evidence of violation of an agreement; it would be easier to differentiate between normal resupply operations and the reintroduction of forbidden forces. In sum, if agreed procedures can be arrived at for normal allowed operations, then the probability of detection of a violation can be greatly improved.

Thus, the verification provisions of the SALT I agreements on strategic weapons have great potential for application to the future arms control measures which are being seriously considered at this time. If the U.S. uses the precedents established in these agreements with imagination, the opportunities for at last taking major steps in controlling the arsenals of the world are manifold. Perhaps surprisingly to some, the Russians apparently agreed to these provisions early in the SALT negotiations, despite the fact they involved a fundamental change in previous Soviet attitudes toward secrecy. In the past, the Soviet Union has allowed its people, and even many officials in high government circles, to have only limited knowledge of its weapons systems. Now, by the two SALT I agreements, it has recognized the right of the United States to have such information and, going even further, has agreed not to put obstacles in the way of our obtaining it. In time this new position could bring about a profound alteration in Soviet society by expanding the circle of those knowledgeable on national security affairs. In the next round of SALT, the U.S. negotiators may not, as they did in SALT I, have to apprise some members of the Russian delegation of the nature of certain Soviet strategic deployments. The U.S. should now take advantage of this new approach by exploiting the verification procedures negotiated in SALT I in seeking further important restraints on the arms race.

Part 3

CHAPTER SEVEN

Perspectives from Europe

Ian Smart

UNDERLYING ATTITUDES IN WESTERN EUROPE

European reactions to SALT were not born in November 1969, when SALT opened in Helsinki, nor Jaunary 1967, when President Johnson first proposed such talks to the Soviet leadership. Their genesis lies in the 1950s and early 1960s, during the period in which Europeans, consciously or unconsciously, were learning to live with growing nuclear forces in a continent divided by a frontier of military confrontation. Attitudes to nuclear strategy have thence evolved which differ markedly from the parallel attitudes most common in the United States.

Although West European governments in NATO have taken an active part in discussions with the United States concerning the most effective way of fighting a defensive land war against the Warsaw Pact, their hearts have rarely been in it. Of the two possible means of deterring a Soviet attack in Europe, the effort to deter by threat of failure—by presenting a high probability that an attack from the East would be defeated militarily—has commanded intellectual attention but little emotional commitment. Most West Europeans have remained unconvinced that a full-scale Soviet attack, even if only by non-nuclear forces, could be halted on the battlefield. In any case, they have consistently been told that, if such an attack were pressed home, NATO would have to use "tactical" nuclear weapons in response, with the consequent prospect that even a successful Western campaign would entail appalling damage to Western Europe's population and territory. Their overwhelming perference, therefore, has been for an alternative approach to deterrence: deterring the initiation of a Soviet attack by threatening, as a probable penalty, an intolerable measure of injury to the Soviet Union itself—injury so substantial as to make the local military outcome of an attack largely irrelevant.

In the United States, the distinction between these two essentially different forms of deterrence—deterrence by threat of failure and deterrence by threat of retaliatory penalty—has perennially been blurred, so that there has seemed to be no obstacle to discussing the "war-fighting" and retaliatory utilities of nuclear weapons as though they were inseparable and as though the latter were dependent upon the former. But West European political leaders and their electorates have rarely, if ever, been willing to devote serious attention to what would happen if the deterrence of initial attack by threat of intolerable penalty should fail. When compared to Americans, divorced by distance from land war against the Soviet Union and eager to rationalize alternatives to a strategic nuclear exchange, West Europeans have been, in a sense, the "purists" of nuclear deterrence.

In the 1950s, the doctrine of "massive retaliation," threatening to respond immediately to *any* Soviet aggression by launching strategic nuclear weapons against Soviet territory, was identified with such Americans as John Foster Dulles. But, the doctrine had its intellectual roots at least as much in Western Europe, and especially in Britain. Within NATO, the associated concept of the "tripwire," providing that conventional forces should do little more than test the resolve of any invading Warsaw Pact army as an intermediate step towards strategic nuclear retaliation, commanded wide West European sympathy. During the 1960s, as the tripwire concept was progressively diluted in reaction to the parallel growth of Soviet nuclear strength and American intellectual doubt, many West Europeans added their explicit or tacit reservations. Finally, in 1967, persistent pressure from Washington and the withdrawal of French representatives from NATO opened the way to formal acceptance of the American "flexible response" doctrine—the notion that NATO should rely upon a range of conventional and nuclear forces capable of responding effectively *in combat* to any type or level of Warsaw Pact aggression. Acquiescence by West Europeans in that step, which implied that the ultimate testing ground for NATO strategy should lie on a European battlefield rather than in the minds of Soviet leaders contemplating an attack, was never more than lukewarm. Thus interest in the conventional and tactical nuclear forces needed to support the doctrine of flexible response—and especially in their American component—has been implicitly limited by the belief that the principal utility of those forces will always be to strengthen the expectation that major aggression in Europe must lead in the end to strategic nuclear war.

As far as SALT is concerned, the most important effect of this common European emphasis on deterring attack by threat of retaliation has been to make Europeans highly sensitive to the political credibility of strategic deterrence but relatively insensitive to the details of the technical and quantitative relationship between opposing strategic forces. West Europeans have wished to be satisfied of two things: first that no matter what preemptive action the Soviet Union might take, the United States would retain the ability to inflict an intolerable degree of destruction upon Soviet territory; and second, that there should be a sufficient and credible probability that any massive Soviet attack on Western Europe would eventually lead to such a punishment. By those standards, and not by any criteria of quantitative "superiority" or "parity," they have assessed developments in the strategic nuclear competition between the superpowers.

Two moments in the history of the strategic arms race during the SALT period illustrate West European attitudes: the debate in 1967–70 over the deployment of an American ABM system, and the rapid growth after 1967 of Soviet offensive missile strength. In the case of the ABM debate, one persistent element in the West European public reaction was a type of anxious irritation—not with reference to America's predicament but with reference to America's preoccupation. Outside technically sophisticated governmental circles, the military arguments for and against ABM deployment fell on deaf ears. What was more generally recognized was the implication, justified or otherwise, that the United States might be about to insulate itself from its European allies, practically and emotionally, by deploying a new defense of its own homeland. The spectre of "Fortress America" seemed, however illogically, to draw nearer. In contrast, the growth of Soviet ICBM strength between 1967 and 1971 left West Europeans almost totally unmoved. Part of their complacency may have been naive: the product of a simple faith that the United States would never allow the Soviet Union to achieve that level of dominance which would permit a totally disarming first strike. Part of it, however, was more rational. They recalled the state of mutual nuclear deterrence which was already asserted to exist between the superpowers in the early 1960s, when total Soviet and American missile forces were far smaller and when potential Soviet second-strike strength was a tiny fraction of that now possessed by the United States. With that in mind, West Europeans were—and are—strongly conservative in estimating the level of potential punishment which either superpower must, in fact, threaten in order to deter the other. The thought that even 100 or 200 thermonuclear weapons might survive to strike Soviet territory has generally seemed to be enough to deter any rational leadership in Moscow.

WESTERN EUROPE AND THE PREPARATIONS FOR SALT

Especially within "expert" groups—technical specialists and their military or executive audiences—West European reactions during 1967–69 to the cautious process by which the superpowers decided to engage in SALT contained predictable elements of alarm or concern. Some European diplomats and politicians apparently feared that Soviet negotiators, concentrating on political rather than technical objectives, would outmaneuver their American colleagues. Others feared that the United States, in order to obtain advantages in terms of the strictly bilateral military balance, might sacrifice some part of its capability to protect allies.

More substantial, however, was a broad, if still inchoate, concern that, quite apart from the military implications of SALT, the United States government might become so intoxicated politically by the long-sought experience of negotiating directly and privately with the Soviet leadership as to diminish the value it placed on political intimacy with West European allies. This fear was not born of SALT alone. In part, it grew up during the negotiation of the Non-Proliferation Treaty, when West European governments repeatedly felt themselves to be excluded, without consultation, from the increasingly intimate discussions between Soviet and American representatives in Geneva and elsewhere. Mr. Gromyko's visit to Washington in late 1966 and the meetings between President Johnson and Premier Kosygin in June 1967 clearly carried the habit of private bilateral discussion to a higher governmental level (as have the Moscow and Washington

Summit meetings of 1972 and 1973). Bilateral exchanges about the Middle East from May 1969 extended the technique beyond the fields of arms control and general diplomacy into crisis management and conflict resolution—as did more private contacts about Southeast Asia. That which had once been characterized as a limited adversary relationship seemed to many to be growing into one of collusive competition.

The implication was that the clear vertical division between East and West, which had seemed to dominate and simplify much of international politics since the 1940s, was being progressively intersected, or even supplanted, by a horizontal division between superpower relations on one level and the network of relations involving lesser States in East and West on another. In such circumstances, the two levels might become capable of movement at different rates, or even, perhaps, in different directions.

Vague apprehensions of progressive alienation from both superpowers aside, the dominant reaction in Western Europe to the 1969 announcement of SALT was welcoming rather than fearful. At least in public, hardly any word of regret or alarm was spoken or written. Instead, numerous political and editorial voices greeted the Soviet-American agreement to meet in Helsinki with approval and relief. Most West Europeans, reflecting their fundamental view of the specific utility of nuclear weapons, were strongly inclined to believe that the Soviet-American strategic arms competition had long since transgressed the bounds of any appropriate rationality. They had seen nothing in the quantitative or qualitative development of the superpowers' strategic arsenals during the 1960s to challenge their security and were therefore eager to find in SALT the evidence of movement toward a more rational assessment. In addition, progress by the United States and the Soviet Union toward reciprocal restraint in their strategic confrontation was widely seen in Western Europe as consonant with efforts to secure a more general relaxation of East-West tensions. By late 1969, those efforts were gathering their own momentum.

"EUROPEAN" ISSUES IN SALT I

Although presumbably conscious of this general European reaction, the United States government, as SALT itself approached, was understandably concerned to calm the fears and doubts which existed within the small group of NATO governmental "experts," especially after incurring so much odium in some capitals, such as Bonn, by its handling of the Non-Proliferation Treaty. It therefore made energetic efforts to satisfy its European allies' desire for close consultation. President Nixon began the process in February 1969, when he gave the North Atlantic Council in Brussels a formal pledge of full consultation, conditional only upon the content of such discussions being treated as a matter of the greatest secrecy. Thereafter, during the later stages of preparation and during the negotiations themselves, United States representatives visited Brussels regularly in order to brief the council on American positions and on the exchanges in Helsinki and Vienna. Not all West European governments were entirely satisfied by this procedure. Some NATO members found—as they had found in other situations before—that the United States government's eagerness to consult turned out to mean little more than a willingness to inform others of what it had already decided to do. On the whole, however, the regular briefings were successful in at least containing nervousness, both on matters of detail and on the general issue of political intent.

It was well that they did, since it became clear during 1969 and early 1970 that SALT, while ostensibly intended to codify and formalize the bilateral relationship of nuclear deterrence between the superpowers, would necessarily touch upon several issues which were of direct concern to West European governments. Two such issues, at least implicitly raised by SALT, were the viability of the British and French nuclear deterrents and the freedom of the Soviet Union to deploy intermediate-range and medium-range ballistic missiles (IR/MRBMs) in western Russia, aimed at West European targets. The British and French governments were naturally anxious that SALT should not, in their absence, impose limitations on the former, while the West German government and others initially believed that SALT should lead to some limitation of the latter.

West European Nuclear Forces

As SALT began, Britain had three operational nuclear-powered ballistic-missile submarines (with a fourth almost operational) to which the formal responsibility for providing the British strategic deterrent had been transferred in July 1969. Each submarine carried sixteen Polaris A-3 missiles, bought from the United States but armed with British multiple reentry vehicles (MRVs) and nuclear warheads. Britain also had Vulcan medium-range bombers, many of them equipped with Blue Steel stand-off missiles, and a number of short-range aircraft (Canberra, Buccaneer, F-4 Phantom) capable of delivering nuclear weapons. Meanwhile, France still relied upon a first-line nuclear delivery force of thirty-six Mirage IVA light bombers. (The first of France's eighteen land-based IRBMs did not become operational until August 1971, with its first ballistic-missile submarine following in early 1972.) Even as SALT began, however, the French government was looking forward to the day when its primary independent deterrent would also consist of less vulnerable submarine-based forces. A total of four ballistic-missile submarines had been approved, three of which were to be in operation by 1974–75, and plans existed for a fifth.

Neither the British nor the French deterrent seemed to be directly at stake in SALT, since neither Britain nor France was a party to that negotiation. SALT could affect those forces indirectly, however, in any one of three ways. In the first place, the utility of British and French forces was inevitably influenced by the size and effectiveness of Soviet defenses. Antiaircraft defenses did not seem likely to figure in the SALT discussions, at least for the foreseeable future. Nor did anti-submarine (ASW) defenses. But ABM systems, the advent of which had helped to bring SALT about, were clearly to be a major subject for Soviet-American discussion. Insofar as Britain or France might envisage the independent use of their nuclear weapons, the size and quality of the Soviet ABM system, particularly if its expansion were not constrained by SALT, would obviously have a greater effect upon their own very small missile forces than upon the very large United States force. In the second place, the British Polaris force was still heavily dependent upon American cooperation. Any move in SALT towards the constraint of superpower cooperation with third countries would clearly concern the British government. In the third place, both British and French nuclear forces might arguably be considered to form some part of the total Western strategic strength. The Soviet Union might seek to obtain American agreement to a limitation of that strength as a whole, and the United States might then wish to transfer some small part of the effect of such a limitation to its nuclear allies. These three problems loomed in the future as SALT began. All, however, were contingent upon Soviet actions, inside or outside the negotiation.

Soviet IR/MRBMs

The second SALT issue of obvious West European significance was not so contingent, in that any move to bring the Soviet IR/MRBM force in Europe within the scope of SALT would obviously have to come from the American side. The 700 Soviet IR/MRBMs then in Western Russia (100 SS-5s and 600 SS-4s, with respective ranges of 2,300 and 1,200 miles) had long seemed to cast a darker shadow over Western Europe than the much larger number of Soviet ICBMs and SLBMs, the great majority of which were presumably targeted on the United States. The immediate impulse of certain West Europeans, especially in Bonn, was thus to call for the limitation or reduction of that 700 as an important Western objective in SALT and to regard the American response to that call as something of a test of Washington's alleged concern for the interests of its European allies.

This impulse was eventually suppressed. The reasons why remain obscured by the veil of secrecy which surrounded the discussions on SALT in the North Atlantic Council. Careful analysis may have shown that these old and inaccurate missiles were a less important component of the Soviet Union's overall nuclear capability against Western Europe than emotion had traditionally suggested. The extent to which attempts to include Soviet IR/MRBMs in SALT might complicate negotiations and delay agreement may have seemed, on reflection, to outweigh any advantage which might come from their ultimate limitation. Above all, however, it presumably became clear soon after SALT began that the inclusion of Soviet IR/MRBMs would greatly weaken the effort of the United States, urged on by its European allies, to resist Soviet attempts to raise what swiftly emerged as the most worrying SALT issue of all to West European governments: the issue of forward-based systems (FBS).

American FBS

Early in the discussions, the Soviet Union introduced the contention that SALT should seek to limit not only those offensive weapons which the West had habitually regarded as "intercontinental" but also any other system with which one superpower could deliver nuclear weapons on the territory of the other. That contention, if accepted, would have meant including all those nuclear-capable American aircraft, on land or at sea, which had sufficient range from their deployed positions to attack Soviet domestic targets. The logic of that contention was (and is) irresistible. After all, the U.S. Navy has long sought to advertise its carrier-borne aircraft as part of the West's overall nuclear strike capability against the Soviet Union. But the implications were calculated to evoke the strongest possible resistance in Western Europe.

American strike aircraft at West European bases and, to a lesser extent, on carriers in the Mediterranean and North Atlantic had always constituted a large part of the capability on which NATO relied for the tactical delivery of nuclear and convential weapons on targets in and around any European battlefield. Arguing on capability grounds, Soviet representatives asserted that these aircraft must be counted as part of American strategic power for purposes of bilateral comparison. Arguing on intention grounds, the members of NATO insisted that they be counted as part of the American contribution to the tactical strength of the alliance and compared, therefore, with some equivalent portion of the tactical capabilities deployed in Europe by the Warsaw Pact as a whole. The NATO contention on this point was permitted to prevail during SALT I. However, it would clearly have been undermined if the United States had endeavored to draw Soviet IR/MRBMs in Europe within the scope of the negotiations.

WEST EUROPEAN REACTIONS TO SALT I

Expert reactions to the Moscow Agreements of May 26, 1972—for example, within West European defense ministries or the disarmament sections of foreign ministries—often seemed to include conflicting elements. Disappointment at the limited arms control effect of the agreements was contrasted with concern about the superficial quantitative advantages ostensibly conceded to the Soviet Union in offensive arms. Satisfaction that there had been no discrimination against those American capabilities of most direct interest to Western Europe (e.g., FBS) and that the ABM Treaty had prolonged the effectiveness of British and French strategic missile forces was offset by anxiety that the stage might have been set for the future constraint of FBS, of West European nuclear forces, or of technical exchanges in the nuclear weapons field between the United States and its West European allies. The United States delegation to SALT asserted on April 18, 1972 that Article IX of the ABM Treaty (which prohibits the transfer of ABM technology to third countries) did not establish a precedent for a parallel prohibition in the case of strategic offensive weapons technology. Equally, the United States rejected the Soviet delegation's attempt on May 17, 1972 to bring British and French ballistic-missile submarines within the scope of SALT limitations. The fact that these issues had arisen, however, encouraged some West Europeans to expect their more substantial resurrection in SALT II, while persistent American assurances to the contrary only reinforced the suspicion that the United States might eventually be tempted to concede the inclusion of FBS in the SALT of the future.

Within broader, politically conscious groups in Western Europe, reactions were both less specific and less ambivalent. Here, the predominant instinct was to welcome the SALT I agreements as a type of superpower endorsement for the process of East-West *détente* as a whole. There was little inclination to be other than mildly curious about their detailed provisions. The important consideration seemed to be what Henry Kissinger pointed out in Kiev on May 29, 1972, when he said: "To put the central armaments of both sides for the first time under agreed restraint is an event that transcends in importance the technical significance of the individual restrictions that were placed on various weapon systems."

Meanwhile, West European public opinion at large responded to the SALT I agreements with a sort of contented apathy. A collapse of SALT would have been a major event, commanding front-page headlines throughout Western Europe. The conclusion of the agreements was material for a short column and a pious editorial. Altogether, the agreements obtained substantially less popular attention in Western Europe than did the opening of SALT in 1969. Since November 1969, a number of other international issues had climbed to a higher place in the priorities of West Europeans. In 1970, the European limelight was occupied by the promulgation of the Nixon Doctrine and the enigma of its relevance to Europe, the opening of bilateral negotiations between the two Germanies and of four-power negotiations on Berlin, the beginning of serious movement towards a Conference on Security and Cooperation in Europe (CSCE) and towards talks on mutual force reductions (MFR) there, the start of formal talks on the expansion of the European Community and the conclusion of West Germany's treaties with Poland and the Soviet Union. In 1971, these issues were joined by growing violence in Northern Ireland, a Franco-British *rapprochement,* the Mansfield Resolution calling for American troop withdrawals from Europe, President Nixon's draconian economic edicts and the reentry of China onto the world stage. Severally or in the aggregate, this galaxy of major international developments seemed to render the subject matter of SALT—the quantitative relationship between the strategic nuclear forces of two superpowers—less predominant in its importance.

East Europeans and SALT

Unfortunately, it is impossible to do more than speculate about East European reactions to SALT I; public comment has been ritualistic, and private views have remained largely private. There may have been some elation—or even relief—at the overt achievement of acknowledged "parity" by the Soviet Union, since the conviction that the United States and its European allies are exclusively peaceful and defensive has not been universal. Against that may be weighed a certain anxiety that SALT might have the indirect effect of ratifying Soviet predominance—and thus freedom of action—within Eastern Europe. Meanwhile, any impression that the Soviet Union's attainment of military parity marked the triumph of a morally superior but beleaguered ideology was presumably qualified by the Soviet leadership's action in concluding agreements on the cooperative management of strategic competition with what had long been advertised as a fundamentally malevolent military enemy.

In at least two respects, the basis for East European reactions to SALT has differed from that in Western Europe. First, the conduct and outcome of SALT cannot have seemed to be even potentially linked to the relative status of lesser powers within the Warsaw Pact, in the way in which they have seemed to be relevant to the status of other NATO members vis-à-vis the United States. Having taken little, if any, part in the formulation of strategic doctrines or in the determination of military deployment, East European governments have no grounds for supposing that SALT can displace them from positions of influence in such matters. Second, there is unlikely to have been in Eastern Europe the same sort of divergence as in Western Europe between the perceptions of military-technical experts and others, simply because East European governments (and *a fortiori* those outside government) have had almost no opportunity to study the technical and military data which constitute the formal currency of SALT. East European reactions are, in fact, likely to have been more coherent than West European, if only because they emerged from a common background of factual ignorance.

This last point may have some wider importance. Soviet commentators on the SALT I agreements, unaccustomed to any narrowly focused public debate about strategic weapons and unequipped with the information needed to conduct such a debate, have seemed to be more sensitive to the wider political implications than their American counterparts—who have, for so long, been involved in permuting a mass of absorbing (and possibly hypnotizing) technical and quantitative information about weapons themselves. East European observers may resemble their Soviet colleagues in this and may thus find it easier to avoid the pitfall of myopic concentration. West Europeans have been divided uncomfortably between the two focal distances, some examining the trees and others viewing the shape of the forest: a fact which helps to explain the divergencies already noted within West European reactions to SALT.

Europe and SALT II: Specific Issues

A relaxed European view of SALT I was encouraged by the extent to which it seemed to match the preoccupation of many Europeans with normalization in their own continent. In general, two processes of negotiation, one between the superpowers in SALT and elsewhere, and the other within Europe, appeared during SALT I to be moving on usefully parallel tracks. SALT I seemed to license the exploration of *détente* within Europe without becoming directly involved in it.

There are several reasons for fearing that neither this essentially commodious interrelationship nor the subjective impression that it exists may survive throughout SALT II. While the courses followed by the superpower and European dialogues remained parallel but arguably separate, interaction between them was a source of consolation or encouragement. The interaction threatens to become a source of anxiety and friction as those courses converge. And convergence is unavoidable, given the coincidence of SALT II with multilateral meetings in Europe: with the Conference on Security and Cooperation in Europe (CSCE) and with negotiations on mutual force reductions (MFR). The CSCE, which emerges from a series of Warsaw Pact proposals reluctantly accepted by the West, has an indefinite agenda. Preparatory talks, attended by all European countries except Albania, together with Canada and the United States, took place in Helsinki from November 1972 to June 1973. The first stage of the conference itself was held during July 1973, and the second of its proposed three stages opened in September. MFR negotiations, in contrast, reflect a NATO initiative, intended to secure the reciprocal limitation of military forces in Central Europe as the result of direct negotiation between selected members of NATO and the Warsaw Pact alone. Preparatory MFR talks opened in January 1973 and culminated, in June, in an agreement that a formal conference should convene in Vienna in late October. Meanwhile, of course, SALT II is under way in Geneva.

SALT II, MFR, and the FBS Issue

Although other problems of overlapping subject matter may emerge later, the most frequently alleged of the specific problems is the potential conflict of interest between SALT and MFR negotiations over the FBS issue: the prospect that the superpowers will, after all, discuss FBS in SALT while others in Europe press for discussion of the same weapon systems under the MFR heading. The problem is a real one, but its form is not simple.

When pressing the FBS issue in SALT, the Soviet Union has apparently had in mind those United States aircraft which could plausibly attack Soviet domestic targets from bases in Western Europe or from carriers in the adjacent seas. There is no evidence of a Soviet desire to discuss the number of nuclear weapons available for those aircraft. Nor, more importantly, is there evidence that Soviet negotiators have tried to argue that the nuclear-capable delivery systems of any NATO country except the United States should be discussed in SALT, with the qualified exception of British and French ballistic-missile submarines. On that basis, the two apparent criteria for including any forward-based system in a future SALT agreement would be that it was under the national control of one of the superpowers and that, operating from its current base and with its own internal fuel, it could attack the territory of the other superpower with nuclear weapons. By those standards, it is only some 500–600 nuclear-capable strike aircraft, including land-based F-4s and F-111s and carrier-based A-7s and (possibly) A-6s, all under United States national control, which would be added to the ICBMs, SLBMs, and intercontinental bomber aircraft already discussed in SALT. United States negotiators might conceivably argue for including Soviet aircraft, such as Tu-16s, which could attack targets in the United States on suicidal one-way missions or, perhaps, by flying on to bases in Cuba, just as Soviet negotiators might then argue for including FB-111 aircraft based in the United States. But SALT clearly does not involve aircraft such as West German F-104s, British Vulcans or French Mirage IVAs which, although they can reach Soviet targets, are not under United States national control.

The MFR situation is quite different. The geographical area of any MFR agreement is likely to cover the territories of the two Germanies, Belgium, the Netherlands, Luxembourg, Poland, Czechoslovakia, and, perhaps, Hungary. It is therefore logical that any NATO or Warsaw Pact nuclear delivery vehicles capable of attacking targets within that area should be considered. The list of delivery systems relevant to MFR would thus include for example, the F-4, F-104, and Buccaneer aircraft and Pershing and Sergeant missiles of all NATO countries and the Il-28, Su-7, and MiG-21 aircraft and Scud missiles of the Warsaw Pact nations (including at least part of the Soviet long-range, tactical, and naval air forces). It would also, of course, embrace the great majority of Soviet IR/MRBMs, as well as British and French SLBMs and IRBMs, not to mention many of the short-range missiles and nuclear-capable artillery pieces widely deployed within both alliances. In all, depending upon the exact definitions used, some 2,500–

3,500 delivery systems might plausibly be listed on each of the two sides. On the NATO side, that total would, of course, include the 500–600 United States aircraft which would also satisfy the SALT criteria. But it would do so because they could attack targets within an MFR limitation zone and not because they were, in the SALT sense, FBS which could attack targets within the Soviet Union. There may be pressure to discuss the same *aircraft* in SALT II and MFR. If there is, however, it will be because those aircraft are at the same time part of two quite different *subjects,* one concerned with targets in the territory of the two superpowers and the other concerned only with targets in Central Europe.

What thus emerges is that the potential conflict of interest between SALT and MFR over FBS is the product of technical chance rather than military necessity. The value placed by NATO on American FBS aircraft is almost entirely related to their ability to strike targets *outside* the Soviet Union, and the fact that they can indeed reach Soviet territory is largely incidental. If that incidental capability, which alone enables the Soviet Union to argue for the discussion of FBS in SALT, were reduced or eliminated by redeploying aircraft or by replacing some of them by alternative types of shorter range, the conflict of interest between SALT and MFR might disappear. Even without that, however, it might not necessarily be to the disadvantage of NATO's West European members to have FBS discussed in SALT. Judging by SALT I, the maximum which could realistically be expected of an agreement on FBS during SALT II would be a freeze at existing levels. If such a freeze were agreed to in that strategic context, it would become harder to press for a reduction in the numbers of these aircraft within the tactical context of MFR, since that would imply a parallel reduction in Soviet *strategic* strength in order to maintain the balance set in SALT. A SALT agreement covering FBS might thus become a lever in the hands of any West European government which wished to exclude American tactical aircraft from a major reduction in the stationed forces of the superpowers in Europe —and a lever, moreover, which would operate in Moscow as much as in Washington.

The real problem of FBS is not, therefore, that any agreement on the limitation (as opposed to the reduction) of American nuclear-delivery aircraft in Europe would be immediately intolerable to West European members of NATO. The problems of FBS lie, in fact, elsewhere: in the bargaining context, in the non-nuclear implications, and in the negotiating process itself.

The problem of the bargaining context is that West Europeans, who regard American strike aircraft in Europe as an important component of the regional military balance there, are naturally opposed to treating them as though they related only to the bilateral, global military balance between the superpowers. If the United States were to accept an FBS freeze in SALT, it would presumably be in return for some further restriction of those Soviet strategic systems, such as land-based ICBMs, which might be launched against American territory. To West Europeans, however, there are much stronger reasons in favor of exchanging any such freeze for some limit on the Soviet nuclear vehicles which threaten their own territories: IR/MRBMs or shorter-range aircraft. To put it crudely, trading an FBS freeze in SALT—to which FBS are, at most, marginally relevant—means giving up the opportunity to trade it in MFR talks or elsewhere for something of direct value to Western Europe.

The problem of non-nuclear implications is probably of even greater military substance. All the American aircraft concerned are capable of delivering either conventional or nuclear ordnance (or even of acting as defensive interceptors). Many West European military commanders attach at least as much importance to their conventional as to their nuclear roles, especially as the improvement of conventional ordnance—in the form, for example, of laser-guided "smart" bombs—increases the variety of possible targets in central and eastern Europe which could usefully be attacked without recourse to nuclear weapons in case of a Warsaw Pact attack. Obviously, there would be strong West European objections to any significant reduction of dual-capable FBS, not the least because removing the only vehicles capable of attacking many targets effectively with conventional armament might actually entail the earlier use of nuclear weapons in case of war. Even a freeze, however, would raise fears in that connection, since it would restrict the ability of NATO to take advantage of technical improvements in conventional weapons by transferring interdiction or battlefield tasks from relatively inaccurate missiles, necessarily carrying nuclear warheads, to highly accurate aircraft systems capable of achieving comparable effects by conventional means.

Whatever the merits of any eventual agreement in SALT on FBS, the problem of the previous negotiating process would remain. Given their substantial interest in the issue and their considerable sensitivity over it, West European governments would demand a degree of consultation during SALT discussions on FBS which would go beyond anything achieved during SALT I or so far tolerable to the United States governmental system. The almost inevitable judgment that consultation was, in fact, inadequate would breed suspicion of American motives and intentions. That problem would obviously be exacerbated insofar as the United States, in SALT, was felt to be exploiting multilateral assets, in the shape of FBS, in an attempt to secure bilateral agreement with the Soviet Union, just as it would become acute if there were any question of a reduction, rather than a freeze, of FBS. But the fundamental issue, existing independently of the details of a SALT discussion on FBS, would seem to be less one of the value of particular weapon systems than one of the relative importance which the United States seemed to be giving to alliance relationships, on the one hand, and to the superpower relationship, on the other.

SALT II and West European Nuclear Forces

The possibility that SALT II may seek to impose some direct limit upon British or French nuclear forces is not likely to be taken seriously in Western Europe; the principle of "no taxation without representation" is as powerful as its history is distinguished. That does not rule out their inclusion in renewed Soviet demands for concessions to offset Western technical and geographical advantages. But technical developments, as well as alliance relationships, now argue against agreeing to such demands. During SALT I, the Soviet Union, in pressing for a numerical advantage in SLBM launchers, seems to have argued first that only this could compensate it for the fact that the United States, because it used forward submarine bases in Scotland, Spain, and Guam and because its SLBMs had a longer range than Soviet SLBMs, could keep a much higher proportion of its SLBM force on firing station at any time—a proportion which has been estimated at 60 percent, as opposed to a maximum of 40 percent for the Soviet submarine fleet. Its secondary contention was that the existence of French and British SLBMs should also be taken into account in setting the Soviet limit. The Soviet Navy, however, has recently introduced a new SLBM—the SS-N-8—whose range appears to be greater than that of the American

Poseidon. This will immediately increase the proportion of Soviet submarines which can be in firing position at any time. Meanwhile, on the American side, the introduction of the much longer-range SLBMs planned for the late 1970s will make the United States independent of its present forward submarine bases. Thus, the Soviet Union will soon have much less reason to argue that the SLBM forces of the superpowers should be compared on any basis other than the number of launchers which they contain, or that the comparison should take account of forces other than those of the superpowers themselves.

What is likely to be taken more seriously in Western Europe is the possibility that SALT II may produce some general restriction on the provision of material assistance to allies in the field of offensive nuclear delivery systems (as SALT I has done in the case of ABM systems). Despite the fact that the effectiveness of British and French strategic nuclear weapons has been consolidated by the low limit imposed in the SALT I agreements on Soviet ABM deployment, the British case, looking to the future, is obviously an acute one. Britain's Polaris force seems to be dependent upon the United States not only for logistic support, but also for cooperation in such areas as navigation and testing. Moreover, a major part of the Anglo-American bilateral agreement on material cooperation in military nuclear matters requires renewal at the end of 1974, at which time there also occurs an opportunity to terminate those parts of the agreement which provide for the exchange of related information. Presumably, therefore, the British government will be watching the course of SALT II in this connection with special vigilance.

Theoretically, a restriction of the kind mentioned could also affect the majority of NATO members in Western Europe, most of whom have been dependent upon the United States for the supply of tactical nuclear delivery systems (Pershing, Sergeant, and Honest John missiles, aircraft such as the F-4 and the F-104, and artillery such as the M-110 203 mm. howitzer), for the earmarking of American nuclear weapons for delivery by systems under allied control in the event of war, and for the provision of information about their operation. In practice, however, it is difficult to conceive that either superpower would give up the whole of its freedom to disseminate nuclear delivery systems or information about them to allies. Such a step, inevitably affecting many of the most important conventional but dual-capable weapon systems on both sides as well as uniquely nuclear systems, would totally alter, and largely destroy, the military basis on which both NATO and the Warsaw Pact have been organized. Anglo-American (or Franco-American) cooperation in the field of strategic nuclear weapons may well be vulnerable to the course of SALT II, but wider cooperation within NATO or the Warsaw Pact on tactical systems seems much less likely to be substantially restricted. Nevertheless, the possibility of any movement towards such a restriction will, within NATO, constitute another source of suspicion and alarm.

EUROPE AND SALT II: THE WIDER CONTEXT

The extent of that suspicion and alarm will depend primarily upon the West European reading of other evidence concerning the United States involvement in Western Europe's military security. Alarm might, for instance, be greatly increased if doubts about the course and outcome of SALT II were amplified by simultaneous movement toward the reduction of United States forces in Europe. If West European governments judge that United States actions with regard to force levels in Europe imply an effort to disengage militarily from Western Europe's security, they will tend to suspect United States negotiators of pursuing a parallel purpose privately in SALT II, at least to the extent of offering concessions which would particularly restrict American ability to support European allies.

Renewed pressure in the United States to reduce the American military commitment to Western Europe may also have an impact upon West European countries' nuclear aspirations. The ostensible, if largely meaningless, codification of strategic nuclear parity in SALT I has already prompted minority groups to argue more strongly for the acquisition or maintenance by West European countries of their own deterrent nuclear forces. These contentious arguments may reach a wider audience if there is any attempt in SALT II to restrict the provision to allies of technical assistance in nuclear matters. By analogy, arguments for the elaboration of independent West European tactical nuclear capabilities may have a wider influence if there is serious suspicion concerning the handling of the FBS issue or, in any other form, an apparent movement towards reducing United States tactical capabilities and commitments in Europe. There have already been suggestions of the possibility that the United States, in SALT II, in MFR, and elsewhere, might pursue a largely covert policy of "Vietnamization" with regard to Western Europe. Whether or not such a policy existed, a spreading conviction that it did could have a divisive effect on United States-West European relations and within Western Europe itself, especially if it were taken to imply nuclear as well as conventional self-sufficiency.

It is broad issues such as these, rather than narrower questions related to particular weapon systems, which are likely to preoccupy interested West Europeans during SALT II. Senator Jackson's plea of November 20, 1972 to the Military Committee of the North Atlantic Assembly in Bonn, when he besought the European members of NATO to interest themselves more deeply in what he called "the central issues of the East-West strategic balance," is doomed to fall on deaf ears. In general terms, Western Europe hopes that SALT II will proceed in a successful manner and that it will yield a more substantial agreement on the limitation and, if possible, reduction of offensive armament. More specifically, however, West European desires for SALT II will be largely negative: that it should not diminish the ability of the United States to contribute effectively to the military strength of NATO, and that it should not impede transfers of military equipment or technology between the United States and its allies. Having little credence in Senator Jackson's assertion that the survival of the American strategic nuclear deterrent itself is at stake, most West Europeans will have little further interest in the details of SALT II negotiations or of a SALT II agreement.

SALT II, MFR, and the CSCE

Ultimately, the most important problem in the relationship between MFR talks and the process of East-West normalization within which the Conference on Security and Cooperation in Europe is ostensibly embedded is one which can only be described as philosophical, since it concerns the meaning of security itself. The ways in which MFR and the CSCE have been conceptualized in advance reflect fundamentally different interpretations of the objective of security in Europe. MFR talks must assume that security is to be reinforced by maintaining or perfecting a balance between opposed military forces. It is, in fact, the *separate* securities of Western and Eastern Europe respectively which are to be pursued. The essence of the CSCE proposal, however, is that, while the several securities of the two parts of Europe remain important, security can also be discussed and pursued as a quality of the European situation as a whole: a situation in which adversity and military confrontation persist, but in which there is some common interest in the avoidance of conflict and in the peaceful absorption of pressures for change. In the long run, the most difficult issue facing European countries may be choosing between the philosophical approaches to security implied, on the one hand, by MFR and, on the other hand, by the process of normalization.

Such a choice will not present itself immediately—and may never do so in an explicit fashion. It may well be that, for some time, MFR talks and the CSCE can proceed in parallel, without noticeable tension between them. But the issues of security in Europe occur in the context of a single territorial region, and they bear directly not only upon relations between different groups of international actors (e.g., NATO and the Warsaw Pact) but also upon the internal structures of those groups. Ambiguity cannot persist indefinitely in such circumstances. Consciously or not, European governments will eventually have to choose between stabilizing a confrontation and seeking to dissolve it.

The significance of this for SALT II is two-fold. First, the potential tension between MFR and the CSCE process clearly complicates the problem of coordinating future stages of SALT with both at once. West European governments are likely to become increasingly uncertain of their own priorities if MFR talks and the CSCE proceed in parallel, and that uncertainty is likely to confuse their reactions to United States policies in SALT. Second, facing the uncertainties which seem bound to proliferate as the opportunities to explore normalization in Europe multiply, West Europeans will at least temporarily become more, rather than less, dependent upon that ultimate confidence in their own military security which, in turn, relies so heavily upon their conviction of a United States commitment to deter attack upon their territory. It is for this reason that some West Europeans have, for example, reacted neuralgically to the possibility that the Soviet-American agreement on the prevention of nuclear war, reached during Mr. Brezhnev's visit to Washington in June 1973, implies a greater United States reluctance to use nuclear weapons in retaliation for a purely conventional Soviet military attack in Europe. The potential effect upon military posture in future combat worries them less than the actual impact upon political confidence during current negotiations.

SALT II and the Atmosphere of Détente

It is exactly on this level of confidence that West European reactions to SALT II are likely to be very different from those to SALT I. SALT II promises both to touch upon sensitive points of direct relevance to the military situation in Europe and to raise broad political questions about United States intentions. Those questions might well be echoed by other developments outside SALT, such as renewed Atlantic tension over trade or monetary policies or over American troop levels in Europe. All in all, the effect could be to strike at that underlying confidence which is a condition even more of prudent political flexibility in Western Europe than of military determination. The impact on both Atlantic and intra-European relations would then be serious.

Many West Europeans might see themselves faced with a choice between recoiling defensively from East-West normalization and engaging in more urgent but less prudent accommodation with the Soviet Union. And the choice would not be unanimous. A wide gap would thus open between the United States, persisting in the development of its own bilateral relations with the Soviet Union, and at least some of its West European allies and friends. The continuation of superpower *détente* would, in fact, have been bought at the cost of Atlantic dislocation, coupled possibly with the disruption of political normalization in Europe and probably with dissension in Western Europe itself.

The alternative is clearly not for the United States to abandon the pursuit of superpower *détente*. If that were done without any apparent change in Soviet policy as a justification, it would have little influence on the independent momentum of the normalization process in Europe —except perhaps in Britain and, possibly, in France. Nor would it have much effect upon West European fears of American disengagement, since those have their independent origin in assessments of American domestic politics. Instead, many West European countries, and especially West Germany, would be likely to sustain their pursuit of normalization in the East-West context, thus diverging increasingly from the United States. And some might even be prompted towards more urgent accommodation with the Soviet Union by the double fear that the United States would still disengage while the Soviet Union, unrestrained by any remaining stake in superpower *détente,* would become more exigent in European affairs. Meanwhile, other West European countries, probably including Britain and France, would strive to reemphasize and refurbish the military security of the West. The result would again be disarray in Western Europe combined with dislocation on the Atlantic level.

It may seem alarmist to suggest that American policies within the superpower context could have such dramatically damaging effects within the West. Why should the process of superpower *détente* not continue to complement and encourage processes of normalization in Europe? Why, indeed, should that *détente* not permit Western Europe to draw away, politically, economically, and possibly militarily from the United States, integrating more closely as it does so, while also constructing bonds of interdependence with an Eastern Europe which has itself been enabled partially to emerge from the Soviet shadow (as well as from Soviet military protection)? The answer is that most, if not all, of those developments might, indeed, be combined. But they will only be so if the United States, in common with European countries, recognizes that the shape and direction of policy is no more important than its timing and presentation.

But normalization and integration in Europe require the taking of apparently substantial risks by West European governments: of domestic embarrassment, or political defeat, or of penalties in external policy ranging from loss of prestige to economic disaster. Many of those risks will not be taken unless the governments concerned have sufficient underlying confidence that, whatever else is at issue, their national securities are not at stake. That confidence continues to emanate, in vital part, from the conviction that the United States attaches higher importance to the military security of the NATO area as a whole than to any other objective of its international security policies. Eventually, the importance of that conviction may be diminished as the processes of normalization and integration generate alternative forms of confidence. Already, integration within what is now a European Community of nine States has reached a point at which it is reasonable to hope that a divorce from the United States would not halt or reverse the process, even if it would certainly disturb it. But irreversibility is far from yet being true of the East-West normalization process, which could still be disrupted by an erosion of West European confidence in American security policies.

It is largely for this reason that the maintenance of an Atlantic relationship on the security level remains a primary objective for so many West Europeans, regardless of their different views on the ultimate role which Western Europe should play in relation to either the United States or the world at large. Whether they believe that some version of an Atlantic partnership is perennially desirable or that Europe should strive instead to constitute some sort of third force independent of both superpowers, the great majority of politically conscious West Europeans would agree that the closest possible association of the United States with their own military security will be a vital support for their preferred national policies during the next few years. The task, therefore, is for the United States and its allies so to manage their policies in the security field—in SALT II or elsewhere—as to ensure that West European fears concerning military security are not brought to any climax before the process of East-West normalization has reached the point at which it serves as an independent generator of adequate confidence.

CHAPTER EIGHT
The Perspective from China and Japan
Morton H. Halperin

Most Asians have never heard of SALT. Even those attentive few in Asian countries who concern themselves with foreign policy questions have not been able to discern any substantial impact of SALT on their country's interests. While the ABM Treaty has had an effect on both China and Japan, it is important to keep in mind that this impact has occurred within a context in which other events have much more significance.

Asia is in a period of rapid and profound change. During the months prior to the signing of the SALT agreements in May 1972, the United States had withdrawn almost all of its ground troops from South Vietnam while mining Haiphong Harbor and launching a major bombing campaign against North Vietnam. At the same time, President Richard Nixon had gone to Peking and opened contact between China and the United States for the first time in twenty-five years. This was followed by the visit of Japan's Prime Minister Tanaka to Peking and the establishment of diplomatic relations between the two major powers of Asia. In the wake of these events the two Korean governments have, for the first time, opened a dialogue which they proclaim is designed to lead to the unification of their divided country.

These international events have occupied the attention of Asians concerned with foreign policy. They have produced in Asia a major concern with the nature of the four-power balance between the United States, the Soviet Union, China, and Japan. SALT is seen as a symbol of closer relations between the United States and the Soviet Union and as a potential factor of discord in China's relations with each of the

209

two superpowers and in Japan's relations with the United States. It is
in this context that it is useful to consider the specific impact of SALT
on the foreign policies of China and Japan in particular.

China and SALT

We shall consider first what the Chinese leaders have said publicly
about SALT and what their attitude to SALT appears to be. Then we
shall consider the impact which China had on the SALT agreements
and the implications of the agreements for American deterrence of the
Chinese nuclear force. Finally, we shall consider the possibilities of
strategic arms control involving China.

China is the only major nation in the world to condemn publicly
and strongly the SALT I agreements as a sham. The Chinese attack
on the agreements has involved a discussion both of their technical
and strategic implications and of their political connotations.

In the first public Chinese statement on the agreements, Premier
Chou En-lai emphasized the limited strategic importance of the accords. He argued that the agreements, in fact, marked the beginning
of a new stage of the arms race between the two superpowers. "The
fact is that the ink on the agreements was hardly dry before one announced an increase of billions of dollars for military expenditure and
the other hastened to test new-type weapons, clamoring to seize nuclear
arms superiority," Chou said, adding that "the agreements marked
the beginning of a new stage in the arms race rather than an effort
to curb it." Other statements have emphasized that the SALT I agreements simply channel the nuclear arms race into qualitative areas, but
the Chinese have apparently not commented on the specific question of
the banning of nationwide ABM systems, which means the abandon-
ment of a China-oriented American ABM system.

The fundamental Chinese criticism of SALT, expressed both before
and after the agreements were signed, is that they are simply a mani-
festation of the efforts of the two superpowers to dominate the world,
both politically and militarily. The Chinese see this same trend in the
Non-Proliferation Treaty and in other arms control agreements in
which the two superpowers have played the leading role in negotiations. They argue that political questions must be settled by a large
number of countries, including the small powers concerned, and that

arms control and disarmament must begin with agreement by the major powers not to use nuclear weapons, to be followed by the elimination of overseas bases and the destruction of all nuclear weapons stockpiles. The Chinese have declared that only if these steps are taken will they be prepared to support the world disarmament conference proposed by the Soviet Union.

These public statements by Chinese leaders seem to reflect a real consensus in Peking that the SALT I agreements are not in China's interest. The Chinese concern at the moment, which is with a Soviet nuclear attack, is not affected by the agreements since the short-range Soviet weapons which now pose a threat on the Sino-Soviet border are not in any way limited by the agreements. The Chinese may fear that a standoff in the Soviet-American nuclear balance will permit the Soviets to devote more resources to development of a nuclear capability against China and make the Soviets more confident that they could use that capability without bringing on an American nuclear response against them.

Politically, the Chinese have been concerned about the danger of a Soviet-American-led anti-China coalition and have moved in their relations with Washington and Tokyo to seek to prevent that. Any agreement between the United States and the Soviet Union is seen by Peking as a danger since it increases the probability that the United States will become at least a silent partner in Soviet moves against China, rather than joining with China and Japan in an anti-Russian coalition. The Chinese position then is clear. SALT makes no contribution to Peking's security and is part of the most dangerous political trend in the world.

We turn now to an American perspective and ask how has the China question affected American policy at SALT and the American ability to maintain an adequate deterrent against China. In this connection we should note that from the Soviet perspective, Britain and France, rather than China, may have been the most important unseen participants. The Russians clearly do worry about the British and French nuclear forces and about the possibility that these forces would be increased in the face of limitations on American nuclear power. On the other hand, as noted above, the Russian nuclear capability against China is not in any way affected by the SALT I agreements, and apparently largely for reasons of geography, if not of doctrine, the Russians do not appear to have ever seriously considered an anti-China area-wide ABM system, although they may have insisted on maintaining the Moscow ABM system in part because of its utility in defending the Soviet capital and political leadership in the event of a Chinese missile attack. To the United States, China has been an unseen presence at the SALT table. The United States had to consider, in the first place, whether any possible agreement to be negotiated at SALT would interfere with its ability to maintain an adequate deterrent against China.

One must consider both the ABM Treaty and the Interim Agreement on offensive forces. The only part of the American strategic posture which has been justified in terms of the emerging Chinese nuclear threat is the ABM. Beginning in 1965, senior officials of the Department of Defense began to predict the early development of a Chinese ICBM capability and to discuss the possibility of deploying an ABM system capable of dealing with such a force. On September 18, 1967, Secretary of Defense Robert McNamara announced that the United States had decided to deploy a light ABM system designed to deal with the Chinese ICBM threat then expected to develop over the next ten years. In the same speech, McNamara ruled out the desirability or practicability of an ABM system directed against the large Soviet missile threat to American cities, but did hold open the possibility that the system could be used to defend Minuteman missile sites. Coming into office in the midst of a public debate about the desirability of this anti-China ABM system, the Nixon administration altered the rationale somewhat by focusing primarily on the defense of Minuteman, but included as one of the purposes of the deployment an area defense against the Chinese threat.

With the opening of the SALT talks, the administration at first indicated that it was not likely to be willing to give up the anti-China ABM in arms control negotiations with the Soviet Union. At one point in a press conference held in March 1969, President Nixon asserted that the anti-China ABM system was critical to American diplomacy in Asia and he asserted that an ABM system could make the United States invulnerable to a Chinese attack. In the end, the United States agreed to give up the possibility of an area ABM system directed against China in order to get the ABM Treaty with the Soviet Union, and in June 1972, Henry A. Kissinger explained the change in policy as follows:

Our estimate of the Chinese nuclear capability is still approximately what it was at the time that Safeguard was developed. Our estimate of the likelihood of our being involved in any nuclear conflict with the People's Republic of China is considerably less than it was at the time that the Safeguard program was submitted to the Congress, because of the political developments that have happened since then, specifically the opening toward China.

Therefore, we accept now that in the overall context of the contribution that this agreement could make toward world peace and toward improving general relationships, and, in the light, also, of improvement of relations with the People's Republic of China, that we could pay this price of foregoing the additional protection that the President requested in his original statement.

We could do this all the more so because if our estimates turn out to be incorrect, we have such an overwhelming retaliatory capability vis-à-vis any other country other than the Soviet Union, that the idea of a third nuclear country attacking the United States is a rather remote possibility.

As Kissinger suggested, the administration would have found it difficult to insist on an anti-China ABM, in light of the changed political relation between Washington and Peking. He also suggested some doubt about the reasoning which led to the belief that the United States could not rely on a retaliatory capability to deter China.

Despite Kissinger's statement that the American estimate of the Chinese nuclear capability has not changed significantly, the posture statements of Secretary of Defense Melvin Laird show a steady decline in the expected Chinese ICBM threat. In February 1970, he stated that a Chinese ICBM flight test "is expected during 1970" and predicted 10–25 ICBMs by 1975. In the following year, he stated that a flight test had not yet been detected, but he still predicted 3–10 ICBMs in mid-1974 and 10 or more in 1975. In 1972, Laird emphasized that it is "difficult to assess either the strategic nuclear threat posed by the People's Republic of China, or how that threat will evolve through the 1970s." He then estimated 10–20 ICBMs by mid-1976.

This slipping estimate of Chinese capability may have influenced the Pentagon's willingness to accept the ABM Treaty, even if it did not affect White House calculations. The Defense Department was also influenced by the fact that the Senate of the United States had shown itself unwilling to appropriate the funds for an anti-China system. Indeed, Secretary Laird indicated that he would not have supported the ABM Treaty, which limited ABMs to two widely separated sites, except for the fact that an area ABM system was not in prospect in any case because of opposition in the Senate.

At some stage, the Chinese are likely to have some operational ICBMs targeted on the United States. Hence, the question of whether or not this was a sensible decision depends on an analysis of how important an ABM deployment against China is for the United States. Supporters of the ABM Treaty could take one of two positions. They could argue that an ABM deployment against China made no sense on its own terms and, therefore, that the United States gave up nothing. Alternatively, they could argue that an ABM against China was of some value, but that value was outweighed by the advantages of an ABM Treaty with the Soviet Union.

Neither the Johnson nor the Nixon administration had spelled out in convincing detail the argument for the anti-China ABM system. At one level, the argument was simply a prudential one, since China would have the capability to destroy American cities and since the United States had the technical capability to build a defense against that threat, it ought to do so. At another level, the argument was related to the credibility of the American deterrent for America's Asian allies and therefore to the prospects of nuclear proliferation.

Proponents of the ABM argued that the United States cannot maintain a credible deterrent against Chinese threats of the use of nuclear weapons against Asian countries if American cities are at risk. Therefore, credibility of the American deterrent rests on the maintenance of a capability to deny China the capability to inflict any damage on the United States.

Opponents of the anti-China ABM deployment argued that such a deployment was not necessary to maintain the credibility of the American deterrent. The credibility of the deterrent against the Soviet Union had not eroded with the Soviet development of ICBMs in the late 1950s. Moreover, the credibility of the American deterrent for countries such as Japan and Australia—the potential nuclear powers in the Pacific—would surely be as effective in relation to the emergent Chinese threat as it is with respect to the fully developed Soviet threat. They argued that the effort to build an ABM defense against China would only serve to highlight the sensitivity of the United States to the defense of its cities, hence, in effect, undermining the deterrent.

The opponents argued further that an ABM deployment would be extremely expensive, costing more than the $4 billion originally estimated, and that the Chinese would find it relatively easy to penetrate the defense by concentrating their relatively small number of missiles on a few undefended or weakly defended cities. Moreover, a small ABM deployment could not be prevented from growing into a large system, and even a thin nationwide deployment would look to the Soviet Union like an anti-Russian defense and hence complicate U.S.-Soviet relations. (It is worth noting that both the Soviet Union and China are over the north pole from the United States and missiles from the two countries enter the United States over the same flight paths.) The degree to which arguments in favor of an anti-China system were taken seriously in the American government and the American Congress may be reflected in the fact that the decision to give up the anti-China ABM met with almost no opposition—no one objected to the ABM Treaty because it precluded an anti-China ABM system.

The Interim Offensive Agreement was seen as having less relation to the U.S.-Chinese nuclear balance than the ABM Treaty. Since the agreement did not prohibit any ongoing American program, it could not have affected any program which the United States considered necessary to deter China. In fact, by limiting the number of Soviet missiles, the agreement reduced the number of targets in the Soviet Union that the United States must concern itself with. Hence in operational planning there would be more missiles left over for targets in China.

The United States now has, and will continue to maintain for the indefinite future, a substantial *damage-limiting* capability against China. That is to say, the United States will be able to destroy a substantial portion of the Chinese nuclear capability on the ground in a first strike should it decide to do so. What the SALT I agreements have done is to eliminate the possibility of the United States' maintaining a credible first-strike capability which would provide a *damage denial* capability against China. The absence of an area ABM makes it impossible to have such a capability. The American force will also be limited by the decision not to deploy a hard target kill capability with its MIRV missiles. Thus while the United States will retain forces sufficient to absorb a first strike from both Russia and China and destroy each country in turn, it will not have the kind of damage-limiting capability against China which it might have been capable of developing in an all-out arms race. From the Chinese perspective, the problems of gaining a confident, assured destruction capability against the U.S. have been greatly reduced.

Whatever agreements are developed in SALT II, they are unlikely to change this basic picture. Substantial reductions in American and Soviet forces would still leave both sides with ample capabilities for deterrence against China by forces substantially larger than the Chinese are likely to have in the foreseeable future. Limits on MIRVs would only underline the inability of the United States to develop a counterforce first-strike capability against China, but would not detract from its deterrent capability. Once the United States abandoned the objective of an anti-China ABM system, the Chinese strategic forces posed, and are likely to pose in the future, no serious restraint on possible arms control agreements to be negotiated at SALT. This fact in itself suggests that it is both unnecessary and probably a mistake to attempt to bring China into the SALT negotiations. The presence of China would open the issue of whether Britain and France should also be invited. This would raise the specter of the five nuclear powers preparing to meet to engage in political, as well as arms control, negotiations. Moreover, the United States and the Soviet Union have now established a tradition of frank discussion of sensitive military issues. Both countries are likely to be unwilling, or at least hesitant, to continue such discussions in the presence of Chinese representatives. In any event, the Chinese, who have thus far taken a polemical attitude towards strategic arms negotiations, would not now join such negotiations if they were invited.

It seems certain that there will be no suggestion from either the United States or the Soviet Union to include China in the SALT II negotiations. If successful, then it may be that at some later stage in the negotiation of reductions, as the Soviet and American forces come down and as the Chinese forces increase in size, it will be necessary to include in an agreement the nuclear forces of China, as well as those of Britain and France. But this stage has not yet been reached and will not be reached in SALT II.

Strategic Arms Control with China

None of this means that the United States should not be giving serious thought to the possibilities of bilateral strategic arms control discussions and negotiations with Peking. The fact that China is unlikely to join the SALT negotiations suggests the urgency of developing another forum in which the United States can discuss issues of this kind with the Chinese government. Some issues, of course, need to be discussed in multilateral forums, and some way undoubtedly will be found to bring China into discussions of questions such as the nuclear weapon test ban and controls on chemical warfare.

But beyond this, it would be desirable to open a dialogue on strategic arms control between the United States and China. Such discussions could be carried on during the periodic trips to Peking taken by Henry Kissinger or other senior officials or carried out through the liaison offices which will be opened in Washington and Peking. It might, however, be preferable to seek an institutionalization of such discussions with meetings in some neutral capital, perhaps in conjunction with the talks on cultural and economic exchanges which have been carried on in Paris.

In an arms control discussion, the United States should first seek an exchange of views with Peking on the nature of strategic deterrence. At a minimum, it would be useful for the Chinese to have an understanding about how American planners view these problems and the basis on which decisions are made to build strategic forces and to target them against the U.S.S.R. and China. It would probably be useful to discuss with Peking the possibilities of negotiating agreements dealing with the accidental detonation of nuclear weapons similar to the Accidents Measures Agreement negotiated with the Soviet Union at SALT I. The United States might also want to propose a hot line arrangement to facilitate communication in a crisis situation. As part of these discussions, the United States might well want to transmit to Peking its own procedures for safeguarding nuclear weapons and preventing their accidental detonation or unauthorized use.

Any effort to discuss these questions will likely come up against the Chinese insistence that the first step in disarmament must be a renunciation of the use of nuclear weapons by the United States and the Soviet Union. The Chinese government itself has declared that it will never be the first to use nuclear weapons and it has called upon the superpowers to follow suit. The Chinese may be unwilling to discuss other issues unless the United States makes this commitment. Moreover, it would be difficult to have a discussion with the Chinese about the American conception of assured destruction and the requirements for a secure retaliatory capability without appearing to be threatening the Chinese by implying that they do not have such a capability. Thus a prerequisite for any serious arms control discussion with the Chinese may be American willingness to renounce the first use of nuclear weapons.

In any event, any arms control dialogue between the U.S. and China will raise concerns not only in the Soviet Union, but also in Japan.

Japan and SALT

The SALT negotiations and the SALT I agreements were not major news items in Japan. The Japanese government expressed its support of the agreements, but neither the government nor any opposition groups have seen any clear and important impact on Japanese security interests. SALT would have an important effect on Japan if it in some way affected the Japanese calculations about whether Japan should become a nuclear power. In order to consider these effects it is necessary to analyze briefly the current attitudes in Japan toward a Japanese nuclear capability and how these might be affected by the SALT agreements.

The so-called nuclear allergy which dominated Japanese attitudes toward nuclear weapons in the postwar period is now almost entirely gone. During the period of the allergy, it was impossible to have a public discussion about whether or not Japan should consider developing a nuclear weapon capability. Any politician who suggested this was even an open question was likely to find himself hounded from office, and no scholar would risk his reputation by putting forward such a proposition.

The situation has now changed. The question of whether Japan should acquire a nuclear force is discussed in relatively hard-headed terms by government officials, bureaucrats, and scholars. The change in attitude is reflected in the fact that Japan signed the Non-Proliferation Treaty only after an intense debate in which many of the leaders of the Liberal Democratic Party expressed their opposition. Japan has delayed ratification ostensibly to wait for the results of the negotiations with the International Atomic Energy Agency (IAEA) on the safeguards arrangements required by the treaty which would involve inspection of Japanese peaceful nuclear plants. However, there will continue to be strong opposition within the Liberal Democratic Party and within the Japanese bureaucracy to ratification of the NPT, even if the inspection problems are solved satisfactorily. Japanese leaders are no longer prepared to give up for all time the possibility of Japan developing a nuclear weapon capability and have delayed a decision on the NPT.

The Japanese government has also opened the door to a possible nuclear capability by declaring that the development of nuclear weapons by Japan is not unconstitutional under the so-called no war provision of Japan's constitution. The government's position is that offensive capabilities are illegal, but that any capability, including nuclear weapons, which was designed to deter an attack against Japan itself is permitted under the constitution. At the same time, the Japanese government has reaffirmed the three nuclear noes: no nuclear weapons on Japanese territory; no Japanese acquisition of nuclear weapons from another country; and no Japanese development of its own national nuclear capability. Thus, there continues to be widespread public opposition to any Japanese nuclear force.

Perhaps equally important, most of the influential groups in Japan have, after sober consideration of the alternatives, decided that it would not be in Japan's interest, at least at the present time, to seek a nuclear weapon capability. In part this view is based upon the extensive public opposition. A commitment of the Japanese government to develop nuclear weapons would stir up very serious social and political tensions serving to unite the opposition groups and possibly to bring on serious rioting and other forms of opposition. There would also be substantial technical difficulties stemming from the opposition of most Japanese scientists to a nuclear capability and from the problem of finding a place within Japan to conduct nuclear tests, particularly in light of Japan's adherence to the Limited Nuclear Test Ban Treaty.

Japanese analysts have also pointed out that their development of an independent nuclear force could not be viewed as simply a complement to the American deterrent. Given the American opposition to independent nuclear capabilities and given the fact that the Japanese capability would have to be justified internally as a device to end Japan's reliance on the United States, a Japanese nuclear force would have to substitute for the American deterrent. This, Japanese analysts point out, would itself create severe difficulties. There is no reason to believe that a small Japanese nuclear force would be a more credible deterrent than an American guarantee backed by the substantially larger American force.

The problems of developing a credible deterrent capability against the large force of either the Soviet Union or the United States are well understood in Japan. Even against China it is pointed out that there is a major asymmetry in that about 20 percent of Japan's population is clustered in three major metropolitan areas centering on Tokyo, Nagoya, and Osaka, while China's population is distributed throughout the country. Thus Japan would be much more vulnerable than China to the threat of a small nuclear force.

Adding to all of these difficulties is the transitional problem. It would take ten years, or at the least five, between the time that Japan made a decision to develop a national nuclear capability and the time that it had at least a minimum deterrent capability actually in operation. During this period, Japan would be particularly vulnerable to nuclear threats and nuclear blackmail as the American deterrent receded in effectiveness and as other governments began to worry about the behavior of Japan when it would have an effective nuclear capability.

For all of these reasons, there is now a consensus among influential Japanese that Japan should not now move to develop a national nuclear force. The major uncertainty which might ultimately lead to a change in this calculation is the role that Japan can play in the world without a nuclear force. The Japanese are well aware of their growing economic power and the fact that it yields increasing political and diplomatic power and responsibility. They are also aware that no country has ever assumed a major diplomatic and economic role in the world without ultimately developing the major forms of military power available. Japan is presently determined to try, but the test of success will be whether Japan is treated as a major world power.

In particular, the Japanese will be sensitive to the U.S.-Japan relationship. If the Japanese conclude that the United States is treating Japan as an equal and not attempting to gain unilateral advantage because of the American nuclear umbrella, then there is likely to be little pressure to move toward a Japanese nuclear force. On the other hand, if the leadership concludes that Japan will be treated as a great and powerful nation only if it develops a nuclear force, then they will be sorely tempted to a move in that direction. Even so it would probably take some major jarring event—an international crisis in which China is seen to have used its nuclear capability successfully for blackmail purposes, or a major action by the United States ignoring Japanese interests and analogous to, but probably even stronger than, the Nixon shocks of 1971—to move Japan to develop nuclear weapons.

Given this context of Japanese attitudes towards a national nuclear force and the events which are likely to change those attitudes, SALT can be seen as having a relatively minimal effect. The SALT I agreements serve to underline Soviet equality with the United States in long-range strategic missiles. It is possible that the Japanese may come to appreciate that the United States has lost its strategic superiority and that it has accepted an interim agreement under which the Soviets have a larger number of strategic long-range missiles. They may then question whether the United States could and would be willing to use its deterrent capability to defend Japan against the Soviet Union or whether the Soviet Union would consider the American deterrent credible when used in defense of Japan.

The SALT I agreements could also raise questions about the continuing credibility of the American nuclear umbrella vis-à-vis China. The United States spent several years trying to explain to Japanese leaders why it was building an anti-China ABM system and why it considered such a system important to the credibility of the American deterrent capability in Asia. Now the United States has turned around and suggested that such a capability is not needed and that the American deterrent against China does not depend on a nationwide ABM system and the capability to deny damage to itself. Having raised the issue of an ABM and then not deployed it, the United States may find some Japanese who will doubt the credibility of the American deterrent vis-à-vis China.

A third way in which the SALT I agreements could affect Japanese thinking about the development of a nuclear capability is the impact that the agreements have on small nuclear forces. The ban on nationwide ABM systems in the Soviet Union and the United States makes more credible the small nuclear forces possessed by China, Britain, and France. The agreements seem to rest deterrence largely on the capability to inflict substantial damage and to suggest that differences in size of nuclear forces may be less important. These implications may convince some Japanese that the Chinese nuclear capability will be more credible against the United States and may, at the same time, make a Japanese nuclear force seem more feasible. Acting against these pressures, however, is the fact that the SALT I agreements, seeming to imply *détente* between the United States and the Soviet Union and part of a general feeling of *détente* in the world, make unnecessary the development of an independent Japanese nuclear force.

As was suggested above, the key variable affecting whether Japan decides to develop a nuclear capability is likely to be the state of U.S.-Japanese relations. It is therefore important to ask whether the SALT I agreements have had any adverse impact on those relations. Here, again one must emphasize that the impact has not been very great. SALT has not been a major issue or a major item of discussion between the United States and Japan. There appear to have been no negative or adverse consequences arising out of the negotiations of the SALT I agreements. From the beginning of the development of the U.S. position in 1968, the United States has fully consulted Japan at the same level and at the same intensity that it has consulted its NATO allies. Indeed, because the consultations were patterned after those with the NATO countries, who had a more direct interest particularly in forward-based systems, Japan has probably been given more opportunity to comment on the American SALT position than it required and than it felt technically capable of coping with.

Hence, there is no feeling within the Japanese government or among Japanese experts that the United States disregarded any Japanese interests in negotiating the SALT I agreements. Indeed, as far as most Japanese can see, no such interest seemed to be at stake.

Conclusion

Over the longer run, the impact of SALT on Asia will stem largely from its impact on Soviet-American relations. If it, in fact, is part of a larger process which changes the very nature of the way in which the Soviet Union and the United States look upon each other and if it generally brings about a rapprochement in Soviet-American relations, then the impact of SALT in Asia, as in the rest of the world, will be substantial.

Part 4

CHAPTER NINE
Future Limitations of Strategic Arms

George W. Rathjens

SALT II began in Geneva on November 21, 1972 with little press or public notice and with virtually no expressions of optimism about early agreement. There appears to have been little progress in the following months. Moreover, notwithstanding the subsequent setting of a 1974 target date for the negotiation of a permanent offensive forces agreement, there are reasons for pessimism about the likelihood of any early agreement of great significance.

First, there is little public and, as far as one can see, little governmental pressure in the U.S. or U.S.S.R. for additional or rapid progress on the limitation of strategic arms. The Soviets appear to be satisfied with SALT I and not to have a strong incentive to move further. While there is some public dissatisfaction in the U.S. with the results of SALT I, and the Nixon administration has stressed the need to reach additional comprehensive constraints, there is no indication the U.S. is ready to propose broad initiatives or seek early agreement.

Second, the easy work of SALT has been done. The negotiation of the ABM Treaty was a "cream skimming" operation facilitated by a combination of favorable conditions not likely to be repeated. The tougher problems, some of which surfaced in efforts to limit offensive forces, proved so intractable that they were handled in a temporizing way in the Interim Offensive Agreement, or not at all. It is these more difficult problems, and perhaps others not broached in SALT I, that will constitute the agenda for future negotiations.

Third, the legislative record on the American side—we have none at all in the case of the Soviet Union—is hardly encouraging. The Joint Chiefs of Staff insisted, in appearances before congressional committees and presumably within the councils of the administration, on certain "assurances" with regard to future programs as a price for their support. If taken literally and adhered to, they will limit greatly what the U.S. might propose and, as a result, what SALT II might accomplish. More widely noted has been the Jackson Amendment to the joint resolution approving the Interim Offensive Agreement, which

> urges and requests the President to seek a future treaty that, *inter alia,* would not limit the United States to levels of intercontinental strategic forces inferior to limits provided for the Soviet Union.

While reasonable on the surface, the passage of the amendment and Senator Jackson's oversight role, which the administration has apparently accepted or at least acquiesced in, foreshadow difficulties because U.S. demands for symmetry or equality in certain areas of strategic arms (numbers of launchers and throw weight) are not likely to be matched by U.S. willingness to accept equality or symmetry in others where it has advantage (notably in access to foreign bases and in the technology relevant to strategic arms).

Finally, Watergate has severely compromised President Nixon's ability to exercise effective leadership. This may prove doubly debilitating regarding SALT: On the one hand, his ability to get congressional support for military programs so that the U.S. can "bargain from strength" is diminished. On the other hand, those in Congress at the other end of the political spectrum, and perhaps especially those in his own party, will be much less inhibited in opposing arms control proposals that they regard as unwise. This will limit not only what the administration can get by the Senate but more importantly what it will propose in Geneva and how it will respond to Soviet initiatives.

But not all the auguries for SALT II are bad. Preliminary sparring need hardly be as time-consuming as it was in SALT I. Procedural arrangements have been established for dealing with problems at both the intra- and intergovernmental levels. In many respects Soviet-American relations are improved. The economic pressures in both countries to limit military expenditures are likely to be at least as strong as they have been over the last few years. And, there is a better understanding on both sides than there was at the beginning of SALT I of the forces and interests that determine the strategic arms policies of the two nations.

With these considerations in mind, there are grounds for optimism about solutions to those kinds of problems relating to strategic arms that have their bases in misunderstanding or failures of communication, but fewer grounds concerning those involving real conflicts of interest between the two powers or—for that matter—between pressure groups within each.

FRAMES OF REFERENCE FOR SALT II

Mutual Deterrence and Action-Reaction

Most American "defense intellectuals" have for the past decade argued that strategic arms policy should be based on the premise of the superiority of the offense over the defense, a view derived from the fact that societies are sufficiently fragile and nuclear weapons sufficiently powerful that defense of population and industry must, but cannot, be nearly 100 percent effective to be "successful." This view has led to the conclusion that a nation can have no realistic hope of limiting damage to itself to acceptable levels in a thermonuclear war with a determined and resourceful adversary. Therefore, the major rationale for strategic forces must be to deter attack by posing the threat of inflicting unacceptable damage in retaliation.

The second element of orthodoxy has been a belief in what Robert McNamara referred to as the action-reaction explanation of the strategic arms race.

Coupling the two beliefs leads to the conclusion that defense or damage-limiting efforts will prove hopeless and undesirable if the adversary has comparable resources. According to the action-reaction theory, any such efforts will be offset by adversary improvement in offensive capabilities. Because lead-times are long and performance of military systems, particularly damage-limiting systems, uncertain, decisions to improve offensive systems will often have to be made based on very imperfect knowledge of intentions and systems performance. Since prudence is likely to require one to assume a high level of performance of a prospective rival's systems but a moderate level of one's own, damage-limiting efforts, or even their possibility, are likely to trigger an overreaction. Thus, the imposition of constraints on damage-limiting systems is held to be an important arms control objective. The conclusion of the ABM Treaty is a testament to the persuasiveness of this line of argument, at least in the United States.

Events of the last few years, some associated with the SALT I agreements, have made it clear that the arms race cannot be so easily explained, nor prescriptions for its alleviation so confidently given, as the foregoing suggests. To the great disappointment of many of the strongest supporters of the ABM Treaty, its conclusion has not resulted in the noticeable slowdown in strategic offensive weapons programs that would have been expected according to the action-reaction theory. Even U.S. MIRV programs, which had been specifically rationalized as being required to penetrate possible Soviet ABM defenses, are proceeding without change. It has become increasingly clear that strategic weapons programs have the bases for their support in a multiplicty of interests and that, once underway, expedient and changing rationales will likely be used to sell them. Thus, MIRVs are now rationalized as being required for flexibility and the two major new offensive weapons programs, the B-1 bomber and the Trident SLBM, as bargaining chips for SALT II.

Bargaining Chips and Sufficiency

It can be expected that as SALT II develops, the orthodox views about superiority of the offense, the action-reaction phenomenon, and deterrence will play a part in the U.S. thinking and very likely in that of the Soviet Union as well. But it is now increasingly understood that the arms development and acquisition process is a far more complex one than a simple model based on these concepts would suggest, and that SALT II will reflect this complexity. What will happen will depend on the emphasis given to the acquisition of bargaining chips; on intragovernmental bargaining processes, including commitments made to get support for SALT I; on perceptions of the political utility of additional agreements and the willingness to initiate proposals; on the seriousness accorded the threat of a first strike; on the extent of concern about limiting damage the superpowers might suffer from attacks by lesser powers or weapons launched accidently; and a host of other factors.

Probably none will be of greater importance than perceptions of the role of strategic arms in world affairs. There have been widely divergent opinions about this, at least in the West, over the last twenty-five years, and there is considerable confusion at present. In the case of the United States, the confusion arises in part because presidential rhetoric has changed since the beginning of the Nixon administration, and because there has been a number of not easily reconcilable inconsistencies in statements and deeds.

A major source of confusion has been in the use of the term "sufficiency" as a criterion for measuring the adequacy of strategic forces. It was used at least as long ago as 1956 to suggest that in consideration of nuclear weapons employed against urban-industrial targets, saturation effects would set in at easily achievable levels, in contrast to the situation with conventional bombs. No useful purpose could be served by a build-up of nuclear weapons in excess of the numbers required to destroy adversary societies. An implication of the concept is that once both sides have "sufficient" strategic forces, neither ought to be particularly concerned if its adversary acquires more.

Early in his administration, President Nixon seemed to accept the concept as a basis for policy and was widely applauded for doing so. Thus, in his first "State of the World" message he observed:

> Formerly, any additional strength was strategically significant; today, available power threatens to outstrip rational objectives.

However, a number of subsequent events have made it clear that the president either was misinterpreted or changed his views. Presumably in an effort to clarify what he meant, he, in effect, redefined sufficiency in his second "State of the World" message:

> sufficiency has two meanings. In its narrow military sense it means enough force to inflict a level of damage on a potential aggressor sufficient to deter him from attacking. . . . In its broader political sense, sufficiency means the maintenance of forces adequate to prevent us and our allies from being coerced.

The second definition greatly expands the range of issues with respect to which strategic weapons have relevance. There are a number of additional examples that demonstrate the administration is certainly not prepared at this time to base its declaratory strategic policy on sufficiency as conventionally defined or, as the president would say, on "military sufficiency." For example there are statements that the U.S. must have strategic forces "second to none," and that with regard to technology, we must maintain superiority. Moreover, requests for additional funding of strategic programs indicate that whatever the declaratory policy, the administration's programs with respect to weapons development and acquisition is not consistent with a narrow or conventional definition of sufficiency.

It would seem reasonable to assume, then, that the American approach to SALT II will be from a competitive perspective despite denials of any intent to seek unilateral advantage. This will also be true of the Soviet Union, for there is not the slightest evidence that it accepts the concept of strategic sufficiency. "More" will be held to be better, and neither government will be disposed to accept agreements that would leave it in a position of overall inferiority as measured by numerical indicators of strength. One may, of course, do so, feeling that it simply cannot match the arms level threatened by the other. In this respect, both nations have advantages. The United States has a larger industrial base and superior technology. The Soviet Union is at a relative advantage in that there is substantial and fairly effective opposition in the U.S., presumably unmatched in the Soviet Union, to large new strategic programs—an opposition having its basis in disillusionment with all things military, following Vietnam; in concern that other national programs should command higher priority; in a discounting of the threat; and in a fairly widespread belief, albeit a minority one and one often poorly articulated, in the concept of strategic sufficiency as conventionally defined, or something very close to it.

With the possibility that one nation may have a net advantage in ability to sustain an arms race, any analysis of the prospects for SALT II ought probably to allow for the likelihood that any bargain finally arrived at will be a somewhat unbalanced one. However, in the belief that no agreement at all is a more likely outcome than a severely unbalanced one, it will generally be assumed in what follows that if an agreement permits advantages to one side, they must be offset by advantages for the other.

Although it is a thesis of this chapter that the primary concerns of the two nations with regard to strategic arms and SALT are similar—to maintain a position second to none—at a secondary level their interests may be somewhat different.

It is certain that much of the expressed U.S. concern about the vulnerability of its strategic forces to a first strike has been exaggerated if not disingenuous. A first-strike concern, like the bargaining chip argument, has been used to generate domestic support for various weapons programs, when the real bases for wanting them are to be found elsewhere: in domestic politics where issues of employment and the viability of large corporations have been at stake; in interservice rivalry; in the Parkinsonian tendency for bureaucracies to grow; and perhaps above all, in the simple belief that increased strategic strength is a politically or militarily exploitable commodity. Nevertheless, it is likely that concern about the vulnerability of American strategic forces to a first strike has been to some extent real and will be a factor of some importance in the future. This is likely, if for no other reason, because those who are really informed talk about it so much that others who are not knowledgeable, but are nevertheless influential, will be concerned.

It is even possible that in our preoccupation with a first strike we may reinforce such fears as there may be in the Soviet Union about the vulnerability of its strategic forces. There is a suggestion of this in reports that one of the consequences of SALT I may be an increase in Soviet interest in defense of its ICBM sites. However, it is likely that there has been less Soviet than American concern about a first strike in recent years and that there is less now. This may be, in part, a consequence of the U.S. not having initiated such a strike when it was closer to having the capability than it now does or is likely to have in the foreseeable future; and perhaps it is because Soviet thinking about nuclear war has not been as much affected as has that in the West by simple models of thermonuclear exchanges which convey impressions of first-strike feasibility that are much exaggerated.

Probable U.S. and U.S.S.R. Strategic Objectives

Whatever may be the reasons, if the judgments are correct, the U.S. approach to SALT II is quite likely to reflect a greater interest than will that of the U.S.S.R. in insuring for itself a near-certain capability under all contingencies of being able to deliver a devastating retaliatory blow following a first strike. This suggests that the U.S. is likely to be somewhat more interested in maintaining forces that have different kinds of vulnerability, a triad for example, while the U.S.S.R. is likely to be more interested simply in more "bang for a ruble."

It is probably also true that the U.S. will exhibit a greater interest than the Soviet Union in the possibility of using nuclear weapons with flexibility and discrimination—in what is sometimes referred to as a "war-fighting" role. Thus, it may place a higher premium on accuracy and timeliness of weapons delivery than does the U.S.S.R.

The latter, on the other hand, will be concerned about forces around its periphery—U.S., other NATO, and Chinese—for which there is no analogue as regards the U.S. Thus, the Soviet Union must be expected to raise the forward-based systems (FBS) problem in SALT II. Concerns about other nuclear powers, particularly China, may make some otherwise acceptable arms control measures unacceptable, particularly large force reductions.

THE QUESTION OF OFFENSIVE FORCE LEVELS

From an American perspective, the priority issue for SALT II will almost certainly be the replacement of the Interim Offensive Agreement with one that will be more acceptable in the long run. Two conceptual approaches are possible: one is based on symmetry and the ABM Treaty is an example. The other approach would permit the two adversaries advantages that are more or less offsetting. The Interim Offensive Agreement, of course, is an illustration. Under the agreement, Soviet superiority in numbers of ballistic-missile launchers is offset by American advantages in areas not covered by the agreement —MIRVs, bomber aircraft, and access to bases around the periphery of the U.S.S.R.

Complications in a Search for Strict Symmetry

The symmetric approach can itself involve two quite different alternatives: one would impose limits that are the same, or approximately so, for both sides on numbers of weapons systems of each type and on their qualitative characteristics; and the second would permit a "freedom to mix." A freedom to mix formula could involve specifying equal numbers of each of several kinds of delivery vehicles for the two sides, with a provision that some numbers could be increased if others were reduced. Alternatively, it could involve even greater flexibility, such as imposing some overall equal limit on strategic offensive forces of the two sides as measured in numbers of delivery vehicles, deliverable payload, numbers of deliverable warheads, or by some more complicated formula, while permitting flexibility as to the proportions of different kinds of delivery systems and warheads. The SALT I Interim Offensive Agreement is illustrative of a limited freedom to mix concept in that it permits, but does not require, the replacement of older ICBMs by modern SLBMs, in this case on a one-for-one basis.

While an approach to strategic arms limitation that is based on symmetry, with or without freedom to mix, has a certain appeal—the ABM Treaty was more easily achieved and has been much less criticized than the offensive forces agreements—an attempt to conclude a SALT II treaty based on rigorous symmetry of offensive strategic systems is bound to fail. The weapons systems possessed by the two sides will in no case be strictly equivalent. Soviet and American missile-launching submarines, even if they each carry missiles that are the same in number and similar in range and payload capability, will not be of identical value, considering that there will be a difference in the availability of bases from which they can operate, an asymmetry that can be rectified to a limited degree, at most, as a result of SALT II. And there are, of course, other significant asymmetries that cannot be affected at all by SALT II, including the facts that American population is more urbanized and that population and industry are more concentrated on or near the seacoasts than in the case of the U.S.S.R. Thus, the most that can be done is to strive for symmetry in specific areas or at least the appearance of it. For quieting public criticism and for political purposes, which may be the most important aims achieved at SALT, appearances may in fact be what matters most.

But even the appearance of symmetry will generally be more difficult to negotiate than the ABM experience suggests. Not only does the ABM Treaty permit essentially symmetric deployments, but in addition, and clearly a compelling factor, neither side had deployed an ABM system with significant capabilities, and the prospects for doing so were remote. The problem of matching what one side will give up or gain with the other's gains or sacrifices will be considerably more difficult in SALT II, and these problems are sure to arise. For example, even if it could be agreed that the intercontinental bomber inventories of the two nations should be the same, there would be the problem that the U.S. would have to give up more (or the Soviet Union acquire more) to reach the same level. In the competitive approach which will probably characterize SALT II, there would be a question of a suitable *quid pro quo*. It could involve the Soviet Union giving up ICBMs (or the U.S. acquiring more). In that case, there would be the issue in intragovernmental negotiations on the relative worth of the two kinds of delivery vehicles, and there would be difficult problems, including those of timing and linkage in negotiating trade-offs between the U.S. and the Soviets.

The problem of the relative worth or utility of different weapons systems would, of course, arise in any kind of a strategic offensive forces agreement other than a simple freeze or a freeze followed by proportionate reductions of all types of delivery systems. Thus, the specification of an overall limit on strategic offensive forces with freedom to mix could be quite complex, since none of the simple criteria referred to earlier (total payload, number of warheads, number of delivery vehicles) would likely be acceptable. Without offsetting concessions by the Soviets, the U.S. is unlikely to accept equating the SS-9 with a Minuteman, which would be implied if the measure were numbers of delivery vehicles. Both sides are unlikely to agree that heavy bombers, such as the B-52s, and large missiles, such as the SS-9, should be counted as the equivalent of dozens of small missiles such as the Minuteman or SS-11, as a simple payload criterion would imply. To make matters more complex, if either payload or numbers of warheads were the criterion, the relative worth would depend on range because of trade-off possibilities between range and payload with respect to bombers and sea-launched missiles. Finally, there is no indication from SALT I that Soviet negotiators would be willing to discuss these matters, let alone negotiate on this basis.

There is an additional difficulty in an approach to strategic arms limitation that attempts to achieve not only overall equality in force levels, but also an approximation of symmetry in numbers of each kind of delivery system for each side. The approach fails to reflect the different geopolitical situations of the two nations and that they have somewhat different interests and motivations with regard to the strategic arms race. In the jargon of game theory, the competition has important nonzero sum aspects, and striving for symmetry fails to take advantage of those features. An asymmetric approach, whether it be based on freedom to mix or otherwise, may permit one side to retain certain forces or move in certain directions that it considers desirable (and which may not be particularly troublesome to the other) without inducing the other to do so. Moreover, if one nation finds certain adversary programs or weapons particularly worrisome, it becomes reasonable to suggest that they be discontinued or scrapped without its necessarily making *identical* compensating moves.

Difficult as they may be, however, the problems of comparing weapons systems when the two nations value them differently are likely to be dwarfed by other asymmetries in their positions. From the narrow perspective of limiting offensive forces, the Soviet Union is clearly in a stronger position than the United States in that the terms of the Interim Offensive Agreement permit it a superiority of approximately 50 percent in numbers of ballistic-missile launching submarines, SLBMs, and ICBMs. In addition, the Soviets have an even greater superiority in payload deliverable with ICBMs. Accordingly, Soviet exploitation of MIRV technology would likely mean the ultimate attainment of a superiority in number of missile deliverable warheads as well. Thus, the U.S. bargaining position is a weak one, and its desire for a more "equitable" offensive forces agreement is not likely to be reciprocated by the U.S.S.R.

Possible Trade-offs or Concessions

Treating the offensive forces level issue in isolation is not a very hopeful approach. The Soviet Union is not likely to be willing to accept a reduction of its superiority in ICBMs unless the U.S. makes compensating concessions in other areas, and as long as one restricts one's purview to quantitative limits on offensive force levels, it is hard to see the *quid pro quo*. The U.S. could reduce its inventory of intercontinental bombers to near the Soviet level of 140 or so; and this might be done with little opposition from the U.S. Air Force if the residual force could be made up of B-1s to replace the aging B-52s. However, such U.S. reductions would hardly seem sufficient from the

Soviet perspective to justify its cutting its inventory of ICBMs to U.S. levels, particularly if this involved giving up the SS-9s as the U.S. would want.

Alternatively, a treaty might be negotiated that would permit an increase in U.S. force levels to something like those permitted the U.S.S.R. This would meet much of the criticism of the Interim Offensive Agreement and would be consistent with the criterion of the Jackson Amendment. There is, however, no apparent reason why the Soviet Union should favor such a treaty, even if it might be accepted in the U.S. as better than no follow-on to the present agreement. One of the very unfortunate features of such an arrangement is that it would increase the likelihood that each side would be induced to keep, or worse yet acquire, weapons or conduct programs which it otherwise might not. Public, bureaucratic, or other interests might argue that what can be done, must be done. This was the Joint Chiefs of Staff's response in June 1972 to the Interim Offensive Agreement. It is also illustrated by the response to the Limited Nuclear Test Ban Treaty of 1963. With underground tests being permitted by the treaty, the U.S. and, possibly, the Soviet Union conducted tests in excess of the numbers that would likely have been carried out if the treaty had never been negotiated. On the other hand, the ABM Treaty offers some hope in this regard. Symmetry was achieved by permitting each nation to build not only the kind of system on which it had started, but also the kind on which its adversary was working. Yet because of congressional opposition, it seems unlikely the U.S. will go ahead with an ABM defense of Washington, and it is possible that the Soviet Union may not go ahead with a second ABM site either. Still, an agreement that would permit a major escalation in force levels is hardly a very attractive SALT II objective.

One is driven then to look for concessions that the U.S. might make on issues other than strategic offensive force levels as a *quid pro quo* for a more "equitable" replacement for the Interim Offensive Agreement. Possibilities are suggested when one considers the advantages the U.S. has in other areas, notably in MIRV technology and in access to foreign bases.

A complete MIRV ban, which included removal of MIRVs already deployed on both the U.S. ICBM and SLBM forces and a complete prohibition on MIRV testing, seems so unrealistic as scarcely to merit comment. A less far-reaching agreement involving, for instance, constraints on MIRV testing, removal of MIRVs from Minutemen, a numerical limitation on MIRVs for SLBMs, and some reduction of SS-9, is a more likely alternative. However, the achievement of some such package would involve very difficult intragovernmental negotiating, at least in the United States.

Concession on the FBS problem, very likely coupled with reductions in intercontinental bombers, would seem a realistic possibility for the U.S. notwithstanding earlier U.S. arguments that SALT is an inappropriate forum for consideration of the FBS issue.

A still more remote kind of linkage—one involving economics—could also be important even if it is not explicitly considered. It is clear that the Soviet Union is greatly interested in securing the benefits of western technology and in improving its trading position with the West through agreements on credits, most-favored-nation treatment, and the export of natural resources. The Soviets might, as part of a much broader strategy of improving Soviet-American relations, accept terms in a strategic offensive forces agreement that would appear to involve some redressing of the "inequities" in the Interim Offensive Agreement.

In the longer term, there is at least one other approach to a treaty consistent with the Jackson Amendment. The possibility of the effective use of bargaining chips cannot be excluded if it becomes credible that with sufficient effort to whip up public concern about the Soviet threat, the administration could generate support for a substantial expansion in U.S. strategic weapons programs. If it then appeared likely that a two- or three-fold expansion in the Soviet budget for strategic arms would be required to stay in the race with us, the U.S.S.R. might, as an alternative, prefer to accept an agreement which would eliminate its numerical advantages. From the perspective of mid-1973, it seems doubtful that the Trident and B-1 programs as presently envisaged would be adequate inducements, and doubtful that still larger or additional strategic force programs could be sold to the public and the Congress unless there were a serious worsening of Soviet-American relations across a broad front.

Moreover, one must be mindful of the criticisms of the bargaining chip approach—that it may be more likely to stimulate an adversary's arms program than to produce agreement, and that a chip loses its value once it has been played.

There is one other theoretical possibility for an agreement being reached in a situation that, from a competitive perspective, seems to favor the U.S.S.R. It is conceivable that the concept of nuclear sufficiency in the narrower, military sense might acquire more support in the U.S., in which case a treaty permitting the Soviet Union superior strategic forces might be acceptable. However, in the absence of a reversal by the administration of its position, the chances appear remote. Certainly, general public and congressional support seems very unlikely at this time.

The Threat to Abrogate the ABM Treaty

No discussion of the prospects for offensive force level limitations would be complete without at least a word on the implications of a failure of negotiations, the more so in that the possibility has commanded some attention in discussions before congressional committees. The U.S. delegation at SALT I indicated that the Interim Offensive Agreement would be unsatisfactory to the U.S. as a basis for a permanent treaty and that failure to conclude a satisfactory replacement could lead to modification or abrogation of the ABM Treaty. Presumably, this might indicate a much heavier defense of Minuteman. Other new offensive programs as well, such as a land-mobile ICBM, might be initiated. Undoubtedly, if SALT II gets nowhere, pressures for such programs will develop. This will be particularly so if the Soviet Union flight tests and deploys highly accurate MIRVs that appear to make possible a successful first strike against the U.S. ICBM force (or if it develops other new weapons that appear to cast doubt on the continued adequacy of U.S. deterrent forces).

In fact, however, there will probably be little change in the directions in which the two nations are moving in the structuring of their strategic postures. Threats to the contrary notwithstanding, it is improbable that the Nixon administration would wish to see the ABM Treaty abrogated considering the undesirable political consequences and the unlikelihood that the Congress or the public would support a large ABM program. This means, in turn, that the threat of abrogation of the treaty is not likely to be a very effective means of putting pressure on the U.S.S.R. to conclude an offensive forces treaty more favorable to the U.S. than the Interim Offensive Agreement. In addition, there is really not much support in the U.S. for mobile landbased ICBMs.

REDUCTIONS IN STRATEGIC FORCES

While the major emphasis in SALT II, at least by the United States, is likely to be on producing an offensive force level treaty that appears more balanced than the Interim Offensive Agreement, attention ought to be given, and probably will be, to the possibility of significant reductions of strategic missile launchers.

In introducing a discussion of reductions, three preliminary remarks seem in order.

First, it is to be noted that the Interim Offensive Agreement notwithstanding, the number of warheads deliverable by the U.S. strategic force will increase by approximately a factor of 2 between 1973 and 1977 when the agreement runs out. The number of Soviet warheads deliverable may grow by as large a factor or even a larger one, depending on whether, and the extent to which, MIRVs are introduced into its missile forces. If strategic strength is measured, as it is sometimes argued it should be, by numbers of deliverable warheads, then a reversal in the build-up of strategic forces requires much more than the Interim Offensive Agreement or a freeze based on it.

Second, if reductions are to result in a significant diminution in the damage likely to result from a nuclear war, they will have to be great indeed. Because of what are commonly referred to as "overkill," "target saturation," or "diminishing return" effects, reductions on the order of 50 percent in numbers of weapons delivered against urban-industrial targets are likely to mean reductions of, at most, 10 to 15 percent in damage levels. Thus, while reductions of, say, 30 to 50 percent in force levels may be politically impressive, and depending on how taken, possibly productive of significant financial savings, they can hardly be characterized as radical or dramatic if the measure is damage-inflicting capability. This will especially be so if, during the period of reduction of missile launchers, the number of warheads deliverable per vehicle doubles.

Third, the two limiting constraints which have permeated discussion of "minimum deterrence" or other low limits on strategic arms, the *n*th country and verification problems, are not likely to be reached in SALT II or for some time thereafter. It is true that at some point Soviet concerns about Chinese and perhaps British and French nuclear capabilities would become an important consideration in limiting force levels, but even reductions by factors of as much as 5 or so would still leave the U.S.S.R. and the U.S. with strategic forces so large compared to those of other powers and, more importantly, so adequate in terms of their destructive capacity, that nth country-superpower relationships would not be changed significantly by the reductions. Cuts would likely have to be even deeper before there would be a basis for concern that evasions that might escape detection could be so significant as to upset the Soviet-American strategic balance. One is led, then, to conclude that reductions of 50 to 75 percent would be "safe" militarily.

There are, to say the least, impediments to reaching agreement on major reductions. The lower the levels of strategic arms, the more troublesome would be the first-strike problem. This is true for each of three components of the triad individually, and also for the feasibility of coordinating a first strike against all. And the lower the strategic offensive force levels become, the more troublesome would be the differences between the Soviet and American positions on the forward-based systems.

Moreover, there would be strong internal opposition, particularly from the military establishment, to reductions on a major scale. However, it could almost certainly be overcome by effective political leadership, particularly if there were no unfortunate events in the next few years that would reverse the improving trend in Soviet-American relationships. The possibility of such leadership on the American side seemed real in the immediate aftermath of President Nixon's landslide victory in 1972, especially in the light of his demonstrated flexibility and capacity for taking new initiatives, e.g., as regards the economy and China. However, the crippling effects of Watergate, noted earlier, now make a U.S. initiative for major reductions in force levels seem less realistic. The conservatism of the Soviet leadership and the fact that public opinion is less informed and less influential suggests that it is also unlikely that an initiative would come from that quarter, although this does not mean the Soviets would not be prepared to consider carefully a comprehensive proposal put forward by the U.S. which appeared to meet concerns of both.

In summary, the prospects for major reductions cannot be judged great. To the extent that possibilities do exist, they depend on the first-strike problem being discounted as something of an aberration, and on the FBS problem being either discounted or handled by agreement.

The next question is the form reductions might take. The two simplest schemes for evaluation and intergovernmental negotiation would be across-the-board cuts by some agreed percentage (equal percentage cuts for each class of ICBMs, each class of submarines, and each class of bombers), and reduction by both sides to equal residual force levels, with perhaps the freedom to mix being permitted.

A proposal for across-the-board reductions would encounter heavy going, particularly from military leaders who could be expected to favor preferential reductions for older systems and, in the case of each service, preferential retention of their own systems.

There would be merit from a broader perspective in the second proposal, reductions to equal residual force levels. However, particularly if flexibility in reductions were permitted, this approach raises the spectre of complex intra- and intergovernmental negotiations. However, if the U.S. and U.S.S.R. agreed on a basic approach to strategic offensive levels based on asymmetry, then the U.S. might favor preferential reductions for both sides in ICBMs because of first-strike concerns. Also, each nation might favor reducing its bombers preferentially because of the high cost of their maintenance and operation, because air defenses are not constrained by the ABM Treaty nor likely to be, and because the bombers are generally not as highly regarded as missiles as symbols of political-military strength.

THE FORWARD-BASED SYSTEMS PROBLEM

Not surprisingly, the question of U.S. and allied nuclear-capable forces deployed around the periphery of the Soviet Union was troublesome to SALT I, and it cannot be brushed aside in SALT II. Even if the FBS issue is never explicitly on the agenda, the asymmetry involved will have a bearing on the resolution of issues that are discussed.

It is an awkward problem for there is persuasiveness in the position of both sides. The Soviets contend that the forces involved and U.S. access to European bases enhance the American potential to deliver nuclear weapons against the U.S.S.R. and that, therefore, the FBS issue is appropriate for SALT. The U.S. claims that FBS should be treated in another forum since the primary mission of the forces involved is not to deliver nuclear weapons against the U.S.S.R., and since the interests and, in some cases, the forces of other nations are very directly involved.

The Conference on Security and Cooperation in Europe (CSCE) and the discussions on mutual and balanced force reductions (MBFR) provide opportunities for solutions consistent with the American position; and it is, in principle, possible that agreements might be reached in these or other forums that would meet some of the Soviet concerns. These might be agreements that could appear advantageous to the Soviet Union if considered in isolation, but they might be balanced by Soviet concessions in a SALT II agreement.

There are other reasons for at least limited optimism about the FBS issue. From the narrow perspective of the Soviet-American strategic balance, the problem is likely to be one of diminishing importance. If one excludes the French force de frappe, the forces that can strike the U.S.S.R. from European bases and the waters near it are not growing, while the true intercontinental capabilities of the two superpowers regrettably are. Therefore, the FBS component, which even now is small in a relative sense, will decline in importance within the total array of forces of concern to the Soviet Union. Secondly, as Trident missiles replace Polaris-Poseidon missiles, the importance of basing submarines in Scotland and Spain (and also Guam) will diminish. In this connection, the Nixon administration proposed in March 1973 that Trident submarines be homeported in the state of Washington. (It may be more than happenstance that this is Senator Jackson's home state.)

Consideration of these points leads to the following conclusions. First, if the Soviet Union presses very hard on the FBS issue in SALT II, it ought to be regarded as partly a matter of posturing—as an excuse to avoid reaching agreements in various areas with which the issue might be linked; as a bargaining manuever; or as some combination of the two. Second, the U.S. could agree to some changes, such as concessions on European basing of missile-launching submarines and perhaps longer-range "tactical" bombers, with very little adverse effect on its military capabilities. This is an obvious example of an area where the nonzero sum aspects of the Soviet-American confrontation come into play. The costs to the U.S. would be small *if* the moves could be handled in a way not to produce adverse political effects in Western Europe, admittedly, in the view of many, a rather big "if." The advantages might appear rather large to the Soviet Union due to its historical concern about encirclement, a concern that may still be strong despite the diminished military relevance of the question.

CONSTRAINTS ON DEFENSIVE SYSTEMS

To those who believe in the action-reaction theory of the arms race and that the best hope for security, at least in the near term, is in the maintenance of adequate deterrent or assured destruction forces, the idea of imposing constraints on the development, testing, and deployment of defensive or damage-limiting systems has had great appeal. As noted earlier, the ABM Treaty is a testament to that belief.

Although somewhat tarnished by the failure, so far, of that treaty to slow offensive programs, belief in the desirability of imposing constraints on defensive systems continues, particularly among those who view the strategic balance as fragile or who are otherwise concerned about the first-strike problem. In the last year or so, this has been manifest particularly in proposals in favor of certain limitations on anti-submarine warfare (ASW), the main argument being that such limitations might lessen concern about the possible vulnerability of missile-launching submarines to preemptive attack. It seems likely, then, that limitations on defensive systems will command at least some attention in SALT II (or III or IV).

Zero ABM

In a way, the most obvious and easily negotiable defensive agreement would be with respect to ABM systems. There has developed substantial sentiment, reflected, for example, in the U.S. congressional hearings on the SALT I agreements, that the levels of ABM deployment permitted by the treaty are so small as to be militarily meaningless. That being the case, there would seem to be merit in modifying the ABM Treaty to require the dismantling of the ABM systems so far deployed and to prohibit any further deployment. Three advantages have been suggested. There would be financial savings; there would be some further reduction in concern about the possibility that a large-scale ABM defense might be deployed at a later date; and there would be some political-psychological advantage since the move would involve some actual disarmament. The first and second advantages would also apply, albeit to a lesser degree, to an agreement to prohibit deployment of a second ABM site in each country. The third would, or course, not.

Since the Congress refused to appropriate funds for an ABM defense of Washington in the summer of 1972 and the administration did not seek funds in the budget submitted the following January, it would appear clearly to be in the U.S. interest to limit ABM deployment to one site each. But in the light of these events, the U.S. bargaining position is very weak, and the administration is likely to be unwilling to make concessions with respect to other than ABM questions to secure Soviet agreement to forego a second site. Certainly any with regard to offensive systems would seem improbable considering both the Jackson reaction to the Interim Offensive Agreement and the compliant attitude of the administration. There are also arguments against reopening the zero-level ABM issue, each of which by itself might be decisive.

There will probably be a great deal of sentiment for leaving well enough alone, at least until the first periodic treaty review in 1977. Neither government is likely to want to expend much political capital to obtain intragovernmental consensus on a zero-level agreement, and reopening the issue in Geneva might appear to be a diversion from issues that each side would regard as having higher priority. In the case of the United States, for example, rectification of the Interim Offensive Agreement would clearly have a higher priority.

The second argument against agreeing on a zero-level position is that the limited deployments permitted by the treaty may, at least in the eyes of some, have military utility. It can be argued that the Soviet NCA deployment may be worth keeping as a defense against Chinese missiles. And the U.S. deployment at Grand Forks, particularly if additional radars were deployed as permitted, might be of some effectiveness in making a first strike against the Minuteman force less credible. This would be particularly germane in the unlikely event that agreement could be reached requiring drastic reductions in offensive missiles.*

ASW Constraints

Putting ABM aside, the other interesting possibilities for constraints on defensive systems are with respect to antisumbarine warfare (ASW) and, to a lesser degree, air defenses. In a number of respects the negotiation of constraints on ASW activity is a more complex problem than limiting ABM systems.

The Soviet Union and the United States could treat the ABM question as strictly a bilateral one, no other nations having deployed such systems and none being in prospect. Even were other nations to develop and deploy ABMs, the ability of the U.S. and the Soviet Union to inflict damage on each other would not be affected. With ASW, the situation is very different. Virtually all navies have some limited ASW capability. For many, including notably those of the smaller NATO powers, it is their principal mission. These forces could be employed against Soviet submarines, considering the egress routes for the latter from their bases, with the exception of those on mid-ocean

---

* There has been so much emphasis during the past few years on the ineffectiveness of ABM defense that it is perhaps worth presenting a simplified quantitative illustration to make the point that under certain circumstances even quite limited defenses could be of some effectiveness. Assume for the moment that an agreement were reached permitting each side to deploy only, say, 200 ICBMs and that the Soviet Union, even with MIRVs, were capable of delivering only, say, 500 warheads in a first strike. Given high accuracy and reliability for the Soviet warheads, virtually the entire U.S. force of 200 could be wiped out in the absence of an ABM defense. But with Safeguard there exists the possibility of a "preferential" defense: the U.S. could elect to defend, say, 25 of its ICBMs. With 100 interceptors allowed by the treaty, this would permit the allocation of four interceptors per silo to be defended. But the attacker, not knowing which particular 25 out of, say, 100 possible silos would be defended, would have to allocate several warheads—perhaps as many as 5, depending on his estimate of interceptor effectiveness—to each defended silo in order to have a reasonable chance of destroying it. In such a hypothesized situation—and recognizing that at least 100 of the attacker's warheads would be employed against the 100 silos not covered by defenses—at least 25, and perhaps 50 or more, U.S. Minuteman missiles could be expected to survive. The attacker could do better by targeting some of his warheads on defending interceptor missile launchers or possibly the ABM radars, depending on their numbers, but even in that case a few Minutemen could be expected to survive assuming reasonable defensive tactics. In any case, the Soviet Union could not count on their being destroyed.

patrol. Thus, there is a possibility that the Soviet Union or, less likely, the U.S. would insist on limitations being applied to the navies of nations other than the superpowers. That this would be the Soviet position is suggested by its demand that the British and French missile-launching submarines be taken into account in considering the Interim Offensive Agreement.

More importantly, there is a great difference in internal support for ABM and ASW programs, at least in the United States. The former had little constituency beyond research and development circles. ASW is, on the other hand, big business, at least in the U.S. Navy and for the industry involved. Thus, efforts to limit such activity would encounter much more internal opposition than was evident in the case of the ABM Treaty.

That being the case, the necessary domestic support for limitations could probably be mobilized only with a vigorous campaign to cast doubt on the continued viability of the sea-based deterrent. Success with such a campaign and the development of domestic support for ASW based on it could be achieved, if at all, only by greatly exaggerating the threat. Limitations on ASW might be the result. However, it is much more likely that the consequences of such a campaign would be unwarranted concern about a first strike with a consequent diversion of attention from more serious threats to security, an exacerbation of international tensions, and acceleration and expansion of a variety of unnecessary offensive programs.

The problem of limiting ASW is particularly complicated because of the fact that nearly all of the effort in the field is directed not at the destruction of missile-launching submarines, but rather at the protection of merchant shipping and surface warships from attack submarines. There is virtually no support at present in the U.S. for reducing capabilities to deal with these latter threats except by economizers who have doubts about ASW effectiveness. In fact, the ASW budget is increasing.

To the extent that there are realistic possibilities for reducing the ASW threat to missile-launching submarines, then, they are to be found in measures that would not adversely affect, to any significant degree, capabilities for protecting surface ships. Identification of such measures is difficult enough, but the challenge is a more exacting one. The Soviet interest in a protracted war at sea would presumably be not so much in conducting ASW as in using submarines to attack U.S. and allied surface ships. Measures to preserve the viability of sea-based deterrent forces would likely be nonnegotiable if they severely reduced Soviet abilities to carry out that mission. This constraint further limits the kind of measures that might realistically be considered at SALT II, particularly with regard to limitations on attack submarines—the systems that are likely to have the greatest capability of destroying missile-launching submarines with something approaching the degree of simultaneity required in a first strike.

The situation is not, however, a hopeless one on technical grounds. One could envisage the negotiation of limits on numbers of high-speed, nuclear-powered attack submarines—the only ones that could trail the missile launchers—without limits being imposed on conventionally-powered, or lower-speed, nuclear-powered attack submarines or on other kinds of equipment useful for ASW in a long war, such as aircraft, helicopters, and mines. And one can envisage prohibitions on trailing and agreements defining sanctuaries in which ASW activity by the superpowers would not be carried out. Measures of the latter kind would be of some utility in allaying concerns about a first strike as long as they were honored. But since changes in force structure require years, neither nation could prudently structure its SLBM force on the assumption that such agreements would never be violated or abrogated.

There is still one other impediment to negotiating constraints on ASW and on attack submarines. It is in the fact that the U.S. has an enormous lead over the U.S.S.R. in virtually all relevant areas except in numbers of diesel-powered attack submarines (which would not likely be subject to limitation). This lead derives from a combination of geographical advantage, operational experience, and more advanced technology. Under the circumstances, the Soviet Union would probably resist limitations, particularly on development, that would have the effect of freezing it in a position of inferiority. On the other side, the U.S. would not be likely to accept limitations, particularly those relating to operations or the exploitation of developed technology, because it would be giving up more than the U.S.S.R. The failure to achieve limitations on MIRVs in SALT I provides an analogy. The Soviet Union appeared to be uninterested in constraints on development and the U.S. in limiting deployment.

In conclusion, there may be some discussion at SALT II of limiting naval activities so that there will be less of a threat to missile-launching submarines. This would likely raise concerns about such a threat that are presently unjustified and from that there might follow a number of consequences that would be counterproductive from an arms control perspective. Moreover, agreement seems unlikely in SALT II because of the powerful forces that would oppose limiting traditional kinds of naval operations and because of the difficulty of identifying measures that would not do so, but which would make missile-launching submarines less vulnerable. The best direction seems to lie in limits on numbers of high-speed, nuclear-powered attack submarines.

Air Defense Systems

The possibilities for limiting air defenses are scarcely more promising. In the U.S.S.R., there are powerful constituencies for maintaining such defenses, and there is a great overlap between the kinds of equipment for continental defense in a central Soviet-American war and the kinds required for other scenarios. Also, there would be problems of verification of compliance with respect to limitations on some items of importance—notably guns and mobile SAM systems. Finally, the asymmetries are very great. Since the Soviet investment in air defense is very much greater than the American investment, large American concessions in other areas would likely be required if there were to be major reductions or other limitations on air defenses.

Constraining the Qualitative Arms Race

General Constraints on Research and Development

Critics of SALT I have argued that the agreements reached have resulted in a channeling of the strategic arms race into new dimensions rather than in its effective limitation, citing the fact that, at least in the U.S., the budget for offensive strategic arms is projected to increase. In both nations, new programs seem to be going ahead with little evidence of any new restraint. Claims of political and military leaders that there must be vigorous weapons programs in areas not proscribed, such as the Joint Chiefs, demand that there be an "assurance" that the nation "maximize strategic capabilities within the constraints established by the ABM Treaty and the Interim Offensive Agreement," also suggest that the issues of development and qualitative changes in weaponry must be faced if there is to be any dramatic slowdown of the strategic arms race.

In addition, many of SALT I's vigorous supporters also argue that limiting development is the next great arms control challenge. Those who have been concerned about the delicacy of the strategic balance have argued that limiting development should command higher priority than further limits on force levels or reductions because it is much more likely that the stability of the balance will be adversely affected by qualitative change than by changes in numbers.

But, however strong the case may be for slowing technological change, it will be difficult. Verification is one problem. It remains a widely held belief in the United States that without much greater access to the Soviet Union than is now possible, or in the near future likely, there will be substantial uncertainty about what is going on in its militarily related research and development facilities. With respect to some limitations on weapons development, notably biological agents, it has been accepted that the risk of noncompliance that might go undiscovered is more than offset by the benefits of constraining agreements. However, a more cautious approach prevails with regard to nuclear weapons and strategic delivery systems. This means that for the present, the only limitations on strategic arms development that are likely to be acceptable are those on certain kinds of tests that can be monitored with some effectiveness with various remote sensors.

Comprehensive Nuclear Test Ban

The most significant precedent is in the Limited Test Ban Treaty which prohibits testing of nuclear weapons except underground. Although in a formal sense the possibility of its extension to include a prohibition on all nuclear tests perhaps ought not to be characterized as a SALT issue, it is a matter of current interest. Discussion is in order, particularly as the military significance and acceptability of a comprehensive nuclear test ban treaty is related to the resolution of other SALT questions. Moreover, the problems of attaining agreement on such a treaty are in large measure bilateral since most other present or potential nuclear powers, France and China probably excepted, can be expected to go along with whatever the U.S. and the U.S.S.R. can agree to.

In a number of respects the situation has changed to make the prospects for a comprehensive nuclear test ban agreement more favorable than when the issue last commanded the serious attention of the two superpowers a decade ago. In particular, as discussed in Chapter 6, technical capabilities to detect and to identify nuclear explosions have improved.

At issue, then, is the question of whether a few tests in the low kiloton range that might be conducted clandestinely by one nation could give it any significant military advantage. If strategic military criteria are used as the basis for evaluation, the answer is "no," at least with regard to the Soviet-American military balance. By now, nuclear weapons design is a fairly mature technology, and accordingly, each additional weapons test is likely to result in only marginal improvements in weapons design. The opportunities for changing the character of weapons inventories are probably greatest with tactical nuclear weapons, but without credible concepts regarding the use of such weapons, it is hard to argue that modest superiority in design or effects knowledge would have much military utility. With strategic weapons, the interest in the low yield end of the spectrum is diminished by the proscription of large-scale ABM defense by the ABM Treaty. A MIRV deployment ban would further reduce the case for additional weapons tests. In any case, the marginal advantage either side could realize through a few clandestine tests would be swamped in the sea of other asymmetries and uncertainties that characterize strategic postures.

If the marginal utility of carrying out additional underground nuclear tests is so low, the question might well be asked, "Why bother with trying to prohibit them?" The answer is in the favorable political-psychological effects that might result and in the fact that a comprehensive test ban agreement would be one more impediment to nuclear proliferation, particularly if some nations which had not ratified the Non-Proliferation Treaty were willing to subscribe to it.

There are ancillary arguments that might be advanced for the U.S.'s, and particularly the Soviet Union's, not favoring a comprehensive test ban at this time. The first is that China and France would be unlikely to accede to the treaty. And secondly, there are claims that peaceful nuclear explosives (Plowshare devices) are important enough economically so that they should not be foresworn; that Plowshare requires further development; and that such development will provide an opportunity for testing devices, the primary purpose of which may be military.

The first argument hardly seems like a valid one on military grounds since there is no case for U.S. or Soviet weapons tests being in any way influenced by the French and Chinese programs, nor is there likely to be for many years.

The Plowshare issue may be a more immediate problem, but it is hardly new. In the early 1960s various schemes were proposed for permitting the peaceful use of nuclear explosions in the context of a comprehensive nuclear test ban treaty, and it is conceivable that an arrangement permitting them could be worked out if a determination were made that the economic potential was very great. There is, however, considerable sentiment that it is not sufficient to justify interference with the conclusion of a comprehensive test ban. This is particularly the case in the United States where interest has diminished in peaceful nuclear explosions for most purposes, a possible exception being for exploitation of natural gas deposits.

There is, of course, a possibility—indeed a likelihood—that the Chinese, French, and peaceful uses arguments and also a claim of the necessity for onsite inspections will be made in intragovernmental negotiations by those opposed to a test ban for other reasons. And either government may make the arguments at the international level if it does not want an agreement. However, such arguments should be regarded more as excuses than as reasons.

A Missile Test Ban or Limitations on Tests

If one turns to weapons test limitations that might have more effect on strategic capabilities, the prospects for agreement are poorer. A major difficulty is the insistence that the U.S. maintain superiority in the relevant technology, a point highlighted in the assurances demanded by the Joint Chiefs as a condition for their support of the SALT I agreements but also reiterated by other administration witnesses. Such superiority is rationalized as being necessary to offset the advantages of secrecy imputed to the U.S.S.R. However, there is not the slightest reason to believe that the Soviets will accept the U.S. position. Thus there is a conflict that would seem, in general terms, to be irreconcilable. Nevertheless, some progress can perhaps be made without the U.S. abandoning its insistence on overall technological superiority, if attention is limited to selected areas where the differences in capabilities of the two adversaries are small or offsetting, of which the nuclear test ban treaty, previously discussed, is illustrative.

The most interesting prospect on the SALT horizon is the limitation of tests of long-range ballistic missiles. The technology involved is one where there are large asymmetries, the Soviet Union having an ability to deliver much larger payloads and the U.S. having a substantial lead in MIRV technology and accuracy of delivery. However, it can be argued that the advantages are offsetting, or soon will be, in view of the Soviet Union's recent MIRV test.

Two kinds of limitations are of interest: on numbers of test firings and on the kinds of rockets and reentry vehicles that can be tested. A particularly interesting kind of agreement would limit numbers of test firings to some low annual quota and also prohibit the testing of rockets and reentry vehicles of types not already tested by some cutoff date. In order to permit satellite and other space launches, exceptions to both kinds of limitations would presumably be required. It is likely that such exceptions could be managed with a very low likelihood that they could be exploited for weapons development.

Compliance with a missile test ban could be monitored with high confidence using remote sensors, especially if it could be agreed that reentry would occur only in certain areas easily accessible to observation. If the quota of firings were low enough—perhaps a dozen per year—such an agreement would greatly slow down the development of missile technology. It could have the particularly attractive quality of reducing concerns about a first strike against fixed land-based ICBMs. In this connection, it is to be noted that high reliability, adequate accuracy taking into account warhead yield, and great confidence in both are required for such a first-strike capability. Attainment of a capability to deliver warheads from a single rocket to separate targets may be a further requirement. It is widely believed that without limits on testing both the U.S. and the U.S.S.R. could have forces that would fulfill the requirements for such a first-strike capability in the not-too-distant future. However, severe limits on testing could extend the period greatly and perhaps indefinitely.

To the extent that there is real concern about the first-strike problem, such limitations would seem attractive. They, or more likely some variant, will possibly receive attention in SALT II, at least at the intragovernmental levels. However, the prospects for agreement are not good. The Soviet Union would almost certainly not agree to significant constraints before it has made and demonstrated substantial progress on MIRVs. Moreover, the U.S.S.R. may never feel sufficiently concerned about a U.S. first strike to be strongly moved to reach agreement. On the U.S. side, one must expect great resistance from the military services to limitations which would slow progress or reduce confidence in the systems for which they are responsible. The resistence is already foreshadowed in the third SALT I Joint Chiefs' "assurance" which calls for "continue[d] testing to insure the effectiveness of new and existing nuclear weapons systems."

Timing and the Prospects for a SALT II Agreement

There is much to suggest that the U.S. and U.S.S.R. will be approaching SALT II rather differently.

There is a widespread American belief that the Interim Offensive Agreement ought not simply to be extended and that, in particular, a treaty of indefinite duration should be negotiated which would limit the numbers of Soviet missiles and the payloads they can carry to much lower levels. Unless there is movement toward acceptance of the restrictive, or military, concept of strategic sufficiency, the pressure for rectification of the Interim Offensive Agreement is likely to increase with time, in the immediate future because of the commitment to early agreement announced in June 1973, and then with greater intensity as the end of the five-year time limit approaches. The pressure will also intensify if the Soviet Union extensively tests MIRVs and begins to deploy them on their missiles. Additionally, the approach of the end of the second Nixon administration may well result in an increasing interest in conclusion of an offensive force levels treaty and possibly other strategic arms limitations agreements. The president is likely to want to leave behind further agreements as a legacy of his tenure in office. Thus, the pressure on the American negotiators in Geneva, until now small, is likely to increase substantially in the years ahead.

In sharp contrast with the American case, there is little if any evidence of any significant degree of dissatisfaction in the U.S.S.R. with the results of SALT I. Hence, a sense of urgency and intensifying pressure from the Soviet side seems unlikely in SALT II notwithstanding its concurrence in specifying 1974 as a target for revision of the Interim Offensive Agreement. The blunt fact is that the Soviet Union now appears to be in a better bargaining position than the U.S. for SALT II, and with time, its position is likely to improve further. To get a satisfactory offensive forces treaty, the U.S. will have to make significant concessions in other areas. With such concessions not being obvious at this time, a significant early agreement seems unlikely.

The negotiations are likely, then, to fill the time available, that is, between now and 1976, and there is no certainty that agreement will be reached even then. Given the apparent Soviet unwillingness to discuss some highly technical matters, and also the fact that many on the Soviet SALT delegation do not have access to the information, the problem of conducting meaningful negotiations and reducing agreement in principle to treaty language will probably be difficult and slow. Recent major changes in key personnel on the U.S. side will also likely be a delaying factor. More fundamentally, it is becoming increasingly clear that U.S. thinking on the broad questions of the role of nuclear arms and the objectives of arms control is in a state of flux, both within the administration and outside it. Until something of a consensus jells on such issues, in particular questions of flexibility, sufficiency, and the acceptability of a policy based on perpetuating the balance of terror, it will be very difficult to make progress. Negotiations may move more slowly than attitudes change. Meanwhile, the arms race is likely to go on with the initiation of new weapons programs which in fact may turn out to be nonnegotiable bargaining chips as they acquire momentum and constituencies for their continuance.

There are possibilities of a reversal of that trend.

Explicit acceptance of the idea of strategic sufficiency, in the narrow sense, and an approach to SALT based on it is one, albeit a remote one. Were such a change to occur, there would be little concern about agreements being equal, and the strategic arms issue would be treated more as a disease than as a race.

Another radical alternative would be negotiation of agreements for such drastic reductions or restraints that the absolute advantage to both powers would be great enough to overcome the fact that one was giving up somewhat more than the other. To achieve an agreement along such lines would require overriding the interests of powerful pressure groups. It now seems unlikely that that will occur: unlikely in the case of the United States because President Nixon is in a poor position to initiate or defend such an approach, even had he the inclination; and unlikely in the case of the U.S.S.R. because it has probably already achieved most of what it can reasonably expect out of SALT—a recognition of parity in strategic strength.

Actually, in the present circumstances, the best hope for a reversal in the strategic arms race may lie in unilateral decisions by either or both of the superpowers simply to cut back on its efforts. Competition for resources could be an important factor for both nations. In addition, public apathy could be important in the case of the United States.

One is led finally then to view SALT II with mixed feelings. Four lines of development are possible: (1) agreement could be reached that would involve major reductions or drastic constraints on weapon programs; (2) the negotiations could drag on for some time producing occasional agreements of limited value; (3) they could degenerate into formalistic efforts—the Conference of the Committee on Disarmament (the CCD) provides a model; or (4) the efforts could be terminated.

Of these, the second or the third seems most probable. They carry with them the unfortunate possibility that bargaining, both intra- and intergovernmental, may result in otherwise unneeded weapons programs. This is particularly likely in the event of the second course, and in that case, the disadvantages of the negotiating process could more than offset whatever benefits there may be in the agreements reached. A judgment about SALT II must weigh that possibility against the hope that really substantial agreements might be reached by negotiation.

It is by no means certain that such moves could lead to agreement. However, a proposal that would result in significant economic savings might appeal to the U.S.S.R. Moreover, the adverse effects of the accumulation of bargaining chips in the next few years may be so severe that SALT II would be judged by many as a counterproductive effort unless rather dramatic agreements are achieved. There is, then, a case for approaching SALT II with the intent of negotiating large reductions and severe constraints on military programs rather than with the expectation of merely rectifying the Interim Offensive Agreement and improving the political climate.

CHAPTER TEN
SALT I: An Appraisal
Mason Willrich

The appraisal of any recent event is always a perilous task. The harsh light of hindsight may soon expose an error in judgment. But SALT does have many meanings, and we must do our best to discover them.

The central meaning of SALT is political. In an overall appraisal of SALT, an enormous array of diverse military, economic, technical, and psychological factors must be filtered through a political lens. In so doing, the light from each factor is diffused and the images become blurred, but the impression one gains is closer to reality.

UNDERLYING FACTORS

The history of Soviet-American diplomacy in the arms control field is replete with postponed negotiations, aborted agreements, and vacuous Summit meetings. Why, then, did SALT I succeed? President Nixon gave Chairman Brezhnev ample provocation for cancelling the 1972 Moscow Summit when he directed the mining of Haiphong Harbor and escalation of the bombing of North Vietnam. Either side in the SALT negotiations could have slowed the pace to make a major agreement impossible prior to the 1972 U.S. elections. Even after Nixon landed in Moscow, either side could have delayed agreement beyond the Summit meeting merely by standing firm on its existing positions during the final hectic negotiating sessions.

Five factors were essential to the successful outcome of SALT I: the mutual interest of the United States and the Soviet Union in preventing nuclear war; the relationship of rough equality or parity between their strategic nuclear forces; the capability of verification of force levels on both sides; the movement that had occurred toward settlement of the German question; and the determination of strong political leaders on both sides to reach agreement. Though each of these factors was necessary, none would have been sufficient by itself to bring about SALT I.

Prevention of Nuclear War

The United States and the Soviet Union have not always fully shared an interest in the prevention of nuclear war. Their mutuality of interest in this respect evolved out of the nuclear arms race itself, and it took many years for the common ground to be widely recognized and accepted by the two adversaries as the basis for agreement.

The use of nuclear weapons against Japan in 1945, which brought World War II to a rapid end in the Far East, made clear to people everywhere the disastrous consequences if mankind failed to prevent this particular kind of violence in the future. In the wake of the defeat of Nazi Germany, it soon became equally clear that the United States and the Soviet Union were on a collision course in protecting or pursuing their respective interests in Europe. Thus, the development and deployment of nuclear armaments were perceived, paradoxically, both as a way to keep the Cold War from turning hot, and as a way to win it. Because of their unprecedented destructive power, nuclear weapons became both a result and a cause of grave international mistrust, tension, and hostility.

In the United States and in Western Europe, possession of a wide margin of U.S. superiority over the Soviet Union in nuclear arms was widely believed to be the strategic foundation for NATO. The American nuclear threat kept Soviet armies from breaching the Iron Curtain and, in particular, kept Soviet tanks from rolling through the Brandenburg Gate into West Berlin, a city which endured year after year of the Cold War as a living symbol of Western freedom and galling proof of Soviet weakness.

But the Soviet leaders knew the source of their military inferiority and found that there was only one way to correct it. The Soviet government began without hesitation to develop its own nuclear arsenal, despite the large appropriation of resources that would otherwise have been available for the development of civilian industry and the production of consumer goods. The Soviet Union achieved the capability of launching a nuclear attack first with bombers, then with IRBMs and MRBMs against West European members of NATO, then with ICBMs against the United States.

Nuclear deterrence became mutual when neither side could launch a nuclear attack against the other without nuclear devastation of its own society in return. The security of the two superpowers became increasingly interdependent, and the prevention of nuclear war was henceforth an imperative in Soviet-American relations.

Functional Strategic Equality

In 1945 it was generally recognized that the American possession of a monopoly of nuclear weapons was a temporary condition. The choice was between an agreement on international control over the development of nuclear energy to be followed by destruction of the American nuclear stockpile and a nuclear arms race that would pit the Cold War adversaries against each other.

The arms race soon became the main battle in the Cold War. Top scientific and engineering brainpower was deeply engaged on both sides. Nuclear weapon and strategic delivery systems chased each other through successive generations of technology, while strategic doctrine adapted as best it could. The relentless development and exploitation of technological options by the two adversaries imparted a momentum to the arms race that was irresistible for many years.

Though pursuing a quite different development path in a different time sequence, the Soviet Union gradually cut into the U.S. margin of nuclear superiority. After the first Soviet test of an H-bomb in 1952, which followed the first U.S. H-bomb test by only a few months, American leaders gradually and grudgingly began to accept the idea that U.S. nuclear superiority was an asset that would probably diminish in value with time. The idea was apparently harder for military leaders and strategic planners to accept than some political leaders, for President Eisenhower clearly foresaw the approaching nuclear stalemate in his Atoms for Peace address in December 1953. The United States could prolong its possession of superiority by a vigorous research, development, and production program, but whether the Soviet Union would ultimately achieve strategic nuclear parity with the United

States was a condition primarily within the control of the Soviet leaders and dependent on their will and determination.

There are three main reasons for this situation. The first is found in the nature of science and technology. The scientific principles governing matter and energy await discovery and application by any man or group of men. Moreover, once a technology has been rather fully developed, a law of diminishing returns applies, and successive improvements usually tend to become more costly while resulting gains in efficiency may be less. The possibility of a breakthrough always exists, but, if exploited, this implies the running of a different technological race. Second, both the United States and the Soviet Union have ample natural resources and scientific skills to devote to the development of strategic nuclear forces, even though the costs of doing so are very high. And, third, nuclear weapons are so destructive that, assuming a perfect defense is impossible, differences between the two sides in deliverable megatonnage eventually become quite meaningless, though when such numerical levels of destructive capability are reached can be the subject of endless debate among technicians.

The determination of successive Soviet political leaders since World War II to achieve a relationship of strategic equality with the United States cannot be doubted. In fact, some of the critics of SALT I argue that Soviet willingness to settle for nuclear parity remains very much an open question even now, while supporters of the agreements argue that SALT I will prevent the Soviet strategic force levels from surging substantially ahead of the United States'.

Had Khrushchev's attempt to install intermediate-range nuclear missiles in Cuba in 1962 been successful, the Soviet Union would have achieved a cheap kind of strategic parity. However, it would have been parity in a very dangerous and unstable form with Soviet missiles so close to the United States in soft emplacements, vulnerable to an air strike, and thus capable of being used only in a first strike. President Kennedy forced the withdrawal of Soviet missiles from Cuba by a combination of local naval superiority and strategic nuclear superiority, both brilliantly manipulated through diplomacy. The humiliation suffered by the Soviet Union redoubled the determination of Khrushchev's successors never again to find themselves in a position of nuclear inferiority in a confrontation with the United States. However, the mid-1960s was a period of rapid expansion in the U.S. Minuteman

ICBM and Polaris SLBM forces. This made the road for the Soviet Union longer and more costly. However, during the decade following the Cuban missile crisis they travelled the distance and achieved approximate strategic nuclear equality, the relationship which was tentatively formalized in SALT I.

Verification of Strategic Force Levels

Though Soviet-American arms control agreements must necessarily be based on common interests, they cannot rest merely on mutual trust. The behavior of its adversary in the Cold War gave each side reasons to be deeply suspicious of the other's motives. It is too early to know whether the present improvement in Soviet-American relations marks merely a temporary truce or signifies the beginning of the end of the Cold War. The legacy of hostility between the two principal adversaries will take years to dissipate.

Therefore, verification by national technical means was an essential factor in SALT I. The Soviet leaders would never have permitted American inspectors to set foot on Russian soil in order to verify compliance with a limitation on strategic armaments, nor would they have passively watched American aircraft overfly Soviet territory for this purpose. Any doubt on the latter score was dispelled by the U-2 incident in 1960. The intransigent resistance of the Soviet government to any verification measures that would involve intrusion on Russian territory meant that unease on the American side concerning the possible presence of Russian inspectors at strategic installations in the United States could be kept beneath the surface. National technical means of verification gives perhaps greater assurances of compliance than would onsite inspection, except inspection of a very intrusive kind.

With strategic force levels already high and without a SALT agreement, verification capabilities might tend to focus decision making on matters of detail, making more difficult decisions which discount the significance of asymmetries between the two sides. With SALT I in effect, however, the situation is changed. Verification of compliance by the other side with agreed force levels may build confidence on both sides.

Movement on the German Question

The primary theater of operations in the Cold War has been Europe, and the nuclear arms race may be viewed in part as a proxy for a conventional war in Europe. At times, progress in nuclear arms control was conditioned on the relaxation of Cold War tensions, while at other times arms control efforts were carefully insulated from some international crisis.

Whether or not related in the rhetoric of political leaders, the policies of the United States, and especially the Soviet Union, on nuclear issues were strongly linked to their fundamental policies regarding Germany. These policies were largely opposed throughout the Cold War. The salient features of Soviet policy toward Germany were the weakening of West German ties to the NATO alliance, the denial of nuclear weapons to West Germany, and the recognition of East Germany as a State, signifying the permanent division of the German nation. The United States placed top priority on integrating West Germany into NATO, while supporting the eventual reunification of Germany. Adherence of both West and East Germany to the Limited Nuclear Test Ban Treaty in 1963 caused difficulties between Washington and Bonn, but none between Moscow and East Berlin. For several years in the mid-1960s the United States government gave its proposal for a NATO multilateral nuclear force (MLF), which would have included West Germany, a higher priority than agreement with the Soviet Union on the Non-Proliferation Treaty, which is intended to prevent the spread of nuclear weapons. Thus Soviet arms control policy has been a useful complement to its German policy, while the United States has been able to obtain the benefits of the Test Ban and Non-Proliferation Treaties only at a cost in terms of its relations with West Germany.

With the election of Willy Brandt as chancellor in 1969, however, the German problem began to move rapidly of its own accord. Without the Brandt government's formulation and skillful execution of *Ostpolitik,* it is doubtful that agreement on SALT I would have been reached when it was. The West German treaties with Poland and the Soviet Union preceded SALT I. The successful conclusions of the four-power agreement on Berlin and the treaty between West and East Germany, which were negotiated in parallel with the SALT talks, were reasonably foreseeable before Nixon and Brezhnev signed the SALT I agreements. Until now the pace and direction of Soviet-American arms control negotiations has been vitally affected by West German domestic politics, but whether this linkage will persist as strongly in SALT II remains to be seen.

Political Leadership

The fifth factor which was essential to the successful outcome of SALT I was a strong political leader on each side who favored agreement. Governments are never of one mind. Men with keen intellects and refined judgment are found on both sides of the decisive intragovernmental issues that arise in negotiating agreements bearing directly and substantially on national security. Of course, there were technical, military, and political arguments for and against every provision of the SALT I agreements.

Given the political weight of the contending forces, many of the major issues were settled only at the very top. The internal battles between various government agencies in order to develop a United States position were just as hard-fought as were the subsequent international negotiations with the Soviet Union based on that position. Similar battles between diverse viewpoints apparently occurred in the Kremlin. In any event, neither side could develop an initial position, much less compromise a position once held, unless the top political leadership was firmly in the saddle and strongly in favor of agreement.

In this respect, President Nixon displayed remarkable judgment and courage, and Henry Kissinger played a vital role in developing policy options for the president and later in negotiations with the Soviets. Following his inauguration, Nixon took his time in thoroughly reviewing previous positions and gradually developing his own. His critics may argue that he wasted precious months while the MIRV was being rapidly developed and irreversibly deployed merely to arrive at much the same positions as President Johnson would have adopted if the Soviet invasion of Czechoslovakia in 1968 had not forced him to cancel his scheduled trip to the Soviet Union to open the SALT talks. On the other hand, Nixon's supporters will assert that such a painstaking process was essential in order to win the confidence of his own administration and the American people.

President Nixon fully embraced the concept of bargaining from a position of strength in SALT I. Accordingly, he committed the prestige of the office of president to the deployment of the Safeguard ABM system, justifying it primarily in terms of the Soviet SS-9 threat. Though he won congressional authorization for the initial deployment by the slenderest of margins in 1969, he thereafter obtained more easily from Congress the authorization for three additional Safeguard ABM sites by justifying them as bargaining chips. Moreover, Nixon determined not to deal with the Soviet Union in strategic matters from a position of weakness on Vietnam. In mining Haiphong Harbor, he gambled and dared the leaders in the Kremlin to postpone the SALT effort and scrap the entire Summit conference if they chose to place a higher priority on Soviet interests in Southeast Asia than on improvements in relations with America.

Brezhnev's position remains more obscure and problematical. There may well have been those who strongly dissented from the decision to go ahead with the Summit meeting in the wake of U.S. escalation of the war in Indochina. Brezhnev proved strong enough to overrule his critics and move ahead to strike a bargain with Nixon. We may not know for several years whether in the process he weakened or strengthened his own position at the top of the Communist Party hierarchy, and this may well depend on whether Soviet-American relations continue to develop or falter.

The Strategic Balance and Superpower Security

What do the alphabet soup of strategic forces—ABMs, ICBMs, SLBMs, and so on—and the related numbers mean? They mean very little to the man in the street, and they can be used by experts to support a variety of propositions which range from the immorality of nuclear deterrence theory to the need for strategic superiority for either side in the nuclear arms race. While the details can be the subject of endless argument, some general conclusions appear reasonable concerning the impact of the SALT I agreements on the U.S.-U.S.S.R. strategic balance.

The ABM Treaty reflects a political conclusion derived from a technical judgment. The technical judgment by the United States and the Soviet Union is that ABM defenses of territory and population against a sophisticated nuclear attack are unworkable. The United States and the Soviet Union finally came to share this judgment after more than a decade of intensive research and development activity and limited ABM deployments costing each nation billions of dollars. The ABM Treaty would have been impossible if either side foresaw a realistic possibility of an effective ABM defense of its territory and population.

The political conclusion is that both sides would benefit if the costs of further ABM deployments and of the additional offensive strategic arms to offset those deployments could be avoided. Without a formal agreement on limitations, both governments apparently foresaw that they would be unable to resist political and military pressures for gradual increases in their ABM deployments, and such deployments would, in turn, generate irresistible pressures for offsetting increases in their respective strategic offensive forces. Neither side foresaw the possibility of obtaining a significant advantage—military or political— as a result of continuation of the nuclear arms race in this particular way.

The ABM Treaty implies recognition by both the United States and the Soviet Union that nuclear deterrence by means of an assured destruction capability is vital to the security of both sides. The ABM Treaty makes it easier and less costly for each side to develop, maintain, and have confidence in its capability to devastate the territory and decimate the population of the other country. Regardless of the morality of such a relationship between two nations, the ABM Treaty is intended to stablize and preserve mutual deterrence, and thereby to enhance the security of both superpowers as they perceive it.

None of the limitations in the Interim Offensive Agreement had an immediate impact on U.S. programs with respect to its strategic offensive forces. The Soviet Union had about ninety ICBM launchers under construction and an active ballistic-missile submarine production program on the date of the agreement. It may be plausibly argued either that the ceilings provided for the Soviet Union in the categories of armaments covered by the Interim Offensive Agreement are at or near the levels which the Soviet leaders planned apart from the agreement, or that the ceilings imposed by the agreement caused the Soviet Union to curtail somewhat its planned deployments of ICBMs and SLBMs.

The question of which side has a quantitative lead in strategic offensive forces is impossible to answer, since the United States is ahead by some measures, while the Soviet Union is ahead by others. The question of which side has a qualitative lead is also unanswerable, though endlessly debatable, since substantial qualitative doubts cannot be resolved except by the use of strategic forces in an actual nuclear war, an environment which cannot be adequately simulated. What we can say about the strategic balance under the Interim Offensive Agreement is that force levels will remain very high on both sides and that, through MIRVing, their destructive capability will probably continue to increase.

The Interim Offensive Agreement makes a start toward limiting strategic arsenals, but what has been achieved is less important than what remains to be done. The ceilings on ICBM and SLBM launchers neither stabilize nuclear deterrence nor reduce the risk of nuclear war. MIRV technology seems to pose the clearest and most immediate threat to the security interests of the United States and the Soviet Union. However, the potential MIRV threat is limited to the survivabiliy of fixed land-based ICBMs. The deployment of MIRVs does not substantially increase the vulnerability of bombers to destruction in a preemptive nuclear attack, nor does it affect the survivability of SLBMs. Thus extensive MIRVing of ICBMs and SLBMs should not be viewed as reducing the capability of either side to inflict an unacceptable level of damage on the other. In fact, the deployment of MIRVs in SLBMs will mean that a single Polaris submarine equipped with Poseidon missiles will be capable itself of launching 160 or more nuclear warheads against separate targets.

Moreover, the deployment of MIRVs on one side may be countered in a number of ways on the other. The vulnerability of ICBMs could be simply ignored, since deterrence is guaranteed by other strategic forces. A dangerous option would be to replace plans to launch ICBMs only after surviving a nuclear first strike with revised orders to launch on warning prior to attack. A less dangerous way would be to dismantle the vulnerable ICBMs without replacing them with increases in SLBM or bomber force levels. The addition of MIRVs to SLBMs and SRAMs to bombers could largely compensate for the reduction in nuclear warheads delivered by ICBMs. But it may be very difficult for either side to give up one element of the strategic triad. More costly ways to deal with the MIRV threat would be to replace fixed ICBMs with land-mobile systems, which is not an attractive alternative to the U.S. in particular, or to defend ICBM fields with extensive ABM systems. Finally, the U.S. and the Soviet Union may agree to limit the development and deployment of MIRVs. This would require relatively quick agreement in SALT II regarding control of a very sensitive aspect of strategic forces in a manner that might be difficult to verify. But in terms of the security of the two superpowers, such a limitation could well be the preferred alternative.

Miscalculation has been a major factor in Cold War confrontations and in the build-up of strategic arsenals on both sides. Moreover, the possibility of miscalculating an adversary's intentions constitutes one of the primary risks of nuclear war. While thus far yielding only marginal benefits in terms of nuclear arms control, the SALT process has already produced enduring results in terms of improved perceptions of strategic problems on both sides. Thus, one of the most significant achievements of SALT is the process itself—a process of intimate dialogue about nuclear arms and arms control which has been constructed and institutionalized in the form of the negotiations themselves and in the Standing Consultative Commission established by the agreements. The ongoing dialogue offers both sides opportunities to understand and to communicate in private on many levels about strategic matters of vital concern.

Global Security

A nuclear war between the United States and the Soviet Union could contaminate the whole world with deadly radioactive fallout. To the extent that SALT diminishes the risk of such a war, the security of not just the two superpowers, but of all nations, is increased.

Then why have the agreements had so little noticeable impact on the world community? The answer may be in part that the security gains of SALT I were largely discounted in advance. Moreover, since the step taken is tentative and contingent, its immediate and direct consequences for global security are minimal. Thus, the larger security implications of the SALT process will emerge only if and when further agreements are concluded.

The significance of SALT I itself can best be appraised by exploring the consequences if the SALT talks had failed. In the wake of a breakdown in SALT, the Conference on Security and Cooperation in Europe would have little chance of yielding constructive results, and it is even more difficult to imagine fruitful negotiations on mutual force reductions. There is a tendency to focus on the potential of the SALT process for weakening the NATO alliance. Such a focus leads to confusion between means and ends. An alliance is a means, and NATO provides a means whereby the Soviet Union is to be effectively deterred from an armed attack against any of its members, especially those located in Western Europe. The end is security from armed attack, and such security may be provided by a variety of means in addition to a military alliance. Thus SALT will increase the security of NATO members if it diminishes the threat of a Soviet attack against them, but if the Soviet threat is diminished, the rationale for the alliance may well be eroded and the alliance itself loosened.

The codification and stabilization of nuclear deterrence, which is the hoped-for effect of SALT, need not destroy the credibility of the nuclear guarantees on which the U.S. allies presently rely. Nor would an unrestrained nuclear arms race between the U.S. and the Soviet Union necessarily preserve the credibility of those guarantees. The maintenance of U.S. armed forces in forward positions in Western Europe would seem to be a more effective security guarantee than the quantitative relationship between U.S. and Soviet strategic nuclear forces.

While the continuation of the SALT process could create major problems for the United States in its relations with the NATO allies, the risk in this respect can be controlled by careful pacing of future superpower negotiations so that they do not outstrip the trend in European politics away from Cold War alliances and toward a broader structure of security. But in any event, United States influence over the pace and direction of *détente* in Europe is likely to decrease in the years ahead.

If SALT I had failed, the American-Sino-Soviet triangle would probably have taken on different proportions in East Asia. Improvement of U.S.-China relations would not have been balanced by improving U.S.-U.S.S.R. relations, and the latter relationship should be the more important. Indeed, U.S.-U.S.S.R. relations would have been set back by a failure in SALT, arousing even deeper suspicion in Moscow of Washington's intentions toward Peking. However, Nixon's journey to Peking, in addition to marking a new beginning in American relations with China, made his trip to Moscow all the more important for the Soviet leadership. Thus, the United States appears to be moving into a position where it may play toward both ends of the Sino-Soviet conflict and seek to improve relations with both its Asian adversaries simultaneously. The SALT process has an important role in such a diplomatic strategy.

The sharp denunciations of the Moscow Summit and SALT I which emanated from Peking should not be taken entirely at face value. China will view any American-Soviet cooperation with suspicion. However, the ABM Treaty precludes either party from deploying an effective ABM defense against China (or the United Kingdom, France, or any other future nuclear power).

Finally, the SALT process is the central feature of a much larger nuclear arms control process that is aimed at preventing the spread of nuclear weapons to other countries, as well as at limiting the nuclear armaments of the two superpowers. If SALT I had failed, the prospects for wide adherence to the Non-Proliferation Treaty, which entered into force in 1970 and which now provides the framework for the global nuclear arms control effort, would have been substantially diminished. That treaty obligates the nuclear-weapon parties to undertake "negotiations in good faith" on measures to limit and reduce their nuclear armaments. The two superpowers would not have a persuasive case for measures to prevent nuclear weapon proliferation to other countries if they could not agree to limit the build-up of their own strategic arms. In this respect, the parties to the Non-Proliferation Treaty will review its operation at a conference scheduled by the terms of the treaty to begin in March 1975. This review conference will provide an opportunity for all the parties to evaluate the progress of the United States and the Soviet Union in SALT II.

Regardless of the posture of the two superpowers, for non-proliferation to be a viable policy those nations which have not acquired nuclear weapons, but which have the capability to do so, must perceive more security in self-restraint than in nuclear armament. In this respect, a variety of political and security issues which are specific to particular regions in the world will probably be more important than the behavior of either nuclear superpower. Nevertheless, the example of the United States and the Soviet Union, where each society is held permanent hostage for the other's security, should provide evidence that the acquisition of nuclear weapons does not necessarily increase and may, in fact, substantially diminish a nation's security.

Nuclear energy is forecast to become the most important primary source of energy in several countries by the year 2000. Without nuclear power, a substantial fraction of the world's future needs for electricity may not be met, and this would have severe consequences for human welfare in many countries. However, the technology for the use of nuclear fuel to generate electric power is substantially the same as that required for the production of fissionable materials for use in nuclear weapons. In fact, the amounts of such materials present in civilian power industries in many countries will soon be much greater than any military program would require. Therefore, the large-scale use of nuclear power in a country necessarily results in the creation for the government of that country of an option to acquire nuclear weapons.

One wonders how the bright forecasts for nuclear power could be fulfilled in a global political environment characterized by several unstable, many-sided balances of terror—the probable result of nuclear weapon proliferation. Fulfillment of the peaceful promise of nuclear energy thus depends on the success of a policy of non-proliferation of nuclear weapons, and such a policy has a double aspect: the spread of nuclear weapons to additional countries must be prevented; and the strategic arms race between the nuclear-weapon powers must be stopped.

BENEFITS AND RISKS FOR SOVIET-AMERICAN RELATIONS

SALT I was part of a breakthrough to new ground in Soviet-American relations generally, and the SALT I agreements provide a new source of benefits and risks, opportunities, and problems in those relations.

A Step in a New Direction

From the outset of the SALT talks, it was clear that neither side was contemplating complete nuclear disarmament or the reduction of strategic forces down to levels of minimum deterrence. If anything emerged, it would be a slice of the disarmament apple. A major benefit of SALT I is simply the change from propaganda and sparring to serious negotiation which finally produced important agreements. In the long run, the fact of agreement will be as important as the particular provisions of the agreements that emerged from SALT I.

The same substantive outcome could not have been reached without formal agreements. The negotiating process led to common understandings on quantitative, qualitative, and geographic constraints which could not have been duplicated in effect by unilateral statements of intentions or expectations. The formality of the agreements substantially increases the certainty and heightens the sense of obligation on both sides. Binding international undertakings provide each side with a concrete basis for determining the behavior it has a right to expect from the other. Moreover, solemn obligations to another nation provide each government with a necessary basis for the settlement of internal differences about what the policy should be and what actions should be taken.

It would be a mistake, however, to overemphasize the legally binding quality of the SALT I agreements. For one thing, the withdrawal clauses in both the ABM Treaty and the Interim Offensive Agreement provide either side with a legitimate avenue of escape if the government concludes its national security interests would be better served by taking prohibited action. For another, it is doubtful that a government would continue to adhere willingly to international agreements which adversely affected the vital interests of its nation, regardless of the legal permissibility of withdrawal.

While the fact of agreement is a benefit, one risk arising out of the SALT I agreements is that whatever is permitted will be viewed by either or both parties as options that must be pursued. The nuclear arms race may thus continue through the loopholes. The seriousness of the risk depends in large part on two issues: whether the aggressive pursuit of options within the gaps or around the flanks would erode the SALT I agreements, hinder achievement of a comprehensive SALT II agreement, or destabilize the strategic balance; and if so, whether the mutual interest of the two sides in further SALT agreements is sufficiently strong to induce self-restraint in these critical areas.

The Stabilization of Nuclear Stalemate

The SALT I agreements achieved a tentative and partial codification of a strategic relationship between the United States and the Soviet Union which is based on nuclear deterrence. Mutual deterrence is simply a technological fact of life, assuming that *both* the United States and the Soviet Union would not be prepared to let each other build toward a first-strike capability. Mutual deterrence provides a minimum condition for major improvements in superpower relations in other fields on a long-term basis. The risk of mutual deterrence and stalemate with respect to strategic nuclear forces, a risk which predates the SALT I agreements, is that one side or the other may seek to gain an advantage in other areas of possible conflict or rivalry. Thus from the American viewpoint, a Soviet-American relationship of strategic nuclear equality without further broad understandings does not eliminate the possibility that the Soviet Union may seek tactical advantages in Europe, the Middle East, or Asia which would work against U.S. interests.

The consequences of a course of action which recognizes and attempts to maintain mutual deterrence should be weighed against the alternative, in the absence of the SALT I agreements, which would be continuation of an unrestricted nuclear arms race with the Soviet Union. During the late 1950s and early 1960s, which was the height of the Cold War and also the time when nuclear arms control first became a serious issue, those in the United States who favored the maintenance of nuclear superiority and those who favored an arms control agreement based on strategic nuclear parity were agreed on one point: the United States could win any production race with the Soviet Union. Those favoring an unlimited arms race believed the U.S. should not give up its advantage, while those favoring arms control believed the U.S. should trade off its advantage in the quantitative arms race for the qualitative gains in security that would become possible through arms control. During the early 1960s, it was believed that the United States could pursue a "guns and butter" strategy indefinitely, while the Soviet Union would have to make the painful choice between the two.

The picture in the early 1970s is radically different. A combination of economic and political constraints has emerged in America which preclude pursuit of both an all-out arms race with the Soviet Union and an effective program to deal with domestic ills afflicting society. The choice between guns and butter is thus one that now must be made on both sides.

Momentum for SALT II

SALT I established a momentum toward some sort of SALT II. The momentum is not very strong, and it could be dissipated by the inherent difficulty of the issues involved in SALT II or by adverse developments in areas of importance to the U.S. or the Soviet Union.

At a minimum, SALT II offers the possibility for completing the codification of mutual deterrence and strategic stability that began with SALT I. The ceilings on fixed ICBMs and SLBMs might be expanded to include bombers, and mobile ICBMs might be prohibited completely. The invulnerability of strategic forces might be assured by some constraints on MIRVs. Initial constraints on ASW might also be possible. Moreover, SALT II creates opportunities for agreement on some reductions in strategic offensive force levels, perhaps through a phasing out of obsolete systems, rather than their replacement with more modern systems.

Given the complexity of the SALT II issues and the manifold possibilities for the occurrence of events that would destroy the atmosphere of *détente*, the risk of failure remains substantial. The consequences of failure would, of course, depend on how each of the parties would choose to behave thereafter. Each side might refrain from any action inconsistent with its previous obligations under the Interim Offensive Agreement. On the other hand, one side or the other might announce immediate plans to deploy ICBMs or SLBMs above the previously agreed ceilings and also to withdraw from the ABM Treaty. Thus, the possible responses to failure in SALT II cover a wide range.

The readiness of the U.S. to take the initiative at SALT II and propose specific and comprehensive qualitative constraints may well be the single most important factor in the success or failure of the further negotiations. In the meantime, self-restraint and caution by both the United States and the Soviet Union in the conduct of their respective modernization programs and other qualitative changes in strategic nuclear forces would tend to preserve the present stable balance. Neither side would then need to act abruptly to correct a deteriorating situation. Unfortunately, there are few indications thus far that either superpower is using self-restraint.

A Justification for Normalization

Another benefit of SALT I is the touchstone it provided for the other accords reached at the Moscow Summit. Capped by the Declaration of Basic Principles of Relations, the specific agreements span the range of Soviet-American relations, including environmental protection, medical science and public health, space cooperation, science and technology, prevention of accidents at sea, and commercial relations. Since the Summit, even more important agreements have been concluded regarding the settlement of World War II Soviet lend-lease debts, very large wheat sales, a trade agreement which requires congressional legislation before it is effective, and the possibility of potentially huge deals related to the extraction of energy and other natural resources in the Soviet Union. Not all of the other Summit accords were expressly contingent on the successful outcome of the SALT I negotiations, though Nixon administration spokesmen occassionally mentioned a link between the SALT and trade. However, SALT I was viewed by both sides and the general public as the main justification for Nixon's trip to Moscow, and it was and is the keystone in the arch.

The complementary risk associated with the Summit accords, taken as a whole, is the broad risk of normalization of relations with the Soviet Union. Are both the United States and the Soviet Union prepared once and for all to move away from the Cold War? Are the leaders of the Communist Party in the Kremlin viewing the process of normalization as a way to obtain a series of short-term gains which will at the same time lull the United States and prepare the way for an aggressive reassertion of Soviet interests around the world? Does the Soviet Union view SALT I and the ensuing process of normalization of Soviet-American relations as a series of tactical moves in a strategy to "win" in other areas? Only the passage of several years will reveal the answers to these questions.

In the meantime, implementation of the agreements already reached, including the SALT I agreements, will create important additional variables in the equation. In particular, it may be noted that the possibility of further steps toward normalization of Soviet-American relations could increase the chances for a successful outcome of SALT II. For example, the broadening and deepening of bilateral trade channels would produce economic interdependencies, but the failure of the Congress to enact most-favored-nation treatment for the Soviets, which has been linked by the Congress to Soviet emigration policy, would mean the trade agreement will not enter into force. This could affect the content and timing of SALT II. If trade is viewed as mutually beneficial, and the trade agreement enters into force, it may provide a beneficial framework for success in SALT II.

In conclusion, it should be noted that the five factors which underlay SALT I—a mutual interest in the prevention of nuclear war, the preservation of functional strategic equality, the possibility of verification, the continuing development of *détente* in Europe, and strong political leadership on both sides in favor of agreement—remain critical in SALT II and beyond in successive stages of the SALT process.

SALT and the American Body Politic

The pace of the SALT I negotiations and the timing of President Nixon's trip to Moscow were influenced by both foreign and domestic factors. The Moscow Summit, like the Peking trip which preceded it, had a large and favorable impact on the 1972 presidential election. It is also apparent that the five-year time limit on the Interim Offensive Agreement will create important implications for the 1976 election. If the Soviet negotiators are reasonably cooperative, Nixon will be in a position to claim SALT II as a major achievement of his second term and an important part of his legacy to the Republican nominee for president in 1976. However, he may be able to avoid blame for a failure of SALT II since the Interim Offensive Agreement does not terminate until after his successor, whether Republican or Democrat, is in office.

In any event, the implementation of SALT and the alternatives for SALT II will be issues in the national debate concerning U.S. strategic defense posture during the years ahead. SALT I may be used by Senator Jackson and others who favor increased defense spending to support the need for modernization and bargaining chips to deal with the Soviets from a position of strength. On the other hand, those in favor of arms control may use SALT I, and the need to extend it, to justify restraint in the development and deployment of new strategic systems. Without doubt, the president is likely to continue to play the leading role in determining not only the U.S. position at SALT II with the Soviets, but also the strategic force posture from which the U.S. will negotiate. However, during the second Nixon term, criticism from Capitol Hill may be more sharply focused and better organized than in the past. The members of Congress are more knowledgeable as a result of the debates on the ABM and on the SALT I agreements, and are likely to be more assertive with respect to a broad range of national security and foreign policy matters.

Nuclear Deterrence Beyond the Cold War

SALT I formalizes a strategic relationship between the United States and the Soviet Union based on mutual nuclear deterrence. The agreements affecting Germany cement the status quo in Europe, namely, two German States. At the same time, both sets of agreements open up vast possibilities for political movement toward normalization of Soviet-American relations, on the one hand, and the construction of a new structure of security in Europe, on the other. From the vantage point of the present, it is impossible to see clearly the structure or content of international security as it may emerge in a post–Cold War political environment. But one issue that is sure to be a primary concern will be what to do about nuclear weapons and about the balance of terror which enforced coexistence during the Cold War years.

A strategic nuclear force is the embodiment of a large amount of technological and economic resources invested over a long period of time. As the major powers slowly inch their way beyond the Cold War, strategic nuclear forces will gradually become less relevant in international politics. Yet as long as nuclear weapons exist in the arsenals of any nation, none of the five present nuclear powers is likely to give them up, least of all the United States or the Soviet Union. Therefore, in a post–Cold War era the language of nuclear deterrence may eventually be discarded, but the instruments will remain.

A nuclear force can be controlled only by rational human behavior through stable governmental institutions. As long as nuclear weapons exist, the destructive potential of irrational behavior or of a breakdown of governmental control over strategic forces will be enormous. A new generation of leaders in the United States or the Soviet Union who may not fully appreciate the meaning of nuclear weapons could produce a very dangerous situation, even though they are well-intentioned and relations between the two countries are generally friendly. The possession of large strategic nuclear forces will thus continue to impose heavy, inescapable burdens of responsibility on the political and military leaders of the two superpowers.

SALT provides an evolving framework within which deterrence can be continuously maintained while strategic forces are gradually reduced and nuclear war is effectively prevented. Thus institutionalized, SALT becomes an essential, enduring part of the structure of peace in the nuclear age, a peace that we may hope will eventually make nuclear deterrence an outworn concept that future generations may safely discard.

Appendix 1

ABM Treaty (Treaty Between the United States of America and the Union of Soviet Socialist Republics on the Limitation of Anti-Ballistic Missile Systems), *with* Agreed Interpretations, Common Understandings and Unilateral Statements

UNION OF SOVIET SOCIALIST REPUBLICS

Limitation of Anti-Ballistic Missile Systems

Treaty signed at Moscow May 26, 1972;
Ratification advised by the Senate of the United States of America
August 3, 1972;
Ratified by the President of the United States of America Septem-
ber 30, 1972;
Ratified by the Union of Soviet Socialist Republics May 29, 1972;
Ratifications exchanged at Washington October 3, 1972;
Proclaimed by the President of the United States of America
October 3, 1972;
Entered into force October 3, 1972.
With agreed interpretations, common understandings, and unilat-
eral statements.

By the President of the United States of America

A PROCLAMATION

Considering that:

The Treaty between the United States of America and the Union of Soviet Socialist Republics on the Limitation of Anti-Ballistic Missile Systems was signed at Moscow on May 26, 1972, the text of which in the English and Russian languages is annexed;

The Senate of the United States of America by its resolution of August 3, 1972, two-thirds of the Senators present concurring, gave its advice and consent to the ratification of the Treaty;

The President ratified the Treaty on September 30, 1972, in pursuance of the advice and consent of the Senate;

The instruments of ratification of the respective Parties were exchanged at Washington on October 3, 1972; and

The Treaty entered into force on October 3, 1972, the day of the exchange of the instruments of ratification, as provided in Article XVI of the Treaty;

Now, therefore, I, Richard Nixon, President of the United States of America, proclaim and make public the Treaty between the United

States of America and the Union of Soviet Socialist Republics on the Limitation of Anti-Ballistic Missile Systems to the end that it shall be observed and fulfilled with good faith on and after October 3, 1972, by the United States of America and by the citizens of the United States of America and all other persons subject to the jurisdiction thereof.

IN TESTIMONY WHEREOF, I have signed this proclamation and caused the Seal of the United States of America to be affixed.

DONE at the city of Washington this third day of October in the year of our Lord one thousand nine hundred seventy-two [SEAL] and of the Independence of the United States of America the one hundred ninety-seventh.

RICHARD NIXON

By the President:
WILLIAM P ROGERS
Secretary of State

TREATY
BETWEEN THE UNITED STATES OF AMERICA
AND
THE UNION OF SOVIET SOCIALIST REPUBLICS
ON THE LIMITATION OF ANTI-BALLISTIC MISSILE SYSTEMS

The United States of America and the Union of Soviet Socialist Republics, hereinafter referred to as the Parties,

Proceeding from the premise that nuclear war would have devastating consequences for all mankind,

Considering that effective measures to limit anti-ballistic missile systems would be a substantial factor in curbing the race in strategic offensive arms and would lead to a decrease in the risk of outbreak of war involving nuclear weapons,

Proceeding from the premise that the limitation of anti-ballistic missile systems, as well as certain agreed measures with respect to the limitation of strategic offensive arms,[1] would contribute to the creation of more favorable conditions for further negotiations on limiting strategic arms,

Mindful of their obligations under Article VI of the Treaty on the Non-Proliferation of Nuclear Weapons,[2]

Declaring their intention to achieve at the earliest possible date the cessation of the nuclear arms race and to take effective measures toward reductions in strategic arms, nuclear disarmament, and general and complete disarmament,

Desiring to contribute to the relaxation of international tension and the strengthening of trust between States,

Have agreed as follows:

Article I

1. Each Party undertakes to limit anti-ballistic missile (ABM) systems and to adopt other measures in accordance with the provisions of this Treaty.

2. Each Party undertakes not to deploy ABM systems for a defense of the territory of its country and not to provide a base for such a defense, and not to deploy ABM systems for defense of an individual region except as provided for in Article III of this Treaty.

---

[1] For interim agreement and protocol between the United States and the Soviet Union, signed May 26, 1972, see TIAS 7504 ; 23 UST.

[2] TIAS 6839 ; 21 UST 490.

Article II

1. For the purposes of this Treaty an ABM system is a system to counter strategic ballistic missiles or their elements in flight trajectory, currently consisting of:

(a) ABM interceptor missiles, which are interceptor missiles constructed and deployed for an ABM role, or of a type tested in an ABM mode;

(b) ABM launchers, which are launchers constructed and deployed for launching ABM interceptor missiles; and

(c) ABM radars, which are radars constructed and deployed for an ABM role, or of a type tested in an ABM mode.

2. The ABM system components listed in paragraph 1 of this Article include those which are:

(a) operational;

(b) under construction;

(c) undergoing testing;

(d) undergoing overhaul, repair or conversion; or

(e) mothballed.

Article III

Each Party undertakes not to deploy ABM systems or their components except that:

(a) within one ABM system deployment area having a radius of one hundred and fifty kilometers and centered on the Party's national capital, a Party may deploy: (1) no more than one hundred ABM launchers and no more than one hundred ABM interceptor missiles at launch sites, and (2) ABM radars within no more than six ABM radar complexes, the area of each complex being circular ind having a diameter of no more than three kilometers; and

(b) within one ABM system deployment area having a radius of one hundred and fifty kilometers and containing ICBM silo launchers, a Party may deploy: (1) no more than one hundred ABM launchers and no more than one hundred ABM interceptor missiles at launch sites, (2) two large phased-array ABM radars comparable in potential to corresponding ABM radars operational or under construction on the date of signature of the Treaty in an ABM system deployment area containing ICBM silo launchers, and (3) no more than eighteen ABM radars each having a potential less than the potential of the smaller of the above-mentioned two large phased-array ABM radars.

Article IV

The limitations provided for in Article III shall not apply to ABM systems or their components used for development or testing, and located within current or additionally agreed test ranges. Each Party may have no more than a total of fifteen ABM launchers at test ranges.

Article V

1.   Each Party undertakes not to develop, test, or deploy ABM systems or components which are sea-based, air-based, space-based, or mobile land-based.

2.   Each Party undertakes not to develop, test, or deploy ABM launchers for launching more than one ABM interceptor

missile at a time from each launcher, nor to modify deployed
launchers to provide them with such a capability, nor to develop,
test, or deploy automatic or semi-automatic or other similar
systems for rapid reload of ABM launchers.

Article VI

To enhance assurance of the effectiveness of the limitations on
ABM systems and their components provided by this Treaty, each
Party undertakes:

(a) not to give missiles, launchers, or radars, other than
ABM interceptor missiles, ABM launchers, or ABM radars,
capabilities to counter strategic ballistic missiles or their
elements in flight trajectory, and not to test them in an ABM mode;
and

(b) not to deploy in the future radars for early warning of
strategic ballistic missile attack except at locations along the
periphery of its national territory and oriented outward.

Article VII

Subject to the provisions of this Treaty, modernization and
replacement of ABM systems or their components may be carried
out.

Article VIII

ABM systems or their components in excess of the numbers 'or
outside the areas specified in this Treaty, as well as ABM systems or
their components prohibited by this Treaty, shall be destroyed or

dismantled under agreed procedures within the shortest possible agreed period of time.

Article IX

To assure the viability and effectiveness of this Treaty, each Party undertakes not to transfer to other States, and not to deploy outside its national territory, ABM systems or their components limited by this Treaty.

Article X

Each Party undertakes not to assume any international obligations which would conflict with this Treaty.

Article XI

The Parties undertake to continue active negotiations for limitations on strategic offensive arms.

Article XII

1. For the purpose of providing assurance of compliance with the provisions of this Treaty, each Party shall use national technical means of verification at its disposal in a manner consistent with generally recognized principles of international law.

2. Each Party undertakes not to interfere with the national technical means of verification of the other Party operating in accordance with paragraph 1 of this Article.

3. Each Party undertakes not to use deliberate concealment measures which impede verification by national technical means of compliance with the provisions of this Treaty. This obligation

shall not require changes in current construction, assembly, conversion, or overhaul practices.

Article XIII

1. To promote the objectives and implementation of the provisions of this Treaty, the Parties shall establish promptly a Standing Consultative Commission, within the framework of which they will:

(a)   consider questions concerning compliance with the obligations assumed and related situations which may be considered ambiguous;

(b)   provide on a voluntary basis such information as either Party considers necessary to assure confidence in compliance with the obligations assumed;

(c)   consider questions involving unintended interference with national technical means of verification;

(d)   consider possible changes in the strategic situation which have a bearing on the provisions of this Treaty;

(e)   agree upon procedures and dates for destruction or dismantling of ABM systems or their components in cases provided for by the provisions of this Treaty;

(f)   consider, as appropriate, possible proposals for further increasing the viability of this Treaty, including proposals for amendments in accordance with the provisions of this Treaty;

(g)   consider, as appropriate, proposals for further measures aimed at limiting strategic arms.

2.   The Parties through consultation shall establish, and may amend as appropriate, Regulations for the Standing Consultative Commission governing procedures, composition and other relevant matters.

Article XIV

1.   Each Party may propose amendments to this Treaty. Agreed amendments shall enter into force in accordance with the procedures governing the entry into force of this Treaty.

2.   Five years after entry into force of this Treaty, and at five year intervals thereafter, the Parties shall together conduct a review of this Treaty.

Article XV

1.   This Treaty shall be of unlimited duration.

2.   Each Party shall, in exercising its national sovereignty, have the right to withdraw from this Treaty if it decides that extraordinary events related to the subject matter of this Treaty have jeopardized its supreme interests. It shall give notice of its decision to the other Party six months prior to withdrawal from the Treaty. Such notice shall include a statement of the extraordinary events the notifying Party regards as having jeopardized its supreme interests.

Article XVI

1.   This Treaty shall be subject to ratification in accordance with the constitutional procedures of each Party. The Treaty

shall enter into force on the day of the exchange of instruments

of ratification.

2.   This Treaty shall be registered pursuant to Article 102

of the Charter of the United Nations. [a]

Done at Moscow   on May 26, 1972, in two copies, each in the

English and Russian languages, both texts being equally authentic.

FOR THE UNITED STATES
OF AMERICA: [1]

President of the United States
of America

FOR THE UNION OF SOVIET
SOCIALIST REPUBLICS: [2]

General Secretary of the
Central Committee of the CPSU

---

[a] TS 993 ; 59 Stat. 1052.

[1] Richard Nixon

[2] L. I. Brezhnev

AGREED INTERPRETATIONS, COMMON UNDERSTAND-INGS, AND UNILATERAL STATEMENTS

1. AGREED INTERPRETATIONS

(*a*) *Initialed Statements.*—The document set forth below was agreed upon and initialed by the Heads of the Delegations on May 26, 1972:

AGREED STATEMENTS REGARDING THE TREATY BETWEEN THE UNITED STATES OF AMERICA AND THE UNION OF SOVIET SOCIALIST REPUBLICS ON THE LIMITATION OF ANTI-BALLISTIC MISSILE SYSTEMS

[A]

The Parties understand that, in addition to the ABM radars which may be deployed in accordance with subparagraph (a) of Article III of the Treaty, those non-phased-array ABM radars operational on the date of signature of the Treaty within the ABM system deployment area for defense of the national capital may be retained.

[B]

The Parties understand that the potential (the product of mean emitted power in watts and antenna area in square meters) of the smaller of the two large phased-array ABM radars referred to in sub-paragraph (b) of Article III of the Treaty is considered for purposes of the Treaty to be three million.

[C]

The Parties understand that the center of the ABM system deploy-ment area centered on the national capital and the center of the ABM system deployment area containing ICBM silo launchers for each Party shall be separated by no less than thirteen hundred kilometers.

[D]

In order to insure fulfillment of the obligation not to deploy ABM systems and their components except as provided in Article III of the Treaty, the Parties agree that in the event ABM systems based on other physical principles and including components capable of sub-stituting for ABM interceptor missiles, ABM launchers, or ABM radars are created in the future, specific limitations on such systems and their components would be subject to discussion in accordance with Article XIII and agreement in accordance with Article XIV of the Treaty.

[E]

The Parties understand that Article V of the Treaty includes obligations not to develop, test or deploy ABM interceptor missiles for the delivery by each ABM interceptor missile of more than one independently guided warhead.

[F]

The Parties agree not to deploy phased-array radars having a potential (the product of mean emitted power in watts and antenna area in square meters) exceeding three million, except as provided for in Articles III, IV and VI of the Treaty, or except for the purposes of tracking objects in outer space or for use as national technical means of verification.

[G]

The Parties understand that Article IX of the Treaty includes the obligation of the US and the USSR not to provide to other States technical descriptions or blue prints specially worked out for the construction of ABM systems and their components limited by the Treaty.

(b) *Common Understandings.*—Common understanding of the Parties on the following matters was reached during the negotiations:

A. LOCATION OF ICBM DEFENSES

The U.S. Delegation made the following statement on May 26, 1972:

Article III of the ABM Treaty provides for each side one ABM system deployment area centered on its national capital and one ABM system deployment area containing ICBM silo launchers. The two sides have registered agreement on the following statement: "The Parties understand that the center of the ABM system deployment area centered on the national capital and the center of the ABM system deployment area containing ICBM silo launchers for each Party shall be separated by no less than thirteen hundred kilometers." In this connection, the U.S. side notes that its ABM system deployment area for defense of ICBM silo launchers, located west of the Mississippi River, will be centered in the Grand Forks ICBM silo launcher deployment area. (See Initialed Statement [C].)

The U.S. Delegation made the following statement on April 26, 1972:

Article IV of the ABM Treaty provides that "the limitations provided for in Article III shall not apply to ABM systems or their components used for development or testing, and located within current or additionally agreed test ranges." We believe it would be useful to assure that there is no misunderstanding as to current ABM test ranges. It is our understanding that ABM test ranges encompass the area within which ABM components are located for test purposes. The current U.S. ABM test ranges are at White Sands, New Mexico, and at Kwajalein Atoll, and the current Soviet ABM test range is near Sary Shagan in Kazakhstan. We consider that non-phased array radars of types used for range safety or instrumentation purposes may be located outside of ABM test ranges. We interpret the reference in Article IV to "additionally agreed test ranges" to mean that ABM components will not be located at any other test ranges without prior agreement between our Governments that there will be such additional ABM test ranges.

On May 5, 1972, the Soviet Delegation stated that there was a common understanding on what ABM test ranges were, that the use of the types of non-ABM radars for range safety or instrumentation was not limited under the Treaty, that the reference in Article IV to "additionally agreed" test ranges was sufficiently clear, and that national means permitted identifying current test ranges.

C. MOBILE ABM SYSTEMS

On January 28, 1972, the U.S. Delegation made the following statement:

Article V(1) of the Joint Draft Text of the ABM Treaty includes an undertaking not to develop, test, or deploy mobile land-based ABM systems and their components. On May 5, 1971, the U.S. side indicated that, in its view, a prohibition on deployment of mobile ABM systems and components would rule out the deployment of ABM launchers and radars which were not permanent fixed types. At that time, we asked for the Soviet view of this interpretation. Does the Soviet side agree with the U.S. side's interpretation put forward on May 5, 1971?

On April 13, 1972, the Soviet Delegation said there is a general common understanding on this matter.

D. STANDING CONSULTATIVE COMMISSION

Ambassador Smith made the following statement on May 22, 1972:

The United States proposes that the sides agree that, with regard to initial implementation of the ABM Treaty's Article XIII on the Standing Consultative Commission (SCC) and of the consultation Articles to the Interim Agreement on offensive arms and the Accidents Agreement, [1] agreement establishing the SCC will be worked out early in the follow-on SALT negotiations; until that is completed, the following arrangements will prevail: when SALT is in session, any consultation desired by either side under these Articles can be carried out by the two SALT Delegations; when SALT is not in session, *ad hoc* arrangements for any desired consultations under these Articles may be made through diplomatic channels.

Minister Semenov replied that, on an *ad referendum* basis, he could agree that the U.S. statement corresponded to the Soviet understanding.

E. STANDSTILL

On May 6, 1972, Minister Semenov made the following statement:

In an effort to accommodate the wishes of the U.S. side, the Soviet Delegation is prepared to proceed on the basis that the two sides will in fact observe the obligations of both the Interim Agreement and the ABM Treaty beginning from the date of signature of these two documents.

In reply, the U.S. Delegation made the following statement on May 20, 1972:

The U.S. agrees in principle with the Soviet statement made on May 6 concerning observance of obligations beginning from date of signature but we would like to make clear our understanding that this means that, pending ratification and acceptance, neither side would take any action prohibited by the agreements after they had

---

[1] See Article 7 of Agreement to Reduce the Risk of Outbreak of Nuclear War Between the United States of America and the Union of Soviet Socialist Republics, signed Sept. 30, 1971. TIAS 7186; 22 UST 1590.

entered into force. This understanding would continue to apply in the absence of notification by either signatory of its intention not to proceed with ratification or approval.

The Soviet Delegation indicated agreement with the U.S. statement.

2. UNILATERAL STATEMENTS

(a) The following noteworthy unilateral statements were made during the negotiations by the United States Delegation:

A. WITHDRAWAL FROM THE ABM TREATY

On May 9, 1972, Ambassador Smith made the following statement:

The U.S. Delegation has stressed the importance the U.S. Government attaches to achieving agreement on more complete limitations on strategic offensive arms, following agreement on an ABM Treaty and on an Interim Agreement on certain measures with respect to the limitation of strategic offensive arms. The U.S. Delegation believes that an objective of the follow-on negotiations should be to constrain and reduce on a long-term basis threats to the survivability of our respective strategic retaliatory forces. The USSR Delegation has also indicated that the objectives of SALT would remain unfulfilled without the achievement of an agreement providing for more complete limitations on strategic offensive arms. Both sides recognize that the initial agreements would be steps toward the achievement of more complete limitations on strategic arms. If an agreement providing for more complete strategic offensive arms limitations were not achieved within five years, U.S. supreme interests could be jeopardized. Should that occur, it would constitute a basis for withdrawal from the ABM Treaty. The U.S. does not wish to see such a situation occur, nor do we believe that the USSR does. It is because we wish to prevent such a situation that we emphasize the importance the U.S. Government attaches to achievement of more complete limitations on strategic offensive arms. The U.S. Executive will inform the Congress, in connection with Congressional consideration of the ABM Treaty and the Interim Agreement, of this statement of the U.S. position.

B. TESTED IN ABM MODE

On April 7, 1972, the U.S. Delegation made the following statement:

Article II of the Joint Text Draft uses the term "tested in an

ABM mode," in defining ABM components, and Article VI includes certain obligations concerning such testing. We believe that the sides should have a common understanding of this phrase. First, we would note that the testing provisions of the ABM Treaty are intended to apply to testing which occurs after the date of signature of the Treaty, and not to any testing which may have occurred in the past. Next, we would amplify the remarks we have made on this subject during the previous Helsinki phase by setting forth the objectives which govern the U.S. view on the subject, namely, while prohibiting testing of non-ABM components for ABM purposes: not to precent testing of ABM components, and not to prevent testing of non-ABM components for non-ABM purposes. To clarify our interpretation of "tested in an ABM mode," we note that we would consider a launcher, missile or radar to be "tested in an ABM mode" if, for example, any of the following events occur: (1) a launcher is used to launch an ABM interceptor missile, (2) an interceptor missile is flight tested against a target vehicle which has a flight trajectory with characteristics of a strategic ballistic missile flight trajectory, or is flight tested in conjunction with the test of an ABM interceptor missile or an ABM radar at the same test range, or is flight tested to an altitude inconsistent with interception of targets against which air defenses are deployed, (3) a radar makes measurements on a cooperative target vehicle of the kind referred to in item (2) above during the reentry portion of its trajectory or makes measurements in conjunction with the test of an ABM interceptor missile or an ABM radar at the same test range. Radars used for purposes such as range safety or instrumentation would be exempt from application of these criteria.

C. NO-TRANSFER ARTICLE OF ABM TREATY

On April 18, 1972, the U.S. Delegation made the following statement:

In regard to this Article [IX], I have a brief and I believe self-explanatory statement to make. The U.S. side wishes to make clear that the provisions of this Article do not set a precedent for whatever provision may be considered for a Treaty on Limiting Strategic Offensive Arms. The question of transfer of strategic offensive arms is a far more complex issue, which may require a different solution.

D. NO INCREASE IN DEFENSE OF EARLY WARNING RADARS

On July 28, 1970, the U.S. Delegation made the following statement:

Since Hen House radars [Soviet ballistic missile early warning radars] can detect and track ballistic missile warheads at great distances, they have a significant ABM potential. Accordingly, the U.S. would regard any increase in the defenses of such radars by surface-to-air missiles as inconsistent with an agreement.

Appendix 2

Interim Agreement and Protocol (Interim Agreement, and Protocol to Interim Agreement, Between the United States of America and the Union of Soviet Socialist Republics on Certain Measures with Respect to the Limitation of Strategic Offensive Arms,) *with* Agreed Interpretations, Common Understandings and Unilateral Statements

UNION OF SOVIET SOCIALIST REPUBLICS

Limitation of Strategic Offensive Arms

*Interim agreement and protocol signed at Moscow May 26, 1972;
Entered into force October 3, 1972.
With agreed interpretations, common understandings, and unilateral
statements.*

INTERIM AGREEMENT
BETWEEN THE UNITED STATES OF AMERICA
AND
THE UNION OF SOVIET SOCIALIST REPUBLICS
ON CERTAIN MEASURES WITH RESPECT TO THE
LIMITATION OF STRATEGIC OFFENSIVE ARMS

The United States of America and the Union of Soviet
Socialist Republics, hereinafter referred to as the Parties,

Convinced that the Treaty on the Limitation of Anti-
Ballistic Missile Systems [1] and this Interim Agreement on
Certain Measures with Respect to the Limitation of Strategic
Offensive Arms will contribute to the creation of more favorable conditions for active negotiations on limiting strategic
arms as well as to the relaxation of international tension
and the strengthening of trust between States,

Taking into account the relationship between strategic
offensive and defensive arms,

---

[1] TIAS 7503; 23 UST.

Mindful of their obligations under Article VI of the Treaty on the Non-Proliferation of Nuclear Weapons, [1]

Have agreed as follows:

Article I

The Parties undertake not to start construction of additional fixed land-based intercontinental ballistic missile (ICBM) launchers after July 1, 1972.

Article II

The Parties undertake not to convert land-based launchers for light ICBMs, or for ICBMs of older types deployed prior to 1964, into land-based launchers for heavy ICBMs of types deployed after that time.

Article III

The Parties undertake to limit submarine-launched ballistic missile (SLBM) launchers and modern ballistic missile submarines to the numbers operational and under construction on the date of signature of this Interim Agreement, and in addition to launchers and submarines constructed under procedures established by the Parties as replacements for an equal number of ICBM launchers of older types deployed prior to 1964 or for launchers on older submarines.

Article IV

Subject to the provisions of this Interim Agreement,

---

[1] TIAS 6839; 21 UST 490.

modernization and replacement of strategic offensive ballistic missiles and launchers covered by this Interim Agreement may be undertaken.

Article V

1. For the purpose of providing assurance of compliance with the provisions of this Interim Agreement, each Party shall use national technical means of verification at its disposal in a manner consistent with generally recognized principles of international law.

2. Each Party undertakes not to interfere with the national technical means of verification of the other Party operating in accordance with paragraph 1 of this Article.

3. Each Party undertakes not to use deliberate concealment measures which impede verification by national technical means of compliance with the provisions of this Interim Agreement. This obligation shall not require changes in current construction, assembly, conversion, or overhaul practices.

Article VI

To promote the objectives and implementation of the provisions of this Interim Agreement, the Parties shall use the Standing Consultative Commission established under Article XIII of the Treaty on the Limitation of Anti-Ballistic Missile Systems in accordance with the provisions of that Article.

Article VII

The Parties undertake to continue active negotiations for limitations on strategic offensive arms. The obligations provided for in this Interim Agreement shall not prejudice the scope or terms of the limitations on strategic offensive arms which may be worked out in the course of further negotiations.

Article VIII

1.   This Interim Agreement shall enter into force [1] upon exchange of written notices of acceptance by each Party, which exchange shall take place simultaneously with the exchange of instruments of ratification of the Treaty on the Limitation of Anti-Ballistic Missile Systems.

2.   This Interim Agreement shall remain in force for a period of five years unless replaced earlier by an agreement on more complete measures limiting strategic offensive arms. It is the objective of the Parties to conduct active follow-on negotiations with the aim of concluding such an agreement as soon as possible.

3.   Each Party shall, in exercising its national sovereignty, have the right to withdraw from this Interim Agreement if it decides that extraordinary events related to the subject matter of this Interim Agreement have jeopardized its supreme interests. It shall give notice of its decision to

---

[1] Oct. 3, 1972.

the other Party six months prior to withdrawal from this Interim Agreement. Such notice shall include a statement of the extraordinary events the notifying Party regards as having jeopardized its supreme interests.

Done at   Moscow   on   May 26,   1972, in two copies, each in the English and Russian languages, both texts being equally authentic.

FOR THE UNITED STATES
OF AMERICA:

[¹]

President of the United States
of America

FOR THE UNION OF SOVIET
SOCIALIST REPUBLICS:

[²]

General Secretary of the
Central Committee of the CPSU

---

¹ Richard Nixon
² L. I. Brezhnev

PROTOCOL

TO THE INTERIM AGREEMENT BETWEEN
THE UNITED STATES OF AMERICA AND THE UNION OF SOVIET
SOCIALIST REPUBLICS ON CERTAIN MEASURES WITH RESPECT
TO THE LIMITATION OF STRATEGIC OFFENSIVE ARMS

The United States of America and the Union of Soviet Socialist Republics, hereinafter referred to as the Parties,

Having agreed on certain limitations relating to submarine-launched ballistic missile launchers and modern ballistic missile submarines, and to replacement procedures, in the Interim Agreement,

Have agreed as follows:

The Parties understand that, under Article III of the Interim Agreement, for the period during which that Agreement remains in force:

The US may have no more than 710 ballistic missile launchers on submarines (SLBMs) and no more than 44 modern ballistic missile submarines. The Soviet Union may have no more than 950 ballistic missile launchers on submarines and no more than 62 modern ballistic missile submarines.

Additional ballistic missile launchers on submarines up to the above-mentioned levels, in the U.S. - over 656 ballistic missile launchers on nuclear-powered submarines, and in the U.S.S.R. - over 740 ballistic missile launchers on nuclear-powered submarines, operational and under construction, may become operational as replacements for equal numbers of ballistic missile launchers of older types deployed prior to 1964 or of ballistic missile launchers on older submarines.

The deployment of modern SLBMs on any submarine, regardless of type, will be counted against the total level of SLBMs permitted for the U.S. and the U.S.S.R.

301

This Protocol shall be considered an integral part of the Interim Agreement.

Done at Moscow this 26th day of May, 1972.

FOR THE UNITED STATES OF AMERICA

President of the United States of America

FOR THE UNION OF SOVIET SOCIALIST REPUBLICS

General Secretary of the Central Committee of the CPSU

AGREED INTERPRETATIONS, COMMON UNDER-STANDINGS, AND UNILATERAL STATEMENTS

1. AGREED INTERPRETATIONS

(*a*) *Initialed Statements.*—The document set forth below was agreed upon and initialed by the Heads of the Delegations on May 26, 1972:

AGREED STATEMENTS REGARDING THE INTERIM AGREEMENT BETWEEN THE UNITED STATES OF AMERICA AND THE UNION OF SOVIET SOCIALIST REPUBLICS ON CERTAIN MEASURES WITH RESPECT TO THE LIMITATION OF STRATEGIC OFFENSIVE ARMS

[A]

The Parties understand that land-based ICBM launchers referred to in the Interim Agreement are understood to be launchers for strategic ballistic missiles capable of ranges in excess of the shortest distance between the northeastern border of the continental U.S. and the northwestern border of the continental USSR.

[B]

The Parties understand that fixed land-based ICBM launchers under active construction as of the date of signature of the Interim Agreement may be completed.

[C]

The Parties understand that in the process of modernization and replacement the dimensions of land-based ICBM silo launchers will not be significantly increased.

[D]

The Parties understand that during the period of the Interim Agreement there shall be no significant increase in the number of ICBM or SLBM test and training launchers, or in the number of such launchers for modern land-based heavy ICBMs. The Parties further understand that construction or conversion of ICBM launchers at test ranges shall be undertaken only for purposes of testing and training.

303

The Parties understand that dismantling or destruction of ICBM launchers of older types deployed prior to 1964 and ballistic missile launchers on older submarines being replaced by new SLBM launchers on modern submarines will be initiated at the time of the beginning of sea trials of a replacement submarine, and will be completed in the shortest possible agreed period of time. Such dismantling or destruction, and timely notification thereof, will be accomplished under procedures to be agreed in the Standing Consultative Commission.

(b) *Common Understandings.*—Common understanding of the Parties on the following matters was reached during the negotiations:

A. INCREASE IN ICBM SILO DIMENSIONS

Ambassador Smith made the following statement on May 26, 1972:

The Parties agree that the term "significantly increased" means that an increase will not be greater than 10–15 percent of the present dimensions of land-based ICBM silo launchers.

Minister Semenov replied that this statement corresponded to the Soviet understanding.

B. STANDING CONSULTATIVE COMMISSION

Ambassador Smith made the following statement on May 22, 1972:

The United States proposes that the sides agree that, with regard to initial implementation of the ABM Treaty's Article XIII on the Standing Consultative Commission (SCC) and of the consultation Articles to the Interim Agreement on offensive arms and the Accidents Agreement,[1] agreement establishing the SCC will be worked out early in the follow-on SALT negotiations; until that is completed, the following arrangements will prevail: when SALT is in session, any consultation desired by either side under these Articles can be carried out by the two SALT Delegations; when SALT is not in session, *ad hoc* arrangements for any desired consultations under these Articles may be made through diplomatic channels.

Minister Semenov replied that, on an *ad referendum* basis, he

---

[1] See Article 7 of Agreement to Reduce the Risk of Outbreak of Nuclear War Between the United States of America and the Union of Soviet Socialist Republics, signed Sept. 30, 1971. TIAS 7186; 22 UST 1590.

could agree that the U.S. statement corresponded to the Soviet understanding.

On May 6, 1972, Minister Semenov made the following statement:

In an effort to accommodate the wishes of the U.S. side, the Soviet Delegation is prepared to proceed on the basis that the two sides will in fact observe the obligations of both the Interim Agreement and the ABM Treaty beginning from the date of signature of these two documents.

In reply, the U.S. Delegation made the following statement on May 20, 1972:

The U.S. agrees in principle with the Soviet statement made on May 6 concerning observance of obligations beginning from date of signature but we would like to make clear our understanding that this means that, pending ratification and acceptance, neither side would take any action prohibited by the agreements after they had entered into force. This understanding would continue to apply in the absence of notification by either signatory of its intention not to proceed with ratification or approval.

The Soviet Delegation indicated agreement with the U.S. statement.

2. UNILATERAL STATEMENTS

(a) The following noteworthy unilateral statements were made during the negotiations by the United States Delegation:

A. WITHDRAWAL FROM THE ABM TREATY

On May 9, 1972, Ambassador Smith made the following statement:

The U.S. Delegation has stressed the importance the U.S. Government attaches to achieving agreement on more complete limitations on strategic offensive arms, following agreement on an ABM Treaty and on an Interim Agreement on certain measures with respect to the limitation of strategic offensive arms. The U.S. Delegation believes that an objective of the follow-on negotiations should be to constrain and reduce on a long-term basis threats to the survivability of our respective strategic retaliatory forces. The USSR Delegation has also indicated that the objectives of SALT would remain unfulfilled without the achievement of an agreement providing for more complete limitations on strategic offensive arms. Both sides recognize that the initial agreements would be steps toward the achievement of more complete limitations on strategic arms. If an agreement providing for more complete strategic offensive arms limitations were not achieved within five years, U.S. supreme interests could be jeopardized. Should that occur, it would constitute a basis for withdrawal from the ABM Treaty. The U.S. does not wish to see such a situation occur, nor do we believe that the USSR does. It is because we wish to prevent such a situation that we emphasize the importance the U.S. Government attaches to achievement of more complete limitations on strategic offensive arms. The U.S. Executive will inform the Congress, in connection with Congressional consideration of the ABM Treaty and the Interim Agreement, of this statement of the U.S. position.

B. LAND-MOBILE ICBM LAUNCHERS

The U.S. Delegation made the following statement on May 20, 1972:

In connection with the important subject of land-mobile ICBM launchers, in the interest of concluding the Interim Agreement the U.S. Delegation now withdraws its proposal that Article I or an agreed statement explicitly prohibit the deployment of mobile land-based ICBM launchers. I have been instructed to inform you that, while agreeing to defer the question of limitation of operational land-mobile ICBM launchers to the subsequent negotiations on more complete limitations on strategic offensive arms, the U.S. would consider the deployment of operational land-mobile ICBM launchers during the period of the Interim Agreement as inconsistent with the objectives of that Agreement.

C. COVERED FACILITIES

The U.S. Delegation made the following statement on May 20, 1972:

I wish to emphasize the importance that the United States attaches to the provisions of Article V, including in particular their application to fitting out or berthing submarines.

D. "HEAVY" ICBM'S

The U.S. Delegation made the following statement on May 26, 1972:

The U.S. Delegation regrets that the Soviet Delegation has not been willing to agree on a common definition of a heavy missile.

Under these circumstances, the U.S. Delegation believes it necessary to state the following: The United States would consider any ICBM having a volume significantly greater than that of the largest light ICBM now operational on either side to be a heavy ICBM. The U.S. proceeds on the premise that the Soviet side will give due account to this consideration.

(b) The following noteworthy unilateral statement was made by the Delegation of the U.S.S.R. and is shown here with the U.S. reply:

On May 17, 1972, Minister Semenov made the following unilateral "Statement of the Soviet Side":

Taking into account that modern ballistic missile submarines are presently in the possession of not only the U.S., but also of its NATO allies, the Soviet Union agrees that for the period of effectiveness of the Interim 'Freeze' Agreement the U.S. and its NATO allies have up to 50 such submarines with a total of up to 800 ballistic missile launchers thereon (including 41 U.S. submarines with 656 ballistic missile launchers). However, if during the period of effectiveness of the Agreement U.S. allies in NATO should increase the number of their modern submarines to exceed the numbers of submarines they would have operational or under construction on the date of signature of the Agreement, the Soviet Union will have the right to a corresponding increase in the number of its submarines. In the opinion of the Soviet side, the solution of the question of modern ballistic missile submarines provided for in the Interim Agreement only partially compensates for the strategic imbalance in the deployment of the nuclear-powered missile submarines of the USSR and the U.S. Therefore, the Soviet side believes that this whole question, and above all the question of liquidating the American missile submarine bases outside the U.S., will be appropriately resolved in the course of follow-on negotiations.

On May 24, Ambassador Smith made the following reply to Minister Semenov:

The United States side has studied the "statement made by the Soviet side" of May 17 concerning compensation for submarine basing and SLBM submarines belonging to third countries. The United States does not accept the validity of the considerations in that statement.

On May 26 Minister Semenov repeated the unilateral statement made on May 24. Ambassador Smith also repeated the U.S. rejection on May 26.

Appendix 3

Moscow: Basic Principles of Relations (Text of the "Basic Principles of Relations Between the United States of America and the Union of Soviet Socialist Republics." May 29, 1972)

The United States of America and the Union of Soviet Socialist Republics,

Guided by their obligations under the Charter of the United Nations and by a desire to strengthen peaceful relations with each other and to place these relations on the firmest possible basis,

Aware of the need to make every effort to remove the threat of war and to create conditions which promote the reduction of tensions in the world and the strengthening of universal security and international cooperation,

Believing that the improvement of US-Soviet relations and their mutually advantageous development in such areas as economics, science and culture, will meet these objectives and contribute to better mutual understanding and business-like cooperation, without in any way prejudicing the interests of third countries,

Conscious that these objectives reflect the interests of the peoples of both countries,

Have agreed as follows:

First. They will proceed from the common determination that in the nuclear age there is no alternative to conducting their mutual relations on the basis of peaceful coexistence. Differences in ideology and in the social systems of the USA and the USSR are not obstacles to the bilateral development of normal relations based on the principles of sovereignty, equality, non-interference in internal affairs and mutual advantage.

Second. The USA and the USSR attach major importance to preventing the development of situations capable of causing a dangerous exacerbation of their relations. Therefore, they will do their utmost to avoid military confrontations and to prevent the outbreak of nuclear war.They will always exercise restraint in their mutual relations, and will be prepared to negotiate and settle differences by peaceful means. Discussions and negotiations on outstanding issues will be conducted in a spirit of reciprocity, mutual accommodation and mutual benefit.

Both sides recognize that efforts to obtain unilateral advantage at the expense of the other, directly or indirectly, are inconsistent with these objectives. The prerequisites for maintaining and strengthening peaceful relations between the USA and the USSR are the recognition of the security interests of the Parties based on the principle of equality and the renunciation of the use or threat of force.

Third. The USA and the USSR have a special responsibility, as do

310

other countries which are permanent members of the United Nations Security Council, to do everything in their power so that conflicts or situations will not arise which would serve to increase international tensions. Accordingly, they will seek to promote conditions in which all countries will live in peace and security and will not be subject to outside interference in their internal affairs.

Fourth. The USA and the USSR intend to widen the juridical basis of their mutual relations and to exert the necessary efforts so that bilateral agreements which they have concluded and multilateral treaties and agreements to which they are jointly parties are faithfully implemented.

Fifth. The USA and the USSR reaffirm their readiness to continue the practice of exchanging views on problems of mutual interest and, when necessary, to conduct such exchanges at the highest level, including meetings between leaders of the two countries.

The two governments welcome and will facilitate an increase in productive contacts between representatives of the legislative bodies of the two countries.

Sixth. The Parties will continue their efforts to limit armaments on a bilateral as well as on a multilateral basis. They will continue to make special efforts to limit strategic armaments. Whenever possible, they will conclude concrete agreements aimed at achieving these purposes.

The USA and the USSR regard as the ultimate objective of their efforts the achievement of general and complete disarmament and the establishment of an effective system of international security in accordance with the purposes and principles of the United Nations.

Seventh. The USA and the USSR regard commercial and economic ties as an important and necessary element in the strengthening of their bilaterial relations and thus will actively promote the growth of such ties. They will facilitate cooperation between the relevant organizations and enterprises of the two countries and the conclusion of appropriate agreements and contracts, including long-term ones.

The two countries will contribute to the improvement of maritime and air communications between them.

Eighth. The two sides consider it timely and useful to develop mutual contacts and cooperation in the fields of science and technology. Where suitable, the USA and the USSR will conclude appropriate agreements dealing with concrete cooperation in these fields.

Ninth. The two sides reaffirm their intention to deepen cultural ties with one another and to encourage fuller familiarization with each other's cultural values. They will promote improved conditions for cultural exchanges and tourism.

Tenth. The USA and the USSR will seek to ensure that their ties and cooperation in all the above-mentioned fields and in any others in their mutual interest are built on a firm and long-term basis. To give a permanent character to these efforts, they will establish in all fields where this is feasible joint commissions or other joint bodies.

Eleventh. The USA and the USSR make no claim for themselves and would not recognize the claims of anyone else to any special rights or advantages in world affairs. They recognize the sovereign equality of all states.

The development of U.S.-Soviet relations is not directed against third countries and their interests.

Twelfth. The basic principles set forth in this document do not affect any obligations with respect to other countries earlier assumed by the USA and the USSR.

Moscow, May 29, 1972

For the United States of America
    Richard Nixon
        President of the United States of America
For the Union of Soviet Socialist Republics
    Leonid I. Brezhnev
        General Secretary of the Central Committee, CPSU

Appendix 4

Public Law 92–448 (Including the Jackson Amendment) Which Approved the Interim Agreement

Public Law 92-448
92nd Congress, H. J. Res. 1227
September 30, 1972

Joint Resolution

Approval and authorization for the President of the United States to accept an Interim Agreement Between the United States of America and the Union of Soviet Socialist Republics on Certain Measures With Respect to the Limitation of Strategic Offensive Arms.

Resolved by the Senate and House of Representatives of the United States of America in Congress assembled, That the Congress hereby endorses those portions of the Declaration of Basic Principles of Mutual Relations Between the United States of America and the Union of Soviet Socialist Republics signed by President Nixon and General Secretary Brezhnev at Moscow on May 29, 1972, which relate to the dangers of military confrontation and which read as follows:

"The United States of America and the Union of Soviet Socialist Republics attach major importance to preventing the development of situations capable of causing a dangerous exacerbation of their relations . . ." and "will do their utmost to avoid military confrontations and to prevent the outbreak of nuclear war" and "will always exercise restraint in their mutual relations," and "on outstanding issues will conduct" their discussions and negotiations "in a spirit of reciprocity, mutual accommodation and mutual benefit," and

"Both sides recognize that efforts to obtain unilateral advantage at the expense of the other, directly or indirectly, are inconsistent with these objectives," and

"The prerequisites for maintaining and strengthening peaceful relations between the United States of America and the Union of Soviet Socialist Republics are the recognition of the security interests of the parties based on the principle of equality and the renunciation of the use or threat of force."

SEC. 2. The President is hereby authorized to approve on behalf of the United States the interim agreement between the United States of America and the Union of Soviet Socialist Republics on certain measures with respect to the limitation of strategic offensive arms, and the protocol related thereto, signed at Moscow on May 26, 1972, by Richard Nixon, President of the United States of America and Leonid I. Brezhnev, General Secretary of the Central Committee of the Communist Party of the Soviet Union.

SEC. 3. The Government and the people of the United States ardently desire a stable international strategic balance that maintains peace and deters aggression. The Congress supports the stated policy of the United States that, were a more complete strategic offensive arms agreement not achieved within the five years of the interim agreement, and were the survivability of the strategic deterrent forces of the United States to be threatened as a result of such failure, this could jeopardize the supreme national interests of the United States; the

314

Congress recognizes the difficulty of maintaining a stable strategic balance in a period of rapidly developing technology; the Congress recognizes the principle of United States-Soviet Union equality reflected in the antiballistic missile treaty, and urges and requests the President to seek a future treaty that, inter alia, would not limit the United States to levels of intercontinental strategic forces inferior to the limits provided for the Soviet Union; and the Congress considers that the success of these agreements and the attainment of more permanent and comprehensive agreements are dependent upon the maintenance under present world conditions of a vigorous research and development and modernization program as required by a prudent strategic posture.

SEC. 4. The Congress hereby commends the President for having successfully concluded agreements with the Soviet Union limiting the production and deployment of antiballistic missiles and certain strategic offensive armaments, and it supports the announced intention of the President to seek further limits on the production and deployment of strategic armaments at future Strategic Arms Limitation Talks. At the same time, the Senate takes cognizance of the fact that agreements to limit the further escalation of the arms race are only preliminary steps, however important, toward the attainment of world stability and national security. The Congress therefore urges the President to seek at the earliest practicable moment Strategic Arms Reduction Talks (SART) with the Soviet Union, the People's Republic of China, and other countries, and simultaneously to work toward reductions in conventional armaments, in order to bring about agreements for mutual decreases in the production and development of weapons of mass destruction so as to eliminate the threat of large-scale devastation and the ever-mounting costs of arms production and weapons modernization, thereby freeing world resources for constructive, peaceful use.

SEC. 5. Pursuant to paragraph six of the Declaration of Principles of Nixon and Brezhnev on May 29, 1972, which states that the United States and the Union of Soviet Socialist Republics: "will continue to make special efforts to limit strategic armaments. Whenever possible, they will conclude concrete agreements aimed at achieving these purposes"; Congress considers that the success of the interim agreement and the attainment of more permanent and comprehensive agreements are dependent upon the preservation of longstanding United States policy that neither the Soviet Union nor the United States should seek unilateral advantage by developing a first strike potential.

Approved September 30, 1972.

LEGISLATIVE HISTORY:
HOUSE REPORT No. 92-1324 (Comm. on Foreign Affairs).
SENATE REPORT No. 92-979 accompanying S. J. Res. 241
        (Comm. on Foreign Relations).
CONGRESSIONAL RECORD, Vol. 118 (1972):
    Aug. 11, 14-16, S. J. Res. 241 considered in Senate.
    Aug. 18, H. J. Res. 1227 considered and passed House.
    Sept. 6, 7, 13, 14, considered and passed Senate, amended,
                in lieu of S. J. Res. 241.
    Sept. 25, House agreed to Senate amendment.

Appendix 5

Memorandum of Understanding Between the Government of the United States of America and the Government of the Union of Soviet Socialist Republics Regarding the Establishment of a Standing Consultative Commission

UNION OF SOVIET SOCIALIST REPUBLICS

Standing Consultative Commission on Arms Limitation

Memorandum of understanding signed at Geneva December 21, 1972;
Entered into force December 21, 1972.

MEMORANDUM OF UNDERSTANDING BETWEEN
THE GOVERNMENT OF THE UNITED STATES OF AMERICA AND
THE GOVERNMENT OF THE UNION OF SOVIET SOCIALIST REPUBLICS
REGARDING THE ESTABLISHMENT OF A STANDING CONSULTATIVE COMMISSION

I.

The Government of the United States of America and
the Government of the Union of Soviet Socialist Republics
hereby establish a Standing Consultative Commission.

II.

The Standing Consultative Commission shall promote
the objectives and implementation of the provisions of the
Treaty between the USA and the USSR on the Limitation of
Anti-Ballistic Missile Systems of May 26, 1972, the Interim
Agreement between the USA and the USSR on Certain Measures
with Respect to the Limitation of Strategic Offensive Arms
of May 26, 1972, and the Agreement on Measures to Reduce

the Risk of Outbreak of Nuclear War between the USA and
the USSR of September 30, 1971, [1] and shall exercise its
competence in accordance with the provisions of Article XIII
of said Treaty, Article VI of said Interim Agreement, and
Article 7 of said Agreement on Measures.

III.

Each Government shall be represented on the
Standing Consultative Commission by a Commissioner and
a Deputy Commissioner, assisted by such staff as it
deems necessary.

IV.

The Standing Consultative Commission shall hold
periodic sessions on dates mutually agreed by the
Commissioners but no less than two times per year.
Sessions shall also be convened as soon as possible,
following reasonable notice, at the request of either
Commissioner.

V.

The Standing Consultative Commission shall
establish and approve Regulations governing procedures
and other relevant matters and may amend them as it
deems appropriate.

---

[1] TIAS 7503, 7504, 7186 ; 23 UST ; 22 UST 1590.

VI.

The Standing Consultative Commission will meet
in Geneva. It may also meet at such other places as
may be agreed.

Done in Geneva, on December 21, 1972, in two copies,
each in the English and Russian languages, both texts
being equally authentic.

For the Government	For the Government
of the	of the
United States of America	Union of the Soviet Socialist Republics

Gerard C. Smith [1]   *V. Semenov* [2]

---

[1] Gerard C. Smith
[2] V. S. Semenov

Appendix 6

Standing Consultative Commission Regulations

1. The Standing Consultative Commission, established by the Memorandum of Understanding between the Government of the United States of America and the Government of the Union of Soviet Socialist Republics Regarding the Establishment of a Standing Consultative Commission of December 21, 1972, shall consist of a U.S. component and Soviet component, each of which shall be headed by a Commissioner.

2. The Commissioners shall alternately preside over the meetings.

3. The Commissioners shall, when possible, inform each other in advance of the matters to be submitted for discussion, but may at a meeting submit for discussion any matter within the competence of the Commission.

4. During intervals between sessions of the Commission, each Commissioner may transmit written or oral communications to the other Commissioner concerning matters within the competence of the Commission.

5. Each component of the Commission may invite such advisers and experts as it deems necessary to participate in a meeting.

6. The Commission may establish working groups to consider and prepare specific matters.

7. The results of the discussion of questions at the meetings of the Commission may, if necessary, be entered into records which shall be in two copies, each in the English and the Russian languages, both texts being equally authentic.

8. The proceedings of the Standing Consultative Commission shall be conducted in private. The Standing Consultative Commission may not make its proceedings public except with the express consent of both Commissioners.

9. Each component of the Commission shall bear the expenses connected with its participation in the Commission.

Appendix 7

Accident Measures Agreement (Agreement on Measures to Reduce the Risk of Outbreak of Nuclear War Between the United States of America and the Union of Soviet Socialist Republics)

UNION OF SOVIET SOCIALIST REPUBLICS

Measures to Reduce the Risk of Nuclear War Outbreak

Agreement signed at Washington September 30, 1971;
Entered into force September 30, 1971.

AGREEMENT
ON MEASURES TO REDUCE THE RISK OF OUTBREAK OF NUCLEAR WAR
BETWEEN
THE UNITED STATES OF AMERICA AND
THE UNION OF SOVIET SOCIALIST REPUBLICS

The United States of America and the Union of Soviet Socialist Republics, hereinafter referred to as the Parties:

Taking into account the devastating consequences that nuclear war would have for all mankind, and recognizing the need to exert every effort to avert the risk of outbreak of such a war, including measures to guard against accidental or unauthorized use of nuclear weapons,

Believing that agreement on measures for reducing the risk of outbreak of nuclear war serves the interests of strengthening international peace and security, and is in no way contrary to the interests of any other country,

Bearing in mind that continued efforts are also needed in the future to seek ways of reducing the risk of outbreak of nuclear war,

Have agreed as follows:

Article 1

Each Party undertakes to maintain and to improve, as it deems necessary, its existing organizational and technical arrangements to guard against the accidental or unauthorized use of nuclear weapons under its control.

Article 2

The Parties undertake to notify each other immediately in the event of an accidental, unauthorized or any other unexplained incident involving a possible detonation of a nuclear weapon which could create a risk of outbreak of nuclear war. In the event of such an incident, the Party whose nuclear weapon is involved will immediately make every effort to take necessary measures to render harmless or destroy such weapon without its causing damage.

Article 3

The Parties undertake to notify each other immediately in the event of detection by missile warning systems of unidentified objects, or in the event of signs of interference with these systems or with related communications facilities, if such occurrences could create a risk of outbreak of nuclear war between the two countries.

Article 4

Each Party undertakes to notify the other Party in advance of any planned missile launches if such launches will extend beyond its national territory in the direction of the other Party.

Article 5

Each Party, in other situations involving unexplained nuclear incidents, undertakes to act in such a manner as to reduce the possibility of its actions being misinterpreted by the other Party. In any such situation, each Party may inform the other Party or request information when, in its view, this is warranted by the interests of averting the risk of outbreak of nuclear war.

Article 6

For transmission of urgent information, notifications and requests for information in situations requiring prompt clarification, the Parties shall make primary use of the Direct Communications Link between the Governments of the United States of America and the Union of Soviet Socialist Republics. [1]

For transmission of other information, notifications and requests for information, the Parties, at their own discretion, may use any communications facilities, including diplomatic channels, depending on the degree of urgency.

Article 7

The Parties undertake to hold consultations, as mutually agreed, to consider questions relating to implementation of the provisions of this Agreement, as well as to discuss possible amendments thereto aimed at further implementation of the purposes of this Agreement.

Article 8

This Agreement shall be of unlimited duration.

---

[1] See TIAS 5362, 7187 ; 14 UST 825 ; 22 UST.

Article 9

This Agreement shall enter into force upon signature.

Done at Washington on September 30, 1971, in two copies, each in the English and Russian languages, both texts being equally authentic.

FOR THE UNITED STATES
OF AMERICA:

FOR THE UNION OF SOVIET
SOCIALIST REPUBLICS:

---

[1] William P. Rogers
[2] A. Gromyko

Appendix 8

Revised Hot Line Agreement (Agreement Between the United States of America and the Union of Soviet Socialist Republics on Measures to Improve the U.S.A.–U.S.S.R. Direct Communications Link), *with* Annex

UNION OF SOVIET SOCIALIST REPUBLICS

Measures to Improve the Direct Communications Link

Agreement, with annex, supplementing and modifying the memorandum of understanding, with annex, of June 20, 1963. Signed at Washington September 30, 1971; Entered into force September 30, 1971.

AGREEMENT BETWEEN
THE UNITED STATES OF AMERICA AND
THE UNION OF SOVIET SOCIALIST REPUBLICS
ON MEASURES TO IMPROVE THE USA–USSR
DIRECT COMMUNICATIONS LINK

The United States of America and the Union of Soviet Socialist Republics, hereinafter referred to as the Parties,

Noting the positive experience gained in the process of operating the existing Direct Communications Link between the United States of America and the Union of Soviet Socialist Republics, which was established for use in time of emergency pursuant to the Memorandum of Understanding Regarding the Establishment of a Direct Communications Link, signed on June 20, 1963, [1]

Having examined, in a spirit of mutual understanding, matters relating to the improvement and modernization of the Direct Communications Link,

Have agreed as follows:

---

[1] TIAS 5362; 14 UST 825.

Article 1

1.   For the purpose of increasing the reliability of
the Direct Communications Link, there shall be established
and put into operation the following:

(a)   two additional circuits between the United States
of America and the Union of Soviet Socialist Republics each
using a satellite communications system, with each Party
selecting a satellite communications system of its own choice,

(b)   a system of terminals (more than one) in the territory
of each Party for the Direct Communications Link, with the
locations and number of terminals in the United States of
America to be determined by the United States side, and the
locations and number of terminals in the Union of Soviet
Socialist Republics to be determined by the Soviet side.

2.   Matters relating to the implementation of the
aforementioned improvements of the Direct Communications Link
are set forth in the Annex which is attached hereto and forms
an integral part hereof.

Article 2

Each Party confirms its intention to take all possible
measures to assure the continuous and reliable operation of
the communications circuits and the system of terminals of
the Direct Communications Link for which it is responsible in
accordance with this Agreement and the Annex hereto, as well
as to communicate to the head of its Government any messages
received via the Direct Communications Link from the head of
Government of the other Party.

Article 3

The Memorandum of Understanding Between the United States
of America and the Union of Soviet Socialist Republics Regarding

the Establishment of a Direct Communications Link, signed on
June 20, 1963, with the Annex thereto, shall remain in force,
except to the extent that its provisions are modified by this
Agreement and Annex hereto.

Article 4

The undertakings of the Parties hereunder shall be carried
out in accordance with their respective Constitutional processes.

Article 5

This Agreement, including the Annex hereto, shall enter
into force upon signature.

Done at Washington on September 30, 1971, in two copies, each
in the English and Russian languages, both texts being equally
authentic.

FOR THE UNITED STATES
OF AMERICA:

FOR THE UNION OF SOVIET
SOCIALIST REPUBLICS:

William Rogers [1]   *H. Dobrynin* [2]

ANNEX TO THE AGREEMENT BETWEEN
THE UNITED STATES OF AMERICA AND
THE UNION OF SOVIET SOCIALIST REPUBLICS
ON MEASURES TO IMPROVE THE USA-USSR
DIRECT COMMUNICATIONS LINK

Improvements to the USA-USSR Direct Communications Link
shall be implemented in accordance with the provisions set
forth in this Annex.

I. CIRCUITS

(a) Each of the original circuits established pursuant to
paragraph 1 of the Annex to the Memorandum of Understanding,
dated June 20, 1963, shall continue to be maintained and
operated as part of the Direct Communications Link until such
time, after the satellite communications circuits provided
for herein become operational, as the agencies designated
pursuant to paragraph III (hereinafter referred to as the
"designated agencies") mutually agree that such original circuit
is no longer necessary. The provisions of paragraph 7 of the
Annex to the Memorandum of Understanding, dated June 20, 1963,
shall continue to govern the allocation of the costs of
maintaining and operating such original circuits.

(b) Two additional circuits shall be established using
two satellite communications systems. Taking into account
paragraph I (e) below, the United States side shall provide one
circuit via the Intelsat system and the Soviet side shall provide
one circuit via the Molniya II system. The two circuits shall
be duplex telephone band-width circuits conforming to CCITT
standards, equipped for secondary telegraphic multiplexing.
Transmission and reception of messages over the Direct
Communications Link shall be effected in accordance with
applicable recommendations of international communications
regulations, as well as with mutually agreed instructions.

(c)   When the reliability of both additional circuits
has been established to the mutual satisfaction of the
designated agencies, they shall be used as the primary circuits
of the Direct Communications Link for transmission and reception
of teleprinter messages between the United States and the
Soviet Union.

(d)   Each satellite communications circuit shall utilize
an earth station in the territory of the United States, a
communications satellite transponder, and an earth station in
the territory of the Soviet Union. Each Party shall be
responsible for linking the earth stations in its territory
to its own terminals of the Direct Communications Link.

(e)   For the circuits specified in paragraph I (b):
--   The Soviet side will provide and operate at least one
earth station in its territory for the satellite communications
circuit in the Intelsat system, and will also arrange for the
use of suitable earth station facilities in its territory for
the satellite communications circuit in the Molniya II system.
The United States side, through a governmental agency or other
United States legal entity, will make appropriate arrangements
with Intelsat with regard to access for the Soviet Intelsat
earth station to the Intelsat space segment, as well as for
the use of the applicable portion of the Intelsat space segment.
--   The United States side will provide and operate at least one
earth station in its territory for the satellite communications
circuit in the Molniya II system, and will also arrange for the
use of suitable earth station facilities in its territory for
the satellite communications circuit in the Intelsat system.

(f)   Each earth station shall conform to the performance
specifications and operating procedures of the corresponding
satellite communications system and the ratio of antenna gain
to the equivalent noise temperature should be no less than 31

334

decibels. Any deviation from these specifications and procedures which may be required in any unusual situation shall be worked out and mutually agreed upon by the designated agencies of both Parties after consultation.

(g) The operational commissioning dates for the satellite communications circuits based on the Intelsat and Molniya II systems shall be as agreed upon by the designated agencies of the Parties through consultations.

(h) The United States side shall bear the costs of: (1) providing and operating the Molniya II earth station in its territory; (2) the use of the Intelsat earth station in its territory; and (3) the transmission of messages via the Intelsat system. The Soviet side shall bear the costs of: (1) providing and operating the Intelsat earth station in its territory; (2) the use of the Molniya II earth station in its territory; and (3) the transmission of messages via the Molniya II system. Payment of the costs of the satellite communications circuits shall be effected without any transfer of payments between the Parties.

(i) Each Party shall be responsible for providing to the other Party notification of any proposed modification or replacement of the communications satellite system containing the circuit provided by it that might require accommodation by earth stations using that system or otherwise affect the maintenance or operation of the Direct Communications Link. Such notification should be given sufficiently in advance to enable the designated agencies to consult and to make, before the modification or replacement is effected, such preparation as may be agreed upon for accommodation by the affected earth stations.

II. TERMINALS

(a) Each Party shall establish a system of terminals in its territory for the exchange of messages with the other Party, and

335

shall determine the locations and number of terminals in such a system. Terminals of the Direct Communications Link shall be designated "USA" and "USSR".

(b) Each Party shall take necessary measures to provide for rapidly switching circuits among terminal points in such a manner that only one terminal location is connected to the circuits at any one time.

(c) Each Party shall use teleprinter equipment from its own sources to equip the additional terminals for the transmission and reception of messages from the United States to the Soviet Union in the English language and from the Soviet Union to the United States in the Russian language.

(d) The terminals of the Direct Communications Link shall be provided with encoding equipment. One-time tape encoding equipment shall be used for transmissions via the Direct Communications Link. A mutually agreed quantity of encoding equipment of a modern and reliable type selected by the United States side, with spares, test equipment, technical literature and operating supplies, shall be furnished by the United States side to the Soviet side against payment of the cost thereof by the Soviet side; additional spares for the encoding equipment supplied will be furnished as necessary.

(e) Keying tapes shall be supplied in accordance with the provisions set forth in paragraph 4 of the Annex to the Memorandum of Understanding, dated June 20, 1963. Each Party shall be responsible for reproducing and distributing additional keying tapes for its system of terminals and for implementing procedures which ensure that the required synchronization of encoding equipment can be effected from any one terminal at any time.

III. OTHER MATTERS

Each Party shall designate the agencies responsible for

336

arrangements regarding the establishment of the additional circuits and the systems of terminals provided for in this Agreement and Annex, for their operation and for their continuity and reliability. These agencies shall, on the basis of direct contacts:

(a) arrange for the exchange of required performance specifications and operating procedures for the earth stations of the communications systems using Intelsat and Molniya II satellites;

(b) arrange for testing, acceptance and commissioning of the satellite circuits and for operation of these circuits after commissioning; and,

(c) decide matters and develop instructions relating to the operation of the secondary teleprinter multiplex system used on the satellite circuits.

Appendix 9

Agreement on Prevention of Nuclear War (Agreement Between the United States of America and the Union of Soviet Socialist Republics on the Prevention of Nuclear War)

The United States of America and the Union of Soviet Socialist Republics, hereinafter referred to as the Parties,

Guided by the objectives of strengthening world peace and international security,

Conscious that nuclear war would have devastating consequences for mankind,

Proceeding from the desire to bring about conditions in which the danger of an outbreak of nuclear war anywhere in the world would be reduced and ultimately eliminated,

Proceeding from their obligations under the Charter of the United Nations regarding the maintenance of peace, refraining from the threat or use of force, and the avoidance of war, and in conformity with the agreements to which either Party has subscribed,

Proceeding from the Basic Principles of Relations between the United States of America and the Union of Soviet Socialist Republics signed in Moscow on May 29, 1972,

Reaffirming that the development of relations between the United States of America and the Union of Soviet Socialist Republics is not directed against other countries and their interests,

Have agreed as follows:

Article I

The United States and the Soviet Union agree that an objective of their policies is to remove the danger of nuclear war and of the use of nuclear weapons.

Accordingly, the Parties agree that they will act in such a manner as to prevent the development of situations capable of causing a dangerous exacerbation of their relations, as to avoid military confrontations, and as to exclude the outbreak of nuclear war between them and between either of the Parties and other countries.

Article II

The Parties agree, in accordance with Article I and to realize the objectives stated in that Article, to proceed from the premise that each Party will refrain from the threat or use of force against the other Party, against the allies of the other Party and against other countries, in circumstances which many endanger international peace and security. The Parties agree that they will be guided by these considerations in the formulation of their foreign policies and in their actions in the field of international relations.

ARTICLE III

The Parties undertake to develop their relations with each other and with other countries in a way consistent with the purposes of this Agreement.

ARTICLE IV

If at any time relations between the Parties or between either Party and other countries appear to involve the risk of a nuclear conflict, or if relations between countries not parties to this Agreement appear to involve the risk of nuclear war between the United States of America and the Union of Soviet Socialist Republics or between either Party and other countries, the United States and the Soviet Union, acting in accordance with the provisions of this Agreement, shall immediately enter into urgent consultations with each other and make every effort to avert this risk.

ARTICLE V

Each party shall be free to inform the Security Council of the United Nations, the Secretary General of the United Nations and the Governments of allied or other countries of the progress and outcome of consultations initiated in accordance with Article IV of this Agreement.

ARTICLE VI

Nothing in this Agreement shall affect or impair:
a. the inherent right of individual or collective self-defense as envisaged by Article 51 of the Charter of the United Nations,
b. the provisions of the Charter of the United Nations, including

those relating to the maintenance or restoration of international peace and security, and

c. the obligations undertaken by either Party towards its allies or other countries in treaties, agreements, and other appropriate documents.

ARTICLE VII

This Agreement shall be of unlimited duration.

ARTICLE VIII

This Agreement shall enter into force upon signature.

DONE at Washington on June 22, 1973, in two copies, each in the English and Russian languages, both texts being equally authentic.

For the United States of America:

RICHARD NIXON

President of the United States of America

For the Union of Soviet Socialist Republics:

L. I. BREZHNEV

General Secretary of the Central Committee, CPSU

Appendix 10

Basic Principles of Negotiations on Strategic Arms Limitation (Basic Principles of Negotiations on the Further Limitation of Strategic Offensive Arms)

The President of the United States of America, Richard Nixon, and the General Secretary of the Central Committee of the CPSU, L. I. Brezhnev,

Having thoroughly considered the question of the further limitation of strategic arms, and the progress already achieved in the current negotiations,

Reaffirming their conviction that the earliest adoption of further limitations of strategic arms would be a major contribution in reducing the danger of an outbreak of nuclear war and in strengthening international peace and security,

Have agreed as follows:

First. The two Sides will continue active negotiations in order to work out a permanent agreement on more complete measures on the limitation of strategic offensive arms, as well as their subsequent reduction, proceeding from the Basic Principles of Relations between the United States of America and the Union of Soviet Socialist Republics signed in Moscow on May 29, 1972, and from the Interim Agreement between the United States of America and the Union of Soviet Socialist Republics of May 26, 1972 on Certain Measures with Respect to the Limitation of Strategic Offensive Arms.

Over the course of the next year the two Sides will make serious efforts to work out the provisions of the permanent agreement on more complete measures on the limitation of strategic offensive arms with the objective of signing it in 1974.

Second. New agreements on the limitation of strategic offensive armament will be based on the principles of the American-Soviet documents adopted in Moscow in May 1972 and the agreements reached in Washington in June 1973; and in particular, both Sides will be guided by the recognition of each other's equal security interests and by the recognition that efforts to obtain unilateral advantage, directly or indirectly, would be inconsistent with the strengthening of peaceful relations between the United States of America and the Union of Soviet Socialist Republics.

Third. The limitations placed on strategic offensive weapons can apply both to their quantitative aspects as well as to their qualitative improvement.

Fourth. Limitations on strategic offensive arms must be subject to adequate verification by national technical means.

Fifth. The modernization and replacement of strategic offensive arms would be permitted under conditions which will be formulated in the agreements to be concluded.

Sixth. Pending the completion of a permanent agreement on more complete measures of strategic offensive arms limitation, both Sides are prepared to reach agreements on separate measures to supplement the existing Interim Agreement of May 26, 1972.

Seventh. Each Side will continue to take necessary organizational and technical measures for preventing accidental or unauthorized use of nuclear weapons under its control in accordance with the Agreement of September 30, 1971 between the United States of America and the Union of Soviet Socialist Republics.

Washington, June 21, 1973

For the United States of America:

For the Union of Soviet Socialist Republics:

RICHARD NIXON

L. I. BREZHNEV

President of the United States of America

General Secretary of the Central Committee, CPSU

Bibliography

There are several sources that provide a great deal of up-to-date unclassified data on strategic arms and arms control. Since the Kennedy administration, the basic U.S. government policy statements issued annually have been the statements by the Secretary of Defense on the proposed defense budget and five-year programs (frequently referred to as the "DOD Posture Statements") and the Arms Control Report of the U.S. Arms Control and Disarmament Agency. The Nixon administration has added two additional documents: the report of the President to the Congress entitled "U.S. Foreign Policy for the 1970's," and the report of the Secretary of State entitled "United States Foreign Policy." The U.S. Arms Control and Disarmament Agency publishes annually "Documents on Disarmament," which is a very useful research tool. Congressional hearings before the Senate Committees on Foreign Relations and Armed Services and the House Committees on Foreign Affairs and Armed Services provide an almost continous flow of detailed information. They are excellent sources for those who already understand the basic terminology and issues. The International Institute for Strategic Studies in London publishes annually "The Military Balance" and "Strategic Survey." Finally, John Newhouse's recent book, *Cold Dawn—The Story of SALT*, merits special mention as an especially revealing account of the White House view and role in SALT I.

Books

Aron, Raymond. *The Great Debate: Theories of Nuclear Strategy.* Garden City, N.Y.: Doubleday, 1965.

Beaufre, André. *Deterrence and Strategy,* trans. by Major-General R. H. Barry. New York: Praeger, 1966.

Bechhoefer, Bernhard G. *Postwar Negotiations for Arms Control.* Washington, D.C.: Brookings Institution, 1961.

Bloomfield, Lincoln, et al. *Khrushchev and the Arms Race.* Cambridge, Mass.: MIT Press, 1966.

Boskey, Bennett, and Mason Willrich, eds. *Nuclear Proliferation: Prospects for Control.* New York: Dunellen, 1970.

Brown, Neville. *Nuclear War: The Impending Strategic Deadlock.* London: Pall Mall Press, 1964.

Bull, Hedley. *The Control of the Arms Race.* New York: Praeger, 1965.

Burrows, B., and C. Irwin. *The Security of Western Europe: Towards a Common Defence Policy.* London: Charles Knight, 1972.

Chayes, Abram, and Jerome B. Wiesner, eds. *ABM: An Evaluation of the Decision to Deploy an Antiballistic Missile System.* New York: Harper & Row, 1969.

Coffey, Joseph I. *Strategic Power and National Security.* Pittsburgh: University of Pittsburgh Press, 1971.

Dallin, Alexander. *The Soviet Union and Disarmament: An Appraisal of Soviet Attitudes and Intentions.* New York: Praeger, 1964.

Erickson, John. *Soviet Military Power.* London: Royal United Services Institute for Defense Studies, 1971.

Erickson, John, ed. *The Military-Technical Revolution.* New York: Praeger, 1966.

Feld, B. T., T. Greenwood, G. W. Rathjens, and S. Weinberg, eds. *Impact of New Technologies on the Arms Race.* Cambridge, Mass.: MIT Press, 1971.

Halperin, Morton H., ed. *Sino-Soviet Relations and Arms Control.* Cambridge, Mass.: The MIT Press, 1967.

Halperin, Morton H. *China and the Bomb.* New York: Praeger, 1965.

Halperin, Morton H., and Dwight H. Perkins. *Communist China and Arms Control.* New York: Praeger, 1965.

Herz, John H. *International Politics in the Atomic Age.* New York: Columbia University Press, 1959.

Hitch, Charles J., and Roland N. McKean. *The Economics of Defense in the Nuclear Age.* Cambridge, Mass.: Harvard University Press, 1963.

Horelick, Arnold, and Myron Rush. *Strategic Power and Soviet Foreign Policy.* Chicago: University of Chicago Press, 1966.

Garthoff, Raymond L. *Soviet Military Policy*. New York: Praeger, 1966.

Jacobson, Carl. *Soviet Strategy—Soviet Foreign Policy: Military Considerations Affecting Soviet Policy-Making*. Glasgow: Robert MacLehose & Company, 1972.

Jacobson, Harold K., and Eric Stein. *Diplomats, Scientists, and Politicians: The United States and the Nuclear Test Ban Negotiations*. Ann Arbor: University of Michigan Press, 1966.

Kahn, Herman. *On Thermonuclear War*. Princeton: Princeton University Press, 1960.

Kintner, William, and Robert L. Pfaltzgraff, Jr., eds. *SALT: Implications for Arms Control in the 1970's*. Pittsburgh: University of Pittsburgh Press, 1973.

Kissinger, Henry A. *The Necessity for Choice*. New York: Harper & Row, 1961.

Kissinger, Henry A. *Nuclear Weapons and Foreign Policy*. New York: Harper & Row, 1957.

Klass, Philip J. *Secret Sentries in Space*. New York: Random House, 1971.

Kolkowicz, Roman, et al. *The Soviet Union and Arms Control: A Superpower Dilemma*. Baltimore: Johns Hopkins University Press, 1970.

Knorr, Klaus. *On the Uses of Military Power in the Nuclear Age*. Princeton: Princeton University Press, 1966.

Larson, Thomas B. *Disarmament and Soviet Policy 1964–1968*. Englewood Cliffs, N.J.: Prentice-Hall, 1969.

McNamara, Robert S. *The Essence of Security: Reflections in Office*. New York: Harper & Row, 1968.

Newhouse, John. *Cold Dawn—The Story of SALT*. New York: Holt, Rinehart and Winston, 1973.

Osgood, Robert E., and Robert W. Tucker. *Force, Order and Justice*. Baltimore: Johns Hopkins University Press, 1967.

Quester, George H. *Nuclear Diplomacy: The First Twenty-Five Years*. New York: Dunellen, 1970.

Roberts, Chalmers M. *The Nuclear Years*. New York: Praeger, 1970.

Schelling, Thomas C. *Arms and Influence*. New Haven: Yale University Press, 1966.

Schelling, Thomas C., and Morton H. Halperin. *Strategy and Arms Control*. New York: The Twentieth Century Fund, 1961.

Schilling, Warner R., Paul Y. Hammond, and Glenn H. Snyder. *Strategy, Politics, and Defense Budgets*. New York: Columbia University Press, 1962.

Shulman, Marshall D. *The Soviet Stand on Disarmament*. New York: Cross Currents Press, 1962.

Snyder, Glenn H. *Deterrence and Defense*. Princeton: Princeton University Press, 1961.

Sokolovskii, V. D., ed. *Soviet Military Strategy*. Translated and with an analytical introduction by Herbert S. Dinerstein, Leon Gouré, and Thomas W. Wolfe. Englewood Cliffs, N.J.: Prentice-Hall, 1963.

Stanley, T., and D. Whitt. *Détente Diplomacy: United States and European Security in the 1970's*. New York: Dunellen, 1970.

Stone, Jeremy J. *Containing the Arms Race*. Cambridge, Mass.: MIT Press, 1966.

Stockholm International Peace Research Institute. *SIPRI Yearbook on World Armaments and Disarmament—1973*. New York: Humanities Press, 1973.

Tsipis, Kosta, Anne Kahn, and B. T. Feld, eds. *The Future of the Sea-Based Deterrent*. Cambridge, Mass.: MIT Press, 1973.

Willrich, Mason. *Non-Proliferation Treaty: Framework for Nuclear Arms Control*. Charlottesville: Michie, 1969.

Wolfe, Thomas W. *Soviet Strategy at the Crossroads*. Cambridge, Mass.: Harvard University Press, 1964.

York, Herbert F. *Arms Control: Readings from Scientific American*. San Francisco: W. H. Freeman, 1973.

York, Herbert F. *Race to Oblivion*. New York: Simon & Schuster, 1970.

Articles and Pamphlets

Brennan, Donald G. "The Case for Missile Defense," *Foreign Affairs*, vol. 47 (April 1969), pp. 433–448.

Brennan, Donald G. "When the SALT Hit the Fan," *National Review*, vol. 24 (June 23, 1972), pp. 685–692.

Brennan, Donald G., and Johan J. Holst. "Ballistic Missile Defence: Two Views," *Adelphi Papers No. 43*. London: International Institute for Strategic Studies, 1967.

Bull, Hedley. *Strategic Arms Limitation; The Precedent of the Washington and London Naval Treaties*. Occasional Paper of the University of Chicago Center for Policy Study, 1971.

Bundy, McGeorge. "To Cap the Volcano," *Foreign Affairs*, vol. 48 (October 1969), pp. 1–20.

Bunn, George. "Missile Limitation: By Treaty or Otherwise?" *Columbia Law Review*, vol. 70 (January 1970), pp. 1–47.

Caldwell, Lawrence T. "Soviet Attitudes to SALT," *Adelphi Papers No. 75*. London: International Institute for Strategic Studies, 1971.

Calogero, Francesco. "A Scenario for Effective SALT Negotiations," *Bulletin of the Atomic Scientists*, vol. 29 (June 1973), pp. 16–21.

Chayes, Abram. "An Inquiry into the Workings of Arms Control Agreements," *Harvard Law Review*, vol. 85 (March 1972), pp. 905–969.

Clemens, Walter C. "SALT, the NPT, and U.S.-Japanese Security Relations," *Asian Survey*, vol. 10 (December 1970), pp. 1037–1045.

Coffey, Joseph I. "Strategic Arms Limitations and European Security," *International Affairs*, vol. 47 (October 1971), pp. 692–707.

Columbia University, School of International Affairs. "The Military Industrial Complex: USSR/USA," *Journal of International Affairs* (symposium issue), vol. 26 (1972), pp. 1–97.

Duchêne, François. "SALT, the Ostpolitik, and the Post-cold War Context," *World Today*, vol. 26 (December 1970), pp. 500–511.

Falk, Richard A., Robert C. Tucker, and Oren R. Young. *On Minimizing the Use of Nuclear Weapons.* Princeton: Princeton University, Center of International Studies, 1966.

Feld, Bernard T. "Looking to SALT-II," *Bulletin of the Atomic Scientists*, vol. 28 (June 1972), pp. 2–3, 50, 54.

Garwin, Richard L. "Antisubmarine Warfare and National Security," *Scientific American*, vol. 227 (July 1972), pp. 14–25.

Garwin, Richard L. *Superpower Postures in SALT: An American View.* Occasional Paper of the University of Chicago Center for Policy Study, 1971. 30 p.

Gray, Colin S. "The Arms Race Is about Politics," *Foreign Policy*, no. 9 (Winter 1972–73), pp. 117–129.

Greenwood, Ted. "Reconnaissance and Arms Control," *Scientific American*, vol. 228 (February 2, 1973), pp. 14–25.

Greenwood, Ted. "Reconnaissance, Surveillance and Arms Control," *Adelphi Papers No. 88.* London: International Institute for Strategic Studies, 1972.

Grewe, W., et al. "Soviet-American Relations and World Order: Arms Limitations and Policy," *Adelphi Papers No. 65.* London: International Institute for Strategic Studies, 1970.

Hahn, Walter. "Nuclear Balance in Europe," *Foreign Affairs*, vol. 50 (April 1970), pp. 501–516.

Holst, Johan J. *Comparative U.S. and Soviet Deployments, Doctrines, and Arms Limitation.* Occasional Paper of the University of Chicago Center for Policy Study, 1971. 60 p.

Iklé, Fred C. "Can Nuclear Deterrence Last Out the Century?" *Foreign Affairs*, vol. 51 (January 1973), pp. 267–285.

Imai, Ryukichi. "Japan and the World of SALT," *Bulletin of the Atomic Scientists*, vol. 26 (December 1971), pp. 13–16.

International Institute for Strategic Studies. *The Military Balance.* London: International Institute for Strategic Studies (annually).

International Institute for Strategic Studies. *Strategic Survey.* London: International Institute for Strategic Studies (annually).

Kahan, Jerome H. "Stable Deterrence, A Strategic Policy for the 1970's," *Orbis*, vol. 15 (Summer 1971), pp. 528–543.

Kahan, Jerome H. "Strategies for SALT," *World Politics,* vol. 23 (January 1971), pp. 171–188.

Kolkowicz, Roman. "Strategic Parity and Beyond," *World Politics,* vol. 23 (April 1971), pp. 431–451.

Kurth, James R. "Why We Buy the Weapons We Do," *Foreign Policy,* no. 11 (Summer 1973), pp. 33–56.

Kruzel, Joseph. "SALT II: The Search for a Follow-on Agreement," *Orbis,* vol. 17 (Summer 1973), pp. 334–363.

Lambeth, Benjamin S. "Deterrence in the MIRV Era," *World Politics,* vol. 24 (January 1972), pp. 221–242.

Larocque, Gene R. *Security through Mutual Vulnerability.* Occasional Paper No. 2, Stanley Foundation, Muscatine, Iowa, 1973.

Myers, Henry R. "Extending the Nuclear Test-Ban," *Scientific American,* vol. 226 (January 1972), pp. 13–23.

Pierre, Andrew J. "Nuclear Diplomacy: Britain, France and America," *Foreign Affairs,* vol. 49 (January 1971), pp. 283–301.

Pierre, Andrew J. "The SALT Agreement and Europe," *World Today,* vol. 28 (July 1972), pp. 281–288.

Rathjens, George W. *The Future of the Strategic Arms Race.* New York: Carnegie Endowment for International Peace, 1969.

Scoville, Herbert, Jr. "Beyond SALT One," *Foreign Affairs,* vol. 50 (April 1972), pp. 488–500.

Scoville, Herbert, Jr. "The Limitation of Offensive Weapons," *Scientific American,* vol. 224 (January 1971), pp. 15–25.

Scoville, Herbert, Jr. "Missile Submarines and National Security," *Scientific American,* vol. 226 (June 1972), pp. 15–27.

Scoville, Herbert, Jr. *Toward a Strategic Arms Limitation Agreement.* New York: Carnegie Endowment for International Peace, 1970.

Shulman, Marshall D. "What Does Security Mean Today?" *Foreign Affairs,* vol. 49 (July 1971), pp. 607–618.

Smart, Ian. "Strategic Arms Limitation Talks" in J. Moulton (ed.), *Brassey's Annual 1970,* London: William Clowes & Sons, Ltd., 1970, pp. 39–52.

Stein, Eric. "Legal Restraints in Modern Arms Control Agreements," *American Journal of International Law,* vol. 66 (April 1972), pp. 255–289.

Wolfe, Thomas W. *Impact of Economic and Technological Issues on The Soviet Approach to SALT.* Santa Monica, Calif.: Rand Corporation Paper P-4368, 1970.

Wyle, Frederick S. "European Security: Beating the Numbers Game," *Foreign Policy,* no. 10 (Spring 1973), pp. 41–54.

York, Herbert F. "The Great Test-Ban Debate," *Scientific American,* vol. 227 (November 1972), pp. 15–23.

Official Documents (in Addition to
Documents Included in the Appendices)

Kissinger, Henry A. Remarks at a Congressional Briefing on June 15, 1972, reprinted in *Hearings on Strategic Arms Limitation Agreements before the Senate Committee on Foreign Relations,* 92nd Cong., 2d Sess. Washington: U.S. Government Printing Office, 1972, pp. 393–416.

Nixon, Richard M. *U.S. Foreign Policy for the 1970's, Report by the President to the Congress.* Washington: U.S. Government Printing Office (annually).

Statement by Secretary of Defense to House and Senate Armed Services Committees (annually); available in the Budget Hearings of the House and Senate Armed Services Committees and since 1970 from the U.S. Government Printing Office.

UN General Assembly. *Report of the Secretary-General on the Effects of the Possible Use of Nuclear Weapons and on the Security and Economic Implications for States of the Acquisition and Further Development of These Weapons.* UN Doc. A/6858, Oct. 10, 1967.

U.S. Arms Control and Disarmament Agency. *Documents on Disarmament.* Washington: U.S. Government Printing Office (annually).

U.S. Congress. *Hearings on Agreement on Limitation of Strategic Offensive Weapons before the House Committee on Foreign Affairs,* 92d Cong., 2d Sess. Washington: U.S. Government Printing Office, 1972.

U.S. Congress. *Hearings on the Military Implications of the Strategic Arms Limitation Talks Agreements before the House Armed Services Committee,* 92d Cong., 2d Sess. Washington: U.S. Government Printing Office, 1972.

U.S. Congress. *Hearings on Military Implications of the Treaty on the Limitation of Anti-Ballistic Missile Systems and the Interim Agreement on Limitation of Strategic Offensive Arms before the Senate Armed Services Committee,* 92d Cong., 2d Sess. Washington: U.S. Government Printing Office, 1972.

U.S. Congress. *Hearings on Strategic Arms Limitation Agreements before the Senate Committee on Foreign Relations,* 92d Cong., 2d Sess. Washington: U.S. Government Printing Office, 1972.

U.S. Congress, House Committee on Foreign Affairs. *Report on Agreement on Limitation of Strategic Offensive Weapons to Accompany H.J. Res. 1227,* 92d Cong., 2d Sess. Washington: U.S. Government Printing Office, 1972.

U.S. Congress, Senate Committee on Foreign Relations. *Report on Agreement on Limitation of Strategic Offensive Weapons to Accompany S. J. Res. 241,* 92d Cong., 2d Sess. Washington: U.S. Government Printing Office, 1972.

U.S. Congress, Senate Committee on Foreign Relations. *Report on the Treaty on Limitation of Anti-Ballistic Missile Systems to Accompany Executive L, 92-2*, 92d Cong., 2d Sess. Washington: U.S. Government Printing Office, 1972.

U.S. Senate. *Message from the President Transmitting The ABM Treaty and Interim Agreement and Associated Protocol*, Executive L, 92d Cong., 2d Sess. Washington: U.S. Government Printing Office, 1972.

Index